RAISE YOU ON
THE RIVER

RAISE YOU ON THE RIVER

Essays & Encounters 1964-2018

Barry Callaghan

Publishers of Singular
Fiction, Poetry, Nonfiction, Translation, Drama and Graphic Books

Library and Archives Canada Cataloguing in Publication

Callaghan, Barry, 1937-, author
Raise you on the river : essays & encounters 1964-2018 / Barry Callaghan.

Issued in print and electronic formats.
ISBN 978-1-55096-786-9 (hardcover).--ISBN 978-1-55096-787-6 (EPUB).--
ISBN 978-1-55096-788-3 (Kindle).--ISBN 978-1-55096-789-0 (PDF)

I. Title.

PS8555.A49R348 2018   C814'.54   C2018-904746-1
                                           C2018-904747-X

Copyright © Barry Callaghan, 2018
Text and cover design by Michael Callaghan; cover photo Shutterstock
Typeset in Garamond at Moons of Jupiter Studios

Published by Exile Editions Limited – www.ExileEditions.com
144483 Southgate Road 14 – GD, Holstein, Ontario, N0G 2A0
Printed and bound in Canada by Marquis

We gratefully acknowledge the Canada Council for the Arts,
the Government of Canada, the Ontario Arts Council,
and the Ontario Media Development Corporation
for their support toward our publishing activities.

Canadian sales representation:
The Canadian Manda Group, 664 Annette Street,
Toronto ON M6S 2C8 www.mandagroup.com   416 516 0911

North American and international distribution, and U.S. sales:
Independent Publishers Group, 814 North Franklin Street,
Chicago IL 60610 www.ipgbook.com   toll free: 1 800 888 4741

For my Crazy Jane, Claire

the stillness between silence
and muteness

the moment desire forcibly
is renamed
grief

the precise space between
those two words

—ANNE MICHAELS

With gratitude to Peter Budd.

Special thanks to Marilyn Di Florio
for her longtime commitment and assistance.

Since no one knows the why of the weather
Or can authoritatively forecast
More than twelve hours of day or night, at most,
Every poor fool is licenced to explain it.
—ROBERT GRAVES

Experiment to me
Is everyone I meet
If it contain a Kernel?
—EMILY DICKINSON

In 2011, when *Raise You Twenty* came off the press, my wonderful publisher through the years was going out of business. The book was not what I had expected. I was told that only 300 copies had been printed. It sank out of site, like a stone. Such is life. Except, I thought, the day will come when I will complete this book the way I want it to be, by keeping a good portion of the 2011 edition, by dropping several pieces, and by adding others... and by giving it a title that remains true to the *Raise You Five/Raise You Ten* series – in the parlance of Texas hold 'em poker: *Raise You on the River* (the "river" card being the last card you can bet on, so-named because it is the card that can send you "down the river"). Here that book is. Being only eighty-one, I expect to publish a volume as intended, *All In*.

CONTENTS

FIRST COMMUNION

My First Communion was in late March or early April. There was wet snow on the ground. I was six years old and I was walking alone to church – my mother had dressed me in a grey suit and a celluloid collar with a big white silk bow. An older boy on a bicycle, a delivery boy, was riding toward me. I had a snowball in my hand. When the delivery boy was about thirty feet away, lost in myself and not giving it a thought, I made a behind-the-back flip of the snowball – as if by throwing it from behind my back the delivery boy would not know who had thrown it. As a throw of perfect timing in a perfect arc it caught the delivery boy on the chest – he rode right into it. The astonished boy got off his bike. I stood in my little grey suit, amused at myself. The boy didn't seem angry, he seemed bewildered, knowing that he had to do something, so he punched me in the chest, knocking me to the seat of my pants in the wet snow. It never occurred to me to fight back – I had done something reckless, and anyway I was too small. All I can remember was sitting in a church pew – my celluloid collar scraping my neck – the seat of my flannel pants muddy and wet, but I was full of wonder – not because I had thrown a snowball at a bigger boy – but wonder at the looping curve of the ball in its flight, my knowing as soon as I'd let the snowball go that it was going to hit home, knowing that the only reason the delivery boy was there riding on the street was to end up caught in the falling arc of light. The punch, the dirty wet pants, were inconsequential. I'd been so entranced by the sight of my perfect snowball that I can't remember taking my First Communion.

Between Trains, 2008

1

THE DEAL

After school my twelve-year-old brother, Michael, sold newspapers as a newsboy. He sold the *Evening Telegram* and *Star*, for three cents each on the corner of Dupont Street and Spadina Road. When Michael turned thirteen, Mother and Father gave him a three-speed bicycle. He quit selling newspapers. He got a job as the bicycle delivery boy for the local drugstore. At eight years old I became a newsie, waiting in the late summer afternoon for a delivery truck to drop off several heavy bundles of newspapers for stacking beside the streetcar stop corner lamppost. The bundles were bound by stiff cords and it took all my strength to snip them.

These were the War years and there were very few men in the houses on the streets close by the corner. They were away dying. I'd noticed that the women on our street, Walmer Road, talked a lot about dying. The working women who got off the crowded streetcars, coming home at the end of the afternoon, talked mainly about their jobs. These women lived mostly alone with other lonely young women in rooming houses, or in family homes with sisters and older women, their mothers or aunts. We lived in an apartment in a fourplex. My father had been too young for the First War and he was too old for the Second War.

The corner was in the shadow of the bridge for a cross-town freight railroad line, and on a hill above the bridge there was Casa Loma, an empty looming stone replica of a Bavarian castle complete with stone stables and a stone wall. The castle had been built on the crest of the city's central escarpment, which meant that it overlooked the shoreline of an ancient lake that had retreated south to what was now the city's harbour on Lake Ontario, which meant that in a sense I was selling the news to workers getting off streetcars on an ancient beach. At least, that's how my father had explained it to me.

The working women, and some men, who bought my papers looked stressed and tired out. Yet some seemed amused by how young I was, how small, calling out the dire headline news in my clear boy soprano voice. The floppy papers I held under my right arm were half the length of my tallness. "*Star, Tely*, get your *Star, Tely*…" I liked the feel of the papers, their smell. I liked the ink coming off on my fingers though, of course, I washed the ink off my hands as soon as I got home. My mother was not having ink smudges on her tablecloth.

One evening, a man with a bent nose, who was thick through the shoulders, planted a baseball cap on my head. He stood back and said aloud, "Perfect. Will you look at that? Perfect. Our little Bowery Boy," and he laughed, told me that I could keep the cap, and the people clustered around me who were waiting to buy their papers laughed, too. I didn't know what a Bowery Boy was but I gladly kept the cap, pulling it down over my eyes, trying to look serious, trying to look like a boy who had to be dealt with. My mother clapped her hands at seeing the cap and my father said I was lucky that it fit me so well and my brother said, "Nobody gave me a cap."

One afternoon, just before five, a young woman who was wearing a cardigan and slacks, not so much pretty as what my mother called pert, "eager with intent," leaned down so close to my ear that I could smell her soap, and she said, "I would like to make a little business deal with you." I didn't know exactly what a business deal was, but I said, "Sure."

"I'm looking every day for a job," she said.

"Yes."

"I have to read the Help Wanted Ads for jobs so that I know where the jobs are, and I need every penny I've got till I get a job."

"Yes?"

"So, what if I gave you one cent for each paper every day and all I'll read are the Help Wanted Ads, and when I'm done I'll give you back the papers perfectly folded and you can sell them again like brand new and no one will know the difference and you'll make a profit like a real businessman?"

For four days she gave me two cents and I gave her two papers. She went around the corner and opened the back pages carefully and read the ads for numbers and made notes, licking the tip of her pencil like my grandmother did (my mother had warned me about lead poisoning, and for years I associated death by lead poisoning with numbers). The young woman stood there for ten minutes, only five steps from the railroad bridge underpass, with the castle overshadowing from far up the hill, and then gave the folded papers back to me, her face bent down close to my face, her hands on my shoulders, looking like she was going to cry she was so tired, but then she let go of me and crossed the street, going home, probably to a room in one of the wartime rooming houses south of the corner.

On the fifth day, she did not get off the streetcar. Perhaps she'd got sick but I chose to believe that she had got a job, that the Help Wanted Ads had worked. As each evening went by, as the streetcar doors opened, I looked for her, but somehow I knew she was not coming back, that I was never going to see her again, and I did not ever see her again.

I sold papers for another three or four weeks, wearing my cap every day. Though I liked calling out the headlines as if I knew what was going on in the world of war before the women and men getting off the streetcar did, I told my mother and father that I wanted to quit. My father asked me if I didn't like having the money in my pocket, the money to buy comic books, and I said I didn't really care about the money, I'd rather play with my friends before going back to school. "So much for being a little businessman," my father said and shrugged. My brother said I was crazy. He had started smoking and wanted his own money to buy cigarettes. My father thought that was okay, because he smoked, too.

I said, "Cigarettes taste terrible. And pennies taste terrible. The copper tastes terrible."

My mother laughed and my brother said, "You really are crazy."

I had thought over and over about the woman and the Help Wanted Ads. I had thought of telling my mother and father about what had happened but I wasn't sure that they would understand how I saw it. Maybe they would tell me that I had done a good business deal. But after all, I thought, to make the deal with the woman, to help that woman, I had fooled two readers every day for four days. I had sold them used papers. To make an extra eight cents. I couldn't get around how I saw it. I had done something wrong to do something right, and for the first time in my life, I wasn't sure that I could tell this, let alone explain how good I felt about this, to my mother and father. For a moment I was upset but then I wasn't. As soon as I decided not to tell them, I began to forget about it. I began to go out to play. I knew that something had happened between me and my mother and father, and though I didn't entirely understand what it was, I knew that I was going to keep what I didn't understand and the smell of that woman's soap to myself.

2018

OUR LADY

I was twenty in 1958. Still too young to drink in a show bar. But there I was in the Town Tavern on Queen Street, sitting at the bar, listening to the great Lady Day sing. Billie Holiday. I was wearing my shades. And a new one-button-roll suit with hand-stitching in the lapels. The knowing bartender took me seriously enough to smile and give me a drink, rye whisky (because that's what my father and his sports-writing friends drank) with water on the side. Billie Holiday, looking drawn but with a white gardenia in her hair, sang a mournful song, and then slumped her shoulders toward the crowd rather than bow. She turned her back and stepped off stage.

The Town Tavern was set up strangely. It was a long room, a wide room, split down the centre by the bar. To the right side of the bar was a dining room, tables with white cloths and little hooded lamps. To the left was the barroom, with chairs at the bar and a lot of room for standing. Because it was Billie Holiday singing for the week, the barroom was crowded. There was almost no one in the dining room, and I could see that Lady Day had sat down to be by herself. I watched, while sipping my whisky, and she stayed by herself. I had an urge and I took it. I told the bartender that I would be back, and I walked to the far end of the bar, took a sharp turn past the indifferent maître d', and went into the dining room. I stood in front of Lady Day, took off my shades, which I intended as a gesture of politeness, and said as calmly as I could, "I wonder, Miss Holiday [this was back in the 1950s] if I could buy you a drink?" She nodded yes and nodded toward the empty chair opposite her. I sat down, a waiter appeared, and she ordered a Top and Bottom. (I later asked the

6

bartender what her drink was, and was astonished when he told me it was half gin and half port.) I ordered a rye whisky with two cubes of ice.

Trying not to stare, I stared at her. At her skin, at a greyness under her skin. Ashes. Maybe it was the drag of hard times, but there was something unfeminine about her face. I felt no yield in the set of her jaw, no give in the set of her bony shoulders that held the slack drape of a sleeveless white gown with spaghetti straps. Yet the whining metallic edge in her singing voice was always belied by a softness, even a submissiveness, at the heart of her every note: the tension of dry ice, each note a different pain, a different ring on sorrow.

Stupidly, having been taught the piano and my catechism by nuns, I thought of The Seven Sorrows of the Blessed Virgin. Our Lady of Sorrows. Our Lady of the Immaculate Heart, whose heart was always painted with seven long knives in it. As in those paintings, Our Lady of the Gardenia, who was sitting across the small table from me, just seemed to Be, expecting nothing, bearing her suffering. I could hardly stop from laughing at myself. I still didn't know what to say. There had been moments, listening to her during her last set, when – apparently exhausted – she'd gone a little hoarse, had slurred her words, but mostly when she'd sung she'd been incredibly articulate, enunciating each syllable, bending phrases into a new shape, a new clarity, making an old emotion new: I had never heard the phrase "the man I love" uttered with such desolate pleasure. I thought of the nuns who had taught me elocution. And so there I was thinking of desolation and love and nuns and staring at her bare arms. Thinking heroin. Brutal lovers and brutal cops. Rapes, her beatings. I thought that maybe I should put my shades back on. Be cool. I drank my drink, sure that I was making a fool of myself. I closed my eyes and heard myself say, "Strange…" and then, as if she were rescuing me from my silence, from myself, she said in a whisper, "…strange fruit…?" "No," I said, "that's not what I meant," embarrassed because she thought that I had meant something so obvious as her best known song. She put her glass to her lips, her eyes on me, but did not drink, as if to say, "Okay, then what did you mean?" before turning to look at the front door, the maître d'.

I stood up, trying to bow gracefully, and said, "Thank you for letting me have a drink with you." I left her there sitting alone at her table, Our Lady of the Gardenia. My sense of ineptitude overwhelmed by the wonder that I had actually sat down for a moment and looked into the clouded eyes of Billie Holiday.

I hurried to the little front lobby and back into the barroom, where I took my chair, regretting that I had not asked her to sing "Easy Living."

The bartender, having watched me go into the dining room, said, "She don't talk much, does she."

"No, she doesn't," I said, and put on my shades.

2018

THE CHAIR

Uncle Ambrose Dee, my mother's brother, was a gentle-spoken house painter. Tall and broad-shouldered, he had been a corporal during the First World War but had not gone overseas. He had driven a motorcycle with a sidecar. After the war, he had driven a motorcycle, then a modish car, a Coupe de Ville. In photographs he seems to have had style, a confident thrust to his body, a confident look in his eye. But he was shy. There were very few women – other than his sisters – in his life. He was also devout, in a straightforward way, without flair, going to Mass every Sunday, and sometimes during the week with one of his sisters, most likely Anna, the oldest, who didn't have a job in an office but looked after the family (both the Dee mother and father were dead by the time my mother was ten), and she ran the big house on Roxton Road. Ambrose ran with the men, though he was not much for the drink, and ran with the horses. His father had loved the trotting horses (keeping Scribbler books closely written with results and times from all the little tracks around Toronto), and Ambrose loved them, too. It was his only vice.

And from about the age of thirty-five, Marie had been his only woman – a gay good-looking woman with good long legs. She never seemed unhappy. She was always smiling. She seemed as subdued in her social needs as Ambrose – satisfied with church dances, summer dances on the boats to Crystal Beach and Port Dalhousie, motor trips to visit cousins in Chicago, the trotting races, and baseball games played in Fred Hamilton Park, which was just behind the house on Roxton Road.

As he was about to turn fifty, Ambrose announced he was going to remain a bachelor until he died. Marie went to their parish priest at the Church of St. Francis (where my parents, Morley and Loretto, had been married), complaining that she had given all of her youth to Ambrose. She asked the priest to tell Ambrose to marry her, that he had an obligation. The priest told that to Ambrose, and Ambrose did what he was told. In his fiftieth year, he married Marie.

At first, they seemed happily enough married. Ambrose had saved money and he bought a house. He had not, however, counted on Marie's two bachelor brothers, Rae and Wilfred. Rae, timid, with an eerie fascination for the wounds of Christ, lived with them as a boarder. "He never talks about anything except suffering," Ambrose said to me. Rae had had terrible acne as a boy, and there were healed red craters on his neck and throat, with black bristly hair in the craters that he couldn't trim. He wore light mauve scarves in the house, even in the summer. Wilfred, however, was outgoing. He lived alone in a room or with them in the house, depending on whether or not he had a job. Most often, he clerked at one of the government liquor stores. He was full of political opinions (all of them angry and abusive, in a hapless way). He had a pencil moustache, wore black vests – sometimes of silk – and loved the trotting horses. He kept Ambrose company at the track, and he had one slightly mad indulgence whenever he won a lot of money. He bought shoes. He bought the most up-to-date stylish shoes he could find. He would wear these shoes for two weeks, three weeks, and then he would tire of them and give them away.

Wilfrid and I had the same size feet. Three or four times a year, wearing my everyday baggy grey trousers and a tired blue school blazer, I would show up – to the amazement of my fellow students – shod in two-tone suede, or "Spectator" black-and-white brogues, or leather inlaid with patent leather, or twin-tassel loafers… Wilfred said to me, "Waste not, want not and since I want nothing, nothing goes to waste." Though he was always angry at the government, I never heard him say an angry word to anyone. Wilfred died of a heart attack, and not long after, Ambrose suffered heart tremors

Marie, though she was in her early fifties, wanted children. She was, as she said, "only recently married." Her search for a child became a cruel affair, for everyone. She went to the Catholic adoption agencies. They thought Marie and Ambrose would be perfect adoptive parents, so, one after another – over a period of three years – young boys entered their house hoping to be wanted, to be liked, to be loved, to be given a home. Ambrose was fairly easy, but Marie always became dissatisfied: not one of the boys could ever conform to her idea of how perfect he should be. She was a good woman, determined, yet at the same time docile, wishing no one any harm. She just didn't have any felt understanding of children. She sent them all back. This was heartbreaking and led to my only angry words with her, because she had asked me to meet one of the boys, and his yearning to please was terrifying to me...his knowing after two months with them that he was losing what he wanted to win with all his heart. When, smiling, she sent him back, too, I told her I thought she was brutal and ruthless, and when she turned to Ambrose for a defence, for the only time I ever saw, he put his head down and said with firmness, "That's it. No more. It's over." It was over. No more children came to the house.

She got into the habit, after each of the children, of soothing herself by buying a piece of furniture...a side table, a pot stand, a bedroom chair...all of which she did not need, and most of which, after a while, she gave away. She continued to be very gay, dressing always in bright colours – favouring cashmere and angora sweaters – keeping her very good legs. Even after Ambrose had a serious heart attack and was confined to bed, she kept her gaiety. Then he was taken to hospital, and after two weeks he died.

At the funeral home, Marie's smile for everyone seemed to be what perhaps it had always been: hysteria. She took me by the hand and led me to kneel beside the body of Ambrose in the casket.

"He looks better now than he ever did," she said.

"I suppose he does."

"A fine-looking man," she said.

"Yes."

"And a good man."

"Yes."

"It was a blessing that he went at last when he did."

"It was?"

"Yes. It was a problem of circulation."

"It was?"

"Yes. His feet were rotting."

"The rot."

"Yes. Black, they were black."

"Were they?"

"Yes."

"Well, I guess it was a blessing he went."

"Yes."

"And he looks very good."

"Yes, he does, and he was a good man."

"Yes."

"Would you pray?" she asked.

"No, I would not," I said.

"No?"

"No. I've no need for it."

"Oh, that's terrible," she said, breaking into a broad smile.

"I know but there's nothing I can do."

"You could pray."

"I can't."

"Can't you try a prayer for him?" and she took my hand.

"Yes, I will."

"To God," she said, and she was laughing.

"No, just a prayer," I said.

Later that week, after the burial, Marie went to see my mother and father. She had with her one of the pieces of furniture she had bought after sending a boy back to the orphanage. It was a chair.

That same night I looked at the chair and said nothing. It was in the hall, near the white panelled wall, in front of the black marble mantel. It was a chair unlike any chair of theirs: a chair done in burnt pumpkin quilted velvet with a high back that was cut straight across at the top, and the sides of the back sloped into the seat, so that the chair had no real arms.

Finally Morley said, "How do you like the new chair?"

I hesitated, smiled politely, but said nothing.

"Oh, come on," he said. "How do you like it?"

"Where did you get it?" I asked.

"Well, I didn't buy it," he said.

"I hope not," I said.

"It would have been too expensive," he said. "Marie gave it to us as a present."

"So, you *have* to use it."

"No, we like it," he said.

"I think it's awful. And you were never crazy about Marie."

"And why is it awful?"

"It's right out of Miami. Or maybe Las Vegas. You're sure, you're going to keep it around?"

"I'm going to leave it just where it is."

I was disgruntled. We both knew that little things like this come between people. He had his view – I had mine. It was an eyesore to be tolerated. I tried to maintain a patient silence.

Then, one night he said, "Look, I know how you feel about that chair and its place in the world, but here's how it is in itself. It is a very ancient style, and I like very much the burnt orange velvet. And what do I care if a hotel manager in Miami has chosen for himself something that I like. I'll never meet him or his customers. The relationship is between me and that chair. That's all. If I write a story, and such a hotel manager likes my story, I'm delighted. That's all."

I tried to hold back my hostility. I knew, or believed, he was trying to tell me something about myself, about our relationship.

The chair remained where it was. It didn't look burnt orange to me. It looked pumpkin.

We didn't speak about it.

A few weeks later, he said, "Look, I like my chair. Here it is. And here I am. Incidentally, a very attractive woman who's lived in many cities, but who's never been to Miami, came by the other night and she said, 'Oh that chair looks lovely there.'"

He knew that in telling me this story he wasn't drawing me any closer to him. He knew I was disappointed in him and resented his refusal to remove that chair. In a small way, the chair had come to stand between us.

Maybe he was telling me that no matter how much we trusted each other there always had to be something that stood between us.

Then Marie died of breast cancer.

I would come around to the house and find him, as I often did, standing in the hall, lost in thought, standing in the petalled light from the stained-glass window at the staircase landing, standing beside the chair. But until the day he died I never saw him sit in that chair.

2007

MARGARET ATWOOD

After a Time

It was a small late-evening gathering of friends at the home of Louise Dennys, the publisher. I was sitting on a sofa, keeping to myself. To my surprise, Margaret Atwood sat down beside me. I had known Margaret for years, I had come to know how considerate she could be, especially to women who had been harmed by ill health or happenstance, but I had never had what I would call an intimate, unguarded conversation with her. Without batting an eye, with all her capacity for directness, she said I would like to talk to you about death, about Morley… about how you are…with his dying. Startled, I said something quick, like… It's when you see your dad, how he's wanting so hard to live, that it gets to you, you realize he's really not well.

She said that she had not been well herself.

I spoke about Morley again, telling her that all my life I had believed that as long as he was alive I could not die, no matter what trouble Morley I was in, but if he was dead, of course…

I opened my hands, as if then, I guess, I'd have to be open to my death.

She spoke about her father. About frailty. And then she asked whether I was going to live in my father's house, and I said, Oh, I'm going there for sure, of course. And she said, I could never do that, live in his house. She shook her head. She touched the back of my hand, a consoling touch, and smiled and stood up and that was that.

After a time her father died.

After a time she brought out a book of poems, *Morning in the Burned House*, and at the heart's core of this book there are poems about her father.

I decided to see if, in a way, I could step inside her skin and come to know a little about how it was with her and her father and his dying.

Salt

Margaret knows about dread, about the things that creep across your heart like mildew shrouded on bread. She knows you, she knows me, she has persuaded us, as her readers, that we are her intimate *others*, conscious actors on her street, who, as children, played murder in the dark and she told us how, when we grew up, we hanged someone for having blue eyes.

She knows all about our mother's sob story, about how she was raped by a swan (the house prankster, the housemaid in the family photograph, put a voice balloon over our heads: inscribed over yours, one word, *Slut*). She knows how we, as her pioneers, stood listening for a voice – even an animal's voice – so that we could mimic something true, while around our feet the *strawberries were surging, huge and shining* and when we bent to pick them our hands *came away red and wet* and you said we

> *should have known*
> *anything planted here*
> *would come up blood* ·

just as she knew that we, in a fit of temper, would stamp our feet on stone in the bush and watch our feet sink up to our knees and you would cry: "Wait a minute. Wait a minute. I own this," as a girl with no hands reached out, attempting to console us.

You, and I, we have been walked and run and hauled through her circle games within games within circles. She is a great one for

play: sinister games of double Dutch, double-cross, or double solitaire with a double-headed man who, of course, has two voices,

> *four eyes,*
> *two sets of genitals, eight*
> *arms and legs and forty*
> *toes and fingers.*
> *Our leader is a spider,*
>
> *he traps words.*
> *They shrivel in his mouth,*
> *he leaves the skins.*

Weave a circle around Margaret at least twice. But watch out. It
may not be enough. With her, it's always feeding time. We, her
people, have been edible from the beginning. She has been wearing the skins of those who came before us for a long time, having
been from the start an expert skinner, a stylist on the prowl. She
is after a word that is neither discursive nor decorative, but a skin-
head word. She is a word stalking a word stalking a word. Bald. It
is in bald statement that she is at her best. In the skinning of
words. Transparent, down to the diseased bone.

Which means that there is a kind of madness in the map of
Margaret's mind – stiletto messages – meticulous, detached,
shouting even in sign languages – all a way of trying to live
through dread out on the edges, where there are

> *only the cold jewelled symmetries*
> *of the voracious eater*
> *the voracious eaten...*
>
> *and here*
> *to be aware is*
> *to know total*
> > *fear.*

Well no, not quite. Not total. Not fear that saps the mind blank. Not what Emily Dickinson meant by BLANK. No. To be like Margaret is to think fear. It's to be knowing about fear, even, at her cleverest moments, to play with fear, to ritualize those skin-head words into dystopic stories or faux fairy tales, to take words and *count them like beads,* to *turn them into statistics and litanies,* to turn them *into poems,* and sometimes to step inside the eye of a camera, her own little solitary isolation cell. There, she's looking to see if we, *because we ate the birds,* are still standing *ankle-deep in blood.* She's looking to stop us in time in snapshots, wherein she will speak to us about our own eating habits and the horrific pain we have inflicted on others. Often at these moments, she speaks in a poised staccato where love itself has become operational. Listen and be wary:

> *I approach this love*
> *like a biologist*
> *pulling on my rubber*
> *gloves & white labcoat*

In fact, she approaches not just love but our perdition on earth as a biologist. The motiveless malignancy that is eating away at our nature, at least in her world, is even more unforgiving than our original disease, Sin – for we have, she has come to see, actually created not just atomic bombs as a perverse extension of our genius but unknown diseases that can and will ultimately kill us because we have no known immunity. We do not know how to protect ourselves from ourselves...

Having had all this bred into our bones through our years of play together in her games, we have been not just her tricksters but her sirens, her straight men and woman, and sometimes her stand-ins for various of her orphans. What else could there be after all that munching of small bones but orphans? (*where did you come from, baby dear?*), and to keep us either busy or amused she has, from the beginning, turned men to pigs or put us at the scene of an ingurgitating sponge attack on Florida, or lain us down beside the deposed King Log and his frogs. She has discovered through us not only a whale under the earth but the little old man who sits in the whale's belly pretending to be a shaman.

And so, rehearsed as we have been, you – without hesitation – answered her call and got right inside Half-Hanged Mary's head, long since schooled to speak in a sly monotone from the end of a rope. Who else but one of us would not only wear a noose for a necklace but actually know how to utter in all solemnity: *John and Mary meet... John and Mary die. John and Mary die. John and Mary die.*

Droll. Deadpan funny, if you've been holed up long enough inside her headbone, and if you have seen what she has seen in the way that she has seen it:

> *My eyes are situated in my head, which also possesses two small holes for the entrance and exit of air, the invisible fluid we swim in, and one larger hole, equipped with bony protuberances called teeth, by means of which I destroy and assimilate certain parts of my surroundings and change them into my self.*

This is like listening to a mad undertaker who is standing at the ready with a deboning blade in hand.

In all fairness, there have of course been times when she has put that blade down, when a love deeply felt has been beautifully embodied by her words:

> *I would like to follow*
> *you up the long stairway*
> *again & become*
> *the boat that would row you back*
> *carefully, a flame*
> *in two cupped hands*

to where your body lies
beside me, and you enter
it as easily as breathing in

I would like to be the air
that inhabits you for a moment
only. I would like to be that unnoticed
& that necessary.

Perhaps it was after such a moment that she said that

we should be kind, we should
take warning, we should forgive each other

But before we have been able to offer absolution and make a sign of the cross, as either defence or blessing, she has taken us off to a picnic. And who should show up – having just got his head back up on the bones between his shoulders – but an ambulatory John the Baptist? John is now, she says, a teacher of Religious Studies.

And close by John, by the water's edge, is her own husband. We discover he is holding a brown paper bag that is weighted down with turnips, apples and…her very own head. Things have seemingly gotten out of hand, for suddenly there we are, in our own shapes, rising out of the water. And I see that you are now Salomé and are carrying your own head on a platter. The picnickers

are staring at you
with fascinated
horror, as
if you're about to pull
off one of your legs
revealing a green and
mossy amputated
stump

You, down among the decapitated, carrying your own head! Who in the world wouldn't cry out? – *Here Mom, here Mom, over here.* But neither Margaret nor your mom, who is busy clothes-pegging her wash to

> *the clothesline you once briefly considered*
> *hanging yourself with*

answers. No one answers. In the long run, our silence doesn't matter. Even if one of us were to answer, even if you were to turn radical and *apply* for another *part* in another one of her plots, nothing would change our situation because (being her constant *others*) our situation is her situation. There is *an erased beach* inside her head and once you are on that beach the only saving grace to be found is *clarity*, the seeing of things as they are, eyes wide open, and then the getting down of those things, in detail:

> *Everything was very clear, clearer than usual, my hands with the stained nails, the sunlight falling on the ground through the apple-tree branches, each leaf, each white five-petalled yellow-centred flower and conical fine-haired dark red multi-seeded dwarf berry rendering itself in dry flat two-dimensional detail, like background foliage by one of the crazier Victorian painters, just before the invention of the camera; and at some time during that hour, though not for the whole hour, I forgot what things were called and saw instead what they are.*

Having had to play so many roles for her, you (and I) have ended up seated inside our own paper tents, surrounded by people howling, some "to summon help, some howl for revenge, others howl for blood..." We inscribe in short-hand our neighbours' natures, *their habits, their histories – we change the names, of course, because…/ we don't want to attract the howlers, but they're attracted anyway, as if by a scent: the walls of the paper tent are so thin that they can see the light of a candle,* the light inside the tent by which we seem to have developed, over time, a more dislocated eye than hers, an eye for seemingly disparate details, because one of us whispers,

> *Yes – meat loaf! Meat loaf, and enemas, and bulb-headed syringes used for what they called "feminine hygiene"*

> *– the three are not unconnected…*

Not unconnected?

How can that be? How can she connect what we, in our own way, have begun to see on her behalf?

By dint of tone, that is how. By the force of her voice, that voice so recognizable, still so eager to assert itself, still so young in its energy though the infirmities of age are now upon her:

> *It's begun to happen, the shrivelling. Only I have noticed it so far. There's the barest pucker in my voice, the barest wrinkle. Fear has entered me, a needleful of ether, constricting what in someone else would be my heart… How much of my life do I have left?*

Her heart constricts into

> *sentence or two, only a whisper.* I was born. I was. I.

This is Beckett in delirium, this is diseased life skinned down to a bare bone – *I* – the only intimation of respite being a sighting out of the corner of her eye of a shark that has nudged a sailor's naked, bleeding leg and then turned away.

There comes an hour, however, when life doubles back on itself, when NO – "the power of what is not there" – is suddenly more than a constriction of the heart, more than fear on stilts, more than dreams of decapitation. A real death is occurring. It stops Margaret's heart with a thud. She sees that *another man's hand coming out of (her father's) tweed sleeve*, and so once again she is standing inside a circle of dread, but this is no circle game. At this moment, a face put on to meet a face will not suffice, this is

> *that clean circle*
> *of dead space you have made*
> *and stay inside,*
> *mourning because it is clean.*

This is the circle within which she was bred by her father and this is the circle within which she will be bereft of her father. This is the circle within which her father

> *was sitting in a chair at dinner*
> *and a wave washed over him.*
> *Suddenly, whole beaches*
> *were simply gone.*
> *…Lake Superior. Last year.*

She has heard this self-reliant, knowing man suddenly cry,

> *Where is this forest? Why am I so cold?*
> *Please take me home.*

This moment of standstill amidst the on-rush of confusion is beautifully embodied by her as a river she swims *in by keeping still, like trout in a current,* a moment in which she thinks that he

> *looks erased.*
> *But somewhere in there, at the far end of the tunnel*
> *of pain and forgetting he's trapped in*
> *is the same father I knew before,*
> *the one who carried the green canoe*
> *over the portage, the painter trailing,*
> *myself with the fishing rods, slipping*
> *on the wet boulders...*

At this moment, there are no doubles, no stand-ins (powerful and persuasive as those voices have been in the past), no notes toward a poem that cannot be written. Suddenly, she has suffered an infestation of grief...

> *He went into the lake, in all his clothes,*
> *just waded out and sank.*

In her shocked mouth

> *grief has made*
> *and keeps on making:*
> *round silent Ohs...*

Look, they are everywhere: Oh. Oh. Oh. Oh.
What else can be said?

Well, much can still be said, because even the very briefest of stories can be a deep way of *saying.* And so she consoles herself with several stories that make no attempt at wryness or slyness:

It was my father taught my mother
how to dance.
I never knew that.
I thought it was the other way.
Ballroom was their style,
a graceful twirling,
curved arms and fancy footwork,
a green-eyed radio.

There is always more than you know.
There are always boxes
put away in the cellar,
worn shoes and cherished pictures,
notes you find later,
sheet music you can't play.

A woman came on Wednesdays
with tapes of waltzes.
She tried to make him shuffle
around the floor with her.
She said it would be good for him.
He didn't want to.

In grief, love *is* – and it is transparent, and so her line in these poems has become as transparent as glass. In grief, there is no place for *putting on your pelt of a bear* (and therefore, significantly, you and I are disappeared – as they used to say behind the Iron Curtain). In these poems of grief there is to be no

sliding in and out of my own slippery eelskin...

No: instead, she now finds herself remembering two long canoes of children who years ago had tipped into the wide cold water where she and her father had paddled...children who, while holding hands in the cold water, had sung till the chill had reached their hearts. In utter bleakness she says:

> *I suppose in our waking lives that's the best*
> *we can hope for, if you think of that moment*
> *stretched out for years.*

She has arrived at that still point

> *where the past*
> *let's go of and becomes the future;*
> *the place of caught breath*

where the trick is to have no trick: as the old blues song said it true, you just hold on to holding on...*and so we do*...she holds on to

> *what we will come to, sooner*
> *or later, when it's even darker*
> *than it is now, when the snow is colder,*
> *when it's darkest and coldest*
> *and candles are no longer any use to us*
> *and the visibility is zero:*

This is the place of caught breath. This is zeroland, but this is also, astonishingly for a poet who is sometimes so bleak, the place where her constricted heart becomes big with the strength of affirmation as she utters a cry... *Yes. It's still you. It's still you.*

This is the YES of a voice thrown into the echo of that huge NO. At this moment of not just clarity of detail but clarity of meaning, she cries out once more to her father... *I love you...like salt.*

She knows that she has performed to a sheet music she thought she didn't know how to play – and she has hit the notes cleanly as she watches her father move

away downstream
in his boat, so skilfully
although dead…
He wears his grey hat, and evidently
he can see again. There now,
he's around the corner. He's heading eventually
to the sea. Not the real one, with its sick whales
and oil slicks, but the other sea, where there can still be
safe arrivals.

Here, splendidly transparent, is the bald force of her grief.
Oh. Oh. Oh.
Yes.
Salt.

2011

IN GOD'S HEADBONE

There is an hour in the country night when the elms along the side roads crack in the cold and the white fields of wind-crusted snow seem to be a moonlit absence. My neighbour, however, who is a pig farmer, tells me that there is no absence to be found in the fields of our back concessions. The land, he says, is never empty. He says he has seen a huge cross drag itself over the hill behind my log house. "Back when I was a boy, when there was no electrical through here, people knew where the demons were, creatures with eyes instead of breasts and one with only a huge foot. My mother told me she'd seen him sleeping in the shade of his own foot. The trick around here is to keep a clear thought, and twenty below in the night will do that for your mind."

I told him that it's true, that at twenty below I see things with uncommon clarity but sometimes I see double, like seeing two birds and their ghosts on a wire.

"Don't worry, the ghosts around here always come home," my neighbour said. "God knows his own."

"Who might they be?"

"I wouldn't name names."

⌐>✦<⌐

I'd bought a 200-year-old log house that was standing abandoned and broken on a side road outside Stratford, our Ontario theatre town. I'd had it taken apart, with each squared pine log numbered, and then moved by flatbed trailer to 100 acres of farmland in this township, one of the last areas to be settled in south-western Ontario. That's what I saw on an old map I'd bought, a map from 1880, where my land was shown as wilderness, Ojibwa territory, and I had the map framed for hanging on a wall in the house.

⤙✦⤚

As the logs of the dismembered two-storey house were dropped one-by-one from the trailer to disappear into the tall yellow rape seed on a summer afternoon, the farmer, a man in his sixties, who worked his pig farm on the next 100 on the same concession road, said with a bemused smile, "I mind you're gonna make a house outta them. There was a log house right here on this spot from a hundred years ago. It was still here when I was a boy. We've been throwing them things away now for years."

⤙✦⤚

In 1840, through to the 1880s, settlers and loggers moved north from the village of Fergus along the Garafraxa Road, now Highway 6, to get to lumber camps and to Owen Sound and the lake boats. In those days, the road was only a crooked ox trail with some corduroying (logs laid side by side) through the swamps, cut and slash through the close bog (those old logs still sometimes heave up through our highway roadbeds in the spring). Often, settlers went northeast along the Proton Trail, from Mount Forest to Hopeville and Dundalk. They had the tenacity of the old country weeds that they had carried with them in their clothing.

By 1859, there were some 500 people in the Township, most of them Ulster Protestant Irish and Scots who spoke Gaelic and some English. There were also Deutschland Lutherans and Mennonites. They squared cedar logs and built homes and small churches, chinking and plastering the walls not only for warmth, but also to keep out the swarming clouds of mosquitoes and black flies. They built log barns to protect their cattle beasts and oxen from bears and wolves.

Those settlers set down the first village around here, calling it Hole-in-the-Woods, with their sawmill on the corner, a post office, a gristmill, and a hangman who had two roan geldings and a hansom cab. He was apparently known as Wishbone, and in his lifetime he was said to have hanged six men, one of whom had committed suicide while in custody but Wishbone hanged him anyway. My neighbour laughed as he told me that story (he had a gift for laughter at stories of great calamity, what he called grim deeds of violence done). "Women in childbirth had it hard," he said. "They died for lack of midwife care, and their babies died, too (*Here* – from words on a local tombstone – *lies a babe / that only cry'd / in baptism / to be washed from sin, / and dy'd)*, and often the babies were buried on the home-farms, sewn into heavy blankets (my neighbour – whose Swiss-German grandfather, a descendant of a long line of mercenaries, had come out from County Cork at the age of twelve in 1860 – showed me, by his mother's testimony, where a stillborn child had been put down one summer in a stand of lean cedars on my land, not too far from the log house:

a
syllable
clapped silent.

That old bush of cedar, ash, and pines was so dense and so trackless that women often got lost while looking for their cows, and some were found half-crazed – driven out of their minds by deerflies, black flies, and mosquitoes – and some were found frozen, and some were never found. I walked into a remnant of the old bush north of the log house, into a wall of warm rot, branches, leaves, boughs, vines…a wall of ennui in which there were openings that only went deeper into what seemed endlessly the same. I found myself feeling like a foundling left on his own doorstep, and I remember thinking that I was no one, a no one from nowhere, no walls, no borders, right there on my own land, lot twenty-two. I declared myself peripheral at the core.

As that bush had been slowly cleared into pockets of clustered farms, Armenian gypsies appeared out of the woods, selling cloth, thread, tea, and spices, while buying furs and goose feathers, hardwood ashes for making soap, and pieces of scrap iron. Then, travellers and lumber mills, and the big boat business in Georgian Bay (my great-uncle was a Lakes captain on *The City of Buffalo* out of Collingwood), taverns, halfway houses and hotels cropped up, and two villages took root in the township: Holstein (that had first been called Hole-in-the-Woods) and Yeoville.

Yeoville was a short walk to the west along my concession road. It was a place of a hundred souls in 1850, with a communal oxen shed on the corner, a post office (in those years, the mail carriers had wonderful names like Plumer Sterne), a blacksmith, a lumber mill and gristmill, a cheese factory, a weaver and carpenter, a general storekeeper, a Methodist church, and two escaped slaves from the Southern states – two brothers, who were known as "honey-dippers" because they were the men who lowered their long-handled spoons into the cesspools under the farmers' outhouses, carrying a sign on their cart: SANITATION SALVATION FOR THE NATION. They were also known as "sweet singers," and at the first wedding in Hole-in-the-Woods they not only sang but one of the brothers did what some called his honey-dipper dance, a high-stepping heel-and-toe while holding to a closed space, like a fugitive making his getaway by going nowhere fast.

The first wedding hereabouts took place because a man named George Boakes came to the door of Maggie Brodie asking for work. The Brodies, trying to clear their meagre acres for wheat, were a large family and Mrs. Brodie, burdened by a brood of girls, said that all she could offer as hospitality was one of her daughters as a wife, to which George said (I have this from my neighbour, who had it from his mother), "There's mules and there's donkeys, and mules balk but donkeys get the work done. Donkeys," he said, "wear a cross on their backs, and you're looking at a man who carries his cross when you're looking at me." The wedding dinner was fresh trout (the Saugeen and all its

branches were full of fish), potatoes boiled in a sugar kettle, rasp-
berries and scones.

Soon, their children went to the new log school, where in
1863 William McKenzie was still teaching in Gaelic as well as in
English. In 1878, a brick schoolhouse was built, and in 1892,
when a man named Duncan Galbraith owned my land, living in
a log house where mine now stands, a bell was put on the school
roof. The disused schoolhouse and the bell are still there on the
south side of our road. But Yeoville is long gone, abandoned and
ploughed under, a hydro pylon and a spring-water pond standing
where the blacksmith's house was, and not so far from the pond
is a scrapyard of cannibalized cars and all that's been left behind
as clues to love and the spillage from dreams: stunned clocks and
torn-up drainage tiles and sickles and hammer heads, springs and
shocks, carburetors and rims, sinks and bowls, pump plungers,
gaskets and rusted licence plates...

⊳✱⊴

It is high country, the highest elevation above sea level in the
province. "I mind we're in God's headbone, where there's a whole
lot of winter a lot of the time," my neighbour told me. He had a
way of speaking – by way of seeing and by turn of phrase – that
was on the slant. He told me that he had a metal plate in his own
headbone: shrapnel at Dieppe. "All these years since, I'm a
wounded man," he said and laughed. "Got a tilt to one eye."

He was right about the winter. This is where driving winds
lower the temperature to twenty and thirty below; the snows get
deep and the drifts high; and wind-curtains of blown snow can
blot out the sun so that it looks like a red wound. Not even the
local holy rollers who insist that they can see blue smoke snaking
across the floor on a Saturday night are apt to suggest that this red
sun should be taken as a sign of the redemptive wounds of the
Lord Jesus: it's a sun that's too cold and bristling with crimson
blood, a blood too shrouded in what looks like powdered ice.

Even today, when snow and ice storms come, some of the concession roads are not ploughed clear and farmers are left snowbound in solitude down lanes of bare black trees. There is a severe, pristine beauty to those leafless boughs in a cloud-free pale winter sky, but it is a beauty only for a mind capable of consoling itself in a lonely dark life – a beauty beyond decay, beyond the pathos and sentiment of fallen red and yellow leaves.

It wasn't until 1951, when Hydro at last serviced all these roads through the winter, that big yellow school buses forced the township to plough open the side roads. For a hundred years, however, wintertime had been a sunless season of waiting for the first spring light to leak through the trees like a streak of spittle low in the sky. With the April thaws had come, oftentimes, the finding of a farmer hanged at the end of his rope, worn out by the winter whiteness of everything, stunned by the pain of sudden sunlight glaring off sheets of ice and huge hanging icicles and, more than anything, by boredom:

> *The only true madness is loneliness,*
> *the monotonous voice in the skull*
> *that never stops*
> *   because never heard.*

It is hard to believe, but in the early, early days, some of these families had tried to stave off the freeze in their first sheds and shacks by building large fires as close as possible to the outside walls. On such a freezing cold night, I, too, find myself hungering for fire, even in this secure house of mine. It is into the heart of a fire that I stare, warmed by the heat that holds so well inside my log walls, and the big field stones in the wall of the fireplace have been so masterfully set by a local mason that they seem to float, as if the bone-breaking weight of farmwork that began a hundred years ago with stone picking could be lifted, could become an act of levitation.

In those days, some men and women, trying for relief, for a little ease from what they called "done feet"…took a pick-me-up mixture of sulphur and molasses to tonic their tired blood, while they simmered on the stove a pot of one tablespoon of salt, one "fig" of tobacco, one pint of urine, which they then applied by sponge to their bodies.

To treat chronic matters that could be deadly, they went right to ground and found remedies for their sicknesses in the countryside's river rodents, in the beaver, because the beaver in its glands carried an orange-brown alkaloid curative that contained high levels of what we now call acetylsalicylic acid, the essential to our Aspirin.

They had found redemptive power in the river rat. Its castoreum, they believed, cured snake and spider bites, gout, liver tumours, sciatica, hiccups, and amnesia.

What's more, the fat of the beaver cured epilepsy, bed sores, and colic.

While beaver blood helped with epilepsy, sleep walking, giddiness, and St. Vitus's Dance.

As for the awful grip of loneliness, my pig farmer had his cure: "When you get to feeling done-in by solitude, just squat yourself down in the woods with a deck of cards and lay out a hand of solitaire on an old stump, and sooner than you can say the word *Amen* somebody will lean over your shoulder telling you to put the black queen on the red king."

><+<

In the spring – always late in these high lands, so that tatters of snow still lie in the ditches as the grasses grow – the hillside in front of the log house is suddenly thick with golden dandelions, and the bobolinks and red-winged blackbirds are back. The stream behind the hill swells, and because of beaver dams there's a shallow black lake of stumps and fallen trunks that shift with the easing of the frost:

and those who have become the stone
voices of the land
shift also and say

god is not
the voice in the whirlwind

god is the whirlwind

at the last judgment we will all be trees.

Some people and some animals go whirlwind strange in April (my neighbour says Aye-prille, as if he were a close cousin to Chaucer).

Old man Smitherton, whose head was also hurt in the War, can be found marching alone through the muck of a ditch. Though he'd fought alongside GIs in the woods at Ardennes, he kicks his legs out like a newsreel stormtrooper as he goes singing, *There are rats, rats big as alley cats, in the store, in the quarter-master's store.*

Mrs. Pitcairne, a maker of macramé owls with pellet-like eyes of polished pine, keeps seeing her dead husband's face in her wash basin water, where he says vile things to her, inviting her to join him in hell, telling her to take her life by her own hand. To make sure she doesn't harm herself, her children nightly tie her to her marriage bed.

And then there are the dead groundhogs found nailed by their tails to the township WELCOME signs, and reports of horses being disembowelled in the night, and the sighting of the complete skin of a horse, including legs and hoofs, draped over a tripod of cut saplings like a druidic offering set among the birch trees.

"But there's the thing I can't never explain, except to say it's in their nature," my neighbour tells me, "is how come pigs, being as intelligent in the same way that horses are certain to be stupid are cannibals, how come for no good reason pigs'll attack and gang up and eat one of their own alive? It's the alive I don't get."

"It's because God is with us," his wife says. "He knows His own."

"She goes on, she goes on," he says, smiling indulgently. She says nothing more. They've been married for well over forty years. I suspect that she is a secret drinker.

The dank April wetness, the last of the frost, eases out of the ground, the emerging stems and stalks become yellow, the tractors rattle and crank down the lanes, and in late May, the black flies die off. My neighbour tells me, "I mind we're in summer soon. I mind our summer is as hard as our winter, blistering like our winter can be bleak." Not nearly so bleak to see, I tell him, as all the motor homes sitting forlornly along so many shoulders of so many concession roads, new mobile homes mounted up on concrete blocks, their wheel casings stripped.

Yeoville is gone, along with the graceful hotels along the highway. The stone schoolhouse across the concession road from me is gone. The villages of Sacket's Corner and Maple Lane that were close by are gone, the sawmill and lime kilns are gone, and so is the Mount Zion church that was down the road to the east, beyond what was a rolling hill, a hill that's been turned inside out, gouged for gravel. It is now a left-behind swamp of lurid lime-green scum attractive to dragonflies.

"I mind it's a colour I've not seen before," my neighbour said, "not a colour to be dreaming in."

For a long while, the closest I could come to these lives was to walk back into the bush where there are giant hares and there are still wolves who howl in the winter, but on such a walk, so that I did not get lost, I would follow a stream – a branch of the Saugeen – where I'd find a dead, decaying beaver in the shallows or I'd flush birds, until I'd get to an eerie stand of gleaming white dead elm trunks in a marsh that was once flooded by beaver dams. It's dried out now, so that the entire ground seems covered by a thick weave and braiding of bleached rushes and bleached long grass. It seems to be a kind of primeval prayer mat, a place to meet ghosts, a place where you might become someone you never knew.

One evening after a walk, as I described this place and this feeling to my neighbour, he turned a little shy, moved to at last feel free to tell me something very personal and he said that his mother had been a dead ringer twice and it had changed her life.

"What do you mean a dead ringer? You mean twins?"

"No, no," he said. "Back in her day, mostly because of how lead poisoning worked, they found there was people stretched out who looked dead as doornails, and so got buried for being dead, when really they were still alive. And they died suffocating in their boxes. So families would tie a string to the hand of the body in the box and run it up through the earth to a bell on top of the grave, and my mother, whose job it was to sit, turned out to be a dead ringer twice. Two people came back to life because of her answering the bell. She came to believe she had a gift for resurrection."

It was not until this last spring – when the foundation of my log house became wet, when the walls at the southwest corner of the basement began to weep – that a local farmer, a douser, a diviner, drove by and I came to really feel I belonged to a life that is almost totally gone, gutted by gravel pits. He was an up-to-date diviner. He travelled with a small packet of welded weaponry carried in an old family physician's bag – coat hangers, iron rods, and a small iron drum casing (he was, among other things, in the employ of

Hydro, who paid him to find lost underground cables). He came to me the old way, with an apple branch cut to the shape of a *Y*, and he walked back and forth through the long grass witching for water. The branch in his hands dipped to the earth and he said, "There's an underground stream and it bends right at the corner of the house. Dig there and put in your weeping tiles." He handed me the branch and told me to try. "Some have the gift," he said.

I held the branch, the fork of the *Y* to my hips, and suddenly it whipped down, and because I was holding it hard, the bark tore in my hands. "You don't need me," the farmer said. "You can find all your own water on your own land as you want." A few days later, excited, I walked the twenty-three acres that were under cultivation, criss-crossing and tracking the underground water as if I were reading the map of the land's body, all the veins, able to feel the pulse of what had been marked as empty wilderness on my old 1880s map. Later, when I sat in the evening watching the fireplace field stones float in the air, I felt at last a real intimacy with the place, with my neighbour the pig farmer, whose favourite song was a complaint about his God-fearing wife that made us laugh,

> *It's hard to kiss*
> *the lips at night*
> *that chew your ass out*
> *all day long,*
> *she goes on, she goes on.*

He had warned me, "This is dark country, and in some ways it's getting darker, since there are people presently here who would steal the time of day."

⌐⊷⌐

I've come to feel at ease, even intimate with that darkness in this country, and the laughter that lurks in its hollows, and also with those dead children who were sewn into blankets, with those women who got lost in the land of dead elms, with the men and women of the old township who had step-danced to the honey-dipper's song of a hope that was always just "six pickles short of a jar," and even with the folks of Luther Marsh to the south who long ago named a township east of me, Melancthon – after Martin Luther's right-hand zealot – "salvation by faith alone" – for the dour Elect, covenanted people on the lip of the abyss! We have ended up as come-by-chance neighbours. I have to say, however, that I cannot imagine who the local people were who settled sections around a cross roads not far from the marsh, calling the home town they built Sodom. What did they have in mind?

⟊

On a hot July day, my ears, nose, and hair being swarmed by cluster flies, I told my neighbour that I missed our winter nights under the clarity of a cold moon. I missed it when everything was white, when there was the promise that things could come clear. He said, "I mind we'll soon find you sleeping in the shade of a demon's foot."

He liked saying that. It reminded him of his mother, but I had to tell him, "Naw, these days the demons have all got done feet."

"So you might say," he said, laughing. "Meanwhile, they're piling up on the other side." Then he winked at me. He had never winked at me. I felt a sudden pang of love for the man, but knew that if ever I were to tell him so, he'd shut down and go away from me into an unyielding silence.

The closest intimacy he'd ever been able to offer me, other than stories about his mother, was to suggest that I watch him kill a pig.

"Divining is one thing," I told him, "but hanging a hog on a hook for the skinning is another," and I declined, which I think hurt him. But he said nothing.

Down the road, another mobile home had been mounted wheeless on concrete blocks.

Gravel trucks were on the rumble, raising plumes of dust.

2017

EMILY THE BAT

We have all walked a country road late at night and looked up and seen swooping shadows. We have shuddered at those shadows, knowing that flying vermin of the night are careening close by, sightless, disease-ridden. We step back, even shrink back, because we suspect all the tales we have heard are true: a bat in the house means horrible death, a bat's bite brings on rabies, a bat caught in a woman's hair must be killed and the woman's head must be shaved clean, and worst of all, some bats, who are manlike spirits risen from the dead, search through the night for open windows and a delicate white throat so they can feed on human blood before the moon goes down…engorged creatures afraid only of crucifixes, killable only by a stake driven through the heart.

All of this, of course, is untrue. There are bats in the Americas that feed on blood, after making a small cut in an animal's flesh, lap up the blood trickling from the wound. But there are no such flying mammals in Transylvania, or anywhere else in the dark forests of Europe.

What is true is that there are billions upon billions of bats throughout the world – flying animals…some who have beautiful ears, and some with the faces of sleek foxes and a down-like fur on their chests, hanging by their thumbs together in great clusters, licking themselves cleaner than house cats. Consider the little brown bat (for whom God is an owl), the two-gram Kitti's hog-nosed bat (popularized as the bumblebee bat), eastern pipistrelles, vesper bats, including the eastern small-footed, Europe's greater and lesser horseshoes, the serotines, shaggy-furred whiskered bat, pallid bats, silver-tipped and stark naked free-tailed bats, the greater bulldog bat of Panama that catches and eats fish, the spectral bat, the greater spear-nosed bat, the hairy-legged vampire who does not suck but bites the cloacal (shit-bearing) cavity of chickens, and the lesser bamboo bat, our smallest living mammal, weighing in at 1.5 grams, forearms 21 to 23 millimetres long, with wings folded, no larger than the terminal joint of the human thumb, pulsing with liver, heart, lungs, brain, blood, bones, testes and penis.

What we have is a garden of eccentrics hanging in Henry Vaughn's "deep but dazzling darkness," eccentrics who wake and career and dive through the night hours, through that space where prophets and poets say they have seen things unseen before. According to that most eccentric of dazzling poets, Emily Dickinson, this is the dark space from which the essential oils are wrung,

> The Attar from the Rose

these are the essential truths that she has tried so hard to tell us "slant," as if her

> Mind were going blind –
> Groped up, to see if God were there –

these – faced with the great BLANK of unknowing – are the truths that she is hanging on to by her thumbs – if only to see if she herself is still there – herself being a reclusive, plain woman with middle-parted chestnut hair, wide-set slightly popping eyes, sparrow-chested…with a manner chaste in love at one moment, yet rapturous at another,

> Wild nights – Wild nights!
> Were I with thee
> Wild nights should be
> Our luxury!

Rowing in Eden –
Ah! The Sea!
Might I but Moor – Tonight –
In Thee!

…she can be this intimate and yet so obscure, she can be open yet elusive…a mystic, a seducer, no sooner self-effacing than imperious…a lesbian? a hysteric? a healer? a heretic? a consumptive? Who knows exactly which? But there she is. Emily in her daytime white dress, small-boned, small-footed, elfin… Emily in all her aspects, a poet to be approached gradually (as "the truth must dazzle gradually"), Emily in uprising in flight, becoming the nocturnal creature she calls herself,

…dun, with wrinkled Wings –
Like fallow Article…

… Describing in the Air
An Arc alike inscrutable
Elate Philosopher…

Empowered with what malignity
Auspiciously withheld…

Beneficent

Emily the bat, emerging out of the cave of night. As all bats operate by sonar, as their ears are their seeing eyes in the night, so too her singular strength is aural, lying in how she hears herself – how she turns a conventional thought, a conventional flight pattern of verse into angular emergence as she swerves to the left, to the right, taking unanticipated breath breaks,

More Life – went out – when He went
Than Ordinary Breath –

Lit with a finer Phosphor –
Requiring in the Quench –

A Power of Renowned Cold,
The Climate of the Grave
A Temperature just adequate…

Emily the bat, made, as all creatures must be made, in the image of God – a hog-nosed elate singer of songs, blind but seeing, a carrier of who knows what malignity or beneficence as she describes the inscrutable arc made by her wings. Within that arc, the dark itself dazzles and is made scrutable and made deep – as Emily by going deep is made scrutable.

2011–2017

ON A SUNDAY
MORNING SIDEWALK

On one of those early Sunday morning sidewalks when there was no one to be found but a latecomer hurrying on his way to church, and a straggler squinting, though the sun was not yet strong, I would see on Yonge Street up ahead coming at me two finger-popping young black men about my age, which was nineteen, Little Lester Odom (sporting H tracks on his arm) and his every day bro, whom he called a blip, "You is a blip, man," Dougie Richardson, whose father had been an Olympics sprinter but Dougie was intending to be a tenorman, stepping toward me with that little pimp-walking hitch to his right hip (a slight drag to his other leg, syncopating his left shoe), his hand out in greeting, calling:

> *I'm cool as the breeze on Lake Louise*
> *I ain't no square from Delaware,*
> *I got lard in my hair.*
> *So gimme five on one cause the other four are sore.*

Over the next year or two, I'd sometimes hear *the breeze on Lake Louise* in Sonny Terry singing:

> *Hooray hooray these women is killing me —*

or Brownie McGhee singing:

> *the blacker the berries the sweeter the juice —*

or J.D. (Jelly Jaw) Short singing:

I'm a snake doctor man, I fly by easy, fly by low –

but day-by-day I was not trying to analyze or think through what I was hearing…the dance for me, like any young man sane and sexual at my age, was in my bones, in the syncopated hitch to the hip, the move of the belly to the jelly roll, to the grinding of coffee not in the counting of stresses and caesuras and such.

Until maybe two more years down the line, when I was standing in the cold stone halls of Toronto's Hart House and I surprised myself by believing that I had just heard Dougie's pimp-walking step on the 2/4 and the reach of full rhymes across the rhythm in a poem by Wallace Stevens that had just been read aloud to an academic crowd:

Sóon / with / a / nóise
like / tám / bour / ínes
Cáme / her / atten / dánt
Býe / zan / tínes

I had heard immediately what I had not heard upon my first reading of this poem – that by stepping with a heavy foot on the stresses, the lines could be bop-walked, particularly with a shift of the stress from *zan* to *By* (pronouncing it *Bye*), which served to enhance to a higher degree the dance rhythm of the four-stress line.

I began in the days following to put not just my eye but my ear to the chalkboard and to the page, so that it was easy, having a look and a hear, to pick up the double beat of T.S. Eliot's favourite percussionist, Sweeney, who was still out there among the nightingales:

Doris:	*You'll carry me off? To a cannibal isle?*
Sweeney:	*I'll be the cannibal*
Doris:	*I'll be the missionary.*
	I'll convert you.
Sweeney:	*I'll convert* you!

This being what my young friend Dougie Richardson (who did grow up to become an outstanding tenorman) would have called "cut time."

⇌✦⇋

That Dougie was on my mind carried me back to my early Sunday morning sidewalks and his callout for a touching of hands or, more accurately, the touching together (so hip) of thumbs only:

Gimme fíve on óne cause the other fóur are sóre.

There are four stresses to his jive-talking, so pronounced you can, if you want, finger-pop on the beat, but unlike *cool as the breeze on Lake Louise* (eight syllables), Dougie's handshake line has twelve syllables, necessitating a change in duration within the line itself (but let me take a break right here, take five in the jive, for a brief word about how the four-stress line, prevalent in song and poetry of a kind in our time, goes all the way back through the Border Ballads – through Shakespeare: everything goes through Shakespeare – to Anglo-Saxon verse, the stresses in the Anglo-Saxon being separated two by two by a caesura, a break – as in "break dancing," with the beat actually – again to use the language of rap – "pumped" by alliteration. To get the effect, read the following lines aloud with a *faux* Swedish lilt:

ne forstes fnaest	*ne syres flaest,*
ne haegles hryre,	*ne hrimes dryer,*
ne sunnan hactu,	*ne sincaldu,*

47

ne wearm weder,   ne winterscur
wihte gewyrdan,   ac se wong seonmaxo
eadig ond onsund.[1]

However, to get back to Dougie's handshake line and the matter of duration, what we hear by reading his line aloud is *Gimme five / on one / cause the other four / are sore*

$$(3) \ / \ (2) \ / \ (5) \ / \ (2)$$

while if we read *cool as / the breeze / on Lake / Louise,* four stresses over eight syllables, the matter of duration demands that the more unstressed syllables there are in a line, the faster the syllables in the line must be spoken, as in, for example, a couplet, syncopated, by the rappers Run DMC:

> *He's the bétter of the bést, best belíeve he's the báddest (14)*
> *Perfect tíming when I'm clímbing I'm the rhyming acrobatíst (16)*

With four stresses to each of these lines, with their fourteen and sixteen syllables, there is no time open for being laid-back, for being cool as any breeze known to Louise.

⤜✦⤛

A persistent question that crops up, especially in academe, is can even the *baddest* of the best rhymers be a serious intellectual

---

[1] From "Phoenix"
Or breath of frost   or blast of fire,
Or freezing hail   or fall of rime,
Or blaze of sun   or bitter-long cold,
Or scorching summer or winter storm
Work harm a whit,   but the plain endures
Sound and unscathed.

climber? In other words, with all that out-front seemingly simple-minded rhyming (so unfashionable among leftover Black Mountaineers and throwback Beats, let alone the academically inclined), can a poet operating in this mode *move*, to any degree, as we read and hear him, in the company of a Wallace Stevens or a T.S. Eliot?

To make a point but not a boast, and because I pretty much knew what I meant to do in my Hogg poems with my own man-child signifier, John the Conqueroo, let me begin with the opening two lines of his "rap," which are actually one line of everyday ıambıc pentameter, broken, syncopated:

> *Í am the Mán who ám*
> *in short I ís*
> *John the Conqueroo Decatur*

The reader hears that this man-child has begun by seeing himself not just as a figure who is mythic in the Delta – John the Conqueroo – but he also has boldly played upon the words of Jesus: (I am who am, *Matthew*), followed by an existential Ebonic assertion of "hisself" in which he is able to turn what seems to be a normal two-beat line into three beats – by willing (as he would deliver it) that old hitch into the line,

> *in short Í ís*

(Emily Dickinson had long since mastered how to play this game – she takes what would have been a two-beat line that would have been played against the three... So *wé must méet apárt – You thére I hére –* and instead uses dashes in her usual unorthodox way so as to cause two breaks in the second and fourth lines,

> *So we must meet apart –*
> *You there – I here –*

> *With just the Door ajar*
> *That Oceans are – and Prayer –*

thereby creating three "testifying stresses" where there were only two regular stresses – carrying on just like my boy John the Conqueroo with his *In shórt Í ís*).

To enlarge on the possibilities open to such poetry, here (hear) is another Hogg character – the street preacher, Jeremiah Stuck – whose meditation on the mysteries of Jesus and Judas – the barebones of the theology – is motored by internal rhyming:

> *But the genius of Judas perceived the applied*
> *logic that eluded*
> *the priestly pedagogic, who wouldn't believe*
> *God'd take two legs,*
> *let alone save the dregs by doing a suicide –*
> *that His benevolent*
> *intention was our subsequent redemption*
> *since back before*
> *man's invention –*

T.S. Eliot has lines of the same intent, except that they move at a different tempo, *andante ma non troppo,* meaning that we have a slow-walking T.S. Eliot with four stresses, eight syllables, from *Ash Wednesday,* where he unabashedly engages the Jesus story by moving his meaning forward through internal rhymes that keep the beat and reach across the rhythm:

> *But the fountain sprang up and the bird sang down*
> *Redeém the tíme, redeém the dréam*
> *the tokén of the wórd unhéard, unspóken*

Eliot, in fact, in the same poem, has gone off as half-cocked as any Big Pun or Jay-Z rhyming fool of a rapper:

Against the Word the unstilled world still whirled
About the centre of the silent Word…

Put that couplet in DJ Marley Marl's ear and on will come, seemingly overpowering to some, the current technology – DJ will be "scratching" and he will be sampling, making his turntables crank and *jolt* and come back, returning on the break, going against the return, making the repeats…giving us T.S. Eliot in a *surround* new *sound.*

Enter the Technology

This is how the getting of the surround sound in rap works: – the standard poetic line, having – as we've seen – a flexible syllable count, is played against a standard – as we've seen – fixed metrical beat, but then – to let the technology go to work at play – the metrics are taken apart – as one might take apart a car only to put the old parts and some new parts back together – through various engineering strategies – to arrive at another but the same car.

Some of these "could be" strategies are: "scratching" – turning by hand of a vinyl record(s) on a turntable…so that the needle can be scratched against, and with, the groove; a rupture, the break beat – which is a solo segment of arbitrary length played by the bass guitar and the drummer; "sampling" – the borrowing of a portion of an already recorded song, that portion being repeated, oftentimes on a loop (this usually being…not an act of copyright thievery but an act of homage to the past); "leakage" – the pumping (boosting) of – among other possibilities – an 808 bass drum, reaching at times for an all-pervading low-frequency hum… All of this leading to the constructing and reconstructing of such strategies into a multiple rhythmic fusion of forces around the ancient skaldic (the rapper's) invitation to chant…loud, Louder, LOUDEST…

There is an irony to this reconstruction – this BOOM DIGITAL SMASH YOUR BRAIN TR-808 DRUM BOOM replete with breaking glass, howls, shrieks, and sirens –

All of these polyrhythmic forces are merged into One, a seemingly overwhelming One, but here's the irony – the rapper's voice does not get drowned out – quite the opposite. It is the rapper who is relentlessly articulate (as many a rock singer, also rooted in the blues, is haplessly a mumbler and slurrer)…it is the rapper who articulates and rearticulates his history – and not just the history of gangs and murders (Biggie Smalls and Tupac Shakur) but the history of rap's "literary" roots back through DJ Kool Herc, Grandmaster Flash and the Furious Five ("Don't push me cause I'm close to the edge"), James Brown, Street Punk, Bo Diddley, doo wop and bebop singers, Solomon Burke and Muhammad Ali, skip rope rhymes, Cab Calloway, Pigmeat Markham, every seventh son of a seventh son, Crow Jane and Howlin' Wolf and John the Conqueroo…

Because rap's rage at the po-lice is always at a white heat (Big Pun might like that little pun), a lot of people think the language of such rage has to lack political subtlety, suffer from social simplicity. But consider Ice Cube's couplet from "Endangered Species":

> *Now kíll ten of mé to gét the jób corréct.*
> *To sérve, to protéct and bréak a nígga's néck.*

Some scholars do talk admiringly of Dryden, of Pope, their skilful deployment of the caesura and how their rhyme endings (*his thick skull – be* thou *dull*) enforce and expand upon the meaning of their heroic couplets – though *the job correct* as it rhymes with *a nigga's neck* may not be as syllabically mono-mono as

Dryden's *skull-dull*, it is (given the context of *kill* and the universal police motto, to *serve and protect*) pretty good, fiercely resonant – forcing home the irony of corrécting a *nígga's néck* by bréaking it.

Just how layered rap in its short narrative can be is evident in Eminem's contribution to Jay-Z's "Renegade":

> *Now who's the king of these rude*
>   *ludicrous lucrative lyrics*
> *Who could inherit the title, put the*
>   *youth in hysterics*
> *Usin' his music to steer it, sharin'*
>   *his views and his merits*
> *But there's a huge interference –*
>   *they're sayin' you shouldn't hear it*
> *Maybe it's hatred I spew, maybe*
>   *it's food for the spirit*
> *Maybe it's beautiful music I made*
>   *for you to just cherish*
> *But I'm debated, disputed, hated,*
>   *and viewed in America*
> *As a motherfuckin' drug addict –*
>   *like you didn't experiment?*

Like, this man Muldoon had stepped off the roof of the Ed Sullivan Theatre in New York where Eminem had just performed for – of all people – *The Tonight Show* – loud with *leakage* – as interlocutor for Ice-T, provocateur, before David Letterman's bedroom crowd, Paul Muldoon came onto the scene, with pedigree from academe, being a rhymester, a professor, of the first degree, lately of Princeton, a poet who knows where he has been:

Were we not weaned too then from
Mandrax and mandrake
or snorted we in the seven
leepers' den
a line of coke…

He is a serious, erudite poet who has a whole lot of cousins who validate him as he validates them:

And I'm taken aback (jolt upon jolt)
to think that Hendrix did it all "by hand."

To think, moreover, that he used four-track
one-inch tape has (jolt upon jolt) evoked
the long, long view…
then there was the wah-wah on "Voodoo Child
(Slight Return)" from Electric Ladyland.

Muldoon has the hitch and he, too, believes that rhyme is what knits together the wit by keeping the time – which allows, as a dropped stitch, the last line:

He sucked, he'll have you know,
the tell-tale sixth toe
of a woman who looked like a young Marilyn Monroe,
her húbby gétting a líttle stroppy
when he fóund them thére in the báck of that old jalópy.

Other papers please copy.

And then he really bops the doodlebob –

The Bangle

I

Between the bream with cumin and the beef with marrow
in Le Petit Zinc
a bangle gleamed. Aurora Australis.
Many a bream, my darling, and many a luce
in stew.

II

Not unlike the magpie and the daw,
the emu loves a shiny doodah,
a shiny doodlebob.

III

So a harum-scarum
Bushman, hey, would slash one forearm
with a flint, ho, or a sliver of steel
till it flashed, hey ho, like a hel-
iograph.

IV

By dribs, hey, by dribs and drabs
the emu's still lured from its diet of fruit and herbs
with a bottle cap, ho, or a bit of tinfoil
till it's in the enemy's toils.

V

Its song ranges from a boom to a kerplunks
Reminiscent of the worst excesses of Conlon Nancarrow.

When I was a boy who had learned how to lie about being under barroom age, back even before I'd met Dougie, I had gone for the first time to a jazz supper club in Toronto, the Plaza Room, to hear Calvin Jackson (pi-án-ist, he called himself), a portly but sturdy black man who liked to ride around town in his Rolls-Royce with his white blond wife up front (this was the mid-Fifties!). The Plaza Room was in the Park Plaza Hotel, the same room under a different name where Paul Muldoon, years later, would meet with an ending – that is, be told oh so politely to take a hike, to get lost – that is both satisfying and apt as an ending to what I have been trying to say:

On my last trip (to Toronto) we went to a disco in the Park Plaza,
where I helped a girl in a bin-liner dress to find her contact lens.
—Did you know that Spinoza was a lens-grinder?
—Are you for real?…
—A lens, I went on, is really a lentil. A pulse…
—Did you know that Yonge Street's the longest street in the world?
—I can't say that I did.
—Well, it starts a thousand miles to the north, and it ends right here.

A Yonge Street ending that could only be, if it were on a Sunday morning sidewalk, a beginning.
Gimme five…

2011

VINCE CARTER,
HE DON'T STING,
HE BUTTERFLY

In the name of the Bee –
And of the Butterfly –
And of the Breeze – Amen!
—EMILY DICKINSON

"It's early early, man."

"More like nearly," a white boy says. "Nearly is what's doing now."

Five or six Raptor bench players are out on the floor shooting hoops.

Four clusters of 48 BOSE speakers in the Air Canada Centre are on 85-decibel sonic overblast.

The white boy standing in the gatewell to Sections 115/116, talking *ghetto noir,* says: "But like, if we'da been on time we'da been *nearly* early."

Boom boom, the man sitting beside me says, *Boom,* laughing to himself.

He has a silver stud in his eyebrow, is eating a candy apple and drinking an $11 cup of beer. "Being here is like being inside a damn boom box." He makes a face. He says that "What I actually am is a discount broker." The woman to the other side of me says gaily, "I'm in bonds."

"Whaa…?" he cries, cupping his ear.

She repeats: "I'm in bonds."

"Shit," the discount broker says, "I thought you were talking bondage."

The starting players are now down on the floor loping and dogging to the basket, doing pre-game layups and little air-treading dunks, getting limber and loose in their satin warm-up pants.

The discount man is patting his foot to the "fattest beat, man" – "*the fattest!*" the relentless thudding of Jay-Z *putting it right in your mouth* sounds while Vince Carter fires up a long practice three-pointer from "downtown" – as the sportscasters like to say – downtown, as in Motown downtown…these are certainly not shots from the twin-half-tonne-pickup-trucks-parked-in-the-driveway-905-suburbia where these amiable thousands of almost all white folks seem to be from, almost all the white folks who are here not only nearly early but more than early to watch teams of almost all tall and taller black folks play.

Carter begins to bop-walk the ball to the looping 808 drum *boom* as he cross-dribbles between his legs, picking up on the skip-rope rhymes in the music. The growing crowd gets settled, easy in their anticipation of the game. The discount man starts talking intently – but to no one in particular – about the wildlife moraine where he lives north of the city, and how he can't wait for the snows to come so that he can go cross-country skiing with his family, family being what he says he likes about basketball, always coming to the games with his family, even if his seats cost him $70. "It's a family game," he says with a strange edge of menace to his tone.

Carter is standing on the sideline, waiting for the opening ceremonies, a white towel draped around his head, cowled like a Redemptorist monk.

When I played school basketball in this town, it was a white boys' game, a game played in badly lit gyms so small people stood up against the walls to watch, and my father – who, like everybody else in town, didn't know anything about the game – asked me one day if all the guys on my team wore those same kind of white running shoes? (Converse All-Stars, the style shoe of the day.)

"It's not a fag game, Dad," I said.

Back then, the only black player in the province who anybody had heard of was Fred Thomas, who had played at Assumption, a tiny frontier college that was big in basketball in Windsor. That team had beaten the Harlem Globetrotters. Thomas, for a time, was my weekend coach in high school. He taught me that the game may look like attitude and shooting "all net"…but it is all in the feet…that is, if you had position, especially in rebounding, you had more than half of everything because you had the ball. In the late 1950s, when I went to Assumption myself, the young players doing wind sprints with me were from parishes in upstate New York or Indiana, real Hoosiers – they wore crew cuts (or flat tops! as if they were crew members from the same Panavision aircraft carrier movie). These teammates of mine told me, with a curl of the lip, that I was a wrong kind of guy because I not only listened to "nigger music" (rhythm and blues) on my record player in my room but I played "nigger ball" (playground, showboat ball), with my hook shot and double pumps, sometimes singing to myself

No gal made has got a
shade on Sweet Georgia Brown…

Those white boys – card-carrying Catholics and mostly McCarthyites – espoused the modest one-hand push shot, the two-hand set shot, the twelve-foot jumper, the under-hand-from-between-the-legs foul shot, the weave, the all-court stall "killing of the clock." Bland-ball. And for all the brilliance of a Bob Cousy, who begat Pistol Pete Maravich (the forgotten precursor of all the present big-time shooters), who begat Larry Bird, it was Glenn Miller-ball back then, "In-the-Mood"-ball, waiting for Doctor J. and Do-Wop, or, more to the point, waiting for

Motown to come to the Los Angeles Forum and go down home with the national anthem before the 1983 All-Star Game.

When Marvin Gaye, with all the arena lights turned down low that afternoon, wailed "the rocket's red glare" to a syncopated hip-hop-inflected back-beat, when he flattened note after note, he deconstructed what had been a sacred text for R&B cover-singers like Pat Boone and opera stars like Robert Merrill. The *ghetto noir* beat had become, by then, not just the backbone of American urban song but the brazen face, too, and basketball, like the music, had become a black urban game, the players as in-your-face with attitude as the music. By the time Michael Jordan came along, by the time Dennis Rodman showed up with his feet always in position, wearing a dozen tattoos and a blond wig, bland-ball was long gone and the ghost of Pat Boone wearing white bucks was walking lost out on Highway 61.

"Do you know," the discount broker with the stud in his eyebrow says, "that the players choose some of the game music?"

"So I hear."

"And they play different music for the offence and different music for the defence?"

"*Vin*-sanity."

"I need ear sanity," the bond lady says and stands up, arms extended.

As if in answer to her silent plea, the house announcer asks the crowd to rise and stand in silence to mark the Twin Towers killings of September 11.

"Ladies and gentlemen," the announcer then says, "would you please remain standing for the presentation of the colours, presented tonight by our own Royal Canadian Mounted Police."

Five stern men in scarlet tunics stride through the crowd onto the floor, arms swinging in lock-stride, carrying the flags. They wheel, snap to attention, and face – two of them with trimmed brush moustaches – the black ladies of the Faith Chorale. The Raptors stand shoulder to shoulder, their long gleaming satin shorts hanging on their long black bodies, their skinny shins, like fat-mama pantaloons. Carter stands out on the wing, slightly apart. The Faith Chorale sings "God Bless America," a tidy rendition, all the antiphonal accents in the right place. Then, fronted by Sharon Riley, they bop-jam "O Canada": they syncopate the *Os*, the *stand on guard,* and turn the song into a shout, a break-beat proclamation…a *praise* song of Canada as it has never been praised before, and some in the crowd begin to *jump up* (the Mounties don't move a muscle, not a flicker of moustache), and Antonio Davis, the black power forward who has worried publicly that his children might lose their American roots in Toronto, begins to smile and bob his head.

Sharon Riley has not only deconstructed "O Canada," she has *torn* it up. Made it "*Yo* Canada" to fist-pumping cheers as Vince Carter tucks his chin down into his warm-up shirt, drawing the shirt up to his nose, hiding his face the way a kid hides, his mouth covered, eyes closed; and later talking to him I say, "You pull your shirt up, it looks to me like you're either play acting or actually praying."

"I pray, man, twice, sometimes three times – in the dressing room, before the starting lineup, and when we do the national anthems."

"A man who pulls his practice shirt up over his face in front of nineteen thousand, to pray, he must have some kind of big botheration on his mind or something to hide?"

"I need prayer all the time, for strength. I pray for my teammates. Before the game, after the game."

"When you pray for strength, you pray to win?"

"No."

"That'd be vulgar?"

"Exactly."

"You pray to be the best you are?"

"For the things I am able to do. I pray for forgiveness."

"You think you need forgiveness…you're warming up for a basketball game and you think you need forgiveness?"

"It's like it's a church, out there on the court."

"And up comes the T-shirt?"

"Right."

"To get publicly private?"

He gives me a big smile. He is beguiling because of that guileless smile, a smile that gives him his air of unknowingness (his razor moustache would be sinister on any other face), a man seemingly free from envy and helpless in the presence of wrong, almost as if he has an incapacity to imagine malice (*and* therefore cannot conceive of retaliation), a man of active good nature, a Billy Budd on the back court, whose self-approving sense of his own singularity is so persuasive that you have to wonder what accusing voice he hears when he says he is asking for forgiveness: forgiveness for what?

Boooooom. Boom.

The whistle blows.

The game begins, a tip-off from the Dream Hakeem to Mo Pete to Carter to Mo Pete. *Swoosh.* Two points. *Boom.* And then a strong rebound and another two points. I am waiting to see if this is going to be a game of one-on-one moves to the hoop, street ball, slam, playground ball, dunk, or a game of the little things – the necessary game if a team is going to win consistently, the game of little things that is played by men who've been in the league ten years – a game of backdoor cuts, hitting the open man, post-ups, setting the pick-and-roll to the hoop. *Boom.* I realize the 48 BOSE bass line is still thumping over the play, through the play. It is like a pulse, electronic *leakage,* a hum that gets to be an ache in the bones. This is *power* embedded in the play (at hockey games, as soon as the puck is dropped the music must stop – otherwise, the league imposes a fine). It's time. If you listen. One pulse for offence, a different one for defence. The pulse is an invitation to power-dunk. It is an invitation to play to the crowd, but "dunks are what you do when you're losing," a wise old pro has said, "and no one cares except the crowd. If you're playing to the crowd when you push the ball up the floor, you're not playing the game to win."

Carter is pushing the ball up the floor, but he is not looking to dunk, not this time. He seems to be looking to make an outlet pass, looking to do one of the little things out on the perimeter of the key, as his teammates clear out to the right, and he holds the ball in his right hand and swings it – as if the globe in his hand is all the world – and then his right foot hooks forward and back, forward and back, and behind the *boom boom* I believe I hear Coltrane, the honk of his horn, *vurun-teeoh,* as he spins left, cross-dribbles, *tee-yu,* and then a bounce, a bounding leap, *aanh.* as he eases in a layup, and later I say to him. "There is a move you make, and what I hear is Coltrane."

"Funny you say that."

"You hear music while you're making your move?"

"Like you say, the beat of a particular song. I have heard it more than I can say. I always play with the beat. I want to be on the music, whether it's R&B, hip-hop, rap, classical, jazz – it's always to a beat."

"Or off the beat!"

"Maybe it's a critical point in the game. I could be humming to a beat to myself, singing to myself. I play with the music. I sit back, I analyze, I am looking at players, their reactions to different situations – things normal players wouldn't do."

I worry about forcing ideas on him, encouraging him to say things he doesn't want to say – he seems so accommodating, still just twenty-four years old, so ready to play along, to skim the scene with that little ingratiating pout to his lower lip. But since I've been told that in school he had a gift for mathematics, and mathematics and music are so conceptual, I want to know, so I ask – can he actually *see* isolated moments of time in the flow and space of the play?

"When I get the ball I always look at the court to see where everybody is standing at that point in time, and I try to pick their brains within two or three seconds. I say time, two or three seconds, because a man is guarding me and I am always thinking, when I go by him, There's the guy on the baseline and the guy who is standing on top of the key, and is that guy going to run, or is this guy going to run? I look at where I am, if I am close to the sideline; I can only go one or two dribbles to the right or it's out of bounds. If I go left, who is going to be there? What is going to happen?"

"Sounds like you're playing some kind of chess in your head?"

"Definitely."

"So the other players are pieces moving?"

"It's how you see what's going on, when you are on a fast break, not exactly in the middle of the court but if you get an outlet and you are running down the sidelines, you might see your man heading you a little bit and you might see two defenders running down the middle and you have the ball inside and you are moving down, and you have got to get your speed up to get by them, then stop, cross over, look to the middle. That's when I see the people moving, and I try to figure out their path before they take it, so I can make mine."

"When you shoot, and I gotta tell you…even as a white bread ball player in college, I sometimes could see that the ball was going to go in before I let it go."

"Yes, yes, all the time. Before it actually happens. Before it happens. I see that when I am in the zone, when I hit five or six shots and after that I am shooting on the beat and I just listen to the reaction of the crowd."

"Like when you let the ball go and you actually turn away – "

"I let go and don't know where the rim is. And when I look, the ball is through the net. All net. Sometimes I don't even look back to see, because I know where it is. I've seen it already."

⌖

During a break in the action, two young boys are led onto the floor by the Raptors mascot and given huge fisherman's nets on poles. Big red and white beach balls fall from the roof rafters. The boys try to net them, zigzagging and running around the hardwood in circles. One boy catches five, the other four, five's the winner. "A fisher of souls," I say to the discount man with the silver stud in his eyebrow. He looks at me as if I am strange.

⤜⚬⤛

I am still wondering what Carter could have done that he has to ask for forgiveness. He won't tell me. But he knows something of what evil is: his first agent, a man named William (Tank) Black, stole $300,000 from him through a pyramid scheme and phoney stock purchases. Carter had refused to believe Black was a thief. "But then it got to the point," says his mother, Michelle, "where even Stevie Wonder could see what was happening." Black went to jail. Carter, as he talks about this, pulls in his pouty lip, he can get a grim look in the corner of his eye, an angry look. "But you just get on with it," he says, sloughing his anger aside. "You do what's got to be done."

Getting rid of that anger, that was too easy, I think to myself.

"My instinct'd be to kill him," I say.

"Not mine."

In high school, Carter played saxophone in a marching band directed by his stepfather (he was offered a music scholarship to Bethune-Cookman College). We talk a little bit about Coltrane and Miles Davis. I tell him that one of the best lines I ever heard was Miles Davis saying, "I just don't know, philosophically, what white people mean when they say – 'Let's have some fun.' – What philosophically is fun?"

"I dunno, I have fun when I'm playing video games, I'm having fun."

"I guess Miles never played a video game," I say, and am about to ask him if he's heard how Chris Morris of the Nets, after a game in Portland, went into a kind of upscale sophisticated cocktail piano bar and said to the pianist, "Hey, can't you play some Picasso?" But then I suspect that he might not find that funny,

65

that he might not want to laugh with me at another ball player, a black journeyman ball player, so instead I tell him a story about myself, how I came to my own dead end as a basketball dreamer. How, in high school, I'd been called "Sweetwater" after a Harlem Globetrotter, Sweetwater Clifton, and that was because of the "sweet" game I played, a game that had been tutored by Fred Thomas, and then I'd gone to college, where I was high scorer and rebounder on the junior varsity team. Then we played one night against an all-black team from Detroit. I had never seen anything like them. It didn't matter how I moved my feet. They were gazelles going by who left me flat-footed on the floor – a white boy who couldn't jump. "They're shooting down instead of up," I'd yelled at my coach. My dream of becoming Bob Cousy was done. Cousy himself was done. As far as I could see, back then, and there, everything was going to change (Carter is now laughing) and it did change.

He gets serious: "I understand what you are saying because I have seen the change. I watch a lot of vintage NBA games and see the change. I see where it's all white at one time and it changes to a few blacks to where it's fifty-fifty, to where it's all black, and some white, and we have our ignorant black people now who say, 'Oh, this is our sport'… I appreciate the black athlete, but I appreciate the white athlete, too. That's how I live. I just want somebody, whoever, who can play."

Carter, of course, lives day to day in the closed, sometimes stultifying world of the young multimillion-dollar star athlete – he has one or two friends who dog around with him all the time. You can tell they are his pals; they not only have a deferential fetch-and-carry air but the stamina to play all-day war games and space games, shoot-'em-up and shoot-'em-down video games (I get the sense that Carter has not felt the need to thumb through a book since he left college, where he says he majored in black studies). "He plays and plays," one of them tells me, but you can see that they are his friends because of how he laughs with them. He doesn't laugh easily with strangers (few professional athletes do, wisely refusing to risk the intimacy that laughter allows or implies). His pals cocoon around him (not the least of whom is his mother, who attends to her reserved seat at every game and has a prime reserved parking space, much to the irritation of some players). He and his friends get into a groove of finger-popping laughter, conspiratorial laughter in which the sly thing that is being said or done is seemingly out in public – though it is understood as an entirely private show of good feeling.

"I was watching you banging with the guys, your friends, and I can see that you love to laugh."

"Yes. That's one thing about me. I even show it on the court, when it can be a crucial situation, everybody uptight, but I am joking and hitting a couple of guys on the head." His willingness to bop high-fives and goof around with players on the other team during a game grates on many of his teammates, but he makes no apologies. "That is how I am. I am having a good time."

"Maybe laughter's a way of fending off fear, fear of missing the last shot. Failure."

"I don't know. I will do anything I can to win but once it's done, I say, 'Okay, next time.' It is what it is. I missed it? The shot? It is what it is. That's it."

Which, of course, has led to the complaint that he "don't sting," that he takes defeat too easily.

An official's timeout on the floor: A boy of about ten or eleven is brought to the foul line. For ninety seconds he is given basketballs as fast as he can grip them, to see how many foul shots he can make. He is so small he doesn't shoot – he heaves. Underhand, sideways. The crowd roars as he makes eleven baskets. Shaquille O'Neal couldn't make eleven foul shots in ninety seconds if his mother's life depended on it. Someone shouts: "Sign him up, he's the Great White Hope."

Charles Oakley was his own grizzled man in Chicago (with the Bulls) and in Toronto. He liked to say, "Jordan is a Bentley, I'm just a used car in the lot." He played like a banged-up stock car. He was a snarler and a growler and he talked tough and he played tough. Not tough like Isaiah Thomas ("When *he* snaps," the big man, Sam Perkins, said, "he's like a thug with a sling blade"), but mean and with grit. For a time, he played boss man under the backboards to Carter's lightsome lad always on the lookout for the Oakley outlet pass, but then Oakley startled Carter by calling him out publicly, telling him and anybody who was listening, "Time to step up in the game and be a man. Be *the* Man!"

Carter said to anybody who was listening, No, he wasn't going to be *the* Man.

Boom Boom.

Carter comes out of the corner and takes the ball at the top of the key, leaning to his left, seeing an opening to the right. He pushes the ball, one swooping dribble, to a jump stop, planting himself, trapped between two Dallas Maverick players, their hands held high, but in a blink he is off the ground in a half-spin backwards between them, and as they reach for the ball he tucks it between his knees, levitating *upward* till, from the side of the basket – which is ten feet off the ground, a red 18-inch iron cylinder – he tomahawks the ball back over his head. Dunk.

The two hapless Mavericks stand like they've been put under arrest on a street corner.

As the crowd *oohs* and then roars, Carter lopes back up the floor with a "Don't-know nuthin'-about-nuthin" deadpan look on his face, but he has signified – he has signified that he is the Man.

And he knows it.

He knows what signifying is. He knows that the signifier has a long history, going all the way back from hip-hop through Shaft – talking the talk of the Man – to Muhammad Ali floating like a butterfly but ready to sting you in-your-face like a bee – to bebop, to Cab Calloway, to Muddy Waters – whose prophesying "muther say he is gon be the greatest man alive." The signifier is the hootchie-kootchie man, the trickster – who "spell *M – A*, child – *N* – that represent – Man." He is the teller of tall tales who is in every black family, in every sporting house, in every chicken shack and barbershop, the black man full of swagger who is going one-on-one with whoever he is talking to, lying, joking, and carrying on. He is all "attitudes and behaviours and bad mouth." He is the back door man. He is the Signifying Monkey or the Great MacDaddy or Peep, the man from DMX, "busting" rhymes "off the top of his dome":

> *I'm like Tyson icin', I'm a soldier at war,*
> *I'm makin' sure you don't try to battle me no more,*
> *Got concrete rhymes, been rappin' for ten years and*
> *Even when I'm braggin I'm being sincere.*

On the court, that signifying talk becomes the double-pump 180-degree spin move and reverse two-handed dunk. That's how Carter was at the Slam-Dunk Contest, and at the Olympics, leaping, legs spread wide, straight up in the face of – and over – the seven-foot-two Frederic Weiss ("the Eyeful Tower") of France. SLAM. *Tyson icin'*. Seven-foot-two made to look like a midget. One-on-one. But Carter, the greatest slam-dunker in the history of the game, not only now refuses to compete in the championship, but generally speaking, he disdains all attitude, shrugs off talk about killer instinct. (When he was eleven years old and running out front in a 100-yard race, he slowed down so another boy could share the prize.) He insists on talking – like he's at a church basement breakfast meeting – about the team. He insists on being sincere. He has no Dudeman bragging in his bones, no rap.

"But in the game you play," I say, "there is nothing more dominating than the dunk."

"Right," and again he gives me that smile.

"Charles Oakley says the game is war, that you've got to play the other guy like he's the enemy?"

"When he said what he said about me, I took my time, and I said, 'Oak, I hear you loud and clear. I gotcha. I'll take care of the rest.' I think I caught him off guard. I was quiet. He was expecting me to be angry."

"Your boys tell me that what gets you real angry is when you lose one of your video outer space games."

"Games is games. What I think on the floor is: kill 'em softly, so to speak. Kill 'em with kindness."

"But Oakley got to the contradiction that's in you. He said, 'You are here to be the Man,' and you said, 'No, I'm not the Man,' but then, you went out and played like the Man. You made the shots, the dunk, the slam, and then you turned back up the floor with that look on your face. Guilty but innocent."

"Just something I've always done."

"Be the Man, but back off from being the Man."

"True."

⌖

Another timeout: A young woman is blindfolded at one end of the floor. Toward the other end, a huge inflatable cordless telephone. She has to find the phone and the crowd leads her on by cheering or booing as she changes direction:

She that has an ear, let her hear,
The words I'm about to speak are black but clear,
I bring light for us to fight the right fight
So that in darkness you might have sight, alright?

The cheering and booing confuse her. She wheels in an arc, doubles back, darts forward, and as time runs out she stands on the sideline at centre court. They take off the blindfold. She sees that she's at the centre of things but that she has lost the game.

"You gotta dial long distance," the discount broker cries.

⌒◆⌒

During the timeout, coach Lenny Wilkens stood among his players and said nothing, but with his wry smile and lifted eyebrow and his arms folded across his chest, he looked like he was doing a Jack Benny take. A patrician Jack Benny, in a hand-stitched Italian suit.

The Raptors are well ahead, and Carter is sitting on the bench, the towel hood over his head. One of the Maverick players flops, he gets brushed and goes down like he has been poleaxed, looking for a foul. The bond woman, who holds a long purple sausage balloon in her hand, yells, "Dennis Rodman was the greatest flopper. No one could flop like Rodman, but other than him, all the floppers are white guys. Don't ask me why. Laimbeer, Danny Ainge, Shawn Bradley. A long tradition of floppers."

In the seats behind the Raptor basket, fans are trying to distract the Maverick flopper at the foul line. They are waving and wagging their own purple sausage balloons. Suddenly, at 1:06 on the timer, with the Raptors ahead, the discount man has decided it is nearly late and with a smile but without a word he gets up and leaves, his family trailing behind him. He looks very happy. As the rookie Carlos Arroyo dribbles out the last seconds at centre court, the BOSE speakers go sonic – *BOOM Zeeowowow BOOM*. The bond woman has twisted her sausage balloon into a crown and she is wearing it on her head. Queen of the boom box.

People empty out of the rows. I wish that I could hear "*Yo Canada*" again. The bond queen seems, for a moment, filled with a quiet stillness, a kind of joy, and I feel light of heart, too.

Later I ask Carter, "Do you ever think about joy, the fact that when you dunk, when you are the Man, you bring joy into the lives of people? That it's possible to do that?"

"Yeah, I know it's possible, and I enjoy it, because that's what I want, too, when I am up there in the air, and doing something different in the air, I get excited myself."

"You know their joy is there?"

"I've felt it, the energy I feel from them after a dunk."

"Do you ever have a moment at night, when you lie down and reflect on this, the effect you have…?"

"I understand the power…when I realize…"

"…you have this astonishing athletic gift."

"It's hard to believe," he says with forceful sincerity.

His look turns inward. I am about to ask him again what he prays to be forgiven for but think better of it. Remorse is not his game. Sorrow is not his game. Maybe he asks to be forgiven for having so much pure talent, a purity he can never measure up to.

"How's this from left field? I want to know if you ever think about death."

He whistles.

"About death?"

I take his big hand in my smaller hand and turn his palm open, and although he is startled he does not take his hand away, and then I draw my finger like a blade across the soft centre of his palm, the long lifeline that hooks behind his thumb, and I say, "If I told you now that I looked in your hand like some kind of voodoo person and said, 'In two years you're going to be dead…'"

"At first it would scare me."

"How scare you?"

"Family, friends, would be gone. There would be no chance to continue, no chance to work hard, to finish. It's a scary thing to think it could ever happen, depending on how you die, whether you die slowly in your sleep, and you start wondering, How am I going to go? You think about all the crazy things that could happen."

He lets his chin drop to his chest, the place he puts it when he is praying. I know he is tired, maybe of me…certainly he is tired of his back, because it is paining, and he is trying not to show it.

"Are you too young to think about the meaning of your life?"

"… The meaning of why I'm here?"

"Which is what?"

"To shine light on other people," he says, smiling broadly.

"What does that mean, to shine light on other people?"

"To let what I've done in my life be a light, to be with people who are in rough times and help them see that there can be light…"

"When you do that thing with your shirt, when you are praying before the game, you said to me before, 'There are times when I make the basketball court into a church?' Is it that kind of light?"

"All kinds of light."

"Sacred light?" I ask, wondering if I haven't bent the moment, turning it awkward.

"Any light possible," he says. "It's a kind of light so people can see you don't always have to have confrontation to get your point across."

We stand together in silence.

No *boom*. Just silence.

"Do you think about life after death?"

He laughs and says, "I wonder what it'll be like, where I'll be. Where will He put me next?"

"What if He doesn't put you anywhere? What would you yourself choose to be?"

"A butterfly."

"How about a bee?"

"I don't want to be a bee. I wanta be a butterfly."

Toronto Life, 2004

FAT CITY

A small Mexican standing motionless under a nozzle asked: "How's the ass up here?"

"Not good. Where you from?"

"L.A."

"How's the ass down there?"

"Good."

Soapless, the two hunched under the hissing spray.

"Are the guys tough in this town?"

"Not so tough. How about down there?"

"Tough."

"Just get here?"

"Yeah, I was in a bar yesterday, this guy's calling everybody a son-of-a-bitch. So I go out and wait for him. He come out and I ask did that include me. Says yeah. So I got him. I mean I just come to town. Some welcome. I don't know, trouble just seems to come looking for me."

Then the man began to sing, repeating a single phrase, his voice rising from bass moans and bellows to falsetto wails. *Earth angel, earth angel, will you be mine?* The song went on in the locker room, the singer, as he put on his clothes, shifting to an interlude of improvisation: *Baby, baaaby, baaaaby, uh baby, uuh, oh yeauhm, BAAAAAAABY, I WANT you,* while naked figures walked to and from the showers and steam drifted through the doorway.

There is a deep sense of "nothing going nowhere" in the stillness of naked men as they stand briefly together in the heavy steam of a white-tiled shower room, men who are small club boxers, who have just come down out of the ring, or out of the gym, sore muscles shining with sweat, crowding together, some-times jocular, but mostly silent, their bruised faces and bodies made more pale by the steam, totally at ease, limp, under the pounding water…talking patter talk about the local broads and small beatings and a referee who was full of shit, the shuffle danc-ing, the clinches…this, the bloodying courtship between men who've been beating on each other in the ring – three rounds, five rounds, ten rounds – the *wanting*, the terrible wanting, the ache of wanting to win:

"You want to know what make a good fighter?"

"What's that?"

"In believing in yourself. That the will to win. The rest condition. You want to kick ass, you kick ass."

"I hope you're right."

"You don't want to kick ass, you get your own ass whipped."

"I want to kick ass. Don't worry about that."

"You just shit out of luck."

"I said I wanted to kick ass."

"You got to want to kick ass *bad*. They no manager or trainer or pill can do it for you."

"I want to kick ass as bad as you do."

"Then you go out and kick ass."

In *Fat City*, Leonard Gardner, a young first novelist, has given the lives of such club fighters a shape that is not sentimental, not sensational. They are lives directly seen and spoken about – lives of slow passage through unfounded hope, elation, self-deception, and breakage in a boxing town like Stockton where there is never any marquee story about boxing, no Mr. Big, where no one bothers to fix a fight, and there are no wise old sportswriters …no, it's a world where young men brought up short by won-dering if they are, in their love lives, adequate to a woman's needs, do 200 consecutive sit-ups.

These are emotionally clumsy men, but they are also men of certain admirable disciplines. They know how to "listen" to their bodies. They know how to punish themselves by getting the grinding roadwork done at dawn, by taking thudding leather medicine balls to the belly, by putting in hours of skip-rope dancing, hours of work on the rat-a-tat small bag, on the big heavy bag...trying to get in shape, to stay in shape – not to better hit another man – but all the better to be able to absorb pain, to be able to take a punch, to be able to get up off the floor, to beat "the count" (time – everything is time...three-minute rounds...and timing...jab, hook to the body, cross...in combinations of two, three shots, step back, do the dance, step in)...and to know with certainty – having taken the other man's "best shot" – that you have become his bullying shadow, that you are on him like a lamprey eel, closing in...cutting down the size of the ring...and then TIME is called...the gloves are dropped, the men are standing in the steam of the shower room as ghosts of themselves...being told that things are looking up, that the bruises around their eyes have faded from purple to yellow...

The young untested fighter in this novel as it opens is Ernie Munger. He prepares himself by toughening his nose with salt: "He snuffed in harsh handfuls, pinched his nostrils shut and...he released the brine from his outraged nose...sneezing and coughing, his eyes watering, he went on dabbing and snuffing."

Then there is the fight:

> Startled by the bell and a shove against his back, Ernie bounded forward. His opponent turned around in his corner, went down on one knee and crossed himself. He rose immediately, his hair, in a grown-out crew cut, standing up like a wild boar's bristles. The two touched gloves across the referee's arm. Ernie, embarrassed about hitting Rosales so soon after prayer, reached out to touch gloves again and was struck on the side of the head. Offended, he lashed out and felt the thrilling impact of bone through the light gloves.

Stirred by shouts, amazed by his power over the crowd, he sprang in, punching, and was jolted by a flurry. He backed off. Chewing on the mouthpiece, he danced around the ring while Rosales charged after him, swinging and missing… His lead sent a shower flying from Rosales' hair. He stepped away and Rosales hurled himself into the ropes.

"Go in! He's tired, he's tired," Ruben [Ernie's trainer] yelled, and Ernie realized he was tired too. He struck out and moved away. Backed into a corner, he was attempting to clinch when a blinding blow crushed his nose. Bent over with his arms around Rosales' waist, he became aware of the referee tugging on him. Locked together, the three staggered about, blood spattering their legs, until Ernie's grasp was broken.

Blearily he saw a gush of blood down his chest. The referee was holding him, looking up at his eyes. "I'm okay, I'm okay," Ernie said through a throbbing nose and began to understand that something was wrong with him. Afraid the fight was going to be stopped, he pushed toward Rosales, there open-mouthed behind the referee, his gleaming body splashed with blood… "Shit, I'm okay. Shit, goddamn it, I'm okay." Then Ruben was in the ring, holding him by the shoulders.

"Tilt your head back. Breathe through your mouth."

He was being sponged in his corner when his opponent, now back in the red robe, came over, mumbling, to hang an arm briefly around his neck.

Ernie's gloves were pulled off and the hand wraps cut away with hasty precision. A grey-haired manager came and peered at his nose.

Ernie was left standing with his head tilted back. Blood still trickling over his lips, he went to a mirror. His nose looked like a boiled sausage about to burst. He went into the shower room and, feeling the pulse of splintered bone, stood with closed eyes under the spray.

Ernie is the protégé of an older over-the-hill fighter, Billy Tully by name, and Tully knows a thing or two because he had, for a while, been up in the big time, but now he's down, and he's been down for so long that there's nowhere to go. Still, he knows how to delude himself. Delusion is how he has stayed alive and sane, it's how he has kept his sense of worth. Ring talk. Bullshit talk like it's savvy talk. It's how they all stay alive, big punchers punching air, big punchers pussy boasting. It doesn't matter to them that they've got muscle cramps from the Greyhound buses they ride, the hitchhiking, getting dumped by drivers on open roads as they go from fight town to fight town, as they hang out in back-alley bars and flophouse hotels, getting brain cramp from being thumbed in the eye, pounded in the face.

Tully is overwhelmed by melancholy, but – since he's no longer a fighter – all he's got left to deceive himself about is his long-gone wife. He's talked himself into believing that his wife...wherever she may be...must still love him... He has talked himself into believing that everything, all the ratshit disappointment he has endured, he has endured for her, that there's been a purpose, and it's all been for the sake of their reconciliation, so that yes, what he wants is reconciliation and he is confident that it will come, he is sure that he will salvage his life.

Tully, being on the cusp of nowhere as a fighter, as a husband, and (like most other of the men) having neither tools nor trade, has had to find work to stay alive in the San Joaquin Valley. He has had to work the harvest alongside wetbacks and wizened blacks, he has had to work on his hands and knees as a weeder with a three-foot hoe in an onion field: "The pain began at his waist, spread down the backs of his thighs to the tendons behind the knee joints...he was falling behind... Tully chopped on with desperate imprecision...it was not the loss of money he feared. It was the disgrace, for all around him were oaths, moans, bellowed complaints, the brief tableaux of upright wincing men, hoes dangling, their hands on the small of their backs, who were going under the same torment…occasionally there was a gust of wind and he was engulfed by sudden rustlings and flickering shadows as a high spiral of onion skins fluttered about him like a swarm of butterflies."

Tully and Ernie, bonded by pain, are also bonded by how they manage to see possibilities where there are no possibilities: they share an inexplicable confidence (delusion?), it is always in the air, it permeates the gym, it's in every punch thrown at the small or big bags:

> Yes, confidence, Ruben believed, that was the indispensable ingredient of success, and he had it in abundance – as much faith in his destiny as in the athletes he trained. In his own years of battling he had had doubts which at times became periods of terror. With a broken jaw wired into silence, he had sucked liquid meals through a tube, wondering if he were even sane. After a severe body beating and a bloody urination in the dressing room, he had wondered if the big fights and large sums he had thought would be coming but never came could be worth what he had already endured. But now Ruben's will was like a pure and unwavering light that burned even in his sleep. It was more a fatalistic optimism than determination, and though he was not immune to anxiety over his boxers, he felt he was immune to despair. Limited no longer by his own capacities, he had an odd advantage that he had never had as a competitor. He knew he could last. But his fighters were less dependable. Some trained one day and laid off two, fought once and quit, lost their timing, came back, struggled into condition, gasped and missed and were beaten, or won several bouts and got married, or moved, or were drafted, joined the navy or went to jail, were bleeders, suffered headaches, saw double or broke their hands. There had been so many who

found they were not fighters at all, and there were others who without explanation had simply ceased to appear at the gym and were never seen or heard about again by Ruben, though once in a while a forgotten face returned briefly in a dream and he went on addressing instructions to it as though the intervening years had never been.

This would be a draining, disheartening tale, a taxing of the spirit, if Gardner were not such a remarkable new young writer. In a sense, the success of this short novel is summed up in that passage about the onions – for the lives of Tully and Ernie (and all of Ruben's fighters) are governed not just by gusts of chance and emotion but by the profound needs and the great virtues attached to those emotions…perseverance, reconciliation, courage, immunity to despair – all of which gives them – even as they are broken and humiliated – a kind of dignity. Delicate in their vulnerability – as butterflies in the fields – their harsh lives briefly transformed.

Ernie, after an out-of-town fight, has come home (somebody somewhere, while he's on the road, has got to be singing "Earth Angel") to Stockton, at first hitchhiking into the night with a couple of lesbian loonies and then travelling by bus into the dawn: "Dazed with fatigue yet alert in the eagerness of coming home, he rode into the city… Ernie rose, and when the bus roared into the depot he was standing at the head of the aisle. He came lightly down the metal steps into balmy air and diesel fumes, and feeling in himself the potent allegiance of fate, he pushed open the door to the lobby, where unkempt sleepers slumped upright on the benches."

The strange effect of this novel about men who are often bewildered as they step out of sleep into their day-after-day body banging and bloodletting, who are often lost in their yearning for a destiny, is that the reader concludes by remembering not their degradation and decline, but how earnestly and with what hope they took a punch and got up off the floor feeling "…the potent allegiance of fate."

There is a noble rectitude to that phrase.

The Telegram, 1970–1978

BLOOD IN THE WORD:
MARIE-CLAIRE BLAIS

In Montréal, I sat down with Marie-Claire Blais for a light lunch at the Ritz-Carlton Hotel. She had just published *Dürer's Angel*, the final book of *The Manuscripts of Pauline Archange*, and we had agreed to meet in the elegant outdoor garden café, tables arranged around a small pond, an easeful gaiety in the air, not just because there were so many fine ladies and their men all in sunlight but because of the dozen or so yellow ducklings pedalling around the pond.

Marie-Claire, my old friend, was wearing a nicely tailored maroon jacket with black trousers and a pale blue silk scarf at her throat. She was without makeup except for a smoky black line around her eyes. The line set off the paleness of her skin. She seemed, in her body, almost passive, waiting in an unassuming stillness, but with an attentive intensity to her shadowed eye.

She laughed as she put down her new book, *Pauline Archange*, and took another drink. "But, Barry, you must take care – to drink so much, we are a danger to ourselves."

I laughed and said, "Of course we are."

She wagged her small hand at me, not in judgment, but out of her concern for a frailty she sees in those around her.

"Take care. We are too passionate, yet too frail. Because, of course, it is our fate to be separate, it is who we must be."

"You know," I said (I've never known how to respond to her insistence on my frailty), "after reading your *Pauline Archange* book, I was thinking about us, this separateness that maybe we share, and I was thinking that maybe what happens to us as writers is that as children we are persecuted by words and per-secuted by our dreams. And maybe we're a lot like your Pauline – we grow up with our family and we are forced to lead a double life. She realizes that by feeding her own fantasies, her own sto-ries, she is betraying her family. We all do it, telling our family tales out of school, an act of treachery."

"I do think," she said, the rhythm of her very good English just a little stilted, "that this is, yes, the condition of the artist."

"And about Pauline" – and I felt a little awkward saying this – "There's a lot of Pauline in you, right, your younger self – as Pauline tells the lies we love to read, the dark lies that are her nov-els, she is also engaged in lying to those who are closest to her."

"Yes, yes. Today, to write novels, confronted by all the temp-tations of life, with our own trepidation, for the writer to actu-ally concentrate, to think, to be observant… It is amazing. You are with your friends, you are not with your friends. You always betray…"

"Is this what your Jean-Le Maigre, the poet, means when he says he wears a crown of lice?"

"Yes, by nature he was born to retreat into himself."

"He went down into the damn cellar."

"Yes," and she drew her scarf closer to her throat.

"So, if I read you right, the writer's got to go down into the cellar of his own darkness to get his work done. And what Pauline says of herself, working within her own darkness, is that she believes she was actually born into the story she is compelled to write. I mean, she's like those little ducklings there in the pond…"

"(…?)"

She stared at me. I'd lost her, so I explained: "See, those duck-lings there, they can't be anything other than what they are, duck-lings, so she can't be anything other than her story, but realizing this, what she hopes to do, see, by writing about her pain, is to free herself, to get out of her own story, to escape the bloodletting – even as she is standing there knee-deep in blood…"

"But don't you think that this is true of everybody who writes," she said, "writes with the awareness of his own blood and flesh? Dostoyevsky wrote with his blood, and without his pain, without that humiliation, his work would not exist."

"That's what Pauline says, too," I said. "That if you hadn't produced your novels, you'd be threatened with the sense of never having existed, for anyone."

"Well, maybe I could not live without the writing."

She said this with stern conviction, but also with a gentleness of tone that belied the sternness in her eye.

"So what is on the page," I said, "is the writer's way out, the public admission of one's pain…"

"Yes, it is a freedom, when it is out…"

"So, the only possibility if you're not writing is…what?"

"Look," she said, throwing her head back, wanting to break for a moment the tenor of our little talk, "life in itself is wonderful. Look at us here. In this garden."

We ordered another drink. She was drinking gin. I was drinking cognac. It was three in the afternoon.

"Just to be alive," she said forcefully, "just to live every day is wonderful enough. But writing gives a value to this life, to my life, a life that would otherwise be, let us say, not full."

"Or, too full of a suffering and a violence that allows for no escape."

"Perhaps," she said.

The yellow ducklings were darting in twos and threes between water lily pads in the pond, feeding.

"Your Pauline says that the sap that feeds her books, it is unjust violence…"

"Well," she smiled, as if she had been asked to explain something that needed no explanation, "we feed off each other from the moment we are born. A child feeds off his mother, children are starved of their dreams…"

"This voraciousness," I said (remembering that it was a word Pauline liked), "is it something in nature itself? Is it something that comes out of poverty? Is it something that comes out of simply being born? That gives rise to monstrousness?"

"This monstrousness, that's what was in my earlier books, *La Belle Bête, Tête Blanche,* but not so much recently."

"Not in *Pauline Archange?*"

"The people in this book are people who have what I would call weaknesses, people with human vices, but they are not monstrous people. I would not say so."

"Some act savagely."

"Well, the priest maybe…"

"The priest, the nuns…"

"Yes."

"They're kind of half-demented in their brutality."

"I denounce, yes," she said with sudden great firmness, "I denounce ferociously any violence against innocent human beings, or against animals. That brutality is a shock to me. But then we also have people who are more subtle. They are not monsters, they are people with difficult weaknesses. Even the priest in *The Manuscripts* is a compassionate man. He has carnal desire that may be repellent but he is not a brutal person. He is, as a matter of fact, weak, and extremely sensitive to pain. He's contradictory. You have people who are carnally weak, who are culpable, who are also compassionate, even very generous, all at the same time. That is what is so interesting for me as a novelist. There are so many levels to human nature. So many contradictions. Contradictions are what fascinate me."

"You want to talk about contradiction," I said. "I mean, there's a point where that crazy priest of yours talks about pity. In his world, what we do is hunt each other down, like panting animals in the jungle, but for him there is always something more than the bestial call. There is something weirdly lacerating, that's what you wrote, and it is pity, the capacity for tenderness, and apparently it's according to this capacity that we're to judge a person, if we are to judge at all."

Another cognac.

"Well, I did believe that when I wrote it."

"Not now?"

"Well, I do think that pity can be treacherous, too. Perhaps we are always trapped. To be trapped, that's a terrible thing, but we must risk it…"

"Like the boy who wants to be the redeemer in *The Wolf,* but that particular attempt at redemption…"

Another gin.

"He is a potential wolf."

"So, now, in your new work you are dealing with people who have potential, who are acutely aware of their own sensibilities, and they try to find the courage to love, but they are thwarted as they try for tenderness because they deceive themselves…?"

"Yes, yes, that's true, but then so many people just don't live at all. They don't try to have any passion. They have no passion. They are just neutral. That's real tragedy."

"But your people are all acting on the urge—"

"Of awareness. Yes. But that awareness, though it's only there for a moment, maybe several moments, it is betrayed by itself. It fails. It is grim. We try to be angels but we are tied to the earth."

"And the urge…is toward consolation?"

"I am not sure we are very good at it."

"You mean, no matter how hard we try, what we've got standing bcsidc us is an empty ladder…"

She smiled sadly, and then laughed, and we ordered more drinks and she sat in her stillness, absorbed for a moment in her own thoughts, and I watched the ducklings dart and circle on the surface of the water, and then she said, " You must be careful. To drink while feeling such melancholy, and to live such passion…"

⌒✶⌒

There is an empty ladder that stands in *Dürer's Angel,* the third book of *The Manuscripts of Pauline Archange,* and that ladder appears in her description of Dürer's woodcut, *Melancholia:*

The details of that magnificent *Melancholia* came rising slowly to the surface of my mind as I stood there beside my mother, drying the dishes, the sullen, unruly angel lost in contemplation, his big fist pressed against his cheek, his hair crowned with flowers that resembled thorns… Seated on the rough, ancient earth, his wings were open but he did not fly… In him, all was violent and passionate meditation, but this was a violence that would be appeased only in labour… When a simple-minded nun said, "Genius verges on madness," I sensed that…in the face of such misunderstanding the spirit of Dürer seemed to me so sad, so vulnerable… An empty ladder stood near the angel, and beyond, the dawn rose over the sea, though the angel was not looking in that direction. His gaze spoke of uncompromising and practical thoughts, and indeed, his appearance bore a closer resemblance to that of a solitary labourer than an angel. The place in which he meditated, moreover, was not a peaceful or a restful one; it was a humble workshop where the entire fervour of his immense genius would shortly awaken. But awaiting that moment, he brooded alone, his only companion a dog whose bones could be seen through its mangy coat and who seemed to share the anxious thoughts of its master, though it feigned sleep. At the angel's feet lay a hammer and saw. Several nails glittered in the shadows.

Nails glittering in the shadows.

Flowers that resemble thorns.

Melancholy.

For some readers, a dankness of the heart.

Yet there is something compelling in Marie-Claire Blais' stories, in her way of looking at things.

What is it that makes her prose compelling?

The answer, I believe, is this: Think of all the great children's stories.

The children in these stories see with an unblinking eye, just as Blais sees with an unblinking eye. To children, a man the size of a thumb is a man the size of a thumb. Hunger is hunger. Violence is violence, and because it is nearly always arbitrary, the violence can be monstrous, but it can also, because it is so arbitrary, be hilarious (BLAM and SPLAT out of NOWHERE).

Children see saints who are at heart whores and whores who are at heart saints, they are loved by grandmothers who are malevolent and prayed for by priests who are pedophiles...and sometimes what they see is almost slapstick, as when the winter comes to Pauline's house and the family's washing is hung over the supper table, so that droplets of water land on their noses while they eat and "Monsieur Poire, rising from the table with the tyrannic majesty of a drunkard, suddenly had his head imprisoned in the leg of his pyjamas"...grim, yes, but also slapstick...however, if they are children like the child Oscar in *The Tin Drum*, they stand apart, they are separate, wearing their crowns of lice, and they spend the rest of their lives madly beating on their drums...

There is all of this in Blais' novels.

Each book is her drum. Rat-a-tat-tat...she says what she sees. Monsters come. Saints and pedophiles go. But, and this is key, there is no call for any kind for retribution.

Quite the opposite.

Blais sees and names those who have sinned and those who are broken, those who have been stunted by a depravity of spirit, and those who have been exalted by the leper's kiss... She describes them all with an unblinking eye.

She refuses to pass judgment.

She offers not scorn, not condemnation, but compassion, as if such deeply felt compassion could be offered by a guileless child, a gift that is disconcerting because the child is wise beyond adult years.

❧

This compassion is conveyed in a singular style, her own style.

A style that is all her own because – in her eye – that is to say, in Pauline's narrative eye (as in the eye of any of her narratives) – Pauline not only sees everything for herself but she sees everything that all the other characters see, too, and often in the same sentence. She's got a fly's eye. It is as if Huck Finn, while telling his story from his point of view, also became Aunt Polly and told her story and then became Jim and told his story, saying what they saw as if he'd seen it for them.

If it is true, and I believe it is, that Huck's voice is so believable because nothing stands between his eye and the reader's eye, then Pauline is believable because nothing stands between her all-inclusive eye – and the reader's eye.

This is not faux-Proust, as some have suggested.

This is pure Blais, and the only thing that has changed over the years is that the Blais eye has ranged further afield, and the sentences, the flow of what the narrative eye is seeing, have grown more assured, longer, braver.

The world has, indeed, become her intoxication, her oyster.

❧

In the Bible, the prophet is exhorted to LIVE IN THE BLOOD. In the work of Blais, the blood is in the WORD, and it is in the WORD, in her story, that she, like Pauline Archange, lives:

> I thought of nothing but that typewriter: it was an old, grey, machine, ugly and battered, but I loved it as if it were a person. As dilapidated as it was, that instrument was a perpetual source of inspiration to me: in its company, I never felt alone, and the moment I touched its shaky keys, my thoughts became mysteriously clear... A sublime peace settled over me the moment I closed the door of my

room…the voice of my mother who was calling me to come and wash the dishes, no longer penetrated the quiet world of my meditation; and even if I did nothing but type out long rows of words, without at all comprehending their significance, forsaking all form as I arranged them on the page for my own pleasure, each word glittered beneath my eyes…my intoxication was complete.

Words glittering, nails in the shadows.
Standing beside us, an empty ladder.

The Manuscripts of Pauline Archange, 2009

ADVENTURES
IN THE TRUDEAU
WORD TRADE

In the early 1960s, young Jerry Goodis, a sometimes flurried, incautious, but always amiable man who was quick with words and at ease with a dollar, had sung tenor with a popular folk group, the Travellers, and for a while the quartet had had great success..."Michael, Row the Boat Ashore," "We Shall Not Be Moved," a revamp of Woody Guthrie's "This Land Is Your Land" ...and other union hall, hootenanny, and picket line songs...but then Jerry Goodis, unafraid of the resentment his ambition incurred among friends left behind – he liked to say that "he had not been born with a silver knife in his back" – had quit the group, those singers of union songs, to give himself over entirely to advertising, where he had made a billboard name for himself – in a time when sensible men wore sensible shoes – brogues with thick soles and tooled-leather toecaps – by successfully promoting a soft pliable shoe, the Hush Puppy; he had also created a same-day service muffler market for Speedy Muffler King ("At Speedy You're A Somebody"); a fast-food market for Harvey's ("Harvey's makes your hamburger a beautiful thing"); and he had leant a certain gravitas to his rise to prominence by not only becoming a senior executive at MacLaren Advertising (General Motors and the federal Liberal Party), but by telling his "true" life story in a brash little book, *Have I Ever Lied to You Before?* by Jerry Goodis, which of course had been written by a ghost – the journalist Barbara Moon.

In 1979, Jerry and his clients – the federal Liberal Party – the party of Prime Minister Pierre Elliott Trudeau – were up to their worried eyeballs in a re-election campaign. They were running on the hapless slogan "The Land Is Strong." They were not just flagging at the polls; they were trailing the supposedly inept "Joe Who?" Clarke and his Conservatives and, most troubling, Trudeau seemed to be distracted, disengaged, even disinterested.

I sat with Jerry on the patio at an outdoor table in the shadow of an Anglican stone church at Prego de la Piazza, a downtown restaurant favoured that spring by the plugged-in and well-heeled.

It was a bright sunshiny day. The white linen of our tablecloth gleamed in the shadow cast by the church.

He ordered a bottle of Chassagne-Montrachet.

Over a bowl of *moules* in a white wine sauce I drank most of the bottle.

He offered another.

I said I thought that would be taking advantage of him.

"Take advantage," he said expansively. "I like it." He patted his soft cheeks, as if he might be freshening himself at his mirror in the morning, and then told me what was on his worried mind.

"It's her, his crazy wife…it's not about the see-through nipples when they're with Castro, it's not just that she disappears with the Rolling Stones for the weekend, I mean, he's crossing the country trying to get us re-elected and she's on the phone all the time…they tell me he whacked her in the eye in the limo, it's all got outta hand, we gotta get it back in hand, she torments him at three in the morning…he's lost touch, like he's losing it, and Pierre Trudeau's not a loser but he's gonna lose."

"And so, you want me to do what?"

"Do what you do best."

"What can I do?"

"We gotta place him, Trudeau, we gotta place him here, like he cares, like he's one of us, here in Toronto."

"He has no story here."

"Make him one, make him a story."
"Like what?"
"I don't know. Think about it."
"I'll think about it."

I spoke to the editor of *Toronto Life* magazine. I asked him if he would like to publish a story by Pierre Elliott Trudeau... maybe, I suggested, Trudeau talking about the ravines of Toronto?

The editor, who had a wry sense of the opportune, said yes.

I should explain how my relationship with Trudeau – glancing, as it turned out over the fullness of time – had come about.

In 1967, after the young Trudeau had been in Lester Pearson's cabinet as the Minister of Justice for about a year, in September – as part of the Expo 67 celebrations – I had attended a brunch in a Montréal hotel given to welcome some thirty poets from around the world. I had written:

> ...in September poets from around the world met in Montreal, and they first came together at a brunch in the Windsor Hotel. There was much to drink and some stoked up on martinis before noon, having been through the grind of poetry conferences before. Then it was time to eat, and as we ambled into a dining room, the English poet, George Barker, muttered, "Now we get the rubber chicken routine." We got beef, but that didn't cheer him up. About half an hour into the meal, just as he was jabbing his spoon at the dessert, there was a clinking of a knife against a glass, and Barker, out of the corner of his eye, noted someone had risen to speak. He poured brandy on his ice cream and kept on eating. But then he stopped and turned to listen.
>
> A slightly built but sinewy man, in an off-the-cuff fashion, was talking about literature and art. He had a kind of

natural grace that finishing schools cannot teach. After listening for about five minutes, Barker asked, "Does he write good verse?"

Realizing he thought the speaker was a Canadian poet chosen to welcome the literary guests, I said, "Poetry… I have no idea. He's the Minister of Justice."

"You mean he's a bloody politician?"

"Yes."

"Uncanny…the man knows what words are."

The speaker was Pierre Elliott Trudeau. I was pleased with my poet friend's response, for I have a certain admiration for Trudeau, an admiration for the way he uses both languages.

It is my view that men who care nothing for the value of words, who distort reality with vague rhetoric, or twist the truth through glibness, are not to be trusted. A man who unwittingly or, what is worse, knowingly falsifies facts, misrepresents his own experience or the experience of others, is capable of any kind of legerdemain. It has been told many times that Prime Minister King was determined that nothing in his speeches would ever be remembered, and so he made them as drab, as toneless, as possible. This ensured that he would not have to account for anything on the hustings. What does this tell us about the man? That he was duplicitous? That he had contempt for the people?

And what do we learn about a politician like Allan Lamport, Mayor of Toronto, who is good for a garbled speech on any subject at the drop of someone else's hat? He uses the language as if it were a punching bag. He smashes into verbs as if they were nouns. He jabs away at facts, but always leaves me with the impression that he didn't hear the question, and even if he had, it wouldn't matter.

John Diefenbaker, ex-prime minister much beloved, is only a degree removed from Lamport. He is the master of dramatic incoherence, and the country discovered that Diefenbaker's government at no time had a coherent policy. Can coherent action ever come from incoherent thinking expressed incoherently? Experience tells us no.

Nor is it accidental that the able negotiator, Lester Pearson, affable though he may be, always sounds somewhat ineffective. He is negotiating with the language, counting on the phrases to recognize the reasonableness of his position and, as a result, show up on time. On the other hand, the style of the Socialist Tommy Douglas is predictably doctrinaire. All his thought is predictable, sheer plod, and the predictable style, always devoid of imaginative surprise, does not make "plough down sillion shine."

Consider the ponderous style of Paul Martin, Pearson's possible successor. Surely there is a kind of weird mastery of language here. What discipline must have been required to evolve a style that conceals the thought behind the words.

If you want to know about René Levesque, read his words carefully. You will discover in the images a secular Jansenist – an old monk in a new, double-breasted business suit talking of the purity of the French spirit on one hand, and the corruption of the materialistic English on the other.

Such is the way politicians use the language and such is the way of democracy. Justice Oliver Wendell Holmes was certainly too harsh when he said that if you wanted to see the human brute at his professional worst, at his most cunning, most self-deluding, then look to his elected representatives. But, listening to these figures day after day I can't help but feel chagrin, and not a little trepidation.

So, it is with relief that I turn to Pierre Elliott Trudeau. He is direct and to the point, he knows what he means and never seems unaware of the implications of what he, or anyone else, is saying. It should have surprised no one that Trudeau, as the Minister of Justice, has taken the criminal code by the throat and made sensible and sweeping reforms.

It is the real satisfaction of the democratic process that every now and then a politician comes along who is impressive, a man who not only has his own voice, but gives clarity to that voice…a man you would invite into the privacy of your home – not because of social prestige – but because you would genuinely like to discover his world.

In Ottawa, in the shank of the afternoon, a little after the appointed hour, Pierre Elliott Trudeau – in boldly striped shirt sleeves – opened the door to his office. He didn't seem distracted or disengaged; he was beaming and he invited us in and told Jerry to take a chair over to the right of the prime ministerial desk. Jerry sat down on the edge of his chair, backed by the prime minister's attendants, two gaunt men of Gallic severity. Jerry's chair faced a sofa on the opposite side of the carpeted room where Trudeau and I sat corner to corner, each with a left leg folded under the right. Between us and above us, an Inuit cloth wall hanging, of drummers, harpooners, and seals.

For a little more than a decade, from round about the election year of 1968, I had – at off-chance meetings during the odd social gathering – bantered with Trudeau…a quick exchange or two of idle anecdotal wit over canapés…and we had eaten supper alone together twice, the tone over these meals casual, amiable. His amiability, however, brought out in me – almost compulsively – a wry, ingrained attitude toward power, always turning me a little pesky – an attitude that had provoked him only once to flinty anger – when I had suggested that his speech writer, Ivan Head, had no gift for his voice. "He makes you sound like Bishop Fulton Sheen after he lost his faith."

Otherwise, this attitude, more often than not, amused him – as when I had asked him over Chinese noodles if he wasn't afraid that his fate as a master of politics might not be that of one of Henry James' characters – a great painter whose masterpiece, a canvas worked on for years, when finally seen in the James story, turned out to be blank. He had deflected this mild impertinence by telling me, "Never mind James, he stole that story from Balzac. And the Bishop never lost his faith."

As for Jerry Goodis and his relationship with the prime minister, Jerry loved Trudeau because Trudeau had, on several occasions, made it clear to men who were more sophisticated, men of political presence who believed they were more deserving of preferment, that he liked Jerry – that he really liked the way Jerry was so openly and even guilelessly himself – a man who – while giving off an air of utter good faith, the air of a man who intended no harm – could be, not duplicitous, but capable of what the Irish call *bull* – (from the French *boule)* – not so much a matter of outright *deception* as the ability to *mislead* while honourably taking the *lead* – or, as Yogi Berra once put it: if you see a fork in the road you take it.

"Barry's gonna make this happen," he told Trudeau. "It's a small thing we're doing, this article, but it can be a big thing, too."

"How long'll this take, how're we going to do this?" Trudeau asked.

"If the way I want to do this is okay with you," I said, "we'll be done and out of here in forty minutes…"

"That quick?" Jerry asked, looking a little disappointed.

"Really," Trudeau said, dubious but pleased.

I had placed a Uher tape recorder and a microphone on the sofa between us.

"I'm taking a guess," I said, "but I bet – you being who you are – that when you were a student visiting Toronto, you went out walking, and I bet you figured out that we have these ravines…"

"As a matter of fact you're right," he said, cocking his head to the side. "I was so bored I went for a walk and I ended up down in one of the ravines."

"Great. We're going to write a piece about how much those ravines mean to you, and how you think about Toronto today, the mystery of the place…"

"Okay," he said with a wry little smile.

"Okay," Jerry said emphatically. "Right. Good."

"So what I'm going to do is… I've got some notes, almost paragraph by paragraph for the way this can be…so, I'll give you the ideas for each paragraph as we go, and you give me the ideas back in your own words, talk them to me, and when we're done, we'll have the piece… I mean, I'll take the tape home and hone everything you say into shape and it'll be you writing about the ravines just like you'd been homegrown in Toronto…"

He was all eagerness, as if this were a new diversion, a new game that was not about politics or re-election at all.

"The first thing is…" I said.

✥

Within weeks, *Toronto Life* published an article *in which,* they said, *our correspondent recalls his days as a visiting student in Toronto, returns in search of the heart of the place and says what he thinks of the city and its people.*

✥

TORONTO
AND ITS RAVINES

by Pierre Elliott Trudeau

The best way to get to know a city is to walk around in it. I suppose I've walked around most of the great cities of the world. I've taken a lot of time doing it, nosing about, looking into things. You must have the curiosity to look into things, but also, there must be something there to look into. I can say that Toronto, even when it was at its narrowest, ingrown and a little mean-spirited, had its character, its own human dimension. Now, when I walk the streets, I see a change, a change of heart.

The first thing that strikes me about a city is the landmarks particular to it, and the use people make of them. In this sense, what impressed me early on in Toronto was the ravines. The ravines are something you discover and then go down into, as I did when I was in the city as a visiting student in the late thirties and early forties. I was amazed that a mercantile town, a place that some people dismissed as a city of shopkeepers, had preserved its ravines, had kept the country alive right in the middle of city life. I was, however, a little distressed to find that Toronto, built on a great lake, had hardly any access to the water. The city, for whatever reasons, had turned its back on the water. It was years before I discovered the islands, and that was sad, because the lake should have been there in the lives of the people and it wasn't. One of the cheering aspects of more recent times, however, has been the opening up of the city's arms, bringing the lake, and the moods that come from being close to the water, into the city. But back when I first discovered Toronto, a visitor didn't get much to hang on to between the ravines and the lake; there were low buildings in a rigid grid-work of commercial streets, and people who talked in the same tones and lived in little pockets. It did seem to be a place of pockets, inland islands, and it was not easy to be in one place in the city and say, aha, here's where the heart beats.

You see, back in my university days, I'd go to Hart House – a lovely building with the feel of old stone and heavy wood, a place where many young people could take the time to learn how to think – and I'd meet my fellow students there, or the professors. They were all good meetings, but I could just as easily have been at a provincial university in Kingston or Poitiers; they were good scholars comforted by closeness yet subdued by separateness. It seemed to me that the university was not tied into Toronto in those days. It was one of those inland islands, interesting in itself, but an island.

The same was true of the CBC. I was completely bemused by the old building on Jarvis Street, that rambling, red-brick honeycomb of offices. People went in and out of there as a kind of clan. They were talented, intelligent and witty, but I was struck by an irony. They were interpreting the country to itself, often with great accuracy and insight. They had connected with the country but seemed to have little connection with their own city. Just like the university, they gave me no sense of being tied into the city.

These are, of course, early impressions from many years ago, but though they are only impressions, I'm sure to this day that those professors and broadcasters didn't quite know where the heart of their city was, either. It might have been Bloor Street, Queen's Park or Eaton's, but you were always looking for the heart and you couldn't quite locate it. That's frustrating when you're a foreigner in a city. You go out at night and you say, well, where's the street with all the lights and we'll go there and we'll explore it because that's where the people come together? Or, when you go out in the daytime, you say, well now, where are all the pretty women going and where do all the businessmen go for lunch? No matter how hard you tried, you just couldn't touch the heart. I'm not saying that a city can't have many hearts because obviously it can, but it's frustrating when a city doesn't seem to know where any one of its hearts is.

I'm saying all of this only to lead up to the impression I now have of Toronto: obviously, it is changing, it is changed. You can feel a heartbeat. You can see the centre booming, you can see the City Hall Square, unlike anything else in the country, and Cabbagetown, which I understand was once the only Anglo-Saxon slum in North America. It is saved and restored, as if to say that there is still a life worth living in the core of the city, and there's Kensington Market. I remember going through those side streets after I became prime minister, feeling a little uncertain and withdrawn because I thought in a market I might just be reduced to "squeezing the flesh" that distancing that's so debilitating to any politician – and instead I was charmed, carried away by the natural vitality of the place and I found myself holding a chicken aloft by the neck, mock-haggling with the storekeepers. You could see right there how the city had changed, all those different faces that had come together, a man's eyes with the light of the Black Sea in them, and then another face from Lisbon, faces from all over, suddenly there together on that side street. They are the people of the place, and their voices are the voice of the place. I've never understood why a person would want to hear only one voice, one tone all his life, and now in Toronto a dozen different voices always surround you. This is how one of the hearts of a city seizes you.

You see, those hearts are communities. I remember about six months ago, when I saw the glass roofs of the Eaton Centre, I said, "We've got to go in there, we've got to take time from these political meetings and just walk around there." That's what we did, and we discovered that it, too, is a kind of community centre, with people moving about comfortably no matter how harsh the cold outside. One of the things that struck me was the greenery, the plants, as if there had to be a part of those ravines close to the heartbeat of the people. The fact is, Toronto has become a city alive in the day and at night. It's a city taking hold of its own potential.

This is what touches me in a city. As people begin to discover their potential, you begin to discover *them*. You pass through the physical city and you try to find your own place in it, but then you realize that the place is in the process of being defined by the people who live there; big buildings are going up and people are being drawn into the canyons. But in Toronto there always seems to be enough open space and sunlight so that the people aren't lost in shadows. And suddenly it's a pleasing and exciting city, surprising as you see it develop, asserting its own special character.

I have to confess, you see, that Toronto has surprised me. If I look back about 10 years, when I was beginning as prime minister, I was amazed to see building going on in Toronto because in my mind Montréal was the city that always had buildings going up. But suddenly Toronto was growing, too. Then, the same thing happened with the people.

I suppose, in a sense, my surprise is shared across the country: Toronto is still called Hogtown, largely because it *was* Hogtown and the people had the reputation of being straight-laced and rather boring. Hogtown is a legend with real roots. There was something sour and sullen about the place. It was hard to meet anyone outside the little group you happened to be with – what someone once called the town's secret living-room culture – and city life seemed to mean little more than working and going back to live in the seclusion of your home, the safety of your home (though Toronto has always been one of the safest cities in the world).

But now, all this has changed. Anyone who cares to look can see it. The people are coming out into the streets and they're beginning to develop a spirit. You can't create spirit through any kind of boosterism. Spirit is one thing a manufacturing city cannot manufacture. It springs out of itself, out of the people, and the people of Toronto are no longer Hogtown. As I look back, I think the coldness I used to feel was all just a matter of process, of building quietly, of getting the heartbeat going, because now, when I am in some small eating place that feels warm, like someone's living room, when I'm with one of my friends, say Marshall McLuhan or Peter Stollery, or when I'm at a friend's house and there's a little musical group after supper, perhaps Liona Boyd plays for us, a woman of remarkable talent, I know that I'm there as myself. The city gives me that sense of freedom. I'm at home; I'm not a foreigner looking for a place to hang my hat or my hopes, and I think, as I'm sure others do, "Gee, what a nice place it is." A city, if it has a heart, should make you feel at ease, at ease with yourself. Now I feel at home in Toronto, so the heartbeat must be there, for me, for thousands.

I remember one day when some of those thousands had come together to see Pelé play soccer. Everybody in the stadium seemed to be Italian or Hungarian or Portuguese or German or Pakistani, people from everywhere. It seemed to be a stadium of the world in a city of the world. It was bigger than any narrow group though they were there in their groupings, and they'd all come out to see Pelé, to see a unique man, to applaud him, to feel bigger because of him. The taste for excellence, the large thing, was there.

On this theme, I would say Toronto is developing a pride in itself that is due and merited. That would, however, be a terrible stage to stop at, becoming smugly proud of being the biggest metropolis in Canada because you have the biggest financial centre and the theatres and the opera and the coffee shops and the media centres and a press that's alive. And I say that about the press, even though we sometimes have our differences, because there are still three newspapers in Toronto, a fact true of too few cities in North America. That means people are reading. I'm not fond of the age of television and if people read newspapers that's good, because it probably also means that they're reading magazines and books. Our civilization must preserve the ability to read. It's disappearing so rapidly, even among our students, but the multidimensional media are a hopeful sign for Toronto, a hopeful sign for all of us. Toronto should be proud of all these things. It's great to be proud of your city and community because that permits you to go on and accomplish things.

But, and I don't want suddenly to sound like a spoilsport in the midst of my enthusiasm, it seems to me that Toronto is at that point where it has to go beyond being proud of itself and pleased with the sound of its own heartbeat. People should sort of say, "Okay, this is our springboard. Now what do we do with it?" I haven't sensed that yet in too many areas in Toronto, that real leap of confidence. I still notice a defensive negativism, as if too many people feel it is easier to be a bit cynical about the future of a country, or a province or the economy or whatever. Cynicism, like irony, is all too often a refusal to realize the possibilities of your dreams about yourself, because there is a risk; you have to say, "Here I am and I'm not afraid." I happen to believe that the people of Toronto will get over their sometimes glib cynicism, that fear of risking excellence, and they will say, "Okay, let's just turn ourselves outward with great confidence."

One way they could do that was put very nicely to an acquaintance of mine by Marie-Claire Blais, the novelist from Québec who lived a long time on Cape Cod. She said that the Toronto-Montréal axis – only an hour-long hop by air – was now richer for her than the tie between New York and Boston, that legendary culture linkage full of ferment. What a fresh way of looking at the possibilities of our community life. However, Mlle Blais made a particular point: you have to have the courage of your imagination to step into both cultural camps. You have to want to be bigger than you are. Rather than that eternal rivalry and pettiness that moves back and forth, we should sort of shake hands along the St. Lawrence and say, "Look, we're big enough to look to the future together, to exchange between ourselves, like Boston and New York, San Francisco and Los Angeles, London and Edinburgh, Paris and Marseilles, Rome and Milan. Those are the possibilities that are open to us if we'll only seize them."

But someone has to show courage and leadership. It can't just be the mayor of Toronto and the mayor of Montréal shaking hands at Grey Cups. The people of Toronto have to say, "Gee, we're an exciting city but there's also this exciting city down in Montréal. Let's go and walk the streets, let's see what we can see, let's have the curiosity to look into things outside ourselves and, above all, let's forget our timidity." This goes for Montréalers, too, who still think Toronto is Hogtown with nothing to do and no place to eat, which, as I said, it is not. Only someone wearing blinkers would say that, someone afraid to look. But neither is Montréal a hub of animosity toward *les Anglais*. Torontonians should be wise enough and big enough to find out for themselves that it isn't true. They should consider the possibilities: Marshall McLuhan and Pierre Dansereau, Marie-Claire Blais and Margaret Atwood, Morley Callaghan and Jacques Ferron, William Ronald and Jean-Paul Lemieux, Harry Somers and Robert Charlebois; if only they would all come out to play with each other, full not only of pride but confidence, what wonderful things they could say, and what wonderful things they could reveal about their cities, and how surprised we would all be to discover how interesting we are. But the risk has to be taken, with self-assurance and not petty cynicism. Just as Toronto should at last open its arms wide to the lake, really take the lake into itself, so too the people should open up to the whole of the country; and Toronto will become the great city it can be if the will and the courage are there.

❧

During the campaign of 1979, as he crossed the country, Trudeau continued to seem flat-footed and distracted: he was being thumped in the polls by "Joe Who?" His advisers at MacLaren in Toronto decided that unless he gave a "heartfelt" speech – "a speech in which he is not aloof and half-dead on his feet" to launch the last week of the campaign, a speech that would be televised to the nation from Maple Leaf Gardens – "then the fat lady can uncross her legs, it's over. We're gonna lose. Fucked, we are!"

Jerry asked me if I would write the speech. I had something more than one week. I decided to turn Trudeau's private disappointment with his beautiful young Margaret into a metaphor for the public's disappointment with him. Discreet but direct, I took up every major social and political question – particularly Québec – as if each were a sorrow he had to share with his family, his neighbours, the electorate. At the end of the week, I read the speech to Jerry. When I was through there were tears in his eyes.

Maybe the speech was great, maybe it wasn't. Jerry was an easy weep.

So I wondered and we waited.

As the days passed, Senator Keith Davey, the "Rainmaker," the *eminence argente* in Ottawa, could not say whether Trudeau was going to read the speech. The Toronto advisers started pushing their noses into their hands.

On the night of the speech, we sat at the south end of the Gardens: among us, a senator who had recently come out of the closet, several local MPs hoping to ride Trudeau's coattails, my father, Morley, and Jerry Goodis. The Ottawa word had come. He was going to read the speech. Sixteen thousand people were on their feet roaring as he stepped to the podium, opening his arms to the crowd. "Tonight," he said, "I want to speak to you very personally…" Jerry clutched my hand. "…personally, so that I can touch the private…" He paused. "…the private places in the heart…the private places of the heart in this great land, that is strong…" Jerry moaned. "The land is strong…" Trudeau went on quickly from the land to problems in the constitution…a talk bereft of sentiment, timing, twist of phrase, or turn of thought, the speech of a politician trying to think seriously out loud. Jerry looked at me, ill with disappointment. "The cheque will be in the mail," he said.

2011

JOHN STEINBECK:
A HAUNTING

It's strange the way a writer gets in your blood, the way he moves around in your life and haunts you, even after you've quit reading him. John Steinbeck still haunts me.

I remember the afternoon I bought a paperback copy of his novel *East of Eden*, and I took it with me down to the old waterfront ballpark that night. I was a ball-hawk kid in those days, a sandlot pitcher with a submarine curve ball borrowed from Satchel Paige. Jack Kent Cooke, a friend of my father's and the owner of the Toronto Maple Leafs ball club, had told me to come and sit in his box along third base anytime I was in the park, so there I was with Cooke, who fussed and fumed and bled with each pitch.

Between innings I started reading *East of Eden*, just to see what it was like, and kept on reading, paying no attention to Cooke's country boys as they whacked the ball around (or not). It was a couple of innings later when Cooke snapped the book from my hand and snarled at me, as only Cooke could snarl – a real hardness in his bright boyish eyes: "Damn it... I hope you read books till you're blue in the face...but damn it, this is my ballpark and this is my box..." He threw the book aside.

I discovered that there were all kinds of things wrong with *East of Eden* as a novel: some of the characters were abstractions; Cathy Trask – the Eve of Eden – was not only grotesquely evil but a calculated monster; the ending was forced and more than a little false. But Steinbeck had hold of something in that novel, something that is bred in the bones of our culture – the curse of original sin, the curse of inherited sin that is cruel and inexplicable, the curse of the open wound that is the Cain and Abel killing – so senseless and yet repeated in generation after generation – and God's challenge to Cain: "Thou mayest triumph over sin."

Steinbeck had the gift for going after and sometimes getting hold of the deeper social mysteries...and if, as in *East of Eden*, he plumbed those mysteries within an awkward scaffolding, the mysteries were there and the mysteries compelled you to read. So, *East of Eden* is a novel, for all its flaws, that has remained in my mind over the years.

⊰✦⊱

For those of us who are curious about how a storyteller's mind works while he builds his book, we have often been given glimpses. For example, Sherwood Anderson of *Winesburg, Ohio*, once wrote: "If I have been working intensely, I find myself unable to relax when I go to bed. Often I fall into a half-dream state and when I do, the faces of people begin to appear before me. They seem to snap into place before my eyes, stay there, sometimes for a short period, sometimes longer. There are smiling faces, leering ugly faces, tired faces, hopeful faces... I have a kind of illusion about this matter. It is, no doubt, due to a storyteller's point of view. I have the feeling that the faces that appear before me thus at night are those of people who want their stories told and whom I have neglected."

We have some remarkable John Steinbeck letters at hand. From January 29 through November 1, 1951, the period when he began and completed *East of Eden*, Steinbeck wrote daily letters to Pascal Covici, his editor at Viking Press. These letters, well and carefully written themselves, are a kind of arguing ground for the story of the novel, for Steinbeck's view of life, for his own life as he was living it from day to day.

*Up and to my desk very early because going to the opening of the World Series today and I don't want to lose any work time. Baseball yesterday, probably the best game I or anyone **ever saw**.*[1] *And I was glad then that I had a full day of work in.*

As the letters develop, you can see that a rush of joyous energy has seized Steinbeck, and that even when he was contemplating the creation of a monster like Cathy Trask – it was, as he said, an act out of joy: *The joy thing in me has two outlets: one a fine charge of love toward the incredibly desirable body and sweetness of woman, and second – and mostly both – the paper and pencil or pen. And it is interesting to think what paper and pencil and the wriggling words are. They are nothing but the trigger into joy – the shout and beauty – the* cacajada *of the pure bliss of creation. And often the words do not even parallel the feeling except sometimes in intensity. Thus a man full of bursting joy may write with force and vehemence of some sad picture – of the death of beauty or the destruction of a lovely town – and there is only the effectiveness to prove how great and beautiful were his feelings.*

You watch the characters of *East of Eden* emerge in his mind – a new Eve, mother of a new Cain and Abel – becoming so real that he talks of them as if they were present in his writing room alongside his wife, Elaine. He is driven by them, led by them even while he is leading them forward on the page. All little events or the large political moments of the 1950s as he reports and discusses them become part of the struggle in Eden, the attempt to triumph over the monster he was so energetically creating in his imagination: *"Once you know that Cathy is a monster then nothing she does can be unusual... Don't you know people like that?..."* Here's how, in the completed novel, Chapter 17 – the chapter in which Cathy's two boys are born – opens, and it is as if Steinbeck were still talking to himself:

---

[1] The Giants beat the Dodgers 5-4, with a three-run homer by Bobby Thomson when they were trailing 4-2 in the third game of their playoff for the National League pennant. They lost the 1951 World Series to the Yankees.

I've built the image in my mind of Cathy, sitting quietly waiting for her pregnancy to be over, living on a farm she did not like, with a man she did not love. She sat in her chair under the oak tree, her hands clasped each to each in love and shelter. She grew very big – abnormally big, even at a time when women gloried in big babies and counted extra pounds with pride. She was misshapen; her belly, tight and heavy and distended, made it impossible for her to stand without supporting herself with her hands. But the great lump was local. Shoulders, neck, arms, hands, face, were unaffected, slender and girlish. Her breasts did not grow and her nipples did not darken. There was no quickening of milk glands, no physical planning to feed the newborn. When she sat behind a table you could not see that she was pregnant at all.

In that day there was no measuring of pelvic arch, no testing of blood, no building with calcium. A woman gave a tooth for a child. It was the law. And a woman was likely to have strange tastes, some said for filth, and it was set down to the Eve nature still under sentence for original sin.

Cathy's odd appetite was simple compared to some. The carpenters, repairing the old house, complained that they could not keep the lumps of chalk with which they coated their chalk lines. Again and again the scored hunks disappeared. Cathy stole them and broke them in little pieces. She carried the chips in her apron pocket, and when no one was about she crushed the soft lime between her teeth. She spoke very little. Her eyes were remote. It was as though she had gone away, leaving a breathing doll to conceal her absence...

After the brothers are born:

Her golden hair was wet with perspiration but her face had changed. It was stony, expressionless. At her throat the pulse fluttered visibly.

"You have two sons. Two fine sons. They aren't alike. Each one born separate in his own sack."

She inspected him coldly and without interest.

"No," she said without emphasis.

"Now, dearie, don't you want to see your sons?"

"No, I don't want them."

"Oh, you'll change. You're tired now, but you'll change. And I'll tell you now – this birth was quicker and easier than I've seen ever in my life."

The eyes moved from his face. "I don't want them. I want you to cover the windows and take the light away."

And then the chapter ends:

The door opened as though she had been standing waiting. She was dressed in her neat travelling dress, the jacket edged in black braid, black velvet lapels, and large jet buttons. On her head was a wide straw hat with a tiny crown; long jet-beaded hatpins held it on, Adam's mouth dropped open.

She gave him no chance to speak. "I'm going away now."

"Cathy, what do you mean?"

"I told you before."

"You didn't."

"You didn't listen. It doesn't matter."

"I don't believe you."

Her voice was dead and metallic. "I don't give a damn what you believe. I'm going."

"The babies—"

"Throw them in one of your wells."

He cried in panic, "Cathy, you're sick. You can't go – not from me – not from me."

"I can do anything to you. Any woman can do anything to you. You're a fool."

The words got through his haze. Without warning, his hands reached for her shoulders and he thrust her backward. As she staggered he took the key from the inside of the door, slammed the door shut, and locked it.

He stood panting, his ear close to the panel, and a hysterical sickness poisoned him. He could hear her moving quietly about. A drawer was opened, and the thought leaped in him – she's going to stay. And then there was a little click he could not place. His ear was almost touching the door.

Her voice came from so near that he jerked his head back. He heard richness in her voice. "Dear," she said softly, "I didn't know you would take it so, I'm sorry, Adam."

His breath burst hoarsely out of his throat. His hand trembled, trying to turn the key, and it fell out on the floor after he had turned it. He pushed the door open. She stood three feet away. In her right hand she held his .44 Colt, and the black hole in the barrel pointed at him. He took a step toward her, saw that the hammer was back.

She shot him. The heavy slug struck him in the shoulder and flattened and tore out a piece of his shoulder blade. The flash and roar smothered him, and he staggered back and fell to the floor. She moved slowly toward him, cautiously, as she might toward a wounded animal. He stared up into her eyes, which inspected him impersonally. She tossed the pistol on the floor beside him and walked out of the house.

Steinbeck said that he had almost hesitated to put her down on the page, but he did, and with a strange kind of love for her, knowing that he was creating her only to rise above her and kiss her off. It was a compulsive and exhausting process for Steinbeck

– and this comes clearly through in the letters – but this is wherein lay his strength as a writer. He knew he had a big story to tell – that the monster within was battling for the promise God had given Cain – thou mayest triumph – and no matter the flaws in Steinbeck's completed work, that perpetual sense of struggle with large issues was a part of his genius.

October 10 – Wednesday: I have noticed so many of the reviews of my work show a fear and hatred of ideas and speculations…it seems to be true that people can only take parables fully clothed with flesh. Any attempt to correlate in terms of thought is frightening. And if that is so, East of Eden *is going to take a bad beating because it is full of such things. I didn't tell you that I got up at four this morning to work on this final Cathy scene – but I did. Couldn't sleep for thinking about it and I couldn't see any reason to lie in bed waiting for daylight. I guess there will be a howl that I am being sympathetic to her. I'm not, really. Just putting it down as it might have happened. There aren't any should have beens. This is the way Cathy died…*

October 17, Wednesday: And Cathy died. I did well over three thousand words yesterday and built a coffee table, too.

The Telegram, 1969–1973

TREE

As I shelter
by the apple tree petals fall,
fall from the apple bough,
white petals fall, my salt tears fall, fall.

Every day I greet the passing
axe children,
children of the axe
who wax tall with my own small children.

I rooted the linden in –
O, Lord, I dibbled her down in the middle of the yard! –
and the linden sprang to the air.
– O, Lord, Lāčplēsis sprang from the linden and Koknesis'
nine sons fair.

Rooted the linden out –
O, Lord, they rooted the linden out of my hand.
Uprooted the linden tree –
and dibbled her down –
O Lord, down beyond the sea.

Beyond the sea –
let it be – let nine boughs be, and bloom across the sea for
Ieviņa, too!
And yet,
when white apple petals fall,

Tree

I say:
ease the spade into the earth here, dig it right here
where we'll hitch the horse,
the homestead and hitch landhome…

Dibble a tree,
it breaks the light, branches broken by hanged men, by fruit –
O yes, where there are trees
someone always breaks, and breaks…

Imants Ziedonis, translated from
the Latvian, *Flowers of Ice,* 1987

A LITERARY LIFE

Of a late November evening two or three years before he died, I was sitting with my father in his library, his old typewriter by the window of the study at the front of the house, and around him were tattered books, photographs, a clutter of magazines, broken pipe stems, the stain of years of smoke on the walls, the drapes drawn against a chill wind. He'd settled into a nest of shawls, chewing on his pipe, feeling the cold deeper in his bones now that he was nearing ninety.

We were talking about the singer Tina Turner.

He said: "She cut loose from that thug of a husband...she's recreated herself, watching her, it makes me want to write, I think creation is something you can pick up on, creation can be contagious..."

The television was on, the sound low, and he had one eye on a college football game somewhere...

"You mean you and your guys in Paris all had the same head cold?"

He chuckled, as he sideways glanced at the screen to watch a wide sweeping run by a scatback in a game he didn't care about, some boy running beautifully, and he said, "Well, what've you been reading?"

"Nothing."

"You read that nitwit today in the *Globe* about Jerusalem?"

"Just the same-old same-old."

"I was going to read this guy Doctorow but then I decided that there's something too secure in writing about brave deeds done back in someone else's time, I put it aside..."

"So it's you, me, and the TV."

"Not exactly…"

"Guess I'll hit the road."

"I was going to talk to you about a thing I've been working on, a way of doing all my talks and stuff about writers over the years, and other stuff, too, without it being like everybody else's old thing…stale stuff stacked together like sliced bread…"

He showed me thirty or more pages of newsprint pages torn in half, torn into little oblong piles of pages that he shuffled back and forth as we talked.

Over the decades, I knew he had written the occasional book review, some newspaper and magazine essays, and the odd column. Also, for more than twenty years, he had appeared on the CBC radio program *Anthology*, invited by its editor/producer, Robert Weaver, to talk about whatever was on his mind. Through the first years of his radio appearances he spoke off-the-cuff, using notes he had scribbled before and after breakfast on the backs of envelopes. Then, after it was suggested that he should think about his archives, he began to type his talks on pink and yellow and green sheets of newsprint, typing sentences that had words left out, on pages that soon had holes – letters like "o" – punching through the papers as ● because his old Underwood roller had hardened to stone over the years. And then he would make corrections on those pages in a ballpoint hand that my mother described as "a slurring of letters in which some vowels just never show up."

"I want this thing to have the feel of my just talking, just that…"

In fact, what he was trying to do was put his horribly typed notes into a kind of offhand narrative flow – as if the reader might be on the telephone with him or sitting with him late at night in his library, listening to him in an easy intimacy as he rehearsed whatever was on his mind…

"And maybe," he said, "I could drop the actual reviews I wrote when I was young, and other later stuff – you know, I remember I wrote a very pointed piece a few years ago about surveillance and the police, and you remember when you were in college I wrote those sports columns for the *Telegram*... Somehow, this thing, if it was set up right, could have a freshness of effect, it could be a new way of getting at a literary life, maybe some teasing anecdotes thrown in..."

He handed me a box of papers.

A few weeks later, we got to work and agreed on how the book should begin: with *The young in one another's arms*...

"And Marquez should be near the beginning, too," he said.

Since we had just come back from a trip to Paris together: "Paris, that piece I wrote about Rodin, that could be great toward the very end..."

⌁

In what turned out to be the last year of his life, he started to write a novel; he'd written a draft of the first hundred pages...it was called *In the Park*. "I like this woman," he said. "She's something new for me, and the park: every great city has a great park and ours is out there in the west end, High Park, and she lives with her lawyer-father overlooking the park..."

"What about your book of talks, the young in one another's arms and all that stuff?"

"It can sit for a while."

Then, he fell and broke his hip.

He convalesced in a nursing hospital. He read novels and all the newspapers, received visitors, and watched the Blue Jays baseball games on a small bedside TV. "I don't get it," he said. "I have never dreamed in words. I've always dreamed in pictures, Monet, Cézanne, Matisse, but last night I dreamed in words, words under my eye, like Joyce obviously dreamed in words, words that had to be the phantoms of his dreaming mind when he wrote *Anna was, Livia is, Plurabell's to be* – because you can sing those words, they sing themselves, they're the music of his dreams about the Liffey River, the Lethe, a music I'd never heard before, the music of Lethe."

The broken bone knitted, he healed very quickly, and after two weeks he was home and walking. He picked up a stack of pages he had written about Solzhenitsyn. He read them. "Great," he said. "Got to get back to this." He did not finish the manuscript himself – but he had set up an anecdotal pace, he had established a tone, and he had revised two-thirds of his talks – so I decided that enough of his intent was there for me to go ahead, to not only complete the text, but achieve the overall effect he had hoped for.

While selecting pieces that best conveyed his habit of mind, I tried to maintain his ongoing conversational tone, and tried to give the feel of a Morley-narrative backbone that was not constrained by chronology. Morley didn't believe in "divisions by decades." He wanted his book to reflect the "way his mind worked," and to achieve that end, he preferred resonance and reverberations to any storytelling arc or any strict thematic unity.

The reader of Morley's oeuvre will recognize that the structure he chose for this text is similar in spirit to the method followed in his *Complete Short Stories*, which he insisted were to be printed without original publication dates. That this process frustrated a certain kind of professional academic pleased him to no end. He liked to think that his short stories were of such consistent quality that no reader would be able to tell which stories had been written first and which had been written last. All that mattered to him was the story in and of itself.

A little over a week after he had reread his Solzhenitsyn piece, after he had gone back to work on the organization of his book, he was found lying in his own blood in the vestibule to the house. Before he was taken to the hospital, he asked for "one of those little Laura Secord rice puddings from the corner store."

After two months in the Intensive Care Unit, after two months in which he lay cocooned inside his bloated body, two months in which he never opened his eyes, never said a word, but squeezed my hand twice, he died.

Silence.

We had talked on the phone or in his living room or library almost every night of my adult life.

He was a great talker.

He was a great listener, too, which is why, I think, women liked him.

I have not been able to describe the silence in the night in my life without that voice, without that talk. But now that I am done with shaping his literary reminiscences, his reviews and his reflections, I have got hold, I believe, of the book that he wanted them to be. I know that his voice is on the page, the tone of his temperament so consistent from the beginning. I hear him on the page as I remember him, and I am sure that Morley's readers will not only recognize his voice but will learn what it was like to sit with him, sometimes in the dark, and to listen to him, and to rejoice – whether you agreed with him or not – in the way his mind worked.

A Literary Life, 2008

SAUL BELLOW,
A GLIMPSE

Saul Bellow, as he took off a black Aquascutum top coat and a black felt alpine fedora with a bright feather in the band, was affable and very much at his ease (though he'd already paid attention to his wristwatch twice) as he then sat down in his Chicago university office and agreed that we could have a chat about alienation and society. He spoke directly to me, yet immediately there was between us a space; he leaned forward from behind his desk, intent on filling that space conversationally – except it was a one-sided conversation, and he was (as he looked again at his watch) the one: "The individual," he said, "like a bird, does not find himself on the outside, alienated and looking for accommodation. He's somewhere in the middle, moving around and suffering. In the middle, that's where his life is. I'm a little like that bird that feeds its young by gashing its own breast; the pelican in mythology. At least, there are elements of my own life in my books. But you don't write good fiction only by feeding off yourself; you must obtain a certain dramatic distance from yourself and your characters."

"Is that distance, that space, what allows for the feel of history?"

"You see, willy-nilly every novelist is an historian. He describes what he sees and acts as a medium, reflecting states of mind or feeling. Today, there's a loss of identity in the air, with people looking for new ways to see themselves and place themselves in society. No good writer could hope to be interesting who avoided these matters. The good writer, you see, is a medium because he stops the gap where religion has gone out – with the enchantment of life, the strangeness of life, and so he has a kind of mystic function."

"Why mystic?"

"Because life is very confusing and badly needs sorting out. People are always plastering labels and pigeonholing things, and this can be useful if you classify correctly, but most of the time the classifications are not correct. Some say I'm a Jewish writer. Well, I simply deal with the facts of my life. I have no fight about being a Jew, but I should hate to think that my characters are so exclusively Jewish that they have no connection with the species as a whole, and I rather think from the response to my last two books (*Herzog* and *Henderson the Rain King*) that I interest a great many people for reasons other than being Jewish."

"I hope so."

"I've also heard it said that I write about alienation. Well, alienation's a rather old-fashioned, romantic idea, and most of the modern ideas of alienation we owe to Karl Marx, to his description of an alienated society. But if someone says he means by alienation being divided against oneself, I have only this to say: that romantic writers have made far too much of this; it's become a posture, and there's something really rather sentimental about it. It's like the vogue for rebellion. It's exploited for the purposes of excitement. Writers are never quite so alienated in their lives as they are on paper. It's part of their being artists to describe themselves as alienated; but you'll find that at the back door they have a perfectly accommodated connection to the social order. They're rebellious only while carrying the picket sign, and quite respectable when they put it down."

"Is that how most so-called alienated people are? Accommodating? They've come to terms before even they know it?"

"I don't take seriously the fashionable cant of alienation. Nine-tenths of it is nothing but cant. There is, of course, genuine human alienation, but it's not the sort of thing that noisy writers and painters and literary critics mean. The fact is, we never leave society. There's no human life without it. We may feel an imaginary estrangement and very often an imaginary independence, but we belong to a civilized society, we enjoy a common history, and if you pretend that you were born yesterday on some Pacific island as some sort of unclothed savage, that can be a very interesting form of madness; but to talk of the artist in these terms is to take up the superstition that the artist is obliged to be a rebel and a separatist and that he must get away from society and pelt it with mud or whatever he has at hand. This is where the whole misunderstanding of alienation *from*, and accommodation *to*, society comes in. Intellectuals, by tendency, are separatists, but it isn't only intellectuals. It's anybody within society who suffers from the conditions of mass living, from barren labour, from filth and squalor, and all those things which are estranging. Those are the real forms of alienation that one can write about."

"Is there ever any force at work outside what we call society?"

"I don't deny for a minute that there is an alienating force in human life. Intelligence itself is an alienating force, and anybody who thinks for himself is bound, up to a point, to be estranged. But on the other hand, that person can have no real life if he assumes there is no common life. So all these literary discussions tend to take place in terms of words like militancy or betrayal. And that's a phony thing. It distorts the facts for the sake of argument. It's not a question of a militant posture toward society, or betrayal by society; it's a question of understanding who we are in society, where we are, and what we are. When I say that I'm certainly not ruling suffering out of the question; without suffering human life would be Bunny Brown and his Sister Sue at Grandma's farm. But seldom does the individual suffer on the periphery. He suffers inside the common life.

"If you ask me how writers are responding to this, like a lot of people, I fall back on de Tocqueville's chapters describing literature in a democracy. He predicted we'd have a mass public needing stronger and stronger stimuli, and that writers and painters and musicians would have to increase the doses all the time, and

lately we've been getting strong shots of violence and sensation-
alism. De Tocqueville also said that the hero with whom we tra-
ditionally identified, the hero of the aristocratic tradition, would
disappear from literature in a democracy."

"Has he?"

"Well, that hero has had a rough time, but then, there is
another side of de Tocqueville's prediction that has not yet come
to pass. That is, that the people as a whole would become the subject for great works. Walt Whitman tried it, but his tradition's run
into rather shallow waters, and nothing of the sort has happened.

"But, a strange thing I think *is* happening. Our civilization
has given a great number of people a private life, the leisure to
organize their own happiness. In their efforts, we see they have
frequently made a mess of their privacy and of the limited scope
of their existence. On one hand, this has become the plague of
American social life, so that many feel a private life is to be strug-
gled with; in the struggle the normal social instincts of people
have suffered a serious privation and there is very little scope for
their activities apart from fraternal orders or associations, temple
sisterhoods, fundraising groups – none of which constitute a normal social or political life.

"What seems to be developing out of this, however, is a personal interest in the public; people may be estranged, but they've
kept their values alive, in relation to others, and so the hero of
society may become society itself."

He stretched his arm, shortening his jacket sleeve so that he
could see his watch, and he smiled and stood up.

I thanked him for his time.

He thanked me for my time, holding out his hand, asking, "I
don't suppose you would ever go to Lachine?"

"No, no reason I'd ever go there. Hardly know where it is,
somewhere close to Montréal."

"That's where I was a boy. Well, goodbye."

"That must have been interesting, your childhood there?"

"Yes."

He put on his alpine hat but not the coat and opened the door to let me step out and then, not going anywhere, closed the door behind me.

CBC's *Show of Shows*, 1964

SAUL SAMMLER, THE BELLOWVIAN MAN

Saul Bellow is a man of high intelligence. It is often said that he is the most intelligent novelist in America. But seldom, if ever, is it said that Saul Bellow can be tedious and tiresomely tendentious and, no matter the honed rhythms of his prose, long-winded. His Herzog…full of angry, eager, and aggrieved verve…a man "fantastic, dangerous, crazed, and to the point of death, 'comical'…" is but a manic scribbler, a dandified noodler hard at stool. He is an epistle freak, sometimes capable of "brilliant" but finally cluttered thoughts, a clutter that has played thin over time.

Now we have another Herzog.

This fellow, however, is longer in the tooth, but his mind's still aquiver with all-encompassing commentary and speculation. His name is Mr. Sammler. He is a Polish Jew, born before the Second World War into a family of lace-curtain east European Jews. He is now, as a survivor of the camps, an aging intellectual living on the upper West Side of Manhattan.

Mr. Sammler ruminates and ruminates and ruminates. He is rampant with observations and consternation, very refined. It is astonishing how much regurgitated information and opinion Bellow has crammed into Mr. Sammler's head. And into the heads of other characters, too – cardboard cut-outs all of them – set up as butts for, and abutments to – Mr. Sammler's way of thinking. Idea. Memory. Ideas. Memories. Skilled and clever. But empty of force.

And so, what of Mr. Sammler?

He is an erudite man in his seventies who had once moved in a rather courtly literary atmosphere in England (he was a friend of H.G. Wells). But that had come after he had survived being buried alive in a Nazi death camp, where his wife had died of a pistol shot to the nape of the neck. At the end of the war, he had taken pleasure in stripping down a German soldier before killing him. As a man of such wide – and early on – awful experience, he has spent most of the hours of the rest of his life musing on what he has been through – refusing in his own heart of hearts to believe that "the centre cannot hold" – even though (and this has been proven to him year after year) "reality is a terrible thing, the final truth about mankind overwhelming and crushing."

Things have got so bad in civic life that a bus ride downtown can lead to assault. Mr. Sammler happens (though he is almost blind in one eye) to spy a black pickpocket working the bus. The pickpocket (a man of some cool and elegance) knows he's been detected, and arrogantly he follows Mr. Sammler home to the lobby of his building, where he traps the old man in an elevator and, without saying a word, in a gesture of brute triumph and contempt, forces old Mr. Sammler to look downward: "The black man had opened his fly and taken out his penis. It was displayed to Sammler with great oval testicles, a large tan-and-purple un-circumcised thing – a tube, a snake; metallic hairs bristled at the thick base and the tip curled beyond the supporting, demonstrating hand, suggesting the fleshly mobility of an elephant's trunk, though the skin was somewhat iridescent rather than thick or rough. Over the forearm and fist that held him, Sammler was required to gaze at this organ."

The notion that old Mr. Sammler – no matter his lifelong gift for observation – the notion that he, while in a panic, while being held forcefully close by the forearm of a large man, could so lucidly detail with only one good eye the heft of the man's testicles, the texture of the hair at the base of his penis, the iridescent skin…beggars all belief. This is not Sammler seeing; this is Bellow enjoying himself, enjoying his own prose.

If this telling moment in such a thin narrative could be read as intentionally comic ("the fleshly mobility of an elephant's trunk") – which it can't – I might not so readily recall a moment of homosexual revulsion that Cecil Beaton recorded in his diaries after he had photographed Elizabeth Taylor at the height of her beauty: "I went forward to this great thick revolving mass of femininity in its rawest…not with anything but disgust and loathing at this monster. Her breasts, hanging and huge, were like those of a peasant woman suckling her young in Peru. They were seen in their full shape, blotched and mauve, plum…"

The great oval testicles, the tan-and-purple snake, the breasts huge and hanging, blotched and mauve and plum…

O Lord.

It could, of course, be argued that the black man's aggressive, insidious, thieving, sexual physical presence is not evidence of some nasty little obsession but is, by and large, symbolic (as nearly all of Bellow's sub-characters are little more than symbolic in their roles as walk-ons), but then the question would be, symbolic of what?

The answer, it seems to me, is not just the obvious one…that the black man is symbolic of the general breakdown, brutality, and crude sexuality of Mr. Sammler's times – a period (of who knows what duration) when all words of hope and desire have been mongrelized, when exclamations of grief and utterances of compassion are so dumbed-down as to be suppressed. No, he is more than that: the black man is also symbolic – and this Bellow certainly did not intend – of a disgust and loathing that Bellow's "mouthpieces" feel for the gross and mediocre world that they – as men of virtuous impulse – are forced to live in (all of Bellow's main characters… Tommy Wilhelm, Henderson the Rain King, Herzog…are his bondsmen, his mouthpieces, they are him).

And so, old Mr. Sammler, having been frightened by the black man, is stimulated to expose his own private parts, that is, his ideational ruminating machine…for he has "a mind that is unusually active," he has "a mass of intelligent views" that he expresses at all times…views and ideas that he thinks he should "state, reiterate, and consolidate – ideas that are historical, plane-tary, and universal…" This is a kind of thinking out loud, as if consciousness could be a sparkleless incantation…a naming of names, a naming of notions, a swarming of "explanations, arrangements, rearrangements…(those) certain minor things which people insisted on enlarging, magnifying, moving into the centre: relationships, interior decorations, family wrangles, Minox photographs of thieves on buses, arms of Puerto Rican ladies on the Bronx Express, *odi-et-amo* need-and-rejection, emotional self examination, erotic businesses in Acapulco, fella-tio with friendly strangers. Civilian matters. Civilian one and all! The high-minded, like Plato (now he was not only lecturing, but even lecturing himself), wished to get rid of such stuff – wran-gles, lawsuits, hysterias, all such hole-and-corner pettiness. Other powerful minds denied that this could be done. They held (like Freud) that the mightiest instincts were bound up in just such stuff, each trifle the symptom of a deep disease in a creature whose whole fate was disease. What to do about such things? Absurd in form, but possibly real? But possibly not real? Relief from this had become imperative…"

Relief indeed!

As the old man lives through his days of quiet desperation that border on terror, all the savagery, the stupidity, the violence, all the smothering slovenliness of thought and deed that is ram-pant in the land, that is pushing him closer to a bewildered death, is being helped along by his acquaintances and relatives, espe-cially his daughter and niece, whose lives are dominated by junk, and more junk, the odds and ends of things and ideas collected and stored in lieu of any real relationships, the contaminating clutter of such junk having been one of Bellow's favourite ideas – signalling how barren the life of his niece is in the big city:

> High-minded, she bored you; she made cruel inroads
> into your time, your thought, your patience. She talked

junk, she gathered waste and junk in the flat, she bred
junk. Look, for instance, at these plants... This botanical
ugliness, the product of so much fork-digging, told you
something didn't it? First of all, it told you that the individual facts were filled with messages and meanings, but
you couldn't be sure what the messages meant... There
was not enough light. Too much clutter. But when it came
to clutter, his daughter, Shula, was much worse...

And on it goes.

With an admission...that No, it was not always necessary for
Sammler to personally thrust himself into every general question
– to assail, for example, "Churchill and Roosevelt for having
known (and surely they did know) what was happening and their
failing to bomb Auschwitz, nor was it necessary for him to ask
why they had not bombed Auschwitz." The fact is they didn't.
They hadn't. Mr. Sammler, of course, knew that as an individual
he was the supreme judge of nothing, but still, all things being
done if not said, "he had to find out for himself," so, as if unable
to help himself, he keeps on asking questions and he keeps on
raising issues, even if "existence was not accountable to him, even
if he would never be able to put together the inorganic, organic,
natural, bestial, human, and superhuman in any dependable
arrangement..."

If, however, Mr. Sammler stalls for a moment, Bellow takes
over. He has to, he has to clarify and catalogue what is happening
because

...the labor of Puritanism now was ending. The dark
satanic mills changing into light satanic mills. The repro-
bates converted into children of joy, the sexual ways of the
seraglio and of the Congo bush adopted by the emanci-
pated masses of New York, Amsterdam, London. Old
Sammler with his screwy visions! He saw the increasing
triumph of Enlightenment, universal education, universal

suffrage, the rights of the majority acknowledged by all governments, the rights of women, the rights of children, the rights of criminals, the unity of the different races affirmed, Social Security, public health, the dignity of the person, the right to justice – the struggles of three revolutionary centuries being won while the feudal bonds of Church and Family weakened and the privileges of aristocracy (without any duties) spread wide, democratized, especially the libidinous privileges, the right to be uninhibited, spontaneous, urinating, defecating, belching, coupling in all positions, tripling, quadrupling, polymorphous, noble in being natural, primitive, combining the leisure and luxurious inventiveness of Versailles with the hibiscus-covered erotic ease of Samoa…

…Dark ruminations now took hold. As old at least as the strange Orientalism of the Knights Templar, and since then filled up with Lady Stanhopes, Baudelaires, de Nervais, Stevensons, and Gauguins – those south loving barbarians. Oh, yes, the Templars. They had adored the Muslims. One hair from the head of a Saracen was more precious than the whole body of a Christian. Such crazy fervour. And now all the racism, all the strange erotic persuasions, the tourism and local colour, the exotics of it had broken up but the mental masses, inheriting everything in a debased state, had formed an idea of the corrupting disease of being white and of the healing power of black. The dreams of nineteenth-century poets polluted the psychic atmosphere of the great boroughs and suburbs of New York. Add to this… Add to this the dangerous lunging staggering crazy violence of fanatics, and the trouble was very deep.

Deep!
He can't stop himself, not for a minute. Mere explication will not suffice, he (or Sammler) must plumb those deeps: "What formerly

(had been) believed, trusted, was now bitterly circled in black irony... People justifying idleness, silliness, shallowness, distemper, lust –" people were turning what had been respectable inside out, and – this was a hard truth – the worst among these people were not just the radical young, but young women:

> Hairy, dirty, without style, levellers, ignorant... Some of the poor girls had a bad smell. Bohemian protest did them the most harm. It was elementary among the tasks and problems of civilization, thought Mr. Sammler, that some parts of nature demanded more control than others. Females were naturally more prone to grossness, had more smells, needed more washing, clipping, binding, pruning, grooming, perfuming, and training. These poor kids may have resolved to stink together in defiance of a corrupt tradition built on neurosis and falsehood, but Mr. Sammler thought that an unforeseen result of their way of life was loss of femininity, of self-esteem. In their revulsion from authority they would respect no persons, not even their own persons.

Through all of this ideational clap-trap and clutter, a basic Bellowvian idea has, in bits and pieces, been advanced: the humane, the sacredness that is at the heart of humanity, can only be confirmed by the determined assertion of and advancement of ideas of communal order, an order that must be sustained and defended by a commonality of high intellectual ambition that, upon examination, is shared by a few good men (never women), men who have bonded together to maintain their devotion to ideas of conduct that have, in our time, been almost totally discredited.

Given such a malodorous state of civic and moral affairs, Mr. Sammler can only think, with the same desperation he felt in the elevator, that "signs could be made, should be made, must be made. One should declare something like this: 'However actual I may seem to you and you to me, *we are not as actual as all that.* We will die. Nevertheless there is a bond. There is a bond.'"

A bond!

This is the pale assertion of a pale idea, a pale declaration by a character who has, over 313 pages, paled into a sign among signs…a symbolic presence among the everyday dolts who are themselves signs of the tedious multitude.

Saul Sammler, the idea man, is the intellectual interior decorator of our time.

The Telegram, 1970 1978

MUNICH:
FEAR AND LOVING
IN FÖHNLAND

A mid-afternoon pale blue sky, a warm south wind. Hunched forward and half asleep, an old woman sits wrapped in a coarse woollen cape in front of her flower cart. She is sitting in the dark under the wall of a Munich cathedral, a red brick wall that traps the wind in the narrow east-side alley (there is a local story: when this cathedral, the Frauenkirche, was completed, Satan rose up out of the darkness, tied the four winds to the doorpost, and went in; when he saw no windows, and no light, he stamped his foot with joy – the human foot, not the cloven hoof – leaving his imprint in one of the flagstones; he went back to Hell to his generals to reveal the good news and forgot to untie the winds) that is now whipping around the old flower woman who is deep in the shadow that falls from the massive cathedral wall that was built through the sale of indulgences. The cathedral has no steeples, only twin towers capped by dark-green copper cupolas, so that the towers look like huge arms reaching to the sky, amputated at the wrists.

Sitting in a small courtyard beer garden under a plum tree thick with pink blossoms, a blond woman says, "These south winds are our worst enemy. They make us tired and moody. Even the birds are tired. It's the kind of day lovers hurt each other. The winds come from the Sahara."

"Over the Alps?"

"Yes. They are warm but on them you can taste the ice."

"When I was a kid, in August, it was always burning hot in August, we'd suck on ice, we'd chip it right off the block."

"You had blocks of ice?"

"Sure, packed in sawdust, and we'd put a block on a table and turn a fan on it – this was way before air conditioning – and cool off the room."

"I once went into a room in August," she says, "in New York. It was very hot, a room all of Jews, and I broke into tears. I ran away."

"Because...?"

"I was only a baby during the war. After all, I did nothing. But I never felt this hatred before, worse than hatred. It was pitying, like I was dying of some secret disease. But I am what I am and, among Jews and many others, German is still a bad name now. Whether we like it or not, we're carriers."

"Of what?"

"Germs. The germ of death. We are Germans. But my brother says I'm crazy. He wasn't born till after the war and he says he owes nobody no guilt and he's right, and I don't feel guilt. It was the look in their eyes like I had sores, and a man I didn't know touched my hair as if he knew me and said, 'You have such lovely blond hair,' and he laughed and that's when I ran away."

There is a wide-shouldered woman wearing a sugar-loaf hat and wedge-heeled walking shoes sitting alone at a table. She gives the waiter a little fluttering wave and he bows from the waist and whispers to us, "It's disgusting. Since this morning she's been eating cakes. And more cakes." He goes to her, smiling, his napkin folded over his forearm. "More cakes?" he says with loud cheerfulness.

"I love it here," the blond woman says, "more than any city in the world."

"Why's that?"

"Because here I can believe."

"In what?"

"That I'm happy."

We are walking into the heart of the town, the Marienplatz, a large square flooded in sunlight, and at the centre there is a tall pink marble column with the Mother of God standing on top. She is cradling her child in the crook of her arm, and she is looking down on stone fish spouting water, on flowers and dwarf trees, on Chinese-red umbrellas, and shopping arcades…balconies, gates, long lean windows, and high up in the carillon tower, life-size dolls are whirling and dancing and jousting – carved wooden figures from a sixteenth-century wedding – and below, on a sub-balcony, enamelled cobblers dance, they are celebrating the end of the Black Death…it is decorative, delightful, it is history (I keep imagining a giant key in the side of the carillon tower) as a giant toy, tradition alive in a doll's house.

"In Oberammergau," the blonde woman says, "they don't dance, they dress themselves up in the death of God."

"You're kidding."

"You must see it. Since the Plague they've played the Passion play every ten years."

"The old play where they blame the Jews?"

"It is impossible to blame the Jews."

"For what?"

"For anything these days. No one will let you."

"The Jews will make mistakes, too. Everything suddenly changes, turns inside out, just like in the old miracle plays."

"There are no miracles. We have only our *maurischen* dancers."

"Who?"

"Our beautiful hunched-up men. You'll see them. They're wooden dolls, and they dance with their legs crossed and their arms scooping up whatever is there."

"Why *maurischen*?"

"Black, maybe the Moors, from I don't know when. Hundreds of years ago. We love dwarfs. They're all over the place in Munich. Look at Cuvilliés," she says as she leads me toward the Isar River. As for Cuvilliés, he was a great architect, an ugly energetic dwarf who built the little rococo hunting castle, Amalienburg, in the city's Nymphenburg park: gold and pastel and pilasters, cluttered plaster moulds, flower buds of gilt, appliqués of porcelain, mirrors reflecting mirrors…eternity over-dressed for the occasion…strange, this zealous, florid love of arti-fice…the artifice bespeaking doubt as opposed to the simplicity of zeal…among a rustic people whose sturdy roots lie in an early settlement of monks *bei den Monchen* – a monastery built beside a toll bridge over the Isar, the tolls collected by a bishop of Freising; and then…by a duke of Bavaria, Henry the Lion, who had attacked and taken the bridge, a crossing point for the lucra-tive salt route…and Henry the Lion, in 1158, had turned the monastic settlement into a trading town.

Soon, with the ruling Wittelsbach family rebuilding and re-furbishing the walls, by 1504 Munich had become the capital of the Duchy of Bavaria, a country town that was then ruled by Wittelsbachs for another 300 years…a town that, as it grew, bor-rowed all the architectural styles available…always a little late, always indebted to the other side of the Alps, to the Italians, and it became a town of collectors and performers, and finally, under the Maxes and the Ludwigs, it became a grand performance in itself, a stage set…baroque overlaid on baroque, rococo foliage spiralling into itself, Renaissance avenues…everything copied from somewhere else…an elaboration upon elaboration…as if such lavish self-indulgence could mask indebtedness…a wealthy provincial city trading in culture as it had traded in salt…a people dressed up in the dreams of other men…stern but dangerous people, so emotionally mercurial, so mystically rooted in their soil.

The city, to this day, is spacious, pleasant, and amiable. Sedate and salacious, filled with treasures and wonderful churches, so clean and so seemingly open to all the influences of Europe, yet it is curiously – and with the humourless conviction of the smug – closed in on itself: a little like their Mad King Ludwig…adrift in his nineteenth-century daydreams, sitting alone late at night in a gondola in the winter garden of the royal palace, a garden dimly lit, a glass-roofed arcade that had been constructed on an upper floor of his palace behind the Marienplatz, an arcade with a little lake where a live swan swam in circles amidst brightly feathered birds, flowering bushes, palms and bay trees and cypresses...with the music of Wagner played softly by a string quartet in another room as the king sat in his gondola staring at a painted moon – but unfortunately, the indoor lake leaked, the water crumbled the clusters of plaster leaves on the ceiling below, staining silks on the walls and warping the inlaid floors...no matter, he was content in his magic garden, a small-boned purse-mouthed man...perhaps not unlike the little man and his wide-hipped woman who are walking ahead of me now along the Thomas Mann Allée, walking in the wooded shelter of tall trees, the woman, with thick ankles, wearing sturdy walking shoes, walking four "sausage" dogs on a leash.

There are riding paths for horses in the park, a Chinese pagoda, a river and a small lake and a beer garden beside the lake, with little ducks feeding along the shoreline, the water a strange milky jade-green in the shallows. Two lovers lie cradled on a bench under chestnut trees, the candles all in bloom. The sun is deceptively strong in the iris-blue sky. Feeding swans are hissing. They have black, cold eyes. The cries of children in pedal boats carry across the water, and their old grannies are sitting at a café on the shore drinking beer from trumpet glasses. Beyond some linden and poplar trees, I can see a copper-green spire. It sits like a conical clown's cap that's been caught in the high branches.

We sit down, the blonde woman and I, beside the river. The water is running fast. There are two older nuns coming along the path. They are dressed in grey skirts with ornate oval wimples around their faces. One of the nuns walks with a cane and has to stop every five or six steps. Two big Rotweillers are barking. The other nun, pausing to wait, has closed her hand around the cross hanging at her bosom. I am reading Thomas Mann's *Doctor Faustus*, a passage where he says there is a curious medieval morbidity in the modern air of Munich: old churches, preserved houses with round towers in the walls and jutting upper storeys, tree-studded squares with cobblestones – an air of continuity that is merely pietistic, a declared defiance of time in a clockwork town… As Mann points out, the town is not modern; it is the past overlaid with a presentness and one can, in the midst of the town's seeming calm, "imagine strange things: as, for instance, a movement for a children's crusade might break out; a St. Vitus dance; some wandering lunatic with communistic visions, preaching a bonfire of the vanities; miracles of the Cross, fantastic and mystical folk movements – things like these, one felt, might easily come to pass… Our time tends to return to those earlier epochs; it enthusiastically re-enacts symbolic deeds of sinister significance, deeds that strike in the face of the spirit of the modern age, such, for instance, as the burning of books and other things of which I prefer not to speak."

Mann, of course, was speaking in a prudent muffled voice about the death camps, seeing them as a re-enactment of sinister moments in the past, indicative of something fearful that is always lying in wait under the eaves of the quaint houses and calm facades…a fear of a boil beneath the cheerful surface…

"Do you mind," the blond woman asks, "if I take off my shirt?"

There are families with basket lunches on the slope of the hill. She lies down in the long grass, folding her blouse into a small pillow. Half naked, she bathes in the sun. An old man wearing a white straw hat is walking a spider monkey on a leash, and only a few feet away, under a weeping birch tree, a young man with red hair sits cross-legged playing a song on a guitar. He has long bony fingers. The two girls beside him are naked. They have full breasts. They are listening with their eyes closed. There is, through the leaves, a little spot of sunlight on one girl's shoulder. Two other naked girls are in the shallow river, letting the strong current carry them. Men and women stroll along the paths pushing baby carriages. On the opposite shore, three dark Turkish men wearing heavy sweaters and felt caps stare across the narrow flow of the river at the naked women. The nun, stopping to rest on her cane, looks at the girls sitting in the grass. She has a wistful look.

"Everyone seems wonderfully at ease."

"And why not?" the blond woman says.

"I don't know. I always thought you Bavarians were strict conservative Catholics. Even the nuns…"

"Maybe it's the wind."

"The what?"

"I told you. The *Föhn*…it leaves us heavy, what you call sluggish, and a little sensual. We are sensual people, you know, close to the earth. We are not afraid of the earth."

"Maybe it's the gaiety of the light," I say.

"What?"

"Sometimes I get the feeling that all the buildings are huge doll houses with proper little string quartets in the courtyards, people pleased with how pleased they are with perfectly dead Dixieland, played by Rip Van Winkle…"

"Who?"

She sits up. Her small breasts are pink from the sun.

"An American guy who fell asleep for twenty years," I say (the night before I'd been on Turkenstrasse in Schwabing, the student quarter, and in a little club five puck-faced men in their middle years had played "Ain't Misbehavin'" and "Beale Street Blues" and "St. James Infirmary," all the old black riffs, the chording, learned by rote from records, collected and catalogued records, and between sets a young man had sat down and played the piano – frenetic and sweating… He'd hit all the right notes, jamming them together, little jack-hammer notes, like the concert pianist Mann once described: "He had accepted the fact that if a horizontal melody of nine bars is divided into three sections of three bars each, they will still produce a harmonically fitting texture." The crowd in the club had listened with a studious air, and then they had applauded wildly, mistaking this mechanically perfect exercise in joylessness for the real thing…and yet, it could not be denied, the room had been filled with genuine laughter and good feeling, with *gemutlichkeit*; no matter that what had been missing was not only a felt syncopation but the silences between the notes, the feel of the real thing), as we sat watching the nuns go down the walk where we heard the sound of horses' hoofs…three riders wearing black jackets and black hats suddenly appeared between the trees and the Turkish men huddled together as the horsemen wheeled around, erect in the saddle, galloping off toward the Chinese pagoda.

"It's always the big shots who break the law," she says.

"You mean they shouldn't be here?"

"No. There are paths for them on the other side of the park but they're showing off."

"The local aristocracy always do," I say.

"No," she says sternly. "They're not aristocracy. They're big shots. Big shots show off. The Nazis were show-offs."

One of the naked girls, now with a blouse thrown over her shoulders because there is a slight chill in the air, is playing the guitar. A man rides slowly by on a bicycle. There is a cage mounted behind the bicycle seat. He stops and lets a pebbly-grey pigeon out and as it circles and then flies toward the sun, he pedals furiously away, toward some place only he and the bird know. I lie back listening to the guitar music and the light wind in the trees, thinking about bonfires, vanities, children's crusades, and other things unspoken…and I begin to read again a remarkable but almost unknown book I'd come across, a wartime journal written by a monarchist and pessimist, Friedrich Reck-Malleczewen, a conservative aristocrat, *Diary of a Man in Despair*, a man killed in 1944 in Dachau by a *genickschuss*, a shot in the nape of the neck.

He had begun the journal in May of 1936 when he was fifty-two…a landowner south of Munich who, like Mann, was obsessed with the idea of re-enacted sinister moments, the eruptions of book burnings and frightful laws, the eruptions of religious fervour and mob rage...as he saw it, a psychic abscess. Beginning with the death of his friend Oswald Spengler, the author of *The Decline of the West*, Reck-Malleczewen's prose is prophetic, vitriolic, and not unlike Céline, full of contempt for the ersatz aristocracy of the 1930s, and condemnation of himself. As a landowner, he had been close to men of influence, and he blamed himself in a 1936 entry for not having had the wit to kill Hitler: "But I took him for a character out of a comic book, and did not shoot...he had the look of a man trying to seduce the cook. I got the impression of basic *stupidity*...the kind of stupidity that equates statesmanship with cheating at a horse trade."

During the war years, he buried his journal in the woods and kept telling himself, as a loyal German: "When the whole truth comes out someday, it will make people shudder...," a truth terrifying to him because – while trying to fathom Hitler and his henchmen – he had been shaken to read of accounts of the sixteenth-century Anabaptist Kingdom of Zion, accounts of

a man named Bockelson, later known as John of Leiden, 1509-1536, who had set up a theocracy and declared himself king. He, too, as a misbegotten failure conceived, so to speak, in the gutter, became the great prophet, and the opposition simply disintegrated, while the rest of the world looked on in astonishment and incomprehension. As with us (for in Berchtesgaden, recently, crazed women swallowed the gravel on which our handsome gypsy leader had set his foot), hysterical females, schoolmasters, renegade priests, the dregs and outsiders from everywhere formed the main supports of the regime.

As with us, Bockelson also surrounded himself with bodyguards, and was beyond the reach of any would-be assassin. As with us, there were street meetings and 'voluntary contributions,' refusal of which meant proscription. As with us, the masses were drugged: folk festivals, useless construction, anything and everything, to keep the man in the street from a moment's pause to reflect.

"Do you think my breasts are getting burned?" she asks.
"No...no, I don't think so."
From where I'm lying, the conical clown's cap, the steeple, is hovering over her belly.
Reck-Malleczewen:

July, 1936

Exactly as in Nazi Germany...the Münster propaganda chief Dusentschnur limped like Goebbels, it is a joke which history spent 400 years preparing. . . the resemblance may not be coincidence at all, but may be determined by some frightful law decreeing periodic draining of a psychic abscess. How much do we really know about the vaults and caverns which lie somewhere under the structure of a great nation – about these psychic catacombs in which all our concealed desires, our fearful dreams and evil spirits, our vices and our forgotten unexpiated sins, have been buried for generations? In healthy times, these emerge as the spectres of our dreams. To the artist they appear as Satanic apparitions.

But suppose, now, that all of these things generally kept buried in our subconscious, were to drive for emergence in the blood-cleansing function of a boil? Isn't this exactly what happened in Münster, so conservative before and after the event? Doesn't this explain how all of this could have happened to a basically orderly and hard-working people, without resistance from those dedicated to the good in life, in the same kind of grim and incalculably vast cosmic convulsion which from the first day of the Hitler regime has not only brought sunspots to affect the weather, endlessly rainy summers to spoil the harvests, and strange crawling things to afflict this old earth, but has also in some unfathomable way turned on its head concepts like mine and thine, right and wrong, virtue and vice, God and the Devil?

August, 1936

I saw Hitler last in Seebruck, slowly gliding by in a car with armour-plated sides, while an armed bodyguard of motor-cyclists rode in front as further protection: face waggling with unhealthy cushions of fat, gelatinous, sick…a moon-face into which two melancholy jet-black eyes had been set like raisins… There was no light in his face, none of the shimmer and shining of a man sent by God. Instead, the face bore the stigma of sexual inadequacy…the rancour of a half-man who had turned his fury at his impotence into brutalizing others. And through it all, this bovine and finally moronic roar of "*Heil.*"

There is a frightful riddle here, and I come back again and again to what appears to me to be the only answer to it: What I saw gliding by there behind his Mamelukes, like the Prince of Darkness himself, was no human being.

The three horsemen appear again along the river. The air is clear, crisp. There's a thin pink cloud in the sky, like a fishhook. A dog lopes through the long grass, a lanky short-haired mongrel. It sits down and whimpers. The horsemen rein to the left, toward the hill. The dog trots on for twenty paces and then sits down. It looks up into the branches of a big tree, whimpers, gets up, and keeps on going.

"You read too much," the blond woman says. "You should relax."

"I relax when I read."

"No, I mean really relax. Empty your head."

"Do you ever get your head empty?"

"No, but I try very hard."

"Isn't that tiring?"

"Sometimes." She laughs as she stands up. "Come on, it's too cold, and too damp when it's cold."

We walk out of the park across a stone bridge and along side streets of stucco and plaster houses in Schwabing, the student quarter…into a little park of bramble bushes and a lone light-green figure, a bronze fisherman…this is Nikolaiplatz; Lenin had lived close by, passing through town for a little while like so many others: Mann, Klee, Kandinsky, Brecht…

Then, by a corner apothecary, we come out onto Leopold-strasse, a street of outdoor cafés and empty rows of vinyl chairs. As she wants an egg shampoo for her grandfather, a man who'd fought in World War I, we step into the apothecary, a shop of elegant jars and a poster on the wall of a beautiful nude woman probing her breast, testing for cancer. There is a parrot perched in the window. The parrot's feet are the colour of grey kid gloves. The owner says the bird is called Cato and that he cannot speak.

"Carthage is safe at last," I say.

Nobody laughs.

As we go out, walking south toward Ludwigstrasse, toward a monument that cleaves the road in two, the blond woman says, "What was that all about?"

"Cato?"

"Yes."

"He was a big-shot Roman senator, the guy who said Carthage had to be obliterated, blitzed. *Delenda est Carthago*. It was the Roman final solution. It's good that Cato should come back as a dumb parrot."

At the Triumphal Arch, the road separates into two *allées*, Geschwister Scholl-Platz and Professor-Huber-Platz…the *allées* commemorating Hans and Sophie Scholl and their teacher, Huber, who were part of a resistance cell called the White Rose whose members had, one night in 1943, painted "Down With Hitler" some seventy times along the avenue, and shortly thereafter they had been arrested carrying fistfuls of anti-Nazi leaflets, leaflets written by the stepson of Kleeblat, one of Reck-Malleczewen's friends, and that stepson and the Scholls and Huber had been jailed and then beheaded.

"That's the Feldherrnhalle," the blonde woman says, pointing down Ludwigstrasse, a broad avenue of restored Renaissance buildings (it is an aspect of Munich that this city's beautiful borrowed architectural energy, bombed and almost obliterated during the war, is now restored and is, therefore, a replica of replicas). The Feldherrnhalle, a graceless military monument of arched alcoves, squats at the head of two streets close by Odeonsplatz and the Opera House.

(In 1923, when a streetcar ticket in Berlin cost 400,000 marks and you could get 4,200 billion marks for a dollar, when fishing by hand grenade in the rivers had to be forbidden, Hitler led his putsch: two thousand marchers met state troopers in front of the Feldherrnhalle. There was a fire fight for twenty or thirty seconds. Hitler fell on the cobblestones and dislocated a shoulder. Fourteen died and Hitler fled to Putzi Hanfstangl's home at Uffing, where he – the man who had described himself at the beginning of *Mein Kampf* as a *Muttersöhnchen,* a little mama's boy – spooned sugar into a glass of sweet white wine and waited for his arrest. In his plea to the court he conceded guilt according to the rule of law, but he appealed to a principle higher than mere law and political institutions, a transcendent historical ideal – "and in the light of that ideal, he was a thousand times innocent." It was a deadly attractive argument to a people who had produced the greatest idealist philosophers of modern times… The call to rally to a principle beyond mere law, beyond politics itself…)

To the left of the Feldherrnhalle, secreted behind heavy doors, there is a very large wine hall with high windows, and perhaps seventy or eighty middle-aged men and women – there's a lady wearing a pillbox hat with a lowered veil – are quite drunk, affably drunk. We order a bottle of wine. When a woman holding a furled umbrella across her lap slides out of her chair to the floor, two elderly men pick her up and sit her back, one holding her hand until she takes a sip of white wine, smiling.

"It's wonderful the way we drink here," the blonde woman says, and she asks for more wine.

"Why?"

"It's the way we make love. We're a stodgy people who are liable to do anything."

"What's anything?"

"Whatever you want. Come on, I'll take you across the road. There's a beautiful church."

It is quiet in the street, as if the wine hall were not there.

"We'll walk behind the Feldherrnhalle; there's a little lane. It's very important. It's called Sneaker's Walk, because in the war if you went in front of the Feldherrnhalle you would have to salute Hitler, and the only way to escape saluting was along this back alley."

We emerge up against an ochre wall and twin towers capped by copper-green cupolas. The ochre seems to hold all the lingering afternoon sunlight. "This is the church Hitler wanted to tear down," she says. "Can you imagine?"

"Well, he wanted to do a few strange things."

"Yes, yes, of course." She walks to the front steps, saying, "Do you want to pray?"

"Maybe, a little. Do you?"

"No, no. I told you there are no more miracles. Anyway, I'm leaving you now because I want to take my grandfather his shampoo. Come and visit him if you like. He has wonderful albums from his own war."

I go in, expecting whorls of gilt, all the usual pillars of tasselled gold and clustered cherubim in the transepts: instead, it is all white, a pristine white...stone drapery and rose petals, the pulpit stairs and marble rails. The pews are empty except for a girl across the aisle, each of us alone in an eggshell whiteness that seems, no matter the careful carving and detail, devoid of definition. An absence. I find myself remembering an afternoon on a northern lake at home, rowing, and then drifting lost in a sudden white fog, feeling befuddled because I was sure I should have seen, with all that white luminous light, something: the whiteness of God's mind…? The girl approaches, asking, "Do you mind if I sing?" She is wearing a scarlet silk scarf. She closes her eyes and sings: *Panis angelicus…*

Astonished, close to tears, remembering myself as a choirboy, I ask, "Do you mind if I sing along with you?"

> *fit panis hominum*
> *dat panis caelicus*
> *Figuris terminum…*

⊰✦⊱

Thunderstorms, curtains of grey rain across the courtyard. It is only thirteen kilometres to Dachau by rapid transit. A dwarf is seated beside me in the car. He is bent over an ivory inlaid pocket chessboard, playing first the white and then the black, playing against himself. By the time we get to the Dachau stop, the rain has drizzled off and there are ribs of gleaming light along the sky. The dwarf goes on up the road into town. I hadn't known that there is a town called Dachau. *Salute!*

The gate to the camp is no more imposing than the curt notice that appeared in the *Münchner Neuesten Nachrichten* in 1933:

> On Wednesday, March 22nd, the first concentration camp will be opened in the vicinity of Dachau. It can accommodate 5,000 people. We have adopted this measure, undeterred by paltry scruples, in the conviction that our action will help restore calm to our country and is in the best interests of our people.
> —Henrich Himmler, Commissioner of Police
> for the City of Munich

148

It was the first of the camps, built over a drained swamp, and the land is still damp and foggy. On a clear day prisoners could see across the country road to the mountains, pink and pearl-grey in the sun on the snow line. The camp was not large, only 900 metres wide and 1,800 metres long, and the "turnpike to hell" was an asphalt street leading to the thirty-four board and batten barracks. After 1942, there were never fewer than 12,000 men and women crammed into lice-ridden beds, and by mid-war there were so many prisoners – more than 30,000 in 1945 and thousands more coming by transport – that 132 branch camps were set up in the countryside, some as far south as Bad Tölz, spa town of healing waters.

When there was no room in the mortuary, the death house, bodies were stacked like corded wood stripped of their bark in the open street and then slung onto the *Moor Express*, and skinhead prisoners harnessed to wagon shafts like mules trotted them off to the "smokehouse" where the small gas chamber stood unused but the crematorium was fired up all day, a stone building, built by imprisoned priests, to the west side of the camp, sheltered in the trees of a lovely pine forest. The prevailing wind back then was westerly so the sweet stench of cooking flesh must have blown back constantly over the barracks...the twin furnaces, like huge red brick bread ovens...the doors now stand ajar, and inside, the rusted iron cradles for the dead... I find myself singing little children's songs I'd been taught during the war...*din don din...*

And then the barracks, running my hands along rough-hewn bunkbeds, walking about among souls of wood from a time when "a police dog determined the destiny of the world," walking about into an alleyway where prisoners had been forced to flog each other... I pick up two small stones and put them in my pocket. A medieval man, Adam of Saint Victor, had said that stones are fallen angels. I have two fallen angels in my pocket. (I hear distant laughter, the laughter of an angel who is drowning in a puddle of water.) "Do you know what laughter is?" one of Elie

Wiesel's angels had asked the last of the living Jews among God's chosen children. "I'll tell you. It's God's mistake. When God made man in order to bend him to His wishes he carelessly left him the gift of laughter. Little did He know that that earthworm would later use it as a weapon of vengeance."

It occurs to me as I stand there in the alley wondering why I am not laughing that Christianity, alone among the religions of the world, began with a murder – the murder of God.

The same desert God who, as the Word, had taken the trouble to rise from the dead, but only to end up playing dumb here during this disaster.

There's been a break in the sky over the camp, a streak of ice-blue light. I am sitting close to a perimeter trench that lay between the prisoners and an electrified barbed-wire fence. Sometimes guards had forced prisoners to fetch their caps thrown into the ditch, promising they would not shoot from the watchtowers. It was a game. Fish in a barrel. They were shot for trying to escape. I do not see the barbed wire but the space between the wires…perhaps it is this that never dies…the space, the silent possibilities between barbed wires… I finish reading the diary, Reck-Malleczewen's record of impotent outrage, a patriot who disappeared into this very place:

> The ghosts of the dead have begun their work, and already the effects are felt in the systematic demoralization of the Nazi ruling structure. For weeks now, the lower echelons of hierarchy, district officials, township leaders, and bastions of the regime generally have been making gestures, meant to be noticed, of disillusionment with the Nazis. Their general demeanour is now supposed to convey disgust, so that everybody may know their dissatisfaction, their unhappiness about the present state of things. Now, in the post office, for instance, the clerk is liable to fling official notices contemptuously to one side, muttering that he has "had enough of this swindle."

The secret behind this transformation? All these gentle-men have in recent days received a letter from a certain "revolutionary executive," informing them that they will be held responsible for their official actions: the previous denunciations and similar crimes have been duly re-corded against them, and that the continuation of such activities will further worsen the consequences for them. By great good luck, I got hold of one of these missives:

"—we possess documentary evidence regarding your activities since 1933, and you will be held responsible for them following the collapse of Hitlerism. The Executive Committee hereby informs you that you will henceforth remain under the most intensive observation. If there should occur a single further instance of activity on behalf of the present regime, or if any additional reports are confirmed of harm done to political opponents, the sentence of death which has been pronounced against you for future execution will be extended to include your entire family. Execution will be by hanging on the day of overthrow of the regime."

It had its effect. These letters were in some incompre-hensible way sent registered mail from widely separated places, so that those sent to Bavaria originated in Inster-burg, while the letters mailed to Middle Prussia evidently came from Baden or Württemberg.

(Meanwhile) the news from Hamburg is simply beyond the grasp of the imagination – streets of boiling asphalt into which the victims sank and were boiled alive…stories of amnesia, stories of people wandering through the streets in the pyjamas they had on when they fled from their houses, crazy-eyed, carrying an empty bird cage, with no memory of a yesterday, and no idea of a tomor-row… And now this is what I saw on a burning hot day in early August at a little railroad station in Upper Bavaria… A suitcase, a miserable lump of cardboard with edges bro-ken off, missed the target, fell back to the platform and broke open, revealing its contents. There was a pile of clothes, a manicure kit, a toy. And there was a baked corpse of a child, shrunk to the proportions of a mummy, which the half-crazed woman had dragged along with her, the macabre remains of what only a few days before had been a family. Cries of dismay, disgust, roars, hysterical outbursts, the snarls of a small dog, until finally an official took pity on all of them and had the thing disposed of.

We breathe the air of death…as the Woman's Organization leader in Obing, a harmless farm village, told us recently when she extolled this Führer of ours because 'in his goodness, he has prepared a gentle and easy death by gas for the German people in case the war ends badly.' Oh, I am not writing fiction. This lovely lady is no creature of my imagination. I saw her with my own eyes: a golden-tanned forty year old with the insane eyes of all this type – I remind you that next to the schoolteachers these female hyenas are among the most rabid of our Hitlerite whirling dervishes… Strange atmosphere, compounded of fear, of resignation, and of a last, bellowing madness… At six in the morning – that hour so beloved of all secret police officials – I heard the bell ringing rather loudly… I was charged with "undermining the morale of the Armed Forces." The cell is two paces wide and six feet long, a concrete coffin equipped with a wooden pallet, a dirty, evil-smelling spittoon, and a barred window high up on the wall. By climbing onto the pallet I can see a minuscule piece of the sky, the barracks compound, a section of the officers' quarters, and behind, a pine forest: a pine forest of our lovely Bavarian plateau, which has nothing in common with this frenzy of Prussian militarism, this pestilence which has devastated Bavaria… We who are buried alive here are not to be granted even the solace of a quiet night. When a door is closed it is slammed shut with full force… I pondered the question of who was responsible for this, who it was whose amiable purpose it had been to deliver me up to the hangman…

As I close the book, this diary of despair, two little boys are playing catch behind me with one of the stones from the parade ground: another fallen angel, this one is once again in flight.

⌖

In the late afternoon, after a slow ride back to Munich, I find that the blond woman has left a single theatre ticket for me. I dress for the opera, Wagner's *Die Meistersinger*, and go sit among grave men – some white-haired, one with a leather left hand dressed in black – and many strikingly beautiful women; though, for all their corn-silk hair and eyes like still water, they have declined or are declining into the shape of their mothers, a dumpling stout-ishness, their skin the dough colour of the back of their hands.

The stage setting for *Die Meistersinger*, a congenial, comic mastersong of delight and conviviality, is so contemporary I cannot believe my eyes…fresh wood, board and batten, scaffolding, the rough-hewn carpentry of the barracks at the camp. But then the overture swells: it is a foretelling of joy.

Die Meistersinger is a strange opera. Hans Sachs, the cobbler storyteller, is the central figure, a man who fashions his songs in the metaphors of his boot shop: a well-heeled tune, a phrase on the last, the counterpoint of cross-stitching. He lives in a medieval town of guilds, and each guild has a mastersinger. But a knight drifts into this tight little conventional world, singing so independently of love and so directly from the heart that he upsets all the singing rules. He meets up with only malice and ignorance among the masters. He is denied membership in the singing clubs. He cannot have little Eva, his love.

This is a trite story and, on the surface, entirely sentimental. But at the core, there is a challenge. All goes awry. Sachs – confronted by the local singing rules that constitute the conventional wisdom – openly urges his fellow citizens to understand and accept that authentic feeling, if it is to be authentic, must have its own rules. At the end of act one, there is, in the streets, a sudden and inexplicable breaking of societal rules: rioting and brawling erupt in Nuremburg. One of Mann's psychic boils has burst.

From this moment on, conviviality is undercut by melancholy. Sachs knows that life is tragic, that the artist's function is to tap into the terrible, to tap into the motiveless malignancy that is in all men: tragedy is the unspeakable that is sung for all to hear – the refusal to retreat into or reside in indifference. In this context, the knight's callow joy is heartbreaking; it is a song sung by a man so impressed by his own declarations of love that he does not know he is already hung from the hook, that the sunset he sees is actually the open eye of the furnace.

In act three, Sachs sings of *Wahn*, the incomprehensible manias that seize men unawares:

> *No matter where I inquire,*
> *whether chronicle or shire,*
> *seeking the reason*
> *why we love the season*
> *of blood, flaying each other*
> *in fallacious anger!*
> *witless on the run*
> *he beats the town drum;*
> *deaf to his own*
> *pain, and grown*
> *so insane he seeks to atone*
> *by breaking his own bones.*

The abscess that feeds the seasons of blood lies just under the skin, and Sachs, appalled by the village brawl, has no explanation for such an eruption of rage. His singular response is: – cheerful acceptance…from a man who has looked into the eye of the oven and knows neither words nor weeping can deflect us from our destiny…and so we might as well laugh and sing a counter song to the wail of woe. Though the opera has at its core a vision of mendacity, of street brawls and lice-ridden dead, it concludes with the fulfilled promise of the overture: at a wedding, there is a surge of laughter and life is celebrated even as life is lost. It is an acceptance of the unacceptable, an affirmation of the infirm.

As the curtain falls, there is an eruption of cheering and applause.

The tall, very erect man beside me, as we stand, is old and lean and severe. He has a hawk's face, the jaw lifted. He has a stiff arm, a sheen to his leather hand. He cannot applaud. He is fierce-looking and infirm.

The blond woman is waiting by a tiered fountain, effervescent spray splashing into a floodlit pool, thousands of little balls of light crashing through the air…

"I want to get drunk," she says. "I want to get drunk and to make love, to make love somewhere out in the open air."

"Any particular reason?" I ask, trying to be jaunty.

"No," she says. "This afternoon, coming back to town from my grandfather's, I wanted to cry, so I cried. Tonight I want to drink."

In a crowded nightclub café there are water-silk-panelled walls and many framed sepia photographs of men, most of whom have moustaches, and old posters boasting of *Schwabylon* and a festival of clowns who had been once let loose to drift in the sky, blowing little tin trumpets. Huge ostrich feathers enclose a postage-stamp Art Deco stage made of a mosaic of tiny inlaid mirrors. A waiter brings a menu shaped as a swan. "See," the blond woman says, "how easy it is to pretend you're happy here."

Each entrée is named after a performer: crab meat and avocado à la Marlene Dietrich; crêpes suzettes and crème de menthe à la Lola Montes (the dancer who had been Mad King Ludwig's mistress, who had died broke in Brooklyn); cooked prawns with cauliflower florets à la Edith Piaf; figs in blackberry coulis à la Josephine Baker…

"You are very lucky to have seen *Meistersinger*," she says.

"Well, it's been a stranger day."

"Did you hate us at the camp?"

"No."

"Why not?"

"I met a little man, who told me that for the great getting up Judgment Day…"

She interrupts, shaking her head, laughing. "No," she says with finality, "there's no Judgment Day. There's only the possibility of thinking you're happy though you know you're not."

"You think so?"

"It's why we sing. Obviously. To make ourselves happy."

"I remembered at the camp, a song from when I was a child…"

"And yes?" she says, brushing her blonde hair away from her eyes and lifting her glass of champagne.

Very softly, so no one else can hear, I sing to her:

> *Hitler,*
> *has only got one ball.*
> *Goering has two but very small.*
> *Himmler*
> *has something similar.*
> *But Goebbels's*
> *got no balls*
> *at all…*[1]

There are tears in her eyes. She is laughing. She puts down her glass.

"You didn't watch out for me this afternoon," she says. "My breasts got all burned, they're red. Shall I show you? No, I won't show you. Let's just be happy."

Toronto Life, 1979

[1] To the "Colonel Bogey" marching tune.

I KNOW NOT WHY
THE ROSES BLOOM

There was an old man called Rosie who had eyes like swamp water. He stood night after night outside the Imperial Theatre on Yonge Street and sold long-stemmed red roses from a seeding box. He was so shabbily dressed the theatre manager spoke to a policeman. "Make him move away. If he won't get out from under my marquee, for God's sake, you should arrest him." The policeman stared at the old man's roses. The old man stared impassively at the policeman. The policeman turned away with a shrug, saying, "What's God got to do with anything."

A PROMISE OF RAIN

Officers of the Ice Palace died during the war: Sedelnikov, Chulpenyev, Belov. Names. Ice on the tongue, silver bells in the mouth, that's what the poet Tsvetayeva said – a name, click of a gun, deep sleep.

Grandmother, at 101, shrivelled to the size of a little girl's crib, called for her brother, great-uncle Victor, who had lost a leg during the siege, clean cut above the knee.

He kept it encased in a lead box in the family crypt, afloat in embalming oils. A respected lexicographer, he visited his leg once a year, lit a candle, said a prayer, and flaunted his affairs with young soldiers in the lobby of Hotel Astoria.

He died despised in an S&M whipping stall at a military punishment club. Even so, he was a compassionate man who talked about evil, how the tear in a needle's eye comes from laughter, and how men like Stalin, Himmler, and now Bin Laden, not only know the evil they do but find it wryly amusing in all its intricacies of device, the way pulling the wings off butterflies is ferociously funny to queerly strung choir boys.

What else could that defiant sign WORK MAKES FREE over the gate of a death camp be but a joke that only killers could enjoy? They knew, they knew, they knew, and they laughed, he said, as they laughed at work, work, the dignity of work in the work camps of Siberia and Cambodia.

What a joke, which is how he thought of his leg, a length of space filled with phantom flex, a twitch, an ache, resurrected in those stalls, as he took the lash so that he could lie down in laughter at the pain of inexplicable, baseless hatred, silver bells in his mouth, ice on his tongue, names: Sedelnikov, Chulpenyev, Belov.

—Hogg, The Seven Last Words, 2001

ROBERT GRAVES:
"O PER SE O!"

I had intended to be in Cork City, but I had not intended to find myself with Robert Graves, a tall big-boned man, nearly eighty, a poet of great proportion, a man who had – according to all reports – lived his life by his wits, that is – he had always, as a writer, lived separate and apart from his countrymen, in Majorca…

Here he was, in Ireland, returned for the first time since the First World War to spend five passing strange days in a hunting castle in the Wicklow hills…where I found that, despite the height of the man and his big head, his sensual mouth with the full bottom lip and the deeply set pale blue eyes, I couldn't take my eyes off his hands…almost ham-handed, the fingers long and thick – peasant hands, all wrong for a poet, yet his fingers are tapered and graceful, and though thick, they are elegant…like the hands of Death in engravings by Kathe Kollwitz…somehow a contradiction self-contained…his hands a powerful presence…of what brute strength? Of what delicacy…?

But I am ahead of how it happened. Early one evening, a plane, a 727, with the bold shamrock on its tail fin, landed at Cork airport. The passengers emptied out. The Aer Lingus crew had kept the poet behind – an apparent courtly concern, so that the grand old man would appear on the top step alone…on view…angular, outlined against the evening light as he walked down the stairs and across the tarmac wearing his hard-brimmed black Spanish hat, a loping stride that seemed to be part playful bravado and partly an old man trying to keep from wobbling on his long legs.

He has a boxer's broken nose, high cheekbones, a mouth down at the corners…curly white hair…and a slight grey stubble on his cheeks and chin – and over the following days that stubble 'was always there – as if he couldn't shave his slack skin too closely, or maybe he just didn't care.

That evening in Cork, at supper at John Montague's row house on Grattan Hill – the acrid smell of coal soot and smoke, the feel of it clinging to one's face on the hillside overlooking Cork Harbour – I found him amiably polite, deferential…but then, not so much deferential as self-enclosed, indifferent as other guests became intent upon friendly seriousness, drawing a sour face at local gossip, at too much noisy talk…in other words, he was engagingly open even as he stood impassively apart from the nine or ten guests around him, which only compounded a nervous confusion among his hosts, who were so determined to be effusive, considerate, and respectful.

After supper in the small kitchen, a serving of onion tart and lamb shank with lashings of good wine, amidst laughter and prodding, he broke open the table talk by announcing, "I'm greatly in favour of the cuckoo."

"Why?"

"He's somehow holy, the cuckoo is," he said, clearing his throat, coughing, "especially in Ireland." He hunched his big shoulders, smirked, and declaimed,

> *And if no cuckoo sings,*
> *what can I care? Or you?*
> *Each heart will yet beat true*
> *year in, year out, we lie*
> *each in a lonely bed,*
> *the vows of true love read*
> *as prayers, though silently,*
> *a well-starred and open sky.*
> *Fierce poems of our past, how can they ever die?*

He had been invited to a hunting castle estate in the Wicklow hills, fourteen thousand acres in a hunch-back bowl of hills south of Dublin, ancient trees and a lake (with a lakeside shrine to two children in the family who had drowned), and scattered sheep and white-tailed deer feeding on the faraway hillsides. He was at the castle to be fêted and to relax – yet, what a confusion of personalities he had to contend with... A beautiful, frenetic titled lady, Tiger, of Anglo-Indian blood, who had great white teeth and a whim of iron; a Vietnamese painter, Saigon-bred, muscular, who had about him the air of a masseur in a downscale health club – who was being allowed to live in – as a homeless houseboy, the resident stud; a striking dusky-eyed Semitic woman, long thick black hair, who – when young – had been a concert pianist in Chicago – who had flown with Graves from Majorca; the poet John Montague – who had in his bones a reverence for great old men – and his young, high-strung French wife; and then there was the owner of the estate, who had the wary look in his eye of the rich man who wonders whether anyone cares...one of the Guinness family, a man of sweet accord, unafraid of wilful women or cocaine, his hair tied at the nape of his neck by a string of purple velvet...intending to depart the following week to his home away from home and other women in Haiti; all held under consideration in the eye of a constantly pacing hermaphroditic Irish wolfhound...teats and scrotum hanging...

The eighty-year-old Graves was always with us through the day and early evening, dressed in black, wearing his black broad hat, writing letters and thank-you notes on a stand set up for him by a window, again a little distant, removed, but it was hard to say if that was because of his age, an old man conversing with himself in his own silence, or perhaps a certain reserve, or, just a sensible defence against a tiring time among too many people shuffling in and out of rooms around him.

One afternoon, the Vietnamese painter, with a burst of bumbling friendliness, demanded of this poet of courtly love as he stood by his writing stand, whether he could still get it up! "Your prick!" he cried. Graves spluttered…he hurried across the room, toward me – though he was not looking at me, he was looking at the concert pianist from Majorca – as he asked me how his old friend Robert Frost was. "Yes," he said, "a good man, a very good man who lived close to the Canadian border…do you ever see him?

"No," I said, taken aback. "Frost's dead."

"Oh dear," Graves said, "Too bad. When was that?"

"Four, five years ago…"

"Oh…"

Over the next two days he asked me the same question, with the same seriousness, and I said, "No, dead…" And he replied… "Too bad." Then he said, "You know, my relative, a man from Boston, he drew the line, the dividing line between the United States and Canada…"

"The border…?"

"Yes, that was a good thing to have done, wasn't it?"

"Yes," I said, "I guess it was. All things considered."

"In short supply, consideration," he said.

"I don't know," I said.

"Neither do I," he said, his eyes wide-open – not in anger, not quizzical, not petulant…just open… Or was he hiding? Was this an old man's way of playing with forgetfulness, or was it a kind of indifference…as perhaps, too, were his idle lines spoken from poems, his quips, his questions out of nowhere…?

But then, with utter seriousness:

> *She tells her love while half asleep*
> *in the dark hours with half words whispered*
> *low as earth stirs in her winter sleep*
> *and puts out grass and flowers*
> *despite the snow, despite the falling snow.*

But then again, out of nowhere, "Hardy," he said, "that's how it all started, with Hardy. And I met him in a bookshop first. And we became friends at once and that was the end of it. He was a sad man, but who isn't? I'm not."

"And how about Siegfried Sassoon, the war poet?" he was asked.

"Yes…very difficult, very courageous but very difficult. He had rather bad experiences in the war. He was shell-shocked. Most people were shell-shocked. Look at me."

We all looked at him. He tugged at the brim of his hat.

Then one night, in the hour following on an elegant supper at a long highly polished oak table, as we sat before an unnecessary fire in the drawing room, Graves rose from his chair for bed, and from the far side of the room, he suddenly sailed his black hat across the room at me, and I caught it and sailed it back, and we did that three times, and then, like a vaudevillian character, he slapped his hat onto his head, said nothing, and did a long-legged quick step out of the room.

I went to bed, too, and reread one of his poems, which is about being a poet, and it ends:

> *Well, he had something, though he called it nothing –*
> *An ass's wit, a hairy-belly shrewdness*
> *That would appraise the intentions of an angel*
> *By the very yard stick of his own confusion*
> *And bring the most to pass…*

Somehow, earlier on in Cork City, and then at this hunting castle, he had brought the most to pass; he had brought on roars of approving applause at his readings, and he had achieved warm approving chuckles during nights around the supper table – as if all who were there around him were in tacit agreement…despite his stumbling, his forgetting of lines, his reading of the wrong poems…and the various moments of silence (vacancies?) he had suffered (?)…that he had, after all, consented to come back to be among these people, to assert, as best he could, that he was, after all, at one with them…and in response there had been three big photographs on the front page of the *Irish Times*, and the president himself had sat in attendance, applauding…as Graves had recited and sung, wanting, uppermost, so it seemed, to laugh, to cause laughter and good feeling…a determination to perform and delight those around him…with a song about *Queen Victoria, very good man*…or a song about a son who attempted to come home and destroy his father with a mournful, idiot refrain, *Ooooooooh… Ooooooooh…*

Sing, yes. Recite, remember, yes. He just did not want to talk, not that earnest prying talk that the earnest and prying go in for…there'd been no such talk at all…not that I'd heard…no words on the loose, no volubility…

> *There's a cool web of language winds us in,*
> *Retreat from too much joy or too much fear;*
> *We grow sea-green at last and coldly die*
> *In brininess and volubility…*

He'd played us for a lark, possessed, as he'd said, by an *ass's wit* – able, in *his own confusion, to call the intentions of an angel* up on the carpet with his quick doggerel songs, or the recitation of a short poem as if it were a song, and by so doing, he'd made others sing, as he, one night, had made me sing for the supper table of ten guests the "Agnus Dei" from the Mass by Gounod (the afternoon before, under the eye of the pacing wolfhound, he had asked me if I knew any sacred songs about forgiveness and sorrow and I'd said Yes, and I'd sung for him, in falsetto, the "Agnus Dei," and in baritone, the "Miserere," to which he'd let out a *Hooray*), and then after my singing at the table he had told a short joke in rhyming Latin (which at least two people – one of them, I think was Seamus Heaney – understood), ending it all again with *Hooray*…and then a priest down from Dublin for the supper pressed him in a kindly but hard-to-the-point way, and he said, "I know all about death. On my twenty-first birthday in the war I was officially reported, Died of Wounds – and I was dead, until they brought me back to life, and so I've been where you've not been. Twice born. *Hooray.*"

In Dublin, dressed again all in black, he was seated between small Paddy Moloney of the Chieftains, who was playing the uilleann pipes, and two tin whistle players, his deep-set eyes, so pale blue, catching all the light in the hotel receiving room…his big hands held over his head, hands made for the earth, ceremonious, clapping, his *Hooray* half-heard in the burble of good feeling among pints and whiskies…and again he sang out because *he had something, though he called it nothing* – Queen Victoria, *very good man* – bump-bump-bumpety-bump-bump-bump… shouting *Hooray*, uncaring – so it seemed – as to whether anyone approved or not:

> "*O per se O, O per se O!*"
> *The moribund grammarian cried*
> *To certain scholars grouped at his bedside,*
> *Spying the round, dark pit a-gape below:*
> "*O per se O!*"

2011

SCHACHMATT

Early morning in a cathedral in Munich: I had gone to Mass to hear Mahler's *First Symphony* for the dead, and during the funeral march I heard a little tune between the requiem notes, the composer's joke, a nursery rhyme…

> *Sonnez les matines, sonnez les matines,*
> *Din don din, din don din…*

After the requiem Mass, with a furled umbrella hooked over my arm, I walked into a park of tall oaks and tailored gravel walks and old men sitting on benches reading. There were large squares of cut stone laid into the earth. It was a huge chessboard, and waist-high wooden pieces stood on the board. A small man, almost a dwarf, wrapped his arms around a castle and carried it through knights and kings and rooks and cried, "*Schachmatt.*" He smiled as he rested his elbows on the head of the black queen. And then he turned to the row of seated old men: "*Der Nächste, bitte.*"

Nobody moved.

It started to rain, a cloudburst. The old men scattered. I opened my umbrella and stood beside the small man, sheltering him from the rain.

"*Sehr gut,*" he said, surprised. "*Danke, danke,* thanks to God, thanks to you."

"There's nothing worse than wet shoes," I said.

"No shoes at all is worse," he said and laughed.

"No: no feet is worse," I said.

He asked me what I was going to do after the rain and I said I had hoped to take the rapid transit to Dachau, the camp.

"It's only twenty minutes," he said, "it's where I live," and he told me he had a small house on the outskirts of the town. I said I didn't know there was a town, I thought there was only the camp, and he said, "So, we must have tea. I will go with you. From my house, from the window, the camp is just down the road, almost out of sight."

"I'll be glad for the company," I said.

"And a schnapps, too," he said, "and we can talk about Mahler."

But we did not talk about Mahler, not on the train, not in his house. Sitting in a parlour waiting for the water to boil and the tea to steep, he sat bent over an ivory-inlaid pocket chessboard, playing first the white and then the black, playing against himself, until he cried gleefully, "*Schachmatt*," turning the board around, touching his lost queen tenderly, but then the kettle began to whistle its little song.

He came back into the parlour carrying a tray, and on the tray a teapot, two cups and saucers, and two glasses of schnapps. The cups were a pale porcelain, white with a gaiety of flowers, a porcelain almost transparent as I held my cup up to the light.

"Beautiful," I said.

"Ah yes," he said, "this is Dachau china, we are world famous for our china."

I drank my schnapps.

He drank his tea, his schnapps, and then went to a sideboard and, as he took down a teacup, I asked, "What did you think the first time you went into the camp?"

He wrapped the cup in old tissue paper, saying, "I understood something about God."

"Oh yes?"

"He's going to need a good Jewish lawyer on Judgment Day."

"God?"

"Somebody," he said, giving me the gift of the cup, "has got to plead His case."

Alone at the camp, built in the 1930s in a drained swamp, I had nothing to say as I stood in a barracks beside bunk beds that were like stacked seed boxes, six men to a box. I had nothing to say standing between the barracks where the prisoners were forced to flog each other, where dead bodies were slung like sacks onto the *Moor Express* and skinhead prisoners harnessed to wagon shafts like mules had hauled them off to the "smokehouse," a stone building sheltered in the trees of a small pine woods that had been planted by imprisoned priests. In the smokehouse, the twin furnaces of warm red brick were open, their little doors hanging ajar. The iron cradles for the dead bodies were rusting. It was not the fire holes that distressed me, but the steel hook that had been driven into a ceiling crossbeam. How many men had twisted, hanging from that hook, as they stared into the fire?

I began to sing out loud to myself in a child's singsong, *Sonnez les matines, sonnez les matines, din don din, din don din...* until a stout woman, arm-in-arm with a frail old man who was carrying red roses, walked into the room, looked at me singing, and said scornfully, "You ought to be arrested."

idea&s, 2008

DEIJA VU

I'd been on a carousel of drink in Munich, seeking laughter at the heart's core of sorrow...what Beckett had call the *rhesus* laugh down the snout, laughter at laughter itself...after days of Mahler and Mozart, pig's knuckles and bar brandy, after a dank hour in a disused salt mine and an afternoon standing where Hitler had stood close to the clouds on the Eagle's Nest balcony, after picking up stones ("they're fallen angels," I was told) in the Dachau concentration camp square and after holding up a teacup of Dachau china to the sun and seeing a point of pure light between painted petals in the thin porcelain, I decided to get myself off this carousel, I decided to fly to Majorca, where Elaine Kerrigan (Gurevitch) lived. She was a woman of dark eyes, a dark mane of hair (*vivio sola durante muchos años*), and great intelligence.

Her house on a high hill in Palma city had lineage; it had been lived in by Gertrude Stein and Alice B. Toklas. A Chicago-born pianist, Elaine had become a companion to poets and story-tellers,[1] and an excellent translator of Julio Cortázar, Borges, Gil de Biedma, and Picasso. She had not only acted as an editor to Robert Graves but was his close friend.

I rented a car in Palma. Stick shift. Alien to me. I was all right driving on a road of easeful slopes. Steep hills were a problem.

Elaine suggested we go down into the city. "Let's do something entirely gauche," she said. "Let's drink a glass of Death in the

---

[1] Her Irish husband, Anthony Kerrigan, taught most of the year at Notre Dame. Something of a poet, he was a brilliant translator, his magnum opus being the translation of the selected works of the philosopher Miguel de Unamuno (seven volumes), for which he received the National Book Award.

Afternoon (champagne with absinth) and try to forget Hemingway." We had no intention of forgetting Hemingway (certainly not *The Sun Also Rises*) but we did – at 3:00 in the afternoon, Lorca's hour – salute the afterlife with a glass or two.

And then Elaine brought me into a cathedral. I stood in that peculiar gloom that is shed like mildew by high walls of cathedral stone and stared into a glass casket. In the casket was a bishop, apparently of established saintliness. They had oiled him, dressed him, and sewn his hair onto his skull. I could not take my eyes off the stitching. When I began to count the stitches I said to the amused Elaine, "I need a drink. The Fundador's in the car, best we go home."

In the car, at rush hour, we headed straight uphill. A stoplight at the top turned red, and then, at last, green. I tried for the clutch and gas, tried to get the pedal pressure and release into *sync*, but shot backwards to the bumper behind. I tried again. Honking. Nothing. Backwards. Bumper to bumper, a long single file. Elaine began to laugh. I asked, "How far's home?" She said, "Half a mile." I said, "Tell the bishop I'll see you there," and got out and left the car jammed into line on the hill.

I never did learn how or where the car ended up, perhaps because as soon as I got to the house I went to bed. I stayed asleep in bed for two days except for two hours when Elaine's son Camilo, a painter, woke me and propped me up and painted my portrait in oils. Burnt umber and burnt sienna was how he saw me.

Elaine rented another car. We drove toward a northern limestone mountain thick with wild olive trees and pines, Serra de Tramunta, and to a village close by the coast, Deià, a cluster of stone houses with red tile roofs. On the outskirts of Deià, the Graves family lived in a good-sized house, two storeys of beige quarried stone, the centre door opening onto stone terraces and orange, lemon, and olive trees. The house, which Graves had had built in 1932 when he was living with Laura Riding, was still called Ca n'Alluny. From 1946 on, he had lived in the house with the woman who'd become his wife, Beryl Pritchard.

Robert stood tall in the door, wearing a white blouse and black trousers. He was not wearing his black hat. Tufts of fine white hair stood out from above his ears. With a guffaw he called out a greeting, "Queen Victoria, very good man. Put 'em up! You look like you've done a bit of boxing."

He had big fists, and they were up in front of his face, and in front of mine.

He bobbed his head but did not move his fists.

Elaine, who was wearing a gay summer dress, her black hair drawn tight to her head, highlighting her good cheekbones but making her seem unusually serious, said, as if to caution him because more and more his mind had been slipping loose, "Robert, Robert..."

I held my arms and fists up to my head, just in case.

He was crooning while wagging his fists rather than jabbing, and then he drew his fists close to his jaw, pursed his lips, puffed his cheeks, and blew soft little explosions of air, "Poof, poof, poof... And so how are you? Come in, come in."

It was a cozy sitting room. Beryl was in her chair. A teacup in hand. We sat on a sofa, myself, Robert, and Elaine in a row. After a bit of banter, he turned to me and said, "Would you sing what you sang at Luggala?"

"Yes, do," said Elaine.

It was getting harder and harder for me to bring off my party trick, to hit falsetto notes appropriate to the Lamb of God, and then switch to a baritone "Miserere" but I took a sip of Fundador to clear the passages.

I began: *Agn-nus dei-ei, agn-nus dei-ei, qui to-lis pi-ca-atta, mu-u-u-un-di*

I realized that Robert, beaming at me as I sang, had placed his hand on Elaine's knee, and with each break in the syllables, he was moving his hand up the inside of her dress, along her inner thigh.

Beryl sat holding her empty cup in her lap, impassive. Elaine did not move, but had her eye on me, as if she were waiting to see what I might do.

I sang the last falsetto note of *the lamb of God* and went into the first baritone note of *Mis-se-re-re, mis-se-re-re no-obis…*

Robert, at the first deep note, had his hand on Elaine's divine portal…

She closed her legs.

I stopped singing.

He withdrew his hand.

I said, reaching for a bottle on a little serving table, "I need a drink."

Elaine undid her hair and let the mane fall loose. Her knees held tightly together, she reached and petted Beryl's knee, as perhaps a comfort from one long-time woman friend to another.

"The Lamb of God," I said, "works in mysterious ways."

Puffing his cheeks, pursing his lips, Robert blew: "Poof… poof…poof…"

2018

COMPARED TO WHAT

a clown's smirk in the skull of a baboon
—e.e.cummings

It was a German Jew, Fritz Haber, 1915,
who invented the chlorine gas delivery
system used to poison French soldiers;
his loving wife, also a chemist, ashamed
of the dead flensed to the bone
by trench rats,
killed herself, lungs filled
with a stench too human.
Three years later he was awarded
the Nobel Prize in Chemistry
and his work led to Zyklon-B,
first put to the kill test in '41.

2017

WHO LOOK ON WAR

This is the place
you would rather not know about…
where the word why shrivels and empties
itself…

As a child growing up during the Second Great War I heard my mother and father singing all kinds of songs from the First Great War. My mother said it was strange but there were not so many songs that anyone eagerly sang about the war against the Nazis – no song except "Lili Marlene" – and that was funny, my father said, because our soldiers were singing an enemy song that everyone said was beautiful because it made everyone feel sad. I didn't think it was funny because the only enemy soldier I had ever seen was on the back cover of my piano conservatory practice book and he had cruel eyes like the eyes of the dog our neighbour kept chained to a steel fence post next door.

Mother had dark eyes full of light. She sang gay war songs from the First Great War when we went to my grandparents, where she played His Master's Voice 78s on the Victrola that had a crank handle on the side: "My Buddy," "Over There," "Mademoiselle from Armentières," "They Can't Beat Us," and the bugle boy song, "Oh How I Hate to Get Up in the Morning." Even my father would sing along with my favourite:

Rosie Green was a village queen
Who enlisted as a nurse,
She waited for a chance
And left for France with an ambulance.

175

Rosie Green met a chap named Jean,
A soldier from Paree,
When he said, Parlez-vous my pet,
She said, I will but not just yet,
When he'd speak in French to her
She'd answer lovingly...

And then we'd all let go in a nasal cry,

Oh Frenchy, Oh Frenchy Frenchy...

I thought this was hilarious because an older boy had shown me a package of *Sheiks*, condoms, French safes, Frenchys, and I thought my mother and father didn't know what they were singing about.

Mother showed me, in an album of photographs that she had cut and pasted as a fourteen-year-old girl, a snapshot of herself, stylishly playful, wearing an army captain's hat, and another snap of Uncle Ambrose in uniform in 1918, astride his army motorcycle. She is sitting up to her neck in the sidecar, which looked to me like one of the tiny boats I had floated in my bath as a baby. I thought this was almost as funny as Ambrose's leggings that were wound like brown bandages from his ankles to his knees.

Years later, after going through that album again with Mother, surprised to see with what verve and swish her sisters were dressed, and surprised, too, at all their young women friends who were outfitted in nurses' uniforms, she gave me a little diary she had kept through the 1916–1918 years.

I knew she had been precocious as an art student at fourteen, but one paragraph took me aback. Amidst girlish entries about tea dances in Muskoka and outings on the sand beach by Scarborough Bluffs, and hugging a pillow at night in the way she wanted to hug a boy and kiss him, she wrote about the war with the angry conviction of innocence:

Thursday afternoon, Sept. 12, 1917

Toots [her older sister] *has a fellow, Fred Ryan, a returned soldier coming to see her... There's a young aviator, nearly 20 yrs, coming to see Toots too. He's up at Camp Borden just now... Oh dear there's nothing but "conscription" around here. It's terrible. I just can't stand the thought of it. To think that after all the men Canada has sent that now they should spring this on us. It sure is coming I guess. I hope Ambrose doesn't have to go. It will be awful if he does. Poor Ronnie Lynn was killed on the 9th. Mrs. Lynn got a letter from him that was written on the 6th. This is terrible. Russia into civil war now. What on earth is this world coming to? Japan is going to join Russia. Dear, what will come of it? I hope the States will help some. We won't have any men left here at all. We know there's few enough as it is, but there soon won't be any. To hear some people talk... in their estimation every last boy should have been sent there long ago. They make me sick.*

As it turned out, an armistice was declared less than a year later, only a week or two before Ambrose was to take a train east to board a troop ship and go over there. Mother's three sisters never married. They stayed at home in the family house for forty years. Perhaps, once the death count at the Somme and Vimy Ridge and Ypres had been completed, there really were not enough men to go around:

> *the long, the short, the fat and the tall,*
> *over there...*

Of an afternoon during the next Great War, my aunt Vera ("Toots" – because she was so gaily tempered) would bring me gifts, often a box containing balsa wood and clear glue. I would spend hours making model planes – fighters, like the Spitfire and Mustang – spreading out plans on the dining room table, learning to squeeze a perfect pinhead drop of glue into a balsawood joint, and one day my father got up from the long table where he wrote, typing on his portable Remington, and in a few minutes when he came back into the dining room he was carrying a silver trophy that he had won as a boy during the First Great War. Engraved on the cup was: *Special Prize – Model Aeroplanes – Donated by Long Branch Aviation School – 1916.* He said he had built a fighter with one set of wings above the other, a bi-plane, and he had painted it cherry red. I asked him if any of his older schoolboy friends had gone to the war as pilots and he said, "No, but Eustace was a soldier. I didn't know him then. But he was in the trenches. He got gassed. Maybe that's why he has his terrible depressions."

Eustace was W.W.E. Ross, the country's first modern poet. Taciturn and stolid, I always thought he came to our house like a keeper of secrets. Sometimes, as a boy, I stayed up late to be close to him when he came by on a Saturday night. He would sit for a long time in silence, and then, as others wrangled, he would slip into a laugh, the wide gape-mouthed silent laugh of a man, my father told me, who had gone through shock treatment year after year trying to cure depressions caused by the terrors of being shelled in the trenches.

One Saturday night, excited because I had been to the after-noon cartoons and seen "Donald Duck in Axis Land," I deter-minedly sang, as if I were Spike Jones making farting noises on his Birdaphone,

> *When der Fuehrer says*
> *We is the master race,*
> *We Heil, Heil,*
> *Right in der Feuhrer's face.*
> *Not to love der Fuehrer*
> *Is a great disgrace,*
> *So we Heil, Heil,*
> *Right in der Fuehrer's face…*

I marched around the living room, saluting like a little Nazi duck, and everybody clapped and then I was sent to bed. I have no idea what Eustace, behind the silence of his laughter, thought, but I learned years later – while going through his poetry notebooks with him – that he did have a wry sense of humour. I asked him if he had a favourite song from the First Great War, and he said yes he did and it was called, "Your Lips Are No Man's Land But Mine."

By then, being almost twenty, I had seen photographs of the death camps and grainy news footage of the cratered moonscapes that had once been lush farms…skeletal trees…like charred tuning forks, a silent music. I had also by then been struck by the spare prose of Hemingway's single paragraph stories from *In Our Time*:

> We were in a garden at Mons. Young Buckley came in with his patrol from across the river. The first German I saw climbed up over the garden wall. We waited till he got one leg over and then potted him. He had so much equipment on and looked awfully surprised and fell down into the garden. Then three more came over further down the wall. We shot them. They all came just like that.

Then I remembered that during the war a man called Titus had tended the big-bellied coal furnace beside the boys' latrine in my grade school. Titus the caretaker, an ex-soldier from the Great War, had muttered, "I am the man at the bottom of things," as he'd thrown another shovelful of coal into the fire.

Every day he'd swept the school floors, an inward look in his eyes, and then he'd gone down to the furnace room and he'd sat in front of the open damper, and sometimes his face was red and covered with sweat as he'd leaned toward the flaming coals, mouth open, smiling. Sometimes he would let me stand close to the fire, too, but when my face got too red, the caretaker had pulled me away. "Go upstairs where you belong," he'd said. "This is no place for a boy." Or, he'd send me out to the lane with a bucket of twisted cinders and clinkers, and one cold winter day he'd said, "Maybe that's what little boys do in purgatory."

"What?"

"Carry souls out to cool in the snow. Maybe heaven is all snow. Maybe God is only a caretaker at the bottom of things."

One early November morning, Sister Caroline, the principal, wimpled in black, had asked Titus the caretaker to read a poem to all the children as they had stood assembled in silent rows in the schoolyard:

> In Flanders fields the poppies blow
> Beneath the crosses, row on row,
> That mark our place; and in the sky
> The larks, still bravely singing, fly
> Scarce heard amid the guns below.

> We are the Dead. Short days ago
> We lived, felt dawn, saw sunset glow,
> Loved and were loved, and now we lie,
> In Flanders fields.

> Take up our quarrel with the foe:
> To you from failing hand we throw
> The torch; be yours to hold it high.
> If ye break faith with us who die
> We shall not sleep, though poppies grow
> In Flanders fields.

There were tears in Sister Caroline's eyes as, at eleven o'clock, bells somewhere close by tolled, and far away we heard a steady *whumpf whumpf whumpf*…and somebody said, "Them's big guns."

That is it.

That's all I knew about the First Great War, until years and years later, years after I had put aside the prankish laughter of childhood so that I would be able to go on playing childish games like a man.

As it happened, I was in Majorca at the home in Deia of the elder poet Robert Graves, who had written about the debacle of the First Great War in his *Goodbye to All That*. We were standing just outside his house at the top of a hill, a simple house with sacks of carob leaning against the wall, a wizened old olive tree by the door. He was a big man, big bones, big hands, and he said hello and put up his fists, his mind drifting on the edge of dementia, but eyes bright: "Up with your dukes!" We began to shadow-box, bobbing, feinting, laughing, and then he paused, pursed his lips, and said, "Poof, poof," as if he were blowing soap bubbles as a child. "Poof." He put down his fists and asked, "Do you know Frank Prewett?"

I didn't know who he was talking about.

"Canadian poet. One of yours. Wartime guy. I published him."

I shook my head.

"Never mind. Come in, come, sing for me."

He liked me to sing, since a meeting we'd had of a few days in Ireland, the "Agnus Dei" in falsetto, like a choir child, followed by the "Miserere" in baritone. *Miserere nobis*, as he again punched the air – "Poof, poof…"

…qui tolis peccata mundi…

Once home from Majorca, I decided to find out who Frank Prewett was, and what he had written, because he wasn't in any of the anthologies.

Then, I was put onto a poem by a friend, striking for the time in its tone, its directness:

> *Hearing the whine and crash*
> *We hastened out*
> *And found a few poor men*
> *Lying about.*

I put my hand in the breast
Of the first met
His heart thumped, stopped, and I drew
My hand out wet.

Another, he seemed a boy,
Rolled in the mud
Screaming, "my legs, my legs,"
And he poured out his blood.

We bandaged the rest
And went in,
And started again at our cards
Where we had been.

Here was a Toronto poet who had first been edited and published by Robert Graves and then praised by Virginia Woolf. Why had I never heard of him?

Then one day, Joe Rosenblatt – who has written poems – not in the voice of a soldier – but in the voices of bumblebees, gorillas, serpents, and fish – asked me if I had ever read *Generals Die in Bed*.

"No."

"Oh, it's the great war novel. The real thing."

"Really!"

I wanted to sing "Oh Frenchy, Oh Frenchy Frenchy," as if I, too, knew something about that war and its generals. Instead I *bbzzzzz'd* about the library like one of his bumblebees and I learned that *Generals Die in Bed*, by Charles Yale Harrison, had been published in New York in 1929 to great praise, a trench story written in the staccato plain-spoken rhythms of a declarative prose line, his eye unaffected by any hint of the sentimentality that has so easily come to be attached in our time to extremes of violence. After the novel appeared, John Dos Passos wrote that Harrison's prose (which I will quote at length) "has a flat-footed straightness about it that gets down the torture of the front line about as accurately as one can ever get it." In the trenches on both sides of no man's land, men feared not just death itself but how they might have to die...by maiming, mange, frostbite, and the rats...death by a hand-to-hand mutilation of the body and a mangling of the spirit...

I have a man at the end of my bayonet.

His shrieks become louder and louder.

We are facing each other – four feet of space separates us.

His eyes are distended; they seem all whites, and look as though they will leap out of their sockets.

There is froth in the corners of his mouth which opens and shuts like that of a fish out of water.

His hands grasp the barrel of my rifle and he joins me in the effort to withdraw. I do not know what to do.

I put my foot up against his body and try to kick him off. He shrieks into my face.

He will not come off.

I kick him again and again. No use.

His howling unnerves me. I feel I will go insane if I stay in this hole much longer...

Suddenly I remember what I must do.

I turn around and pull my breech-lock back. The click sounds sharp and clear.

He stops his screaming. He looks at me, silently now.

He knows what I am going to do.

A very white light soars over our heads. His helmet has fallen from his head. I see his boyish face. He looks like a Saxon; he is fair and under the light I see white down against green cheeks.

I pull my trigger. There is a loud report. The blade at the end of my rifle snaps in two. He falls into the corner of the bay and rolls over. He lies still.

I am free.

Some 20,000 men lay dead after the battle at the Somme, to say nothing of the battle for the Ypres Salient in 1914, where the Germans lost 25,000 child soldiers…child-bodies blown apart for the Fatherland…hundreds upon hundreds of arms, hands, a hobnailed foot, legs, a face, a head, buried in the mud.

And so the question is Why? Why did the men, the writers and critics and scholars, who shaped our taste through the decades after that war, who told us what to read – men of influence like E.K. Brown and A.J.M. Smith – why did they consign this work from the trenches to a great gap of unknowing? Why did Northrop Frye, who seemed to know everything about anything, say little or nothing in all his essays, all his commentary – about these wartime writers? Why did he ignore Prewett and Harrison and actually dismiss Eustace Ross as a poet of little consequence, old W.W.E., my childhood pal who wrote:

> *After the Battle*
> *After the Battle the soldiers danced and ate up the*
> *enemy's dead. No one tried to stop them. "Help!"*
> *cried one of the corpses before it was devoured.*
> *The way lay clear before them. Action dictated*
> *solely by consideration in doing just one thing.*
> *So that corpse too was eaten and the dance continued.*

Perhaps the answer lies in a little story about Frye himself.

One day during the First Great War he was playing the piano in his family house. His mother was listening, full of admiration. The postman came to the door with a letter that said Frye's older brother had been killed on the Western Front. His mother went into shock, she went deaf. She never heard Frye play the piano again. He never wrote about his brother, or about battle stories from the war, or the music that came out of war.

Across the land, a silence about the lambs.

People forgot where the Salient was, where Armentière is, even Tipperary…

Only in recent times have I come to an understanding of what Titus the caretaker saw when he sat at the bottom of things, mouth agape, staring into the fire.

We Wasn't Pals, 2001

KHISHCHUK AND UGOLOV, 1984: A LEGAL FRAGMENT

In the early morning two battalion foot soldiers were asked to assist the officers Maxim Khishchuk and Victor Ugolov in an unprovoked killing of enemy children. These officers, sportsmen, were trap-shooting with double-barrelled shotguns. The foot soldiers flung the babies of regional women into the air as the officers cried, according to civilian witnesses, Pull-BLAM. Recrank, Pull-BLAM. Re-crank. Over the course of an hour, Khishchuk in direct hits outscored Ugolov and secured a wager they had made that morning: Officer Khishchuk shot Officer Ugolov and then killed himself. The two foot soldiers gathered twenty of the scattered dead and built a pyre in a pumpkin field to burn the bodies of the children after rolling a gasoline drum forward through the pumpkin vines, but superior Officer Valentin Felikosovich Voino-Belyayev shot the two soldiers dead. Voino-Belyayev was convicted of dereliction of duty for not supervising his sub-officers, Khishchuk and Ugolov, and also with murder in the case of the two soldiers, whose adjutant argued successfully that they were only carrying out orders with diligence and dispatch. The foot soldiers' families were granted half-pensions. Voino-Belyayev, accorded leniency, was sentenced to ten years of reconstructive re-education in a corrective labour camp. He asked to be blindfolded instead and put before a firing squad but his anti-social request was denied. He was transported in leg chains. The dead were buried in an unmarked grave. The battallion retreated, leaving the increment of victims to the pumpkin field.

Hogg, The Seven Last Words, 2001

INDIANS

The play is called *Indians*. It's by Arthur Kopit, the young man who had such success some years back with *Oh Dad, Poor Dad, Momma's Hung You in the Closet and I'm Feelin' So Sad*. He has another success with *Indians*; performances are sold out.

The lights come up: Buffalo Bill is walloping the backside of his white bronco as he canters around prairie mounds, yelping, hallooing. It's Buffalo Bill in his Wild West Show, Buffalo Bill the Indians' bosom pal, the greatest hunter the plains has ever known. He's laughing uproariously. But he's in pain. His Red Men friends are dead or demoralized. He, Buffalo Bill in his tasselled and feathered buckskin garb, has sold them down the river to Washington. He didn't necessarily mean to, but he did. Just as he'd hired himself out as a crack shot to European gentlemen dudes to kill 100 buffalo with 100 shots. He hadn't meant to do harm but he'd done so. He'd subsequently stood stricken and bewildered as Indians in the territory starved for want of meat. Trying to atone, Buffalo Bill has given the battered old Indian chiefs star billing in his Wild West Show, and now, here he is – laughing and hooting – desperately haunted by guilt because the Indians, in the wake of Congressional cunning and corruption, have been decimated.

Buffalo Bill, galumphing around on stage, obviously bears a message in his placard person and it is this: the white man, lusting for land and blood, in his savage contempt for coloured peoples, has committed genocide. The implication, of course, is that the American white man is still prepared to kill those coloureds who stand in his way, to kill much as Buffalo Bill did, with a self-appointed grandeur, with a terrifying self-anointed innocence that is not so much unawareness as wilful stupidity, turning all his slaughterhouse escapades into a spangled pageant of the Wild

West to be played at popular prices. Which is why audiences, out for a night of soul-cleansing entertainment, end up colluding with clichés!

It is through this pageant that Buffalo Bill takes us back into American history, to the Senators who went west at Bill's request to meet with the starving Indians. There, in the bibulous tones of Bible-pounding preachers – treaties be damned – they put the Indians in their place; one step closer to the grave.

There are moments on this stage, so full of claptrap and tomfoolery, when the Indians cease to be hopeless props in the white man's pernicious story, only to become props in the white man's *mea culpa*. Sitting Bull suddenly descends from the skies. He half stalks, half staggers through a clever denunciation of those who have tried to deracinate and eradicate his people.

The audience, rising to every cliché, loves Sitting Bull. They love all the hapless Indian chiefs, toothless, broken, hurling charges at the white man, at the white audience. The audience applauds, especially when truly damning moments in history are burlesqued, as if slapstick deprecation and mockery might make evil easier to ingest. When the president appears on stage riding a mechanical horse, pretending to be Wild Bill Hickok, the audience hoots with contempt, with derision. How could anyone hold in esteem such a dim-witted leader? The audience laps it up as a sad irony is hammered home: the Indians, noble suckers to the end, had believed that if they could only get past the mendacious Senators to the Great White Father, all would be rectified, put right. And here he is: the White Father, an all too familiar liar, a cheat, a conniver, a corrupter, the president!

This ends as it must, with Buffalo Bill standing among the frozen corpses of Indians murdered by the army. Bill moans, he pleads his good intentions, purposes, he excuses himself, asks for forgiveness, asks for admiration, asks for reconciliation. Ghosts haunt his every hour. His face is a harrowed mask, the eyes weary, his mouth hangs open, he collapses, playing with picture postcards, beads, bits of buckskin – all the detritus of the tribes of the West.

Who can deny this bald indictment? Who can deny that policies designed – either mendaciously or through stupidity – to destroy the Aboriginal peoples persist? But what of this play, this exercise in slapstick flagellation, so slick in its easy scoring of moral points? When you get down to it, the play is no more than a sideshow itself – a bauble. You laugh and hoot, deride and cry; you never feel pity or terror. A question looms. Is it reasonable to expect that people who have never seen an Indian, let alone killed one, can feel anything more than received remorse for what the U.S. cavalry did and represented?

Such remorse, such guilt can have no depth, cause no lasting pain, no purging, leave no scars. It is all too easy, too pat; a distress too comforting. Applied art. Angst without consequences. Meant to make remorse, even guilt, pleasurable. In a word, this is all too cheap. But this is the moral strut of our times, this mealy-mouthed appropriation of collective guilt. Audiences crowd into the theatres to beat their breasts for the six million Jews lost in the death camps, for the Dresden firebox, for the strange fruit hanging from poplar trees in the southern breeze, for the Trail of Tears…sucking up easy guilt, cleansing themselves through a theatrical cliché-ridden self-righteousness.

That such a shallow stage piece as *Indians* should be a marquee success on Broadway, that the accusatory posturing of Rolf Hochhuth in *The Deputy* and his all too easy slanging of Churchill in *Soldiers* should move indignant men and women to accusation, to calls for renunciation and retribution…to a general massaging of the guild glands…! Who are these people who pack into plush seats to hear themselves denounced for crimes they did not commit? Who are these people who take this play, *Indians*, not only as an allegorical comment on these Vietnam times but as an exercise in shaming and moral uplift?

I recall Norman Mailer's description of the people he linked arms with as he marched on the Pentagon to protest the war in

Indo-China. He confessed to confused self-communion and drunkenness as he was about to be arrested. Who were the men and women beside him in this righteous citizen army? "Good old American anxiety strata – the urban middle class with their proliferated monumental adenoidal resentments, their secret slavish love for the oncoming hegemony of the computer and suburb, yes, they and their children, by sheer ineptitude, the *kinks* of history, were now being compressed into more and more militant stands, their resistance to the war some hopeless melange…and their children…in whom Mailer had some gloomy hope. These mad middle-class children with their lobotomies from sin, their nihilistic embezzlement of all middle-class moral funds, their innocence, their lust for apocalypse…"

After Mailer, what can I say that hasn't already been said. So I leave the last word to that hill country fine poet, Hayden Carruth:

Only now and in bad luck
do we see the importance of a good fuck.

The Telegram, 1969–1995

GAMAL ABDEL NASSER: AGOG IN EGYPTLAND

Agog

During those days early in 2011, when the wired-up world was agog at the sit-down revolution in Tahrir Square in Cairo, I heard more than one commentator complain, "But who is Hosni Mubarak, what do we know about this man?"

The various answers never amounted to much: President Mubarak was a general like the president before him who was a general named Sadat who had been assassinated by Islamic extremists (the Muslim Brotherhood), a general from the same army as the generals who had brought military rule to Egypt in 1952.

I don't think that I heard anyone ask what had happened in 1952. Nor did I hear during those eighteen days of round-the-clock coverage anyone speak of Gamal Abdel Nasser to ask who he had been and what he had had to do with 1952.

As a matter of fact (I was, of course, not wide awake the whole time), I have no recollection of anyone explaining that it was Nasser and other generals who had overthrown a king named Farouk, so that they might expel the British army that had occupied the country and had controlled the Suez Canal for seventy-two years.

I did not hear anyone explain that it was President Nasser who had (to an agog world) nationalized the canal. I did not hear anyone, in any discussion of how important the present-day treaty between Egypt and Israel is, mention that Israel, acting as the aggressor, probably hoping to curry favour and influence with the French, had joined with the French and the English in an invasion of Egypt that was intended to take back control of the canal (Canadian commentators seemed to have forgotten entirely why their prime minister, Lester B. Pearson, was awarded the Nobel Prize for Peace).

There was so much that went unsaid over those eighteen days… I heard no one speak about the American refusal to support the French, English, and Israeli invasion in 1956, or the American refusal to support the building of the High Aswan Dam, or the support of that dam and the Egyptian military by the Soviet Union, or Anwar Sadat's diplomatic entry into Jerusalem…

I had intended not to reprint my little review/essay on Gamal Abdel Nasser written in August 1970, a month before he died…thinking that readers would not remember much about those times, who the politicians were and what was going on, but then, after those eighteen days of some most extraordinary immediate reporting, I thought that perhaps a little such information might still be useful. And besides, all of this has raised for me a forgotten journalistic disappointment: in late August 1970, in Cairo, one of President Nasser's confidants – a man I'd come to know – Mohamed Heikal, the editor of *Al Ahram*, had arranged that I should meet with Nasser in mid-September after my being in Beirut and Amman. I got trapped in the Black September War in Amman and Nasser died.

Such is life.

Gamal Abdel Nasser

We know too little about President Gamal Abdel Nasser of Egypt. Too often the general is viewed as a pawn in American or Russian foreign policy. As a case in point, after Nasser accepted the Rogers formula for ceasefire in the Middle East (proposed in December 1969), some journalists said that the United States should be congratulated, not only for its initiative but for re-asserting American influence in Cairo. On the other hand, others argued that Nasser was the reluctant victim of Kremlin arm-twisting, that the Russians were scared of direct military confrontation with the U.S. And still others said that, no, this was wrong, for the Russians weren't scared at all; what they were really after was a ceasefire to be used as a screen while they strengthened their political and military hands in Egypt. These views, no matter their perspective and their limited truth, have a common thread and a common failing, in that President Nasser is presented as little more than a dupe being buffeted about by the Big Powers. Such theories are not helpful, either to Nasser's foes or his friends, if only because they simplify the situation and neglect the political acumen of the man who stands at the core.

There is, for example, much evidence that until recently the Americans were flagging diplomatically in the Middle East and only rallied in response to Nasser's initiative. Twelve months ago Nasser scorned the idea of a ceasefire with Israel. Last February 1969, he ruled out recognition of Israel. Diplomats were in dismay. Then in May, Nasser, to the surprise of the Americans, indicated a willingness to negotiate. He followed through very quickly and by late May he had publicly laid down the conditions for a ceasefire to, among others, an independent American journalist – and those conditions were the very essence of what would become the celebrated Rogers formula (this interview, filed in Cairo by NET, was not shown in the U.S. until the middle of June). The interview's existence makes clear that Nasser had long since shaped his policy and intentions.

But to go back: after Nasser's May Day speech, the U.S. went to work diplomatically, but so did Nasser, especially in Libya and in Russia. The question is: Had he become diplomatically active out of strength or weakness? Well, he secured the support of the radical Libyans, and from the Russians he received a military build-up that made the balance of power along the canal relatively equal. Was this window-dressing to hide a drainage of power at home or was it a last stage of recovery for Egypt after the Six Day War defeat? It is my view that Nasser, by May, thought himself in a strong enough position – as the secure general among generals, as the leader of his nation – to offer to negotiate. The Egyptian populace, especially the emerging middle class, supposedly so rabid in its hatred of Israel, did not buck him. The much-predicted Arab split did not materialize (Libya was the key here). Nasser had made it very clear that he was strong – militarily, politically, and economically.

There are even some who believe that Nasser is so strong right now that he has been able to openly adopt a policy that is revolutionary in terms of recent Arab history. Atallah Mansour, the Arab writer for the Israeli newspaper, *Ha'aretz*, says this: "Nasser has made a revolutionary move – and if most Jews and most Arabs don't see it, then that is their funeral. It's the first time since the beginning of the conflict, fifty years ago, that a military Arab leader has said yes to anything proposed by the West – and he has said it publicly." Even so, you might say, it is entirely possible that the whole Nasser performance is misguided, that he deludes himself, and that the Russians, whether he thinks so or not, intend to use the ceasefire to build up militarily along the canal and therefore dig deeper into Egypt. As I have already indicated, I doubt this and I would guess that even if the Russians believe they are manipulating Nasser for their own ends, they may be in for a surprise. Of course now I'm in the realm of guessing, but, as is obvious, I think Nasser a rather formidable politician. Mr. John Kimche, a well-known authority on Mid-Eastern affairs, encourages me to think this way in his recent book, *The Second Arab Awakening*.

Mr. Kimche, of course, is taking a scholarly view of the Middle East. He covers quite a lot of history, from the First World War to the recent rise of guerrilla nationalism. He is trenchant about the roles the Germans, Russians, and English played over the past fifty years. As for the Egyptian army's surge to power, led by the so-called Free Officers, especially Lieutenant-Colonel Nasser and General Muhammad Naguib…a surge that resulted in the overthrow of King Farouk (1952) and the establishment of the Republic of Egypt (1953) with Gamal Abdel Nasser as its first president; as for the story of King Abdullah outfoxing the English and getting them to create TransJordan (now the Jordan of King Hussein); as for the Great Powers trying to use Zionism (and the death camps) for their own political ends and failing; as for the Americans entirely misreading, through the formation of the Baghdad Pact, the strategic importance of Egypt after the Second World War, he is informative and convincing. In his analyses he is in command of large amounts of complex information, of the kind that can have been gathered only after many years in the area.

Mr. Kimche is certainly sympathetic to the Israeli fact and presence (though he regards the Israelis as bumblers in foreign policy). He is quite disapproving of the aims of President Nasser. He acknowledges Nasser's political mastery, but views Nasser the general not as a true social revolutionary (no matter the land and educational reforms supported by the army) but as a kind of empty imitation of Bismark. This is a limited view of both Nasser and Egyptian history, but because he is so harsh, it is interesting to read his analysis of what went on in 1954, 1955, and 1956, for these are the truly emergent years of Gamal Abdel Nasser. Mr. Kimche takes Nasser very seriously as a political force. All Mid-East scholars do, but he has some new views on how Nasser operates.

The popular conception of what happened in 1956 is this: The John Foster Dulles Middle East policy shapes up as an incredible blunder. He gave a missionary's turn to the Truman Doctrine, which was meant to assume commitments to Greece and Turkey that Britain had abandoned – and by so doing – contain Russian influence. Dulles, playing John Wayne in a Wall Street vest, made fundamental strategic mistakes. The Baghdad Pact was rooted in a basic misunderstanding of the rise of Arab and especially Egyptian nationalism. It was formed of countries along the northern tier of the Arab world, and Egypt was left out, for Dulles discounted the strategic importance of the Suez area. Further, he disapproved of Nasser's neutralism in the midst of the American moral struggle against Communism. But before the pact had been formed, back in 1955, an Egyptian fort in Gaza had been almost wiped out by the Israelis. This encounter, so we are told, led to a formal Egyptian request to the Americans for arms. It became apparent that the U.S. was not going to answer this request. Dulles was making a firm lesson clear to Nasser. The Egyptian president, however, took the initiative and concluded agreement with the Russians, through Czechoslovakia. Hence, we are told, Dulles drove Nasser into the embrace of the Russian Bear.

The next stage in events, as they are usually presented, came over the next six months. The Americans, together with Britain and the World Bank, agreed to finance the first stage of the High Dam at Aswan. Plans, we are told, had been completed when suddenly without warning the United States withdrew its offer of aid (June 1956). Critics of American policy blamed Dulles and Zionist pressure in Washington. The rebuff was insulting, and Nasser returned the insult by nationalizing the Suez Canal Company. The British, who had already completed a phased withdrawal of almost 80,000 troops from the canal area – begun with the signing of the Anglo-Egyptian Defense Agreement of 1954 – prepared for invasion (Anthony Eden called Nasser "the Hitler of the Nile"). The French, as if suicidally inclined since their interests in the area (Algeria!) were already on the verge of collapse, prepared for invasion. The Israelis joined the invasion force. The result, of course, was a debacle. The British and French were sandbagged by Eisenhower's refusal to back the invasion. Nasser emerged from the 1956 war stronger than ever, and, apparently was driven to the Russians once more, and fell further into the embrace of the Bear: the Russians were financing the Aswan Dam.

This outline of events, I believe, constitutes the general view of what went on in 1956. What is interesting is that, once again, Nasser is pictured as little more than a leader catching-as-catch-can; the initiative, the crucial decisions, the mistakes or success are credited to everyone but President Nasser.

Mr. Kimche has an altogether different view. He looks back to the spring of 1954 and says that Israel was then a relatively minor problem for Nasser. More urgent was his need to consolidate his political authority in Egypt and in the Arab world as a whole. The British still occupied the Suez Canal Zone, and the Muslim Brotherhood opposed him internally. Nasser, therefore, began negotiations with the British for evacuation. By July, the British agreed to leave, but on the understanding that the Constantinople Convention of 1888 guaranteeing free shipping would be honoured. The Muslim Brotherhood, of course, denounced Nasser. He played his hand slowly and carefully. In Cairo, thirteen young Jews had been arrested for acts of spying and sabotage (in Israel, this developed into the celebrated Lavon Affair, in which Israelis and especially Ben Gurion tried for some years to determine who had actually set up this hapless group in Cairo). Just at the point when the Muslim Brotherhood criticism of Nasser reached its peak, he struck by announcing that the Jewish spies had been arrested and that they were in league with the Brotherhood. Brotherhood leaders, now presented as traitors, were either executed or imprisoned. Nasser had consolidated his home position and he was rid of the British, which raised his star in other Arab countries.

Then came the 1955 Baghdad Pact. Nasser regarded this alliance as a direct attempt to mobilize outside Arab opinion against him. At the same time, in Cairo, the right-wing military men (either sympathetic to the Brotherhood or actual members) were ordering raids against Israel. These raids led to the Israeli reprisal attack in Gaza, mentioned earlier. It is Mr. Kimche's view that the Gaza defeat did not send Nasser after American arms. On the contrary, the Israeli show of strength (as it was intended by

Moshe Dayan to do) prompted many of Nasser's closest advisers to urge an immediate military alliance with the West, and this would have involved a peace settlement with Israel. Therefore, the Gaza raid, rather than ensuring future Egyptian-Israeli hostility, nearly brought about a truce. But, says Mr. Kimche, Nasser rallied from the shock of Gaza and went through the Chinese to the Russians with a request for arms. The Russians not only agreed to an arms shipment of a size undreamt of in the Middle East, but entered into arrangements for the future industrialization of Egypt and the financing of the High Dam at Aswan. While this was going on, Nasser also made his well-known arms request of Dulles, and Dulles acted as expected. He turned it down. Nasser then presented his government with the only alternative, Russian aid. If Mr. Kimche's analysis is correct, the dupe in this affair was not President Nasser but John Foster Dulles.

The same is true of the Aswan Dam crisis of 1956. In this instance, Dulles favoured financing the dam. It was Senator Lyndon Johnson who opposed it (in response to American cotton growers and to Zionist pressure: the implication of Mr. Kimche's argument – though he doesn't go into it – is that while Zionist pressure was an important factor in American politics, it had no real effect on this situation). John Foster Dulles was now convinced that Soviet influence had to be countered in Egypt (Dulles, when he was not just plain wrong, was given to closing the barn door long after the horse had fled). Nasser entered into these negotiations and they went on into 1956, but what is not well known is that the Russians, late in 1955, had publicly declared that they were prepared to undertake the financing of the dam, regardless of other efforts. This was part of the 1955 arms agreement, and since then Soviet aid has been high, and higher than could ever have been expected from the Americans. But Dulles went on negotiating, over six months, on the understanding that the Russians would play no part, despite their arms presence, in the building of the dam. By the time Dulles caught on, the British were evacuating the canal. When Dulles, so beautifully trapped, rejected any American involvement in the dam, Nasser, in calculated righteous rage, nationalized the canal. As far as Mr. Kimche is concerned, Dulles had played the perfect fall guy. Nasser was not only able to take a moral position, but the direction of the canal and enormous Russian aid in money, advisers and arms. It had been a masterpiece of political manoeuvring. While the western world believed Nasser was being heaved about like a medicine ball, he was actually consolidating a triumph.

Mr. Kimche's view of the president could not be more cynical and, therefore, has its own very serious limitations. He is entirely unconcerned with the development of Nasser's social revolution. He treats Nasser as if he were no more than a very crafty political pro. But it is because Mr. Kimche is no advocate of Nasser that his view is interesting. For one thing comes clear: any careful examination, and even an uncomplimentary one, finds Nasser at the centre.

The current concentration on American and Russian strategy and the self-congratulatory American air certainly have their place. But both views, in tried and failed fashion, overlook the political centrality of Gamal Abdel Nasser. The central question for me, then, is this: Having initiated the peace talks, having brought about a ceasefire, just what is it that President Nasser hopes to gain? How does he intend to develop the situation to his advantage?

The Telegram, 1970

HOGG SEES
TWO BLIND MEN

Now it is their own city and even the blind can feel free.
So the two blind men who have never been outside the walls are
walking toward Dung Gate. Beyond is the ridge that
overlooks the ruins that lie in the long grass
at the bottom of Dung Hill Cliff, the ruins of David's
house. The men hurry, holding each other by the arm, asking
soldiers the way south. They go out through the Gate.
They want to stand on the ridge and hear below them the voice
of their forefather who had also held the city. They go on a long
way, talking excitedly, but then they grow silent, and soon
stop. The road has petered out into rubble. They don't know
where they are, but they hear voices, low, whining
voices, children, coming closer, circling them.
—Ask which way's the road.
—They hate us, they'll lead us over the cliff.
—What'll we do?
—Don't move.

The Hogg Poems, 1978

AT FULL TILT: JOYCE CAROL OATES

Possession they call it…hands move to disembowel a passing whore or strangle the neighbour child…alleviate the chronic housing shortage…

—W.S. BURROUGHS, *Naked Lunch*

There is a housing shortage inside Joyce Carol Oates' head… somebody comes, somebody's got to go…by daybreak in the morning she finds strangers sleeping four or five to a room, bunk beds, cots in the halls…"My head," she says, "at times it seems crowded, there is a kind of pressure inside it, almost a frightening physical sense of confusion, fullness, dizziness. Strange people appear in my thoughts." As they enter the hallways, the walls sweating from the humidity, she insists that there are "no conventions, no traditions, only personalities…" she hears their whispering, their whingeing, the threats, their conniving…but listening is not enough…she says she also needs to draw them, their faces, she has this compulsion, it comes over her, "I've drawn several million faces in my life, and I'm doomed to carry this peculiar habit with me to the grave…"

Given these apparitions, this crowd of faces, it's a wonder that she is not half-crazy, but then again…think of how she appears to be: almost timorous, deferential, glad to be welcomed as she walks into a room, walking in the shadow of her husband, who lives in her shadow… So maybe she is half-crazy…(she has insisted that one of her books was outright possession by a storyteller, a certain Fernandes de Briao, *who*, she said, *didn't exist* – but he was nonetheless the author of *Azulejos*, stories that had, she said, never been written...and since they had never been written, she'd "translated them"), Briao's voice joining the hundreds upon hundreds of other voices in her dozens upon dozens upon dozens of novels and stories – can she remember them?...by name, by place, by broken heart? – can she remember who was drowned, who got disembowelled, who drove an ice pick into...whom...and yes, can she remember who was strangled...all of them gone now, gone down...to alleviate the housing shortage? "I am addicted, yes," she says, "to the need to get rid of the little stories that crowd my head"...to be *rid!*...one can only hope that, if only for a moment, there will be a *riddance*, a time when no one new shows up...a time when there'll be an empty room...a silence, a silence that perhaps could become a force...a presence itself...so that she may know within herself what it is like to be wordless (it is little known that Oates has a sister who is autistic – and Yes, she says, her sister has played a role in her life – "I often write about twins. My sister looks like me. She was born on my birthday. She's eighteen years younger than I am. And she's never uttered a coherent word. She is my opposite number. I'm called prolific and she's never spoken"), but then there's a tell-tale knock (she's got more than a little of the Poe Gothic in her), a pounding on the door. She sees the face of a man who believes in "soul murder," and then a Tattooed Girl who is "in a panic tinged by wonderment," a lothario senator, a serial killer gone bucolic in the brain, Snow White doing blow, or Marilyn Monroe, or a fool for porn – a fool for Christ..."like enthralled children" they are liable to show up...overnight...it's an everyday risk (any landlord could have told her that) and even worse, what will she do (as she bears witness – in the religious sense – to her own voices), what will happen if she surprises herself (as her characters so often end up surprising themselves) and, without thinking, she opens the wrong door only to find that the Man in Possession of the Room – say, this guy of hers, the serial killer Quentin P, who calls himself Q – P – , wants to know, "How come there's some man's liver in your lap?"...and she, trying for a little *sangfroid* – thinks of saying, No, no, you've got the wrong book, that's *Naked Lunch*, but instead she says, absolutely dead-pan, "I know him, he is one of mine, another one of those men I've written about…guys who live the life of normal, average men, men who work at daily jobs, in garages, in lumberyards, driving trucks, taking orders from others, trying to make money like you'd try to suck moisture out of some enormous unname-able thing, pressing sucker-lips against it, filled with revulsion for what you did, what you must do, if you want to survive," *suck on the unnameable!*…that's what the most demented of all her houseguests, Q – P – is doing, that serial killer, when he sets out to create, of all things, a "true Zombie":

> A ZOMBIE who would pass no judgment. A ZOMBIE who would say, "God Bless you, Master." He would say, "You are good, Master. You are kind & merciful." He would say, "Fuck me in the ass, Master, until I bleed blue guts." He would beg for his food & he would beg for oxy-gen to breathe. He would beg to use the toilet not to soil his clothes… He would never laugh or smirk or wrinkle his nose in disgust. He would lick with his tongue as bid-den. He would suck with his mouth as bidden. He would spread the cheeks of his ass as bidden…we would lie beneath the covers in my bed in the CARETAKER'S room listening to the March wind & the bells of the Music College tower chiming & WE WOULD COUNT THE CHIMES UNTIL WE FELL ASLEEP AT EXACTLY THE SAME MOMENT.

The final, persuasive thing about her fictions, however, no matter how mendacious, mewling, or depraved her characters are, is that they are creatures of a specific place. This is the strength even of those stories that don't quite work…the voices are always rooted in a place that is deeply documented, deeply felt in the details – whether it is rural Pennsylvania, the northeast rust belt neighbourhoods, the scrub towns and squalid suburbs embedded in the landfill countrysides of upstate New York or the upstate towns with the ludicrous names…Utica, Rome, Syracuse…

> Taverns and gas stations and automobile/truck/motor-cycle dealerships adorned with fluttering banners, house trailers propped up on cinder blocks in the pine woods, bungalows, habitations that appeared to be no more than concrete foundations in the rocky earth, like bomb shelters. There were bait shops, yet more taverns, roadside wood-frame churches, bullet-ridden road signs, lakeside cabins, small boats on trailers, junked vehicles in the ditch by the side of the road, mattresses at the roadside, abandoned furniture as if families had thrown off their chains in a frenzy of repudiation and loss.

Each voice in its place is working at full tilt…each is the voice of a person in pursuit of "what we call your personality…it's not like actual bones or teeth, something solid. It's more like a flame"… These people have their dream of themselves in which they discover, unfortunately, that the more they become big with voice (as in pregnant), the more they fear they are going to flame out, destined to be diminished (as in stillborn), to fail. The end of times for these people is not perdition; as they stand in the ashes of their ambition, feeling more and more like imposters in their own bodies – even the craziest among them – as if life were forever conducted in a grade school classroom – gets an F:

> BUNNYGLOVES who I had such hope for, him being the first (of my victims), convulsed like a madman when I pushed the ice pick at the angle in the diagram through the "bony orbit" above the eyeball (or what ever it was, splintering bone) & screamed through the sponge I'd

shoved and tied in his mouth…but he did not regain consciousness, dying in twelve minutes… My first ZOMBIE – a grade of fucking F.

These are people who have almost no depth of memory of themselves…they are exactly like the towns they live in…where at each crossroads there are directional signs stacked on top of directional signs, route numbers and mileage distances cross-angled – their lives are pointed in every and all directions – with body parts scattered along the shoulders of the roads – hub caps, mufflers, an old shoe, bits of shining broken chrome, a discarded neck brace, the black quarter-moons of blown sixteen-wheel truck tires, a T-shaped cross with plastic flowers tied to it to remind all passersby… Here is a place of pedal-to-the-floor fury, the place of a nameless hit-and-run death, flowers encased in cellophane – here is where only a forlorn voice is heard: "I will settle for redemption, whatever that is."

Oates has borne witness to her society by giving herself up on the page to the voices she has housed in her head, voices that cannot be controlled just as dreams cannot be controlled. Even now, as if she were a religious ecstatic, she finds the voice of the man who has just housed himself in bunkbed H "hypnotic, ravishing, utterly inexplicable."

STORYTELLING

A Conversation with Joyce Carol Oates

BARRY CALLAGHAN:
I have known Joyce Carol Oates since 1973, when she had written perhaps four novels, but now it is a convention of our time that Joyce Carol Oates is a dynamo, and this sometimes leaves people not knowing what to say about her novels, her stories, her criticism, her poetry, or how to approach her. It seems to me that this astonishing body of work can only be seen, in the American context, as a kind of Balzackian vision. The range of experience that is offered to us through the lens of her vision is extraordinary. In a recent novel she's got inside the voice of the young black man, in another recent short novel she's exploring the world of a senator and politics, and of course she has written about boxing and violence and psychopaths, and there is a beautiful scene of youthful sensuality between girls in another recent novel called Foxfire. *Recent, recent, recent, it's incredible. And so, my old friend, Madame Balzac, how are you?*

JOYCE CAROL OATES:
Well, thank you.

I was reading through various things that you have written over the years about writing, about your own concerns, and I came across a remark you made about Joseph Conrad – or, a remark Joseph Conrad made that you quoted – when he was particularly depressed while writing Nostromo. *He said that writing is the conversion of nervous force into language. You said that this is so profoundly bleak an utterance that it must be true. What does that mean?*

Well, certainly on a kind of neurophysiological level we have to have nervous energy to create, but I was probably being somewhat facetious, you know, a little bit, but when Conrad was talking about the writing of *Nostromo* he was speaking of a time in his life that was extremely difficult – he had taken on the task of writing this enormous novel, which is not much read today.

Only in graduate school.

I doubt that it's being read even there; it's so long. Students would prefer to read *Heart of Darkness*, which is quite thin. So it was an extraordinary task for him and I think he was expiring in the midst of it. And those of us who are writers – I am sure you, Barry, have had the experience, too, perhaps often, as I have – it's almost a matter of each hour, each day, getting through that which you have set out to do, hoping you will achieve at least half of it, and sometimes it feels as if this nervous energy is almost consuming itself. If you didn't have the work there, where would the energy go? You must feel this way sometimes.

About every morning when I wake up.

Go back to sleep.

If only I could. Which is another way of saying that we confront failure often in our lives, and you have remarked that the artist, perhaps more than most people, inhabits failure, degrees of failure in accommodation and compromise. My father was fascinated by failure, too. He wrote at length about failure, the panic, the dreadful chill a man feels if he thinks he is marked for failure – the little deaths that all our failures are – and, for him, the trick was to not develop a secret love for those little deaths, but to just live with them. What is your fascination with failure?

I got interested in writing about boxing a few years ago because most boxers are failures. They are losers, and not only are they losers but they are physically injured, so it's a sport that's a kind of paradigm of human effort, where at the very height of boxing's pyramid there are a few people whose names you would know, so-called great champions, but most of the participants are not successful and it seems that most people, if they are trying anything halfway ambitious, are probably not going to succeed, but I feel that there's a certain way of looking at what we do that's humble and modest but also realistic; we try to do the very best we can, but we may have to be satisfied with that which we can do. We just keep trying, this is what we live with, those little deaths, as you say.

Who was it who said that most critics are failed writers and the rejoinder was –

– so are most writers. That was T.S. Eliot. Someone said to him, "Most critics are failed poets," and he said, "Most poets are." But he meant himself, too, in kind of a humble way, but if we do a lot of revision, and you keep revising, as I do, and keep trying, you know, making it better, there may be a point at which it reaches the ultimate. It's fully realized as far as you can do it. So then, that's one hour, and there is a feeling of great happiness, but all the effort before that, there may have been twenty hours, they are incomplete and dissatisfying, so it's like nineteen times out of twenty, one is inhabiting a degree of frustration and dissatisfaction, and then, there's this one time when it works very well and you set it aside and then go on to the next page, the next paragraph, but I think it's all part of the process of writing. Like reading, in love with the process of reading, or listening to music. It's not that you want it to end or want any kind of product.

Well, very often, when you talk about writing, and you talk about the process, you take it to another dimension. For example, when-

ever you speak about Emily Dickinson, and you love the poetry of Emily Dickinson...

Yes.

...you begin to talk about writing as a form of transcendence. You have drawn a distinction between the exploration of the world through the eyes of someone like Whitman...the exploration of what you described as the exterior world, and Dickinson, as the exploration of the interior world, and soul.

Yes.

For all that you might say about process, you do have an almost religious view of the possibilities of writing.

I think so. When it goes well and when we feel that we are really immersed deeply in the work, we transcend our own egos. We don't think about ourselves. We are becoming the work itself and I think of Whitman as very expansive, sort of the North American continent, just out there and very broad and, shall we say, macho, in the best sense of the word. Is there a best sense of the word?

I'm happy to play straight man. Yes.

And then Emily Dickinson is the poet of inwardness, of spirituality, and I am not going to say femininity because that sounds a little sexist, but the two of them almost divide the whole arena of poetry and most people oscillate between the two poles. One has this characteristic long line, which is very incantatory and almost biblical. The other has a very short and elliptical and enigmatic line with slant rhymes and mysterious sounds and even strange punctuation.

Does this religious sense of things – I have in mind another Ameri-can writer you have spoken of, Flannery O'Connor – does this lead to a curious tension between the tragic vision and the comic vision and, if someone is so committed to a sacramental view, as Flannery O'Connor was, to a comic view of human affairs?

There is a certain detachment. I probably don't have that. I am much more likely to be immersed in the individual. I don't have that estrangement, or the perspective that allows me to even want to be apart from my characters. D.H. Lawrence spoke of the nov-elist being in a scrimmage, down there in the roughness of life. I feel that that's my rightful place. It's sort of afterward that I see what I have been writing about, how people are jolted out of their complacency, the routines of their lives, by some event…it's like grace entering our gravitational fields and it jolts us out of who we are or who we had thought we were and we become other people, in some cases more noble, or more reckless, different. But I don't always set out to do that. That seems to be something that happens as a consequence of the writing itself.

But grace does enter into the lives of people?

I think so. Sometimes as a sign of grace and sometimes there may be an actual bearer, another person, who brings grace into our lives in ways that we haven't anticipated, or it might be a dream or it might be an accident, like a physical accident, or something that you see, but it also can be a person who is the bearer of grace unknowingly. It doesn't necessarily mean that there's a conscious intent. So, I have been exploring that lately, and the novel that I wrote last year, *Zombie*, was an attempt to get into a voice very radically different from any I had done before. I had never writ-ten from the point of view of a psychopath before. I may have written about psychopaths and some of my best friends, in fact, may be non-practising psychopaths, in which case you can't tell them from ordinary men. I was wondering if the psychopath didn't represent an evolutionary phenomenon, they haven't quite developed what we call conscience or the ability to identify sympathetically with other people. It's not that it's anybody's fault. It's just that some of us are, I mean, most of us are born with a capacity for identifying with other people or with animals. If most of us saw a suffering animal we would feel great compassion and want to alleviate the pain and help the animal, whereas a psychopath literally doesn't feel anything, or wants to make the pain greater so that he gets more control over it, but I think most psychopaths, by their very nature, just don't have that ability to make the leap to another person and why that is – some think it's genetic – I don't really know. In *Zombie* I thought to go to a radical extreme, waiting for some element of grace to touch this man who is a serial killer, and something does happen and he is about to confess and it happens very quickly, and when I was writing it I didn't know that he would just look out the window where he sees a detective and another man, and it's just the posture of this older man who is like a father that triggers in the serial killer, suddenly, the sense of remorse and conscience just like a flame, and he's actually going to confess but his lawyer stops him, and I thought, you know, when I was writing it, I was really kind of trembling because I thought, it's going to have a different ending, its own inevitable ending, and then the lawyer says, Don't talk to them.

Couldn't you stop the lawyer?

Well, it's a realistic novel set in the United States. Couldn't you stop the lawyer? That's…

Almost an appropriate bumper sticker for our times.

The answer is yes, if you pay him.

And you didn't have the funds?

No, it's just that it seemed to happen so suddenly, and then the reality crushed upon me that no, this is not a realistic action.

For all these moments of grace that enter into your work and your vision, you really have got the handle on a sense of collapse, not apocalyptic collapse but collapse and failure in the American psyche, in the American cities, but part of the mysterious tension for me in all your work is that, even in the last book, your faith in the individual's capacity, whether it's through an act of grace or not, to keep disappearing into America to discover himself, or herself, is unbreakable.

I think so. I think there are infinite spiritual capacities in individuals, and from the outside we may sometimes look like failures and ruins but you don't really know what's inside a person. This is not so in my zombie character, who doesn't, in a sense, have any spiritual depth to him; he has lurid fantasies and he has moments of intense excitement, most of them sexual excitement, but he doesn't have what we would call a spiritual life, but he is an extreme character, and most of the people I write about are people like all of us; they have these capacities to achieve bonds and sudden relationships with other people that are… It's like clasping hands and you don't know what you are going to do until the moment that it happens, like there is a narrative that enfolds us, carrying us along. We don't know where it's going to be bringing us.

And one of the things that happens among such characters, and it's part of being a writer, is the extension of compassion?

Oh yes, definitely. You get to like all your characters, don't you? All of them.

And this compassion, I was thinking about your novel Black Water. *It's the story of a senator and it has its – I suppose – references or resonance in recent American political history, but it seems to me that it could be read as the failure and drowning of the liberal dream in America.*

That's a way of putting it. That's so true, yes.

And there are sections in the novel where very acid remarks are made about our current political time.

Yes.

The rise of neo-conservatism…

Yes.

…which seems to be marked by many things, but not compassion.

Absolutely. In our country, I don't know about your country, but in our country there's such a political ploy of dividing people – blacks against whites, Jews against blacks, blacks against Jews, men against women…

And the poor against the rich.

The poor…

And the rich voraciously against the poor.

It's mainly the rich against the poor. The poor people in our country are just not organized. They don't even vote. People on welfare in these communities are not organized politically; they just don't get out and vote. I don't know why it is. It's just a malevolent and poisonous way of conceiving of a society. The philosophical principles are so inhuman in every way, but it's a time that we are living through, beginning with Ronald Reagan and accelerating and I don't know where it will end. We have had a...

It's reaching its fruition here in Toronto, in Ontario, a man named Harris.

I'm afraid that's what we have been hearing, but usually in our politics, in our history, there has been a pendulum swinging back and forth, somewhat slowly, between liberalism and social generosity and the opposite, which is suspicion and paranoia, like the Cold War and the Red Scare of the 1950s, and then back toward a kind of generosity of spirit, the 1960s, a sort of boom time in our country, and then back the other way. It's a cyclical thing.

How has it happened that an incredible meanness of spirit and lack of compassion has attached itself so successfully to the evangelical spirit among many Americans and Canadians?

I don't know how I would answer that. Christianity is supposed to be a religion of compassion and identification, but there is a side of Christianity that is very punitive, and it's a religion that does believe in hell so, from the point of view of that side, the punitive side, a Christ who says, "I bring not peace but a sword," divides people; it may be something like that. It's also bound up with xenophobia, with white people celebrating white skin and being afraid of other kinds of people and attaching that spuriously, immorally, to Christianity.

Speaking of punishment, one aspect of life that you have been fascinated with, and I am fascinated with, is boxing. Boxing appals many people. As a matter of fact, someone, a woman, asked me if there were two or three things I had shared with my father that I had passed on to my son, and I said, "Well, my father had told me never to lie, which I told my son," and then I said that my father had never hit me as a punishment, ever in my life, and I had never hit my son, but my father had taught me how to fight, how to box, and I had taught my son how to box, and one of the first things I did with him about the age of six or seven, when I gave him boxing gloves, was hit him hard, so he would know what it was like to take a punch.

Yes.

…and would know what pain was, and that it didn't hurt as much as he thought it would.

Did he hit you back?

Yes, after his first gasp, and then I got this gasp from the woman, "Oh, my God, my God." Now you happen to know something about boxing…as a matter of fact, the last time I was in your office in Princeton you had a marvellous photograph of yourself with Mike Tyson.

That's right. Let's quickly amend that and say it was Mike when he was twenty years old, before life caught up with him. Well, obviously boxing is such a myriad culture. I mean, there's so much to say about it, but it is the art of self-defence and it is an art, and when I wrote about it, when I was interested in it very keenly, I approached it as a woman, of course, very excluded from its world and just looking at how men express themselves in terms of this art. It's very stylized and very arcane. It's very unnatural. When a boxer meets a fighter, when a man is trying to hit another man and doesn't have any training, he's fighting naturally. He's doing all sorts of wrong things, but the boxer is doing things that are not natural, and he is the one who is going to win, and that's interesting, too. It's a sort of symbol, maybe, of the artistic element, going against nature, learning, and when I knew Mike Tyson the kind of training that Mike did was just extraordinary. In one hour, the arduous, exhausting training that he was doing – one hour out of how many thousands and thousands of hours? – that's not natural fighting. That's not unleashing aggression but really cultivating a strength and cunning. So, boxing is all these things; it really appeals to me on many, many levels.

And the absorption of pain?

Well, the absorption of pain is very, very important, and I am wondering, since I have never boxed and you obviously have, I would guess that you don't even feel the pain in the role of boxer. I mean, if you got hit suddenly right now, not defending yourself, the pain would be probably extreme, but in boxing you might not even feel it. You absorb it. That absorption, the masochism of an athlete, whether male or female, enduring pain in order to rise above it, and to discipline oneself, is not the same as, let us say, the masochism of a woman who allows herself to be brutalized by a man in a kind of acquiescent, subservient way. It's not the same thing at all. The word "masochism" is inadequate. The overcoming of pain through training and conditioning and different kinds of discipline gives us great pleasure. It's not that I'm any kind of an athlete but I do like to run and running is an activity where you can push yourself and you think, Well, I just can't run any farther, but then you think, Well, I can't go any farther, but you think, Well, I can at least run to that rock. So you are always pushing yourself, but it isn't necessarily anything that's self-punishing. It's more like you are coming above a certain level. You thought you could do this but then you find out you can do a little more. The word "masochism" is not adequate to explain that.

The pushing of yourself through pain can even lead to a kind of ecstasy, too.

Oh, yes, it's a wonderful feeling, especially if your knees don't go.

And that applies to all violent sports, the knees have it, but do you think that boxing really is a sport?

I have never really thought of…

Or is it really a taboo world that…

You play tennis, or people play football, you play baseball, but nobody plays boxing. It's a misnomer, and Tyson himself thought that boxing was not a sport. He thought he was like a gladiator, and this awakened in him, and I have to reiterate – when I knew him he was very different from the person he seems to be now. He was extremely intelligent and thoughtful, a historian of boxing. Here was a young man who would watch boxing tapes and films going way back to the 1900s in the evening. Night after night he was learning his craft, and he had great respect for the boxing champions of the past. He really, really admired them immensely, as I guess we all do when we watch them. So it's complex, and I suppose on one level we all identify with the boxer who is putting himself on the line and exposing himself to humiliation as well as injury, in the way that we all do, but not so explicitly.

And finally, what boxers share, and we may all share this with them, if we are lucky, is that boxers, the winner and the loser, if they have really exchanged pain in a fight, love each other.

They do because one has given the other the fight. They made the fight possible.

There's real compassion there.

Right, right. I am thinking of certain, almost iconic moments – Rocky Marciano and Jersey Joe Walcott, hugging each other, and Marciano had actually won the fight but his was the face that was all bleeding, because he was a bleeder, and also all the emotion, the exhaustion, the distress they lived through, they really respected each other. It's absolutely true. When I have worked on something that has caused a good deal of emotional distress, when I am all done with it, I feel a sense of elation and gratitude that that was given to me to live through, though at the time I was living through it, when I didn't know how it would end, I wouldn't have been able to have that feeling. So when a fight is all over, then, one looks back on it with a good deal of gratitude that some tremendous challenge was given to us.

So can you look at yourself as a writer and your struggle with yourself and your struggle with your individual works as a kind of match?

Well, each novel is. The hardest novel I wrote in recent years is called *What I Lived For*, and in that novel I was in a man's psyche – for quite a time. That novel is about 600 pages long – an Irish American with a drinking problem and problems with women, but his name is not Barry Callaghan.

Haw.

I got into this person who is very profane, very profane and even obscene, and he had a lot of trouble with women, but women loved him and men loved him, too. He had a generosity of spirit that was all mixed up with male chauvinism and other things that were not wonderful, but still this generosity of spirit, which I sort of associate with the Irish-American strain and that world that I am partly from – since I'm partly Irish American – and I had never written about that before, the residue of Catholicism. He is so completely anti-Catholic and he never misses an opportunity to say something a little sarcastic about the Church, but when it comes right down to it, he's still Catholic and he still is worried about going to hell and he's still thinking about the things he was thinking about when he was eight years old, and while I was writing I was sort of suffering. Somehow, each day was a kind of purgatory. It was like a purgatory. It was amusing, you could say.

In what…

In the way of the insights I got, that is, he thinks, suddenly, when a woman loves a man she just loves him, without any criticism, but then if her love is withdrawn she starts seeing him for what he really is and he's not so attractive after all, but when a woman loves a man, it's as if he's just wonderful, and she loves every part of him, every little character flaw or trait or whatever. It's fine, and to be basking in the love of a woman like that is just – it's just so very wonderful. Then he thinks a little while later, well, women are such dopes. You know, they're such dopes to love somebody like me. Like, they're not really looking at me, and I thought that, too, is probably so, that women are such dopes that we are willing to – I've got to – how did I get into this? Let's swerve 180 degrees away to another perspective. Let's take somebody like Ted Bundy. Ted Bundy is this notorious serial killer who probably killed 100 girls and women. Nonetheless, hundreds of women were writing him love letters, and when he was on trial in Florida there were always rows and rows of attractive young women in their twenties and they just were adoring him. I don't see that men would do anything like that. I don't see that men would sit in a courtroom and idolize some dreadful woman who had killed a lot of men. I think the deep masochism of women is something that, as a feminist, I find very distressing but I know it's out there in the world. I'm interested in writing about it, so when I got into this novel and was seeing women from the point of view of the male prism, I saw women very differently from the way I would see myself for my friends, and I don't think I would have had that insight without writing the novel.

If women are driven to some extent by a deep masochism –

Some women.

Some women, never yourself, I'm sure.

Well, I guess I'm deeply masochistic or I wouldn't be a writer.

And if this is a way of punishing themselves, what would be the same drive in men?

I really don't know. To me the only way to explore questions of such complexity are in the novel, because it's a layered thing. My character in *What I Lived For* is living a life minute by minute by minute, so he has different thoughts that are layered and some of them are repeated, a kind of incremental repetition. But to give you an answer in a kind of journalistic way is very difficult. I don't mean all women are masochistic all the time and I don't necessarily mean that it's even a cultural thing, but it does seem to be a predisposition. It may be partly genetic. It may be that our intelligence, education, and culture are going to help us overcome some of this genetic acquiescence, the feeling that we acquiesce to the brute or some large, almost primitive emotions like that, that we try to get away from as women, who have become more independent and, as I said, more educated, but that's a very complex issue. Have you ever thought of these things?

I have often thought that women, while they may adore their men, they certainly are very knowing about one aspect of their men, and that is, by the time men are nineteen or twenty, they have surrendered nearly all of their adolescent dreams.

Really?

They may have one or two left.

Oh, Barry.

I hate to bring the news from Damascus to you but—

I thought that it was the opposite. I thought that when a man got to be fifty he was still in his heart about fifteen years old.

Exactly, exactly. That's the point. A man – this is the whole problem for women. A man will show up still wearing his peewee-baseball championship jacket from when he was twelve years old.

If it fits.

Worse, even if it doesn't fit he will wear it and he will talk about several moments in his boyhood life that are particularly significant to him, and this is why some men end up leaving their wives and inexplicably taking up with bimbos.

Bimbos? We don't use that word.

Oh, dear.

Not P.C.

What happens is that a woman, maybe of thirty-three, will suddenly say to her husband, "I can't stand that story about your peewee baseball team anymore. Don't tell me that boring story anymore."

No, she just thinks that.

No, no, this time she says it.

She says it.

Then the relationship is over and he goes out the door and finds some nineteen-year-old…

Who has never heard the story.

…who has never heard the story. And for three nights or three months in a motel he tells her all his stories. Which are all his failures. He wears, in effect, his jacket.

That's right.

And his life goes on like that afterwards.

That's right.

These dreams are what men live by and this is a terrible burden for women, that they have to keep silent and perpetuate these boring failed dreams.

If you're nineteen years old, you haven't heard it before, so it's a fresh thought.

It's tough to be a woman, but it's tough to be such a man, you know.

Well, I felt when I got done writing my novel that it was very hard to be a man, because a man is always in this competition with other men, jockeying for a position, and my character was only about 5'9, or maybe really 5'8, which is my height, so he's always kind of standing a little taller, and then the cruellest thing in a novel that's filled with obscenities and awful things, the cruellest thing is that another man who is about 6'3, who doesn't like him, says, "You dwarf." My character, his deepest fear was that another man would know that his whole life was spent in the terror that a taller man would say to him, "You dwarf."

In his heart he is big, but he knows, as we all know, that the world will diminish the dwarf if it can or, if it can't, many in the world will turn the dwarf into a fascist hero.

They are all seeking…

Redemption…

About which they have almost no idea…

Conversation, International Festival of Authors, Toronto, 2002

CÉLINE

I have seen photographs of Louis-Ferdinand August Restouches taken just before he died in 1961, when he was ill and living in shabby seclusion on the outskirts of Paris. In these photographs there is a grey stubble on his chin that catches the slatted light from a shuttered window. The stubble is silver against his putty-coloured skin. His lips are curled at the corner into a snarl. A parrot, out of its cage, pokes through his papers on his desk, but he is paying no attention to the parrot...his eyes are fixed...perhaps on a point of stillness in the last of his dark, comedic hallucinations.

This man, Céline, was born in 1894 in the Paris suburb of Courbevoie, the son of a minor insurance clerk and a crippled lace merchant. His parents being poor, he was taken out of school and put to work at twelve. As soon as he reached the military age of eighteen he joined the cavalry, the Twelfth Regiment of the Cuirassiers, and fought for three years in World War I, managing to survive the trenches at Ypres...the moonscape reek of dead men who'd rotted in the mud, the stench of shit and blood... He came out of it all with a partially paralyzed right arm, crushing migraines, and impaired hearing (tinnitus): "I listen to (the buzzing) become trombones, full orchestras, marshalling yards...," a steady roaring he had to listen to for the rest of his life...

In 1918, he returned to Paris to enter medical school. He concentrated on infectious diseases, infancy fevers, and public hygiene. Upon graduation he married the daughter of the director of the school, but before setting up practice he travelled to Cameroon, the United States (studying social medicine at the

Ford factories), and Cuba. Returning to Clichy, he chose to prac-
tise among the squalid and the impoverished. He dispensed pills
during the day and began writing during the night. He treated his
patients with concern and consideration, often forgiving their
debts, but he forgave no one else anything, certainly not his fellow Frenchmen, who were, in his eye, little more than lickspittle
morons,

> a hodgepodge of filth like me… Vicious and spineless,
> raped, robbed, gutted, and always halfwits… We don't
> change a bit! Neither our socks nor our masters nor our
> opinions or, if we do, too late to have it matter. We're born
> followers and die of it! Soldiers without pay, heroes for all
> humanity, talking monkeys, tortured words, we're the
> minions of King Misery! We're in his grasp! When we're
> foolish, he squeezes… His fingers forever around our
> necks, it's hard to speak… No way to live…

In 1932, he published *Voyage au bout de la nuit* (*Journey to the
End of the Night*), a remorseless, caterwauling, caustic indictment
of all that he had so far surveyed…the *End of the Night* became
his burnt-out memory book of soured grief, old battlefields, of
men who had been treated like cowardly shit-bags by their brain-
less generals, his memory book of a broken-down trading post at
Bambola Bragamance, his memory book of assembly line boredom in a Detroit auto plant and of asphyxia at being surrounded
by so much stupidity…he rants at cyanotic men and sclerotic
women, at sordid nature itself…the ordeal and ordure of it all…
he bares his fervid meanness…his mocking contempt for the
cockeyed folly of any and all sycophants and patriotic apologists
for battlefield gore…he exudes delight at the buffoonery of
death…"Death is part of me," he cries. "Yes, the dance of death"
– but he did not mean the grim dance of silhouetted black figures
against a bleak Ingmar Bergman sky, where (to use Bergman's
own words) *death waves a scythe like a flag* – no, Céline's dance

is a shaking of the bones, it is raucous, abusive, rollicking...
appallingly vicious yet farcical: – "It *makes me laugh*. That's
what you mustn't forget: that my *danse macabre* pleases me,
like an immense farce... Believe me, the world is *funny*, that's
why my books are funny, and why fundamentally, I am full of
joy..."

Funny! As in highjinks?

Joy and gallows laughter at the *danse macabre*?

To get the hang of such laughter, we might lend an ear to
Beckett (our poet of ordure and decrepit infirmity):

> The bitter laugh laughs at that which is not good, it is the
> ethical laugh. The hollow laugh laughs at that which is not
> true, it is the intellectual laugh...the mirthless laugh is the
> dianoetic laugh, down the snout – Haw! – It is the laugh of
> laughs, the *resus purus*, the laugh laughing at the
> laugh...the saluting of the highest joke, in a word the laugh
> that laughs – silence please – at all that which is unhappy.

Céline knew how to take his joy neat with no ice, how to rut
in all that is unhappy – it is there in his garrulous, scatological
vituperation...the joy he feels is in his prose line itself...its breath
stoppages...the ellipses...the exclamation points!!! – the dashes –
all these act as a back beat to his laughter, his slanging, his sneer-
ing mockery of the established literary tones of the time –
Verlaine, to one side, tightening his sphincter, and Malarmé to
another side, who has no sphincter...the staid sonorities of
Mauriac and the drawing room harmonics of Proust – it was as
if Ornette Coleman had taken apart the ballroom arrangements of Woody Herman and Duke Ellington – which is why –
particularly after *Mort à credit* (1936) (*Death on the Installment Plan*) – many writers – and not just French writers (André
Gide, Jean Genet)...but American, too...took to Céline: Henry
Miller rewrote *Tropic of Cancer*, Céline was cited by Vonnegut
in *Slaughterhouse-Five*, he was praised by Norman Mailer and

William Burroughs, imitated by LeRoi Jones in *Dante's Inferno*, and Philip Roth said, "To tell you the truth, in France, my Proust is Céline. There's a very great writer. Even if his anti-Semitism made him an abject, intolerable person. To read him, I have to suspend my Jewish conscience, but I do it, because anti-Semitism isn't at the heart of his books, even *Castle to Castle*. Céline is a great liberator. I feel called by his voice."

Céline's voice! His line, *révolté* in the early Thirties, suddenly became corrosive in its anti-Jewish vileness (I say suddenly because in the earlier *Mort à credit* and *Voyage au bout de la nuit* – the word "Jew" had appeared only once and "kike" not at all) – a vileness that erupted in the very late Thirties…

All the same, you need only consider a little more closely, the pretty puss of the average *kike*, male or female, to remember it forever… Those spying eyes, lyingly pale…that uptight smile…those livestock lips that recall: a hyena… And then out of nowhere there's that look that drifts, heavy, leaden, stunned…the nigger's blood that flows… Those twitchy naso-labial commisures…twisted, furrowed, downward curving, defensive, hollowed by hate and disgust…for you!…for the abject animal of the enemy race, accursed, to be destroyed… Their nose, the "toucan" beak of the swindler, the traitor, the felon…the sordid schemes, the betrayals, a nose that points to, lowers toward, and falls over their mouths, their hideous slots, that rotten banana, their croissant, their filthy kike grins, boorish, slimy, even in beauty pageants, the very outline of a sucking snout: the Vampire… It's pure zoology!…elementary!… It's your blood these ghouls are after!… It's enough to make you scream…to shudder, if you have the least inkling of instinct left in your veins, if anything still moves around in your meat and your head, other than pasty lukewarm rhetoric, stuffed with cunning little tricks, the grey suit of bloodless clichés, marinated in alcohol…

Grins of the kind you find on Jewish pusses, understand, aren't improvised, they don't date from yesterday or from the Dreyfus Affair… They erupt from the depths of the ages, to terrify us, to draw us into miscegenation, into bloody Talmudic mires, and finally, into the Apocalypse!…

This is Céline in full stride…the vilifying scourge – milking every ugly Jew libel and *kike* cliché available to him – it is disgusting – and yet – he is so scabrous, so over the top… Could these ratpickings, this gregarious ranting, be his *opera in vout*, could this be what he meant by farce, by *funny*? Farcical or foetid, here we have the mystery inherent in the man's work: – why do so many writers (and readers) – non-Jewish and Jewish – feel a kinship with such a loathsome little *kike-meister*…

Perhaps the answer (listen for the *resus purus*, the Haw, the laugh laughing at the laugh) lies in the fact that…he is certainly not *for* the people…but he is decidedly, and right from the beginning, one *of* the people: even when he is vituperatively hysterical, even when his anecdotes (he is never telling a "story") are at their most malignant and mendacious…he does not draw back, he does not – in his own voice – recoil and stand aloof. Céline loathes his reader, that is a dead certainty…but he also seeks his reader's loathing…he works hard to cultivate his reader's contempt, he hungers for the leper's kiss…(consider how Céline anticipates the great pederast and thief Jean Genet – who willed himself into abnegation and abasement – who sought heroic grandeur by attempting unparalled baseness: declaring – "I refuse to take delight in a man's suffering if I have not yet shared in it. I distrust the saintliness of St. Vincent de Paul. He should have agreed to commit the galley-slave's crime instead of merely taking his place in the irons.")… So, the thing to note is this… Céline never shuns his readers…they are, no matter what, his intimates…he is always telling the despicable mob that their *we* is his *me*…: (it's as if Jonathan Swift, while the

Yahoos up in the trees were pelting him with fresh handfuls of shit, spoke of them as *we – we* Yahoos). If we look to *Death on the Installment Plan* (*Mort à crédit*) or *Guignol's Band*…it is *we we we* like a little pig all the way home. He is the scourge who has lain down among swinish lapdogs, who – as he cries out that what he wants is to be left alone – has got down among the wretched and the retching…*us*…whose vomit he takes full in his face, "the whole stinking stew." He kneels beside the dreadful pawnbroker, Titus Van Claben, that gross, greedy, drugged-out, self-promoting capitalist…he *is* right there with that creep, that toady, with *him*: "Wow!… We tottered, *we* crawled, raving and gasping. It was complete madness…the usual meanness among the great heap of worm-eaten sods *like me*, bleary, shivering and lousy, who come defeated from the four corners of the earth…"

⌒✦⌒

In 1944, after Marshall Pétain's Vichy government had been propped up in exile at the Hohenzollern castle of Seigmaringen in southern Denmark, Céline – who had been ferreting about like a low-life burglar on the lam, hiding out in a Paris suburb – pretending for a time to be a Québécois travelling salesman – dispatched himself to Denmark where he hung out his shingle as a doctor in the shadow of the castle walls…while dedicated anti-Semites, like the editor Pierre Drieu la Rochelle, turned *La Nouvelle Revue Française* into a place for collaborationists to hang out their mingles…while pro-Nazi anti-Semites of the deepest dye, Robert Brasillach and Lucien Rebatet, published *Je suis partout*…while Maurice Chevalier (of later Ed Sullivan fame in America) sang and hoofed his way across the boards to amuse the occupying army…

Céline proceeded to live modestly with Lucette, his young second wife…keeping two vials of cyanide in his pocket…keeping his beloved cat, Bébert, close.

During the day, he worked in a desultory way at being a doctor. Through the night, he survived the fires of '44, the carpet bombing, the cauldrons of flame caused by RAF-Bomber Harris in his bunker who was hard at work at the obliteration of the countryside, its rail lines and its castle town, the family farms and cess pits.

At the same time in Paris, Jean-Paul Sartre had denounced Céline as a paid *collaborateur*. That was a bald-faced lie, but no matter – Céline was sentenced in absentia to death. (George Steiner has suggested that Céline was nobody's patsy, telling us that Céline – while he "was at a soirée" in Berlin in 1942 – had berated the fascist leader, Doriot, complaining that Doriot was inept when it came to the rounding up of Jews, that the Jews had to be swept away like shit – and then – later – as a guest of the German legation, he had "leapt to his feet and performed a dazzling imitation of the Führer's voice and gestures, and instructed his terrified hosts that Hitler would lose the war," and finally, to the horror and rage of all…he had dismissed Hitler as "a cataclysmic clown.")

After the war, in 1950, Céline, defenceless as an exile in Denmark, was fined, shackled, and imprisoned. Whatever property he had in Paris was confiscated.

However, in 1951 a French military tribunal reviewed his case and exonerated him. He was allowed to return to Paris, where he opened an office out among the underclass of the underfed and badly housed in the Paris suburb of Meudon-Bellevue.

Shunned as an anti-Semite and traitor by an ever-burgeoning crowd of Gaulists, righteous *petits advocats*, former "fighters" for the *resistance*, and advocates for a New Left, he had – and wanted – almost no one in his life but his few patients…whose illnesses, whose infections gave him a curious, if perverse comfort: "When people are well, there is no way of getting away from it, they're rather frightening…when they can stand up, they're thinking of killing you. Whereas when they're ill, there's no doubt about it, they're less dangerous." He consoled the ill by charging them next to nothing for their care; he consoled himself by indulging in an exuberant gallows laughter as he saw "…signs of coming events! Little appetizers…prostates, fibromes, tumours of the bronchial tubes…of the tongue…sweet little cases of myocarditis…pure joy!… Cancer of the throat…they howl…"

He wrote furiously by hand, filling – over a period of ten years – several thousand pages in a crabbed script, taking upon himself the role of *chroniqueur* (early on he had written: "The greatest defeat, in anything, is to forget, and above all to forget what it is that has smashed you…") – completing in 1957 a "fiction founded in fact" – *D'un Chateau l'autre* (*Castle to Castle*), the first book of an intended trilogy…a chronicle set in 1944 during the Occupation, during end-of-the-war blanket bombing by the RAF.

Castle to Castle is a hallucinatory anecdotal rant, a romp…an excoriating account of calumny crossbred with rank stupidity…a report on apocalyptic buffoonery…

> …the sirens never stopped blowing…but the RAF was looking for the bridge…at that precise moment…no razzle-dazzle!…dropping their strings of bombs over the bridge…straight down…every which way…three, four planes at a time…how did they manage to miss it?…their bombs sent up geysers! the Danube was boiling! and the muck splashing all over…just then, I remember exactly, a detachment of prisoners came up in the opposite direction…with their *Lansturm* guards…Russian prisoners and old Boches…so tired!…so tired!…all skin and bones the whole lot of them, dragging their feet…and all in rags…the Krauts with guns, the others without… where were they going?… Someplace…we asked them…they didn't understand…they didn't even hear the bombs…how could you expect them to hear our questions?… They were going along the same bank, that's all…in the opposite direction…while Marshall Pétain…

that disastrous cacochymic paranoiac!...ha ha! Pétain, back-lit by burning skies – fearless, he seemed, out for a stroll...but only because he was stone-cold deaf, totally unaware... surrounded by faces!...the treachery, the villainy, the degeneracy, the stigmata!...provocateurs!...talking big, bragging, and then all of a sudden, humble, crawling... chameleons, snakes, vipers...that's what they were...they molted before your eyes...– these *collaborateurs*, deserters, and congenital convicts...

they all stomp through Céline's occupied little moated castle, his mind, *collaborateurs* who bivouac in the rancid corridors of his memory bank, deserters who prowl those secret catacombs that mimic the actual ancient castle...headed up by one of the ubiquitous Hohenzollerns, "a creature who was half witch, half mole..." a creature last seen fleetingly by rocket fire...hurrying down a long hall where

unperturbed a cheerful movie director and his starlet copulate...and a mad surgeon...another character! A fraud...he'd been a general on the Russian front for six months...in command of a *panzer* team...and for six months he'd been chief surgeon of the enormous S.S. hospital in Hohenlychen, East Prussia...a clown!... I sent a friend of mine...extremely anti-Boche...to watch him operate...this S.S. surgeon, Gebhardt, was very skilful!... nuts?...definitely! in his super-hospital in Hohenly-chen there were six thousand surgery patients, a city, four times the size of Bichat!...he staged football games with one-legged teams...war cripples...he was cracked like the supermen of the Renaissance...he excelled in two, three rackets...tank warfare, surgery...ah yes, and singing!... I heard him at the piano...very amusing...he improvised...there I'm a good judge...during the Hitler period the Boches came close to developing a race of such

Renaissance men…this Gebhardt a mad surgeon was one of them!…a man stretched out, all dishevelled and unbuttoned, puking and gasping…and on top of him, straddling him…a surgeon!…well anyway a man in a white smock getting ready to operate on him…forcibly!…three, four scalpels in his hand…head-mirror, compresses, forceps!… Behind him, up to her ankles in sludge and urine, his nurse…

Céline…the pariah…abhorrent to all…was there – on the castle grounds, with his ear to the ground…writing down all that he had heard and seen – without reserve or remorse…in an unrelenting recitation of everyday abominations, of abject wonks who were on the loose with weapons in both their hands… These pages are Céline's dispatches from the hell's kitchen of his heart …this is his conjuring up of the great castle world *complet* as an insane asylum…where he is caught up in a *danse macabre*…a gallows gavotte led by those horrible collapsed aristocrats, the Hohenzollerns…who are the genuine article of the bluest blood among the bloodied…cruel…grasping…monstrous!…*nom de Gott*…the whole line!…all of them "fryers of duchies!…cloven-hoofed!…it was when they stopped being devils that their family collapsed!…it is the same with all empires…" He can see the Russians, just like the Hohenzollerns, slipping…

they put on airs, they wag their tanks, they dialectalize…they'll see…Lenin!… Stalin!…*history*…no end of intent, no end in sight…endless trains…soldiers and soldiers…every branch of service, every nation…and prisoners…barefoot, their feet hanging out…sitting in the doors…hungry too! always hungry! and horny!…and singing *Lili Marlene*!…soldiers of the European *ragout*!… of twenty-seven armies…let them sing! bump! travel! in armoured trains, cannon the size of a house, bristling giants!…dinosaur cannon with two, three locomotives

apiece… And always more trains, one after the other…
engineers, artillery…and still more…whole armies! with
their hairy, bare feet sticking out!…yelling, demanding
girls!…it could have been child's play for them, one bomb,
to blow up the whole station!…marmalade!…blow the
whole mess to pieces!…all these trains switching and
shunting…the switches demolished!…to start all over
again!…

Amidst these cataclysmic events, as he gets down on paper
what he has seen, he is almost cataleptic in his contempt for the
hilarity of it all – the wild thrusts of ambition…never mind the
bravado, the power binges… He has long since figured out how
history works…it is simple…it is so mundane as to be ludicrous…all you have to do is check the lineups for stamps at the
post office…if you've been in power for any length of time
you'll know when you're done…*kaput*…you'll get the message
the day after your head – as it were – appears on the block –
because there it'll be – you'll see…there, on a postage
stamp…you'll know that the collectors, the scavengers, are all
out

> in the biggest cities and the smallest holes…lines and
> lines are collecting Hitler stamps, all prices!…the jig's
> up!…there must be millions of Adolf Hitler collections in
> Germany!…they started years in advance! at the very first
> damn foolishness… Diviners, magicians? don't waste
> your time!…the stamp's the thing…tells you the whole
> story ten years in advance…the vultures, the collectors…
> The stamp's the thing, fevered movements, the future is in
> the mail, scavengers assemble the detritus of mangled
> lives…

In the castle, old Cassandra is crying victory through broken
teeth…poets have become nattering gob spittle priests…generals

are puppets on parade in a clown show, the clowns are high churchmen, the high churchmen are extortionists, and all such are fresh-faced pimps for power... Yes, Céline is crying out to his parrot who is stomping around on his writing desk, there is no escape from history, the stamps have been licked by the ass-lickers...

As his chronicle comes to an end, Céline – who has "grown sensible enough to be a coward forever" – is holed up with that old parrot in his cramped Paris apartment...he is consulting with his last two surviving patients – a half-paralyzed, doddering old matron and her companion, a seventy-two-year-old woman of a certain style, Madame Armandine. She tells Céline that another doctor, a surgeon, has actually been trying to prep her for an operation that she doesn't want but – make no mistake – it is an operation he wants – and he has warned that he will use force if necessary – to cut off her cancer-riddled breasts. And why? For her own good, of course. Her own good! She has come to Céline as if she were a last survivor of the cankered times, saying, "...they wanted to take off both breasts...see here, those people have cancer on the brain...all they can see is cancer! Maniacs! Luckily I stuck up for myself..."

Céline revels in her "perversity of character," in her refusal to agree to go under the knife – her refusal to do the right thing and knuckle under to the agents of good health and public hygiene, her refusal to surrender any part of her diseased life...not even as death approaches:

> I can see she's a little nervous...in fact she's definitely cracked...but she's got a kind of youthful vigour for sev-enty-two! cancer and all...and even a certain coquetry... that plaid skirt, for instance...pleated! and the blue on her eyebrows and eyelashes!...and her raincoat, more blue!... and the colour of her eyes...china-blue...and makeup on her cheeks...pastel pink!...you get the picture?...and smiling like a doll...pert and comely...she only stops

smiling long enough for her little spells of *hee-hee!...hee hee*, before she lifts up her skirts...hoopla!...and her petticoats!...and bends back! – She does a complete backbend! as supple as can be!...and up goes one leg, an Eiffel Tower, straight as a die!...

As she remains *en pointe* to the sky, Céline applauds her... there she is standing "with her leg in the air – she fixes her eyelashes, her eyes, beauty!...a pencil stroke to her eyebrows... she seems to have absolutely everything she needs..."

He wonders what Madame Armandine had done out in the world...

He won't ask...

Somehow, living on death's installment plan, she had paid her dues...

Louis-Ferdinand August Restouches – Céline – soon to be "three feet below the ground himself.... streaming with maggots," suddenly, if only for an aberrational moment, surges with *resus* delight down the snout...he yells at Madame Armandine, "Bravo... Bravo," and then goes back to curling his lip at the world.

The Telegram, 1969–2005

THE FARCE GROWN
MORE GLORIOUS:
SACCO AND VANZETTI

the Shark at savage prey, the Hawk at pounce,
the Gentle Robin, like a Pard or Ounce
Ravening a worm.

—JOHN KEATS

In 1921, Nicola Sacco and Bartolomeo Vanzetti, two immigrants from Calabria, were at work in Boston, one as a pattern cutter in a shoe factory and the other as a barrow fishmonger. Vanzetti, who wore a big bristling moustache, was expansive, hard-working, well-read in the literature of radicalism, and had bright friendly eyes. Nicola Sacco, wary, more pessimistic, and close-mouthed, cropped his hair close to his round skull. He wore an overcoat with a velvet collar, but was by no means a dandy. Vanzetti wore a similar coat, but his collar was of plain cloth, a plain man given to guilelessness. Both were olive-skinned. Both spoke a halting English. Both were mild-mannered in their domestic lives, but in the streets, in their politics, they were militant anarchists, agitators for revolution at a time when anarchists were feared, widely thought of as a menace to the economic order, the public good. Sacco carried a gun. Vanzetti carried a gun.

Two years earlier, in 1919, several bombings had apparently been coordinated by anarchists. That, at least, was the approved public story. The FBI – under the aggressive direction of the young J. Edgar Hoover – arrested between five and ten thousand foreign nationals (no accurate records were attempted) in what came to be known as the Palmer Raids (after the then Attorney General). The government had been, like all authorities since the 1890s, engaged in demonizing and persecuting anarchists as if they were not just "heretics" within their society but "destructive revolutionists" who carried bombs and were trained in revolutionary ballistics. During the Palmer raids, anarchists of every stripe were arrested. None, however, were ever found guilty of the bombings.

No matter: in December of that year, a ship, the *Buford*, sailed from New York with 249 "aliens" aboard – men and women (and their children) who had been described in the press as "blasphemous creatures who not only rejected American hospitality and assailed her institutions, but also sought by a campaign of assassination and terrorism to ruin her as a nation of free men." H.L. Mencken said contemptuously to his fellow Americans that they were now a nation running scared…that they were "engaged in a grotesque pogrom against the wop, the coon, the kike, the papist, the Jap, engaged in an even more grotesque effort to put down ideas as well as men – to repeal learning by statute, regiment the arts by lynch-law, and give the puerile ethical and theological notions of lonely farmers and corner grocers the force and dignity of constitutional axioms."

Watch out! Mencken warned. Watch out for "what happens invariably in democratic states when the national safety is menaced. All the great tribunes of democracy, on such occasions, convert themselves, by a process as simple as taking a deep breath, into despots of an almost fabulous ferocity… Democracy seems bent upon killing the thing it theoretically loves…"

><*<

Early in the spring of 1921, Bartolomeo Vanzetti and Nicola Sacco, while handing out anarchist leaflets, had been arrested by Boston city police, locked up, and though they spoke only a halting English, they had been grilled by detectives into the night. The next day they were accused of the murder of a factory paymaster and a company security guard at the Slater and Morill shoe company; the two company employees having been shot three weeks earlier during a daytime holdup at the factory in South Braintree, Massachusetts. Police said the crime – robbery and murder – had been carried out by a five-man gang. They said Sacco and Vanzetti were members of that gang. They never identified the other three holdup men. Nor was the payroll money – $15,776.51 – ever found. The arresting officers said that Sacco was linked to the killing by his gun and perhaps Vanzetti through his gun, too. They said that both men, when asked questions at the scene of the crime, had not only been confused and confusing in their reluctant, heavily accented answers, but under questioning they had contradicted themselves and, about some details, had lied. Furthermore, by shifting their eyes away from the police and by hanging their heads, they had worn the look of guilty men.

><+<

In the dock, Sacco and Vanzetti stood charged with murder before Judge Webster Thayer, who appears to have taken upon himself a mission (he had specifically asked for the Sacco and Vanzetti case), having boasted before the trial had begun that he would get "the bastards."

In his courtroom, Judge Thayer allowed the prosecution to berate and vilify the two immigrants. He allowed the prosecution to play on social and ethnic prejudice, he allowed the prosecutor to play into and exacerbate the prevalent Red hysteria, he allowed the prosecution to distort ballistic evidence (in his final summation, while instructing the jury on legal procedures, he, too, distorted the ballistic evidence), he reminded jurors that the accused had been anarchist draft dodgers who had fled to Mexico during the Great War, and he told the jurors that they needed, as patriots, to never forget that "American soldier boy…

who had given up his life on the battlefield of France." He then
said of Vanzetti: "This man, although he may not have actually
committed the crime attributed to him, is nevertheless morally
culpable, because he is the enemy of our existing institutions."
The jury brought in a verdict of guilty. Judge Thayer sentenced
the two men to be strapped to the electric chair and killed. Judge
Thayer, quoted afterwards in sworn records, boasted: "Did you
see what I did with those anarchistic bastards the other day?"

Across the United States, the verdict was applauded. H.L.
Mencken said American public opinion could be plainly put:
"Being wops, they got what was coming to them."

One of the great law professors of the day, Edmund M. Morgan
of Harvard, unsettled by the blatant hostility and bias shown
by Judge Thayer, and the jury's verdict, wrote: "Against a mas-
terful and none too scrupulous prosecution was opposed a
hopelessly mismanaged defense before a stupid trial judge,"
while "the jury, largely under the influence of this misconduct
and bias...returned a verdict contrary to the great weight of the
evidence."

Judge Webster Thayer took note.

Felix Frankfurter, soon to be a Justice of the Supreme Court,
wrote: "By systematic exploitation of the defendants' alien blood,
their imperfect knowledge of English, their unpopular social
views and their opposition to the war, the district attorney
invoked against them a riot of political passion and patriotic sentiment; and the trial judge connived at – one had almost written
cooperated in – the process."

The legal establishment to which Frankfurter and Morgan
belonged – as it would be (and is) in any entrenched legal community – was made up of men of moneyed and intellectual
influence, men of preferment and power who had positions,
property, and the prestige of the law itself to protect. Even more

consequential, Boston was also Brahmin country, the Brahmins being a particular caste embedded in that city, a caste that had its own unforgiving and unyielding character. Justice Oliver Wendell Holmes of the Supreme Court, who had invented the term "Brahmin," described the caste as a group of families who were not only distinct from any other group in New England, but they differed, he said, from any other aristocracy in the world.

A Brahmin, Edmund Wilson said – as he tried to account for that difference while writing about Holmes in his book, *Patriotic Gore* – is a man who, from generation to generation, maintains a high and select tradition of scholarship that allows him to become a preacher, lawyer, doctor, professor – "a man of the first water." "Some rough ambitious young boy may come to college from the New England countryside and prove able to compete with a Brahmin, but this is rather an exceptional event, and if one finds a young man with an unknown name, not coarse and uncouth like other countryman, but slender, with a face smooth and pallid, features 'regular and of a certain delicacy,' whose eye is 'bright and quick,' whose lips 'play over the thought he utters as a pianist's fingers dance over their music,' whose 'whole air, though it may be timid, and even awkward, has nothing clownish,' you may be sure that his mother was a Brahmin."

It was within the circle of this very self-interested, hard-nosed, if often effete, and almost always self-serving caste that debate over Judge Webster Thayer and his handling of the two foreign anarchists had begun. As that debate continued, not surprisingly, matters of law – the upholding and maintenance of processes and precedents within the law – became as important as matters of what most would call justice, remembering that H.L. Mencken had alerted his fellow citizens to the fact that "we do live with a government that is not of men but of laws," and though that is taken as a comfort by the ordinary man or woman…it is best to realize that "it is men who are set upon benches to decide finally what the law is and may be…and then the farce only grows the more glorious."

In 1923, a committee to defend the rights of the two anarchists was called, to be headed by a conservative lawyer of considerable reputation, William G. Thompson. The committee sat and then in its report called into serious question Webster Thayer's abilities as a trial judge. Subsequently, a motion was made for a new trial. Under Massachusetts's law, however, only Judge Thayer could grant a new trial.

In a 25,000-word opinion, Judge Thayer denied the motion.

In 1925, a young Portuguese criminal named Madeiros, in prison on conviction of murder, submitted a confession: "I hereby confess to being in the South Braintree shoe company crime and Sacco and Vanzetti was not in said crime." He told the story of the holdup and murders, and it seemed certain that Madeiros had been associated with the Morelli gang, notorious in the neighbourhood for a series of such robberies.

In 1927, the two anarchists having been in jail for six years, Governor Fuller of Massachusetts responded to an increasingly widespread furor among left-wing labour leaders and liberal intellectuals in America and in Europe by forming an advisory committee. This announcement was generally welcomed because the committee was to be headed by a Brahmin of more than a little distinction, A. Lawrence Lowell, the president of Harvard, whose family had a history of concern for, and support of, individual liberties.

The president, however, went to extraordinary lengths to develop arguments against the condemned men, and then, when fresh evidence pointed in the direction of their innocence, he deliberately suppressed that evidence from his report. What shocked the president and his committee was not Judge Thayer's conduct in the courtroom – his open hostility to the accused – but the fact that he had let his hostility be known: he had breached not the principles of justice but the principles of propriety and decorum...

⌖

Sacco and Vanzetti had become a *cause célèbre* among workers, among socialists, among liberals and intellectuals of the left, among distinguished professors at home and the leaders of radical political parties abroad. Appeals had been launched, brief strikes and demonstrations had been organized well into 1927, when the number of such demonstrations increased as the day of execution neared: in Warsaw, Melbourne, Cairo, Havana, Beograd, Moscow, and Buenos Aires. Pleas were made and protest marches were endorsed by Albert Einstein, Henry Ford, Stalin, Thomas Mann, Mussolini, John Dos Passos (who wrote to a friend: "until… A. Lawrence Lowell is to be assassinated and the Business School destroyed and its site sowed with salt…etc."), Dashiell Hammett, Clifford Odets, and H.G. Wells of England, who – stiffening the backs of the Brahmin caste – condemned supporters of the conviction as Americans of "underdeveloped minds, the minds of lumpish overgrown children… They had lived in an atmosphere where there is no subtle criticism of conduct and opinion, where everything is black and white."

In city after city, vigils were being held in support of the condemned men: through August of 1927, a thousand protesters in New York were beaten back from the steps of City Hall by police; upwards of 300,000 New Yorkers stayed home from work; 16,000 workers went on general strike in Rochester; Chicago police had to use tear gas to control rioters; workers shut down several mines in Colorado. With time running out, the counsel for the defendants decided on a last-ditch legal tactic.

On August 10, Justice Oliver Wendell Holmes, who had a reputation as a "liberal" among his fellows on the 1920s Supreme Court, received an appeal from that counsel for a writ of *habeas corpus* and, ten days later, he received another appeal for an extension of time in order to apply to the Supreme Court for writs of *certiorari* and for a stay of execution while the application was pending.

Both of these Holmes denied.

In the first instance, he said that he had "no authority to take the prisoners out of the custody of a state court having jurisdiction over the persons and dealing with the crime under a state law," and in the second, Holmes said he "thought no shadow of a ground could be shown on which the writ could be granted."

These appeals had apparently been made in the hope that the justice would recognize an analogy between the Sacco and Vanzetti case and a Southern Negro case of a few years before, in which he had formulated the majority decision in granting a writ of *habeas corpus* for five men convicted of murder in a court that, as Holmes had said, was dominated by a mob "ready to lynch the prisoner, jury, counsel and possibly the judges if they did not convict." He declined to accept this analogy, saying that the prejudices alleged in the Massachusetts court were not really the same thing, adding that in any trial some prejudice could be alleged.

And anyway, the justice – sounding miffed – wanted to know… Why was so much fuss being made over Sacco and Vanzetti when "a thousand-fold worse cases of Negroes come up from time to time, but the world does not worry about them."

"My prejudices," he wrote in a revelatory letter to his friend Harold Laski, "are against the convictions, but they are still stronger against the run of the shriekers… The *New Republic* had an article that seemed to me hysterical… So far as *one who has not read the evidence* [my italics] has a right to an opinion I think *the row has been made idiotical*, if considered on its *merits*, but of course it is not on the *merits* that the row is made, but because it gives the extremists a chance to yell."

Justice Holmes had clearly inferred in his letter to Laski that he did not think it necessary for him to *read the evidence* given at trial to decide on the *merits* of an appeal concerned with that same evidence – one might well assume that he did not read a *New Republic* report from Dedham Jail where the condemned

Sacco and Vanzetti were being held – a report that attempted an impression of the two men as they readied themselves to die.

The reporter, Bruce Bliven, found that the jail was set amidst countryside parks and ponds, lilacs and elms:

> It does not look like a prison, this nondescript, rambling structure, painted white and grey, and, like the houses, set back in a lawn, with a curving driveway and wooden stables at one side. It looks like a private school – or do all private schools look like prisons?… A guard lets us in – an elderly, silver-haired New Englander, like a lobsterman come ashore.
>
> From the cell blocks they appear, these two most famous prisoners in all the world, walking briskly, side by side… They are in prison garb, they look well, seem in good spirits. Both are of average height, both black-haired, both somewhat bald in front, a baldness which somehow gives them a mild domestic air…
>
> Unless the governor of Massachusetts acts to stay the process of the law, these strong and healthy men, eager and full of life, will sit in the electric chair, their heads tonsured, their trouser legs split, for the electrodes, and say farewell to life. Thus the state will take its Old Testament revenge for a murder which someone committed seven years ago.
>
> That they did not have a fair trial, there is no doubt whatever. No intelligent man has ever read the record of what happened in the courtroom, coming to the case with an open mind, without being convinced that these two were the haphazard victims of a blind hostility in the community, which was compounded of "patriotic" fervor, antiforeignism, and hatred of these men in particular because, as Professor Felix Frankfurter has summed it up, they denied the three things judge and jury held most dearly – God, country and property.

Vanzetti's English, if not always idiomatically correct, is (now) fluent and, on the whole, accurate. Sacco, perhaps, does not do quite so well, but it is fair to remember that most of the time they try to say things that are not too easy, even in one's mother tongue. You must not be deceived by an accent, or by the workingman's easy way they have of sitting on a hard bench as though they were used to it. These are book men. Their political faith is philosophic anarchism, and they know its literature from Kropotkin down. In this year's graduating class at Harvard, there will not be twenty men who, on their own initiative, have read as many difficult, abstruse works as these grey-clad prisoners...and we go on to speak of a famous Italian wine: and one says, "When you are free, you will perhaps go back to Italy and drink again the Lacryma Christi?"

"When we are free..." says Vanzetti thoughtfully. *Tick tock!* Thirty-one days to live! *Tick tock!* Thirty days to live...lately they have been given an Italian lawn-bowling set, which they use during the hour and a half they are permitted to be out of doors. "It is good," says Sacco, and Vanzetti corroborates. "It makes you sweat."...

He has a hatred of injustice... He is opposed equally to Mussoliniism in Italy and Sovietism in Russia, and for the same reason: he is against any rule supported by force. They do not believe in force, these two men who (according to the state's official theory), after a lifetime of sober industry, on a given day suddenly turned murderers to get money "for the cause," when the cause didn't need it, planned a crime which bore every earmark of the expert professional, didn't get any of the money when it was over, and made no effort to hide or escape afterward.

And now they are to die... And so we stand up and shake hands and say goodbye. "Goodbye." "Goodbye."

And they walk away toward the cell block – Sacco and Vanzetti and the unseen grey-robed figure which is ever at their side, and we go out into the glorious June evening, to the car and the chauffeur and the road home.

⌐⋇⌐

Seated on Death Row, two days before he was hooded and killed, BartolomeoVanzetti wrote in broken English: "If it had not been for these things, I might have live out my life talking at street corners to scorning men. I might have die, unmarked, unknown, a failure. This is our career and our triumph. Never in our full life could we hope to do such work for tolerance, for joostice, for man's onderstanding of man as now we do by accident. Our words – our lives – our pains – nothing! The taking of our lives – lives of a good shoemaker and a poor fish-peddler – all! That last moment belongs to us – that agony is our triumph."

⌐⋇⌐

The two tonsured men being dead, a eulogy by John Dos Passos appeared in the Marxist journal *New Masses*:

> *THEY ARE DEAD NOW*
> *… They are burned up utterly*
> *their flesh has passed into the air of Massachusetts their dreams*
> *have passed into the wind.*
> *"They are dead now," the Governor's secretary nudges*
> *the Governor,*
> *"They are dead now," the Superior Court Judge nudges*
> *the Supreme Court Judge,*
> *"They are dead now," the College President nudges*
> *the College President.*
> *A dry chuckling comes up from all the dead:*
> *The white collar dead; the silk-hatted dead;*

the frockcoated dead
They hop in and out of automobiles
breathe deep in relief
as they walk up and down the Boston streets…

❦

In Boston, in December of the year after the execution, Justice Oliver Wendell Holmes wrote: "[Felix Frankfurter] is convinced of their innocence – but I was not convinced that too much talk had not been made on the theme. The *New Republic* recurs to it from time in time. But the *New Republic* strikes me as having become partisan in tone of late judging from an occasional glance… I *come* [my italics] *nearer to reading it than I do reading any other newspaper – but I can't be said to read that.*"

❦

It is unlikely that Holmes and his fellow Brahmins, in the immediate years following, ever read through a trilogy of progressive novels, *U.S.A.*, by John Dos Passos, who, while telling the story, uttered a lament for Sacco and Vanzetti, a lament for the days of protest, a lament for the nation:

> *the scribbled phrases the nights typing releases the smell of the*
> *printshop the sharp reek of newsprinted leaflets the rush for Western Union stringing words into wires the search for stinging words to make you feel who are your oppressors America*
> *America our nation has been beaten by strangers who have turned our language inside out who have taken the clean words our fathers spoke and made them slimy and foul*

248

their hired men sit on the judge's bench they sit back with their feet on the tables under the dome of the State House they are ignorant of our beliefs they have the dollars the guns the armed forces the power plants
they have built the electric chair and hired the executioner to throw the switch
all right we are two nations

The police had arrested two men and had wanted the two men killed.

The judge, hearing the police charges, had made clear to the jury that he wanted the two men killed.

A distinguished Justice of the Supreme Court, though he had refused to read the trial evidence, had upheld the processes due to the court and had therefore upheld the integrity of the law.

By doing so, he had sanctioned the killing of the two men.

The farce then, and in all such cases since, has only grown more glorious.

Life does take farcical turns, the farcical knows no ends. John Dos Passos, the fellow traveller and the outspoken radical of the 1920s and 1930s, the defender of the two doomed anarchists, who was the illegitimate son of a prominent lawyer, came into his legitimacy by inheriting upon his father's death the family's farm in the Virginia Hills. By the 1950s, he had not only become a conservative but he had found a way in his heart to support that scourge of radicals, real and imagined, Senator Joseph McCarthy, who, as a lawmaker given to subverting the law, made Judge Webster Thayer look like a piker.

The Telegram, 1968, 2011

DEAR HEARTS
AND GENTLE PEOPLE

We are an unassuming people, glad to be of use, deferential, a bit obtuse. We tell no stories of captains of the soul crying "Eureka" as they kill the wild things of the air and earth. Our angels are of stone. Abandon is not our strong suit. Destiny is always open to negotiation. When we gamble, we gamble on a sure thing: we buy more life insurance for ourselves than any other people on earth. Why? Because we are going to die. With measured gusto (such contradictions are a Canadian art form) we bet our lives on going to the grave. Intrepid, industrious, we dig down into the earth seeking procedures for the underground in cellars, pits, and tombs.

1.

In Alice Munro's story "Images," a young girl and her father are checking their trapline for muskrats. He carries dead rats in a dark sack slung over his shoulder. Then, another man comes down a hill and there is something scarifying about him. Hatchet in hand, he is hacking at the air. He says he is looking for the Silases family, says he hates them, fears them. The girl and her father walk with the hatchet man to his home. In the middle of a field, angled like a lean-to over the ground, is a roof, and under the roof they go down a flight of steps into a cellar. He lives in the cellar. He is mad. He has burned his own house down and has blamed it on the Silases, but there are no Silases: they are a clan who never were. They are his waking nightmare, and he is afraid to sleep because the Silases may come and get him. He waits with his hatchet and his shotgun. He says he is not lonely. He has taught his cat to drink whisky. He says, "I don't say everybody should live in a hole in the ground, Ben. Though animals do it, and what an animal does, by and large it makes sense."

2.

Ethel Wilson seems to be of an entirely different temperament – sensible shoes and cucumber sandwiches. Her story "Haply the soul of my grandmother" is set out of the country in foreign territory – but the man and wife in the story, who are on vacation, are drawn immediately to a tomb: "What she breathed was not air but some kind of ancient vacuum…she suffered from the airlessness and a kind of blind something, very old, dead…" In the baked, yellow aridity of the hills, in the valley of dead kings, deep down inside this tomb, husband and wife are silent as they stand over an ancient sarcophagus. Then they go out of the tomb, only to be attacked by vicious bright-winged insects, and a mendicant who holds a small object before their faces, an object wrapped in winding cloths; it is a small human hand hacked off below the wrist. They leave Egypt confined to a closed, almost airless train compartment, the husband ill and tormented by his nightmares of the severed hand.

3.

"River Two Blind Jacks" by Dave Godfrey is set in a mill town and logging camp where Albert Godspeed and Reginald Couteau are brawling; each wields a grapline hook, a steel claw that they use to catch logs. "Albert had longer arms and he hooked out Reginald's left eye like you'd spear an onion out of the pickle jar. The eyeball and muscles dangled down Reginald's cheek and Reginald pretended he was about fit to die. That fooled Albert and he let down his guard enough to get one of his own eyes hooked out for his foolishness... When we finally got them apart they was both blind in one eye and gouged over the rest of their bodies..."

Later, as part of an annual fall ritual, the French and English loggers choose their champions. Godspeed and Couteau go into the dark woods. Couteau – with boughs and branches – covers over a deep pit, an old trap for grizzly bears. Godspeed falls in and breaks his leg and Couteau, assured and complacent as he sits by a fire, waits for his enemy to die. But Couteau has been sitting atop a companion bear pit; the fire burns through those boughs and the boughs collapse and Couteau falls in. Days later the dying men, deep in their twin pits, hear heavy footsteps; each claims to hear his supporters; they promise each other a cruel death. But it is a grizzly bear. The men wait, entombed in the animal traps.

4.

Entombed in the pits and hollows of one's life!

In the anthology at hand, it is true of Margaret Laurence's African native, who, to avoid the honourable discharge he deserves, has murdered his captain so that he can be condemned to a jail cell in the only home he has known – the army. It is true of Hugh Garner's retarded Willie Heaps, who is driven, in his mad evangelical hatred of himself, to castrate pigs and then to castrate himself; and it is true even of Mordecai Richler who, at casual reading, seems to have nothing in common with the maimed and the entombed. But his characters are caught in the inescapable trap of his ridicule. His acid scorn is so unrelenting that few of his people – skewered for laughter – are allowed any dignity. In some ways, Richler's characters live in the most airless room of all.

5.

These brief observations are occasioned by the appearance of two collections of short stories: *Dance of the Happy Shades* by Alice Munro and Oxford's *Canadian Short Stories*, edited by Robert Weaver. Munro is a young writer whose tales are conventionally told but they are deeply felt.

The Telegram, 1968

CALGARY:
AFTER THE FALL

At the east end of the Calgary Mall are two small grassy knolls, several silver spruce, and four yellow wooden benches. There is a blind Indian standing in the shade of the spruce. He is tapping a red-and-white collapsible aluminum cane. He has been trying to find a bench in the sun. Except for an unshaven white man who is wearing a whiplash neck brace, there are only Indians on the knolls asleep in the sun or sprawled drunk on the grass, their hats and feathers beside them. The blind man kisses the cross of his red plastic rosary that is hanging around his neck as the upper air fills with delicate lunch-hours bells, played over an amplifier in a glass booth two blocks away by Irene Besse, *carillonneur.*

> *You must remember this,*
> *A kiss is just a kiss.*

The blind man taps straight toward a wall to the west, unhesitating, as if he were intent on disappearing into a two-storey brick wall that he has never seen, a wall that has been painted over with a dream of yellow and ochre fields, green foothills, a blue sky bleeding red, white clouds and white birds, and leaping out of the sky, a rainbow that falls to root over the head of the white man who is wearing the neck brace.

HAS ALBERTA'S SUN SET?

Calgary Herald

It was a province of high-rolling entrepreneurs, posh restaurants, and executive jets. Workers

254

lured by high-paying jobs and the prospect of
speedy promotions descended in droves from all
parts of the country, often arriving in cars packed
to the brim with family and belongings...

Has the whirlwind transformation been tem-
porarily subdued or has it vanished forever, leaving behind half-finished office buildings in the
downtown core and thousands of empty apartment units?

It is the lunch hour, it is drizzling. There used to be tall old
trees and a row of large sandstone houses along the Bow River
road but now there are empty asphalt parking lots. The hookers,
walking in a thin line, are carrying open black brollies against the
rain. Determined joggers angle their way between the umbrella
spokes, heading out of a parking lot. The hours pass. Late at night,
the lamps high above the lot cast a putty light on the concrete
walls of a shopping depot as a cluster of young girls work the cars
and pickup trucks, their arms folded, trying to keep warm.

In the boom days, hookers had stood three deep on these lots
and on certain of the city sidewalks. "That was bizarre," Bill
Mitchell, the successful gallery owner, says. "The Ladies of the
Strasse were so thick it was like a convention. They all wore white
timber-wolf coats and that was great if you were a furrier, but
only up to a point, because it got to be that no self-respecting
woman in town would wear a timber-wolf coat downtown
because you'd either be propositioned or pounded into the dust
by some hooker whose corner you happened to be standing on
by mistake. Mind you," he says, "the girls working the streets are
not the ladies, shall we say, of certain prestige dining rooms,
where you'd find this businessman with a very attractive, no-
trash, impeccably groomed, and very tasteful woman, and you'd
think, 'My God, that guy has a gorgeous wife,' but after you are
there enough, either this woman had a multitude of husbands or
another trick going for her. Such women, however, are terribly

discreet in this hysterically discreet town, because the oil industry, in a curious way, is very domestic. You don't play with dynasties, because Alberta is community property, which can keep your nose pretty clean, but these discreet delights are not the women of the boom. The boom children kept the construction workers content, but now the sky is full of empty lots and empty arms."

At three in the morning, a tall black girl is facing the dark river. Her name is Ché Luelle Craig – Ché Lu on the street. She is wearing silver stockings and a short skirt. "You be needing a little sleaze to please?" she asks. She has braided, beaded hair and carries a little sequined purse with a horseshoe clasp. We walk to the town's tiny Chinatown. The Golden Inn Restaurant is still open.

She has been on the streets for two years. "Man, back then we was having to really strut our stuff, it was tough just getting elbow room on the curb, but now you hang your sign out for hours and hardly get a peep."

"What're the men like?"

"You mean what do they do?"

"Whatever."

"The first rule is, don't never look no john in the eye, especially here in this town, 'cause they get all nervous and fuss and eat up your time, or get weird and bust you upside your head. A whole lot of heads get busted giving head in this town."

"Where you from?"

"Detroit."

"Where you going?"

"I dunno. I be going when I'm going."

"Half this town's on the move."

"One of the strangest tricks I done, this dude he says he wants to go out by the airport and get off watching planes and I say, They's no planes at two o'clock in the morning…but he says he wants to get off in this particular field out by the airport, so he's standing there in the high grass with his pants down aroun' his ankles, staring at the nothing that is absolutely happening up in the sky." She begins to laugh. "And the next minute there's god-damn giant rabbits going by in the night, man, great goddamn rabbits. Big like this, man," and she opens her arms wide.

"They must have been hares."

"That's what he says, but they look to me like they be ghosts going by, a herd of ghosts, man, and I let out a yell."

"You weren't seeing things?"

"Sure, I was seeing things, at the same time this guy is haul-ing his pants up around his throat, he was seeing things, too, and they got red eyes."

"Maybe they were getting out of town like everybody else."

"Man, they was moving *into* town, they are heading straight *down*town, and all of a sudden my guy yells, holding his pants so he don't fall down, 'Sweet Jesus, I have seen the angels and His saints,' and I say, 'Shut up your mouth with all that shit,' and he starts in on how this here is life after the fall…after the fall this and after the fall that…and I don't know what the fuck he going on about."

The city has no centre, though there is a Centre Street. Office workers stroll on the Mall, where there are tacky shops, sum-mertime food stalls, street singers, sex and leather stores, a few trees, and two or three vacuous public sculptures. At night, the Mall is deserted. Even at midday, most other streets seem empty. This is because so many downtown offices and indoor plazas are connected by "plus-15s," enclosed walkways suspended at least fifteen feet over the streets. These much-admired tunnels in the air are appropriate to people with tunnel vision – moles in mid-air – single-minded men and women who work hard all day, take an exact hour for lunch, who stay in the city to get exactly what they want, and then go either to the bedroom suburbs at the end of the day or another city at the end of the year.

MILLIONS NEEDED TO PURIFY WATER
GLOBE AND MAIL
Calgary Mayor Ralph Klein has refused to drink
water from the Bow below Calgary and agrees
that the river is heavily polluted…runoff from
storm sewers has polluted the Bow so badly that
young trout cannot survive in it.

As you meet these busy people, they seem to be free-wheelers, independent and ready to move, but this belies a tendency to cluster like prairie chickens. For all its apparent openness, Calgary is a closed town in contention with itself; caustic and yet courtly, prickly and yet polite and pliable, often openly loony yet closed around shared achievement, and achievement is marked by money. They like to talk about work and money, and money and work. When they talk about politics, it is – not surprisingly – the politics of work and money. After Mayor Ralph Klein climbed to the top of the Saddledome as a fundraising stunt, he said: "I'd only do this for money," and then, as an afterthought, "or maybe love." It is also a violent place. Transient men wear "shit-kickers" and brawl in bars and hang out in motel rows and places called Taco Time, Apollo Muffler, Chubby Chicken, Grab Feast, and Kanadian Kar Kare Klinic.

These workers – whether white collar or grease monkey – dress down – the women look like their suits and skirts have been designed by the Eaton's fashion department, where tradition is a trend, while the men wear mostly jeans…jeans to work, to the bars, to the big convention halls in the borderline posh hotels – and what these people do when they are not working is abort, divorce, and commit suicide more than in any city of comparable size in the country. In recent months, the murder rate has risen 500 per cent, yet they are determinedly law-abiding in open, demonstrable ways. Always in a hurry, they will not jaywalk. Whether it is noon or two o'clock in the morning on an empty street, they will stand like lonely prairie chickens on a curb. They will not cross against a red light.

THE NORTH WEST MOUNTED POLICE
CALGARY: CANADA'S FRONTIER METROPOLIS
Surveillance and protection of the Indian was one of their chief mandates...[A] white man was tried for the hideous murder and mutilation of an Indian prostitute. In spite of overwhelming evidence to the contrary, the Calgary jury found the defendant, a popular local man, not guilty.

Hugh Dempsey is fifty-three and married to a Blood woman. Tall, gangling, with thinning hair and long bony fingers, he has shrewd eyes, quick and perhaps cunning, but he is dedicated to his craft, history; an honest man in a hurry, padding softly in his moccasins, tough-minded, but sometimes yielding – he keeps regular shoes ready for meetings in the Glenbow Museum, shoes he leaves unlaced.

"One thing I find amusing," he says, sitting with his long legs crossed, "is people who haven't been here too long complain about the American influence and yet the American influence has been here right from the beginning. When Calgary was built in 1875 it was as a North West Mounted Police post, but the first letters mailed by Calgarians to people in Toronto carried American postage stamps because there was no postal service. You threw your mail into a box at the local store and the first person who was heading south gathered them all up and took them down to Fort Benton, put American postage stamps on them, and sent them to Ontario.

"For several years after that, in southern Alberta at least, the majority of the population was American." He folds one hand over the other on his knee. "The cowboy came up here packing his gun everywhere, but he found that absolutely nobody here wore their guns into town and, if he did, he'd look foolish. Some of the gunfights we had in Calgary were hilarious." He opens his big hands, flexing the fingers, enjoying himself. "In the 1880s, there was a shortage of women at a cowboy dance and one man known as The Kid started dancing with this girl and kept dancing with her and wouldn't share her and finally a range detective complained and The Kid slugged him, so the range detective went home to get his gun and came back two hours later, still a bit drunk, and started waving this gun around and The Kid escaped by crawling through the guy's legs, going out the door. It sounds like the Keystone Kops, it was our Wild West."

He gets up to take a book from the bookshelves, but he can't find it, shrugs, sits down, and stretches his legs. "As soon as the city got the boom period, from 1906 to about 1912, Mount Royal became the first real elite community in Calgary, but it was really known as American Hill. That was the nickname," he says with the satisfaction of a man who knows that he is in possession of an underlying truth that others lack. "It doesn't show on any maps but that whole area was known as American Hill.

"A great many of these Americans came in and built the great big mansions up on the side of the hill, and it was wonderfully paradoxical because the streets of Mount Royal were named after people from the battle of the Plains of Abraham, all very, very British, very Canadian, but the whole place was known as American Hill because of the American domination, their influence."

"Then this is fundamentally, at its root, an American town?"

"I've always thought it was American."

"Philosophically?"

"Yeah, an American town with British standards."

ON THE BULLETIN BOARD,
SARCEE RESERVE HOCKEY ARENA
CHARLOT, FLATHEAD CHIEF

We were happy when he first came. We first thought he came from the light; but he comes like the dusk of evening now, not like the dawn of morning. He comes like a day that has passed, and night enters our future with him. His laws never gave us a blade of grass, nor a tree, nor a duck, nor a grouse, nor a trout. How often does he come? You know he comes as long as he lives, and takes more and more, and dirties what he leaves.

After three days of what felt like warm sunshine, suddenly it is snowing (the weather in Calgary shifts more radically from day to day than in any other city in the country). It is cold and slushy along the rough Sarcee reserve road. Harley Crowchild, tawny-skinned, in his early forties, is wearing a black hat, his hair is tied at the nape of his neck. He takes off his hat and sits behind a small desk in the reserve arena, a little wary and yet guileless in his earnest need to talk about the spirituality of his people.

"What word," I ask, "do you use to describe the white people?"

"Our description doesn't come out as white people," he says. "This word that's been developed to identify the white people, we say *I k'ohali.* I know before the white people came, 500 years ago, Indians used to have meetings every so often and this old man predicted there's people that's coming from across the ocean. 'These people have no colour to their skin,' he said. 'Other races of people have colour, except white people have no colour.' So, it sort of refers to a certain part of animal fat. *I k'o* means fat, the white part of the fat, the colour of the fat people. *Holi* might mean people, race of people."

"Do you think there's ever been any real communication between the white people who settled Calgary and the native people?"

"The only communication," he says, the lids of his soft dark eyes closing, "was at the treaty that was signed in 1877 at Blackfoot Crossing. Even people that's been in Calgary for a long time, some don't know any history of the Indian people in this area."

"Have you ever stood in downtown Calgary and looked at those buildings and thought, Jesus, what kind of mind created that?"

"Right. They're creating what we might call in our terms a wilderness. In the white man's term, where we live out here, is a wilderness, but we call it natural surroundings. But when I go down there, it's more like a wilderness or jungle. You have to watch out for that animal going by which may be a car, might swallow you up, run over you, and kill you. And the air itself is very, very bad, and some old people have said it's not really progress, it's destruction if they cut everything down and then put trees inside big glass rooms which they call gardens." He hunches across the desk with quiet certainty. "Actually, they destroy nature and then recreate it to their liking. Indian people would rather not live in a city because it's not clean spiritually. If you want to protect your spiritual being, go to where the air is clean, where things are the way it was first created. Everything in the downtown is polluted – water, air, food. It is mind-boggling when you see these buildings go higher and higher and higher, and then you think of the future. You see, it's been predicted by Ioke, an old man, about sixty years ago. He said, 'My grandson, take this little pail outside. See that sand, bring it in. I want to tell you what's going to happen in the future.' So the young fellow brought in that pail of sand. 'I'm going to show you,' he said. 'This is Calgary.' He poured some sand. He grabbed some more in a little pile. 'This is Edmonton. This is Regina. This is Vancouver. These big towns are getting bigger now. These towns, they'll be bigger cities in the future,' he said, 'and then there's going to be a punishment. This sand, the way it's piled, that's the way it's all going to end in the future.' That prophecy goes through my mind whenever I go to the city of Calgary. It's all going to be a pile of rubble again within our future. The thing we don't know is when. We're not allowed to know but it's going to happen."

"So when Calgary was booming, everything got worse?"

"We knew things were going to get worse."

"The happiness of the downtown businessmen is only a sadness for you."

"We dread the times when the wind changes directions. You can see the smog, the pollution line over the city, just a big cloud of dirt, but when the wind changes and blows this way, it enters my mind all the time."

"Now that the boom has come to a halt, it's a good thing."

"Right. For the majority of our people it'll be a sigh of relief."

"YES WE CAN," PROSTITUTES
DECLARE AFTER COURT WIN
TORONTO STAR

Sporting "Yes We Can!" buttons, opponents of Calgary's prostitution bylaw are toasting its defeat in the Supreme Court of Canada. The buttons are part of a campaign by the city and the Calgary Chamber of Commerce to promote economic growth. "The mayor wants to put the city back to work and so do we," lawyer Tony Managh said wryly.

During Stampede Week, an intersection on the Mall is cordoned off and named Rope Square. Stage cowboys stage a shootout in the street and then Harley Crowchild tells the crowd that they are going to see an ancient religious dance. A boy, linking twenty-three wooden hoops around his legs and arms, becomes a swooping eagle. When the dance is over, the master of cowboy ceremonies says, "Thank you, Harvey...you folks out there should visit the tepees on the Stampede ground where you can see how these people live, and talk to them."

In the late afternoon, several hundred men and women sit behind the tepees on a grassy slope, watching beautifully feathered dancers. A Blood elder says to the people on the slope, "I would like to share a funny story. Our elders are wise, they know all about animals, and birds, and living things. One day, two boys found an animal they'd never seen before. It was a monkey, and they took it to an elder and asked him what it was. He told them to come back in four days, and then put the monkey on its back and saw that it was a boy, rolled it over on its stomach and saw that it had a tail like a cow, and when the boys came back, he said, 'I know what this animal is. It is a cowboy.'"

There is an extraordinary garden on the fourth level of a bank building above the Mall, a two-storey, glass-enclosed garden. It is a huge diorama, a still growth of shrubs, dwarf trees, sculpted children, shallow pools, ferns, pink hydrangeas and calla lilies, laminated benches, wood planking, and interlocking bricks. It is humid, lush, but strangely dead: the air is stale and devoid of scent; sloped walls face reflecting glass towers; the ceiling is not a clear expanse of sky, but spray-plastered girders and air ducts; the controlled lighting comes from overhead spotlights; and it is windless...nothing moves, not a leaf, not a fern...no birds, no breathing sound, only the incessant rush of motor-driven water. People don't stay long – a frail young man reading religious tracts, a cruising homosexual boy carrying his lunch in a brown paper bag, women resting their feet between stores. This is the Devonian Gardens – hub of above-ground tunnels – created by the people who also painted the rainbow on the wall of the western sky.

I sit on one of the benches in a grove, close to a monkey puzzle tree, the water running, little sculpted animals poised in the shrubbery, and read a novel by John Ballem called *Alberta Alone*. It opens with an eastern horseman driving into Calgary at the opening of the Stampede. In the middle of the morning rush hour he stares in disbelief: a small herd of steers is in the middle of the road, held by cowboys.

A rider twirls a lariat and a steer buckles down to its knees as the noose settles around its neck. One of the riders dismounts and swings a hammer in a short arc to the steer's head. The steer wobbles, the man slits its throat, blood gushes, and soon ten steers are piled across the intersection. A horseman drives a pitchfork into one of the carcasses. A sign is nailed to the wooden handle: THE EAST CAN'T ROB THE WEST OF THIS MEAT. The rider who has done most of the butchering points at the Ontario plates of the eastern horseman and says quietly, "Tell them back there, we're through being screwed."

The easterner is in Calgary to write about the Stampede, but he confesses, "My mind keeps scratching at the political unrest out here. Maybe that's the real story." He discovers that the real story is a political conspiracy. Ottawa is trying, unilaterally, to take over Alberta's oil and gas industry. A cattle baron and breeder (whose federalist daughter is sterile) declares, "We don't *have* to remain a colony, shipping our raw materials to feed the insatiable industry of eastern Canada. We have a choice. This great country – Alberta – that Ottawa is determined to bring to her knees can go it *alone*." The *Calgary Herald* declares: "ALBER-TANS OPTING OUT OF CONFEDERATION." The cattle baron's plan to take power, in a conspiracy involving genetic war-fare and lurid photographs of a homosexual prime minister, is paralleled by the actual violence in the dark Calgary side streets (a rodeo clown's eyes glare "ferally from his painted face" – he is a rapist who kills women – a clown whose pet monkey mastur-bates before a crowd and then goes berserk). The story ends with a helicopter dogfight over Stampede Park as the (homosexual?) prime minister departs to the ironic singing of "O Canada."

What is interesting about this somewhat lurid adventure novel, aside from its pace and feel for political violence, is its set-ting, Calgary. There is no other fiction in our literature set in Calgary. There are novels and scenes in Medicine Hat, Regina, Edmonton…but Calgary, as a city, does not exist in the imagina-tion. A city that has no imaginative shape has no meaning, no presence. In a very real way, Calgary – though it is certainly *here* – does not exist.

Along from Jacques Funeral Home, the Little Chapel on the Corner, there is a private homosexual bar called Dick's. Sitting with two other young women, a very pert girl from Penticton says she has been engaged for a year to a restaurant owner in San Diego. "But I broke it off because I felt like a reserved table. Now I get a lot of lesbian passes. There are a lot here, career women like me." She is wearing an elk's tooth on a heavy gold chain. She rolls the long tooth between her thumb and forefinger. "And I will tell you something else. When I first came here, a little girl waiting to get married, I went to all the evening courses at the college, but it wasn't to get ahead. I am ahead. That's why I'm here, I'm the best in my business. My friends and I went because of boredom. I mean, this is the capital city of boredom at night for a woman. There is nothing, and I mean nothing, to do."

John B. Ballem, one of the most influential lawyers in the Oil Patch, has a studied self-assurance but, when he came to Calgary in 1954, he was "sort of unknowing, and I flew all night and had this damned big Great Dane with me on the plane. I got off about eight o'clock in the morning and a lot of people said, 'I see you've got your spare horse with you,' but anyway I got into a cab and drove down to the Palliser Hotel. It was the day of the Stampede parade and I wondered what in the world I'd gotten myself into." By 1962, he was in partnership with Peter Lougheed, who was about to become premier of the province.

In the late 1960s, he began writing fiction. "I certainly never had any formal training. The closest I came to it was when my wife enrolled in a writer's correspondence course and she used to get assignments and I would look at those." He has published five novels, and *Alberta Alone* has sold almost 50,000 copies. His office, on the thirty-sixth floor of the Scotia Centre, is proper in the corporate sense; large, with a view of the city, and he has hung unobtrusive – if not altogether bland – contemporary paintings on his walls.

"Do you know," I say, "you are the only writer who has ever set a book in Calgary?"

"I've never thought of that," he says, settling onto a sofa. "That's funny, I'm surprised. I think you're right and I find that extraordinary."

"Writers touch the spirit of a place."

"I suppose they do."

"There's a fierce violence in this city," I say, staring at the gaptooth skyline, the tall buildings, the empty lots. "You feel it if you're a stranger."

"There's underlying resentment. Absolutely. You can scratch that anywhere, just go beneath the surface."

"You feel it in nearly all the bars in town."

"Yeah, you could have a donnybrook any time. So I think that in my book the violence is appropriate."

"Could it be politically organized, as you suggest in the novel?"

"Yeah. It nearly was."

"And would there be public support?"

"If the federal government moved in on the oil wells and gas wells, that could ignite the feeling. There's no deep-rooted racial animosity or any of those things, but an economic event, economic animosity, money, strangely enough, that would do it. I've always felt that this is the oddest thing about the whole situation. These bitter feelings are based essentially on economic considerations. Not racism, or religion," he says, getting up and leaning over his empty polished desk. "Not the things men are supposed to go to war for. It's all economics."

"Sometimes," I say, "I think you guys in the Oil Patch sit here three floors above ground, suspended in the air, up with the Devonian Gardens, self-enclosed in a glass house."

"There's that aspect to it. It's a super-state, whose starting point is the possibility that somebody might develop something, be successful, be rich. That's their starting point. Somebody may get rich. Then they get frustrated and blame it on an alien or hostile government. A lot of these people are driven, like a guided missile."

"If you were writing a love story in Calgary and were looking for images of tenderness, where would you locate two lovers in this city?"

"I would probably put them out south on a nice ranch," he says.

"No, I mean in the city?"

"In a high-tower office."

"Come on, this is a lovely office, but it's not the metaphor for love."

"Of course not, but you could have a very nice love affair, an arrangement between two very high achievers, who are competitive."

"Look, the great scenes in *Doctor Zhivago* or *Anna Karenina* or *Madame Bovary* suggest metaphorically everything that love should be. The dream. An office tower does not do that."

"Oh, I agree."

"The Nova Building does not connote love."

"No, it doesn't," he says, laughing.

"Who could court in the Devonian Gardens?"

"They could court at the art gallery."

"Where?"

"At the Glenbow Museum." He knows he is reaching.

"They could duck between the wigwams."

"How about a nice bar?"

"You'd agree that architecture is a language."

"Oh yes."

"And over the years people tend to create a city in their own image."

"Yes," he says, "and this is what has happened here, too."

VIOLENCE GROWS IN
DOWNTOWN GAY COMMUNITY
CALGARY HERALD
Growing violence in Calgary's gay community has police worried... Police say the attacks are concen-

trated in Central Park and the vicinity of the six to
eight restaurants and private clubs in the surrounding area known to cater to a homosexual clientele…
Police say they have been told there may be 50,000 or
more homosexuals in Calgary.

John Ballem gets up from the sofa and walks over to the
window. There is a gaping hole in the ground below him, a hole
surrounded by board siding. "The town's gone through a lot,
and about two or three years ago this whole city was a hard-hat
construction site. They were tearing everything down and building up again and you just went from gaping hole A to gaping
hole B and things that had been there for years were no longer
there. When I first came out here in '54," and he points out the
window, "the building that I worked in is now that hole down
in the ground, that was the old Imperial Oil building. Those
two buildings next to it, the white ones that are now empty,
they were the most modern buildings in Calgary, brand-new,
and so it's all happened like that and it's all changed."

"Well, surely part of the nature of a small town is its roots.
How can you have roots in a rootless town?"

"I feel I've got roots. I feel I'm a pioneer practically out here."

"But you see my point?"

"Well, I think the roots are, oddly enough, in the industry.
The oil industry is essentially rootless, in the sense that people are
transient, but it also is a super state of its own, and if you're in the
Oil Patch, then you really have this affinity for each other. It's a
community feeling, it is the oil industry. It may be somewhere
else in another couple of decades, but right now it's here."

The First Baptist Church is on 4th Street, across from Central
Park and the Parkside Continental Restaurant. A few years ago,
Anita Bryant, the popular singer known for her orange juice
commercials, spoke out against homosexuals in this church, but

today homosexuals are playing catch in Central Park and dancing at night in the Parkside Continental while male hookers stand in the shadows of old trees. A few luxury cars with electric, tinted windows cruise close to the curb. Transvestites loiter at the door to the Parkside, where there is a shabby bar, a small dance floor surrounded by stalls and by floor-length mirrors. Men cradle each other, snapping their hips in the heat to the disco beat while two enormous fat men wearing leather jackets sit with their eyes closed in one of the stalls, puffy faces shiny with sweat.

Homosexuals are no longer closeted in Calgary but they tend to be domestic and settled, sharing property and discretion. There are private clubs – Dick's on 17th Avenue has a young, orderly clientele, and very close by, as a separate operation, there is Jay's Relaxation Centre, a steam room. "But the Parkside," a young executive, with a razor-sharp crease in his trousers, says, "is a watering hole for some of the not terrifyingly interesting people in town. It's a lot different from when this was a city of 200,000 and the closet doors in the Oil Patch were four inches of solid oak, when the first gay meeting place was in a basement and you had to have sponsors, which meant you hit the streets till you picked up a couple of sponsors, and the club had a record player and a salad bowl. It was enough to make you slam your closet door and die inside in the dark. But now," he says, "the city has put in the biggest vapour lights you'll ever see on 13th Avenue, and it doesn't bother the queens that there's all this light. If you want room service you just shout out the windows. At least you can see what you are buying. It's all part of the matrix of the city. After all, what would Calgary be without a few flamboyant ribbon-clerks out on the streets?"

CALGARY'S HOTEL REVENUE
SHOWED SIGNIFICANT DROP
CALGARY HERALD
Calgary hotels had a significant greater decline in revenue in March than other major cities in

Canada… Room revenue in Calgary fell 35.8
per cent from March, 1982. Food revenue fell
23.1…

I am in the Palliser Hotel, at the Women's World Body
Building Championship. The Palliser is a railroad hotel named
after a wealthy Irish immigrant landowner, John Palliser, who
led an expedition between Lake Superior and the Pacific from
1857 to 1860: his report, published in 1863, received scant
attention. The Palliser was once among the most famous hotels
in the country, built when Calgary was a CPR boom town, and
the impressive station, adjoining gardens, stockyards, and spur
lines all over town made the CPR the focal point of city life.
From a cluster of tents and 500 people in 1884, Calgary became
a town of 50,000 by 1914, putting up easily carved Paskapoo
sandstone buildings, creating a booster ethic, a rage for real
estate, and a construction industry (as in the 1980s) too big for
the strength of the city's base economy. The collapse of the boom
by 1914 threw thousands out of work, and the city settled into
a slough, half-asleep, until it became an oil boom town in the
late 1950s.

The Palliser, once posh, is sad, tacky, and shabby. The rooms
have been redone but the hotel has no élan; lean leatherette
chairs sit in the lobby facing thick columns wrapped in card-
boardy gold-flecked wallpaper. In the main convention hall,
under high ceilings, a chandelier, and gold mouldings, several
hundred people have taken chairs to watch the Women's World
Body Building Championship. *Sold out*, it has been the hottest
ticket in town.

It is a curious crowd, listless and strangely flabby for such an
event: men wearing jeans too loose in the seat and women
wearing elasticized halter tops or sheer rayon blouses. They
crane, trying to get a glimpse of the fourteen oiled women on
stage – tall, tanned, one of them black – who have come from as
far away as Holland, Denmark, Finland, and France, to be judged

for muscularity, shape, and proportion in categories of hit poses, the relaxed state, and free posing to music. Some are strikingly beautiful, despite unlikely names – Georgia Fudge from Florida, who is regal, in a camp way. Their glistening flesh, flexing into knots and bulbs of rococo landscape, is neither male nor female. "This is not the tits, teeth, and tiara set, I can tell you," a fey young man says. "This is an auto mechanic's view of the body, all chrome, bumps, and lumps." Each woman has the guise of power but not potency, the oiled sheen of sexuality but not sensuality, the energy of discipline but discipline rendered static. Perhaps these contradictions account for the strange air in the audience: little bursts of applause from pudgy people who seem bored even as they applaud. The aging basketball legend, the seven-foot Wilt "The Stilt" Chamberlain, is the chief judge. He stands up and takes a bow. The black woman is declared champion, and on the way out of the hotel, walking toward the parking lot across from the Cove strip bar on 10th Avenue, an older woman says, "This city's the saddest place. So many people who were no one thought their lives would boom here. But the boom's over and they're still no one. The city has no personality. How can parking lots have a personality?"

The city is, in fact, a patchwork place, gutted by those who profess to love it most – the promoters and entrepreneurs. Its vitality lies in contradictions: transients talk about their roots; the Oil Patch lawyers speak of power, yet impotence is in the air; sexuality is for sale among the small herds of hookers and lone boys who lurk in hotel corridors, but there is no sensuality, not in the sensible box-suited women or the tall blank towers. The people work hard to turn a profit – among a population of more than 400,000 adults, an incredible 134,000 are enrolled in evening college courses, eager to improve and get ahead – but the city is at a standstill, emptying out, and, unless the price of oil rebounds, the civic boosters will be left muscle-bound and poised in hit poses in empty parking lots.

KLEIN SCRAMBLES TO
PLUG INVESTMENT LEAK

Calgary Herald

The city hall source said [Mayor Ralph] Klein is
worried that Calgary is quickly being tarnished as
a "one-hit wonder" city that will never get over
the recession from which the rest of Canada is
recovering.

"There's something you don't understand in Toronto," a real
estate salesman says. He is wearing a big sunburst belt buckle,
and in the middle of the sunburst, in brass letters, is his name:
WILBUR. "This city is in the middle of the world. It's not like
New York, that thinks it's the centre to everything and isn't.
We're only 900 miles from everywhere – Fiji, Australia, Caracas,
Tokyo, New York, or Paris. The whole world is only 900 miles
away. We're dead centre, see, it all depends on how you look at
things."

In these dry flatlands and foothills, men and women worry
about their lives in images of water: homeowners are advised to
"abandon ship," politicians scramble to "plug investment leaks,"
businessmen bemoan "the ebb in the economy," and hookers
complain about being "flushed down the tube."

At night, in a Red Top taxi on 16th Avenue, the driver says, "I
got here too late, the bubble's burst, the economy's gone under."

"Where'd you come from?"

"New Zealand."

"All that way?"

"Yeah, for the work, but there was no real work."

"Why don't you go home?"

"Can't afford to."

"So, what'll you do?"

"What I'm doing. The only thing I really miss is the sea. In
New Zealand I was always close to the sea and life's easier if you're
close to the sea."

"But you're surrounded by water," I said.

"Where?"

"Look at the stores. In the windows."

"What for?"

"Water."

"Where?"

"Look."

"I'll be damned."

There are waterbed stores all along the avenue, and there are waterbed stores all over the city.

"Half the city," I say, "seems to dream at night on their own little seas. I met a man a week ago who said he had five waterbeds. He didn't like them but his wife and sons did, and every night he dreamed he was drowning because he'd never learned to swim, and when he told his wife that they had to get rid of the bed because he couldn't sleep, she told him to learn how to swim."

CALGARY'S OFFICE SPACE DISASTER
WITH SIX MILLION SQUARE FEET EMPTY
THE MAYOR TRIES TO
PREVENT PANIC
ALBERTA REPORT

"This has been our fourth major boom," Hugh Dempsey says. One foot has slipped out of his floppy moccasin. "The first occurred when the railway arrived in 1883. It lasted for a couple of years and then went semi-dormant. The next was a very small boom, at the beginning of the 1890s, with the actual construction of the railways north and south, but then Canada itself slipped into a recession late in '91, which started to change again with Laurier in '96, with his policy on immigration, and then in 1906 it started galloping, and until 1913 it was going flat out, complete."

"As I read history," I say, "that parallels the most recent boom."

"Completely. It stopped very suddenly in the middle of 1913. Apparently, the number of vacant offices in Calgary at the end of 1913 was adequate to serve Calgary right up until after the Second World War. Then, after the war, after the discovery of Leduc No. 1 in 1947, things took off again."

"A year ago you couldn't get an apartment in this town."

"And now we have a twelve per cent vacancy rate. As a historian, I can almost predict what's going to be in the next day's paper, because all I have to do is turn back to 1913 and see what happened on a parallel day."

"Are Calgarians aware of this cyclical situation?"

"No, I don't think so. The average person isn't interested in history."

APARTMENT VACANCY RATES SOARS
CALGARY HERALD
Calgary's apartment vacancy rates will hit a new high...the highest in the country... The owners of Calgary's 47,486 apartments are in for a gloomy year.

The Mall is not long. At one end, it becomes an avenue of lots broken by stores, an avenue blocked by a brick fortress, the old armouries, and beside the armouries, a poured-concrete planetarium, which has, for some reason, a statue of Wolfe – the sickly English general who, at Quebec, had dreamed of military martyrdom, of immortality, if only he could get himself down and dead in the ground – at the door. In the darkened theatre I watch a sound and light show – the emergence of the universe – a curved spatial heave of birth in an explosion of molten light, which becomes earth and water and time hurtling toward collapse into a black hole, and then redemption in another explosion of light...or perhaps it is only a disappearance of the light into a silence beyond infinity.

When the lights come up, I am alone in the theatre with a young man, his black hair in twin braids.

We sit outside at the feet of General Wolfe (who had succeeded in getting himself killed). He says he is a Sarcee and we talk about dreams and death, and life as a dream in death. I tell him about a group of Protestant Orangemen near my farm back home who had, out of mischief and some malice, buried an old King Billie parade horse – with its white fetlocks and hoofs stuck up in the air – in the sacred ground of the Catholic graveyard. The horse hadn't been found until mid-December when its hoofs could be seen against the snow, when it had to be dynamited to get it out of the frozen ground. He laughs and says, "That's the way people do," and so he tells me about Charcoal, a Blood who he said had been hanged for murder and buried in the ground by a Catholic priest, though the court had promised that the tribe would be able to lay out Charcoal's body up in the open air, and then he says, "It is hard enough being baptized while we are alive, because not only our lives are broken but our spirits, too, and then, after we die we are buried down in the ground." He laughs again. "This way our spirits are trapped forever, it's what you white people want." He takes off his hat and wipes the sweatband. "There've been some graves opened," he says. "Some people have dug open the graves so the spirits can float free. It's against the law. Our eternal life is against the law."

"Which do you prefer?"

"About what?"

"The light coming out of the black hole or silence?"

"I'm for silence."

COWTOWN HERITAGE GOING TO WASTE
CALGARY HERALD

Calgary is the city of back-pocket dreams, back-pocket champions: women's body building, car-crash championships, Sweet Adeline barbershop quartets, championship blacksmith competition, world championship of wild cow milking – there's a deep desire in this town to stand tall in championship shoes, somebody's shoes, anybody's shoes. But often, things are done all wrong (at the Stampede the only craps game in the casinos is played not with dice but on a numbers wheel, taking dice out of the game, defeating the *raison d'être*); and not surprisingly, an authenticity earned by others is too easily appropriated and assumed: during the railroad boom, Calgary called itself "the Denver of Canada," then it became the "Dallas of the North," and lately the "Bay Street of the West" – the braggadocio of boosters and Babbitts…

Because the newspapers said it would be a "Weekend of Champions," and because Willie deWit is, in fact, the amateur heavyweight boxing champion of the world, I went around to meet him, expecting a slum child in a sleazy gym. But Willie deWit, in this consummately middle-class city, is working out in a woman's aerobic emporium called Body Magique, part of a downtown fitness centre owned by Mansoor Esmail, a small dark man from Uganda. As I watch girls in leg warmers swing their arms to a disco beat, he says that he'd been in charge of a physical fitness institute in Uganda.

"Yes, but what do you know about boxing?"

"I was a boxer."

"You were?"

"Yes."

"Who taught you to box?"

"Idi Amin."

He leads me to a room big enough to contain a boxing ring and one light and one heavy punching bag. Harry Snatic, Willie's coach, is in the room. He is a heavily set, curly-haired Louisiana man in his late forties, who fought for a while as a welterweight but now works in the mornings as a dentist.

"How'd you get all the way up here?"

"Where?"

"Calgary."

"I didn't come here. I ended up in Grande Prairie. I was a dentist, and I saw Willie hitting the bag in Jim Murrie's Spa, so we got to know each other."

"But how'd you get to Grande Prairie?"

"A very slow train."

Willie deWit is in the ring, six-foot-three and 201 pounds, square-jawed, boyish. A sparring partner is in the ring, too, shuffling and snorting. Willie wears a white T-shirt, the sleeves cut off at the shoulders. Deacon, his black sparring partner, wears red suedine shoes, red socks, and red satin shorts, and his small wad of pocket money is tucked into his left sock for safekeeping. Snatic calls them over and gently Vaselines their noses and cheeks. Willie, the son of a gravel-crushing-company owner, smiles shyly and turns to look approvingly at a *Rocky III* poster on the wall.

"That was just a movie," I say.

"Yeah?"

"Yeah."

"It better not be."

Snatic takes a stopwatch out of his pocket and calls time. Willie and Deacon circle and Deacon flicks his left into Willie's face, lunges, flicks again, and does a little stutter-step. Willie waits and snaps off hard combinations, his hands fast. Snatic calls time, and the boxers walk in tight circles, heads down, snorting, and then begin again, with Deacon sneaking in a fast short left hook, and Willie hits him hard, driving him back, but it is clear that he does not know how to slip a punch, and when he throws a right hook he ends up off balance, his left hanging like a wounded wing. He fights well out of the corners and he can hit very hard but, as Snatic calls time, Willie's nose is bleeding.

"He's green but there's no amateur in the world who can beat him," Snatic says. "Nobody can hit like him. He's got a dream punch."

"What about Sunday's fight?"

"He'll have to be sharp, this guy was Golden Gloves in Alaska."

"This fight's big?"

"Any fight's big. Nobody wants to fight Willie, he's the most feared amateur boxer in the world. He hits too hard, he's got a heavy punch."

On Sunday, he is supposed to fight Rick Meshen, a young man who was once the Alaska state champion, but on Friday night Meshen's coach calls to say that there has been a bus accident – a couple of blowouts – near a small town called Moscow, Idaho. Meshen will not be able to make it, the coach says, because the bus had gone off the road and broken an axle. On Saturday afternoon, the coach calls again and says that he and Meshen are still in the bus and have only sixty-eight dollars and it is impossible to get to Calgary. But later the coach confesses, "There was no accident. We did not have Meshen with us. He was in a bar fight in Boise and he got kind of beat up."

On Sunday, before a mere 1,400 people, Willie is in the ring with a lugubrious, shuffling Lionel Washington from Wyoming. They dip a shoulder, feint, bob heads, lumber in and out of the corners. Willie hits him a heavy punch close to his kidney, Washington winces, the roll of fat around his waist wobbles, and after two rounds, Washington sits down on the canvas and quits. The crowd boos, sneers. In an instant, Washington seems to have forgotten that he has just quit, or even where he is. He's stepped between the ropes and leapt out of the ring. He has somewhere to go, a bar, a town, another sit-down. Willie is standing in the centre of the ring; he is still champion of the amateur world. He is in the embrace of Harry Snatic, dentist from Louisiana.

A man leaving the arena snarls, "This is a town in which there are a lot of fights, but it is not a fight town." The Weekend of Champions ends with several awards given out at centre ring: the one for The Best Loser is given to a young man whose name actually is Babbitt.

At dawn, the clouds appear as if they were pale water stains in the sky as hot air balloons hover over the outskirts of the city, great teardrops of colour.

Close to Fish Creek in the southeast, in a field of long grass, men in white coveralls are directing a giant fan into the mouth of a long length of pink and red polka-dot nylon. The balloon begins to hump up and then to slowly lift and tilt over its basket that has propane jets braced to it. The jets are turned on, blasts of flame heat the air until the full balloon shimmies and begins to pull upwards. I get into the heavy wicker basket and sit down and the pilot fastens a wooden tabletop over my knees, spreads a white linen cloth over the table, and invites aboard a chef who is going to serve me a champagne breakfast up in the air. This will be my way of getting out of town.

As the balloon and its basket draw off from the ground, the chef pours for me a flute of champagne, and then sets out a plate of diced pan-fried hash browns with rosemary; and these are the side-dish to a plump gorgonzola and mushroom omelette that is fluffy and light. The pilot, controlling the propane jets, takes the basket over the top branches of tall trees along the Fish river bank, and then, well up in the air, we drift on the wind current southeast of the city, raising a flute to the farmland, to the foothills and the range of mountains to the west, and to the far-off valleys inlaid with ice and snow.

Back to the east, the tall glass towers of the city catch the sun – blazes of light, cutting to the eye – but below the light a smear of dun-coloured smog still hangs over the city from the day before. As the chef serves pears in Pernod with coffee, as the silence – except for the *shush* of a light wind – fills me with ease and well-being, I think, "Why not here, in this balloon, in a moment of blessing close to the morning sun, why wouldn't someone from the city, why wouldn't someone after the fall, want to begin a love story here, free-floating, up here in the air?"

Saturday Night, 1983

THE MARINER

When I was a child, I sat on the peaked roof of the garage behind my house so that I could stare at the full moon. I don't know why I sat on the peaked roof. Perhaps I thought I'd be closer to the night sky. I just wanted to sit there and stare at the pale wafer of a moon.

I know I thought one night that the moon looked like a communion wafer.

But I didn't think that meant anything.

The moon was round and white and the wafer was round and white and that was that.

Then my mother said to me, "Do you see the man in the moon?"

And I said, "No," but after a while I said, "Yes."

"He's only there when the moon is full."

"Where's he go?"

"I don't know. He goes away and everything changes. The moon shrinks and grows horns."

My mother smiled, as if she were telling me something, telling me a truth that couldn't be spoken until I spoke it for myself.

And, of course, that's how it turned out.

I learned you can get hurt on the horns of the moon.

I learned that there are many moons: spooning moons, blue moons, harvest moons, and I've heard howls by the light of a yellow dog moon.

I've hung my hat on the horns of several half- and quarter-moons, only to watch the moon go down to the sea and my hat go out with the tide.

I've mused on those moving tides under the moon.

I've tried to put words to the tidal movement of other minds than mine, to make the moon and their voices mine, and in so doing, to give them their voices in mine.

That is, I've tried to translate.

And what is to translate?

To find a rhyme for reason and a reason for rhyme.

It is to sit, like a wise child, on a peaked roof as if it were a peak in Darien and stare at the moon.

It is to swim in the tidal movements of another man's mind, to enter into the great oceanic unconscious of his being.

Some translators dog-paddle, some do the dead man's float.

Entranced by the full pale cold light of the Pavlovi moon, of Pushkin, or the Marteau moon, or Brault's or Akhmatova or Ouellette's or Voznesenski's... I've done the backstroke.

Face up, eyes out of the water, easy to breath.

But swimming blind, swimming backwards.

Half-incompetent when it comes to the languages of other men, unable to see deadheads in the water, believing I'm going east when I've veered west, etc., etc....

What I've needed, and have been lucky enough to find, is a wise old mariner. A man in the moon, who has looked into the languages of men in a way that I can't, who has said warningly, "Shoal...dead calm...undercurrent...squall," as I've backstroked through unknown waters.

More and more as the years have passed, a face has grown into the face of the man in the moon – and strangely enough (as all such matters are meant to be strange) that face has become the face of a man born on the prairies (of all places), a greybeard given to home-brewed beer and playing the harmonica and occasional doggerel...but nonetheless, a translator who carries *Harrap's* entire in his head.

And so, I've not only been able to tell my mother that I've learned about the horns of love, but also – at that ecstatic moment when I've realized the right word has found the right word, when the gift of tongues has been given – I've seen that the round white moon and the round white wafer, though seemingly rent, can be both sole and whole, and for that I have much to thank the mariner for, my man in the moon, Ray Ellenwood, aficionado of French, professor at Atkinson College.

So, I would like to offer him this little bit of moonshine, translated from the Russian of Anna Akhmatova:

> *A chill on my helpless heart*
> *Yet I am walking on air.*
> *And I wear my left glove*
> *On my right hand.*

2017

GOOD MEN
GONE WRONG

Robert Nixon, the Ontario government house leader, is a good man. He's not a stern man but a good, solid soul: a penny saved is a penny-earned kind of man. Since no one who wins lotteries has earned anything, the lotteries offend him. He has to live with them and accept their profits, but he's ill at ease. In fact, though business is booming, he'd rather not have the increased profits of recent months. He says they offend his United Church sensibility. So, you can imagine what he'd think of companies reselling Ontario lottery tickets to eager buyers in the United States and doing so for profit. He wouldn't like it at all. He wouldn't act unfairly – since he's a good man – but if someone told him the companies were breaking the law or cheating people or destroying the integrity of the Ontario Lottery Corporation, why, he'd act…he'd want legislation – something like Bill 115 – to outlaw them. And that's what he got during the last sitting of the legislature. The only problem is, and it is a problem for a good man, Bill 115 was predicated on fudged facts or no facts at all, to say the least.

The minister responsible for Bill 115, John Eakins, stood up last July 3 and told the house that the Ontario Lottery Corporation (OLC) had "received thousands of complaints from U.S. residents." He said so as if that were a fact. Then he introduced the bill, surely intending good work, surely intending to protect the integrity of the Ontario Lottery Corporation. He got his information from the president of that corporation – Norman Morris – who, to protect that integrity, had earlier gone to the police.

On March 3, 1986, he was quoted in a police warrant as saying that Winshare Club of Canada was "conducting an illegal lottery operation" and "approximately 8,500 written enquiries were made by American residents to OLC, of which approximately 2,500 were direct complaints and enquiries [sic]." The U.S. Postal Service had already been fed this piece of news... for they warned that postal inspectors were going to move against lottery ticket "bootleggers" because "the Ontario Lottery Corporation estimates it received 8,000 complaints from U.S. citizens..." In a compendium prepared in consultation with the OLC to help formulate Bill 115, the 8,500 American enquiries – or 8,000 complaints, or the 2,500 direct complaints and enquiries – had become "several thousand complaints annually, *mostly* [italics added] from Americans."

Those "thousands of complaints" began to take on a life of their own, becoming a rolling hairball of innuendo. Since John Eakins had spoken of them in the house to justify introducing the bill, they were accepted by members of the legislature and the press. When, however, Morris appeared – in February of 1987 – before a house committee, he said, "During 1984, we received literally thousands of enquiries from U.S. residents, over 2,000 of which were complaints or enquiries." Then under cross-examination, he said, "In 1984 we had 7,815 written enquiries from U.S. residents." He was asked, "Enquiries? That is not a complaint." He replied, "Of that number, the complaints and specific enquiries about mail-order operations totalled 2,205. Of that number, 236 were clear-cut complaints in 1984. We also had another 100 telephone complaints."

The implied thousands of complaints – whether 8,000 or several thousand or 2,000 – had become 236. In fact, it has been substantiated (through a separate legal proceeding) that the OLC has only 137 documented complaints. The OLC stated, however – under oath – that it had not ever attempted to substantiate any of these alleged complaints to see if they had any legitimacy. All the other figures bandied about were never more – by the OLC's own admission in this other proceeding – than "estimates." Given the mailing by all the companies such as Winshare – some 20 million pieces annually – that is a .00069-per-cent complaint ratio. Canada Post functions with an error factor of three per cent.

This startling piece of information about non-information deterred no one. The bill was rushed through the committee and those slippery thousands stuck to the wall. It has to be said – so that good men will understand – that the government's legislation was based on… why not be kind and call it a lapse in information…? And as a result several companies and a good man, George Yemec, were maligned. Not at all what Robert Nixon had in mind, I'm sure.

What the Liberals had in mind and what has happened is passing strange. A civil servant appointed by the Conservatives came to the Liberal government with evidence of complaints and chicanery by smart boys getting rich… parasites on the public gaming purse. The NDP – their moral hackles up – would support it. Everybody would be happy, the body politic cleansed. But did the government believe all it was told? Did the minister? Did the lottery corporation and its lawyers advise him wisely? Is such a bill even constitutional? (Clayton Ruby, the well-known constitutional lawyer, says no.) Did anyone ask? (Apparently not.) And when George Yemec, representing the companies, said the bill would wipe out 1,000 jobs, why did John Eakins so jocularly say that such jobs didn't exist? Did he blush when hundreds of employees showed up at the House, offering their bodies as proof of their existence?

The bill did not receive third reading because Tory members threatened to filibuster it… Something went wrong, something the good man Robert Nixon should be embarrassed by.

But who are these companies and what do they actually do?

About ten years ago several entrepreneurs realized there was money to be made by selling Ontario ticket-purchase services to Americans. After all, Ontario lotteries are among the best in the world. U.S. lotteries tax all prizes at source and pay off the big winnings as twenty-year annuities. Canadian lotteries deduct no taxes and pay their winners immediately in full. This more than made up for the constant lower value of the Canadian dollar.

George Yemec and others began an industry that now brings $60 million American a year into Ontario. As a result, he and the others employ almost 500 people directly and generate at least 500 other jobs among suppliers of paper products, mailing services, computer services, telephone systems, and so on. The charges for ticket-purchase services are set by market competition. They charge what the wallet will bear. They rely on repeat business and commitments from contented customers who subscribe for weeks or even months at a time. The companies depend on satisfied, steady customers. This new industry expanded rapidly, and by 1984 officials of the Ontario Lottery Corporation were vowing to stamp out the sale of Ontario lottery tickets abroad. But they had no peg to hang their Corporation hat on until December 1985, when a Maine resident named Norman (Chubby) Gallagher picked the winning number in Lotto 6/49 but failed to order in time. Gallagher claimed the ticket-purchase company, Winshare Club of Canada, had cheated him out of his prize. The incident made headlines; there were images of a handful of sleazy con men operating from smoky back rooms. The Peel Regional Police, the Ontario Provincial Police, and the Ministry of Consumer and Commercial Relations investigated the incident. No charges were laid. In these foggy times you have to repeat it; no charges were laid because no one found any evidence that would justify laying them. But the damage was done. Despite the fact that, as Yemec said, "the Better Business Bureau has had a triple-A rating on us for many years," the OLC began pushing for legislation to outlaw the sale of Ontario lottery tickets outside the province. That's when the OLC produced their statistics...those 8,500 letters of complaint and enquiry from U.S. residents. The OLC told Eakins that it was against the law for the companies to send tickets and prize money across the border…when, at the very same time, the OLC itself was doing just that:

Question: "And you regularly send/receive the tickets in the mail and regularly return the cheques to the people who win through the mails?"

OLC vice-president: "Yes."

Question: "And that you know to be illegal under the United States law, do you not?"

Lottery counsel: "No, it isn't illegal."

The OLC continued sending material through the U.S. mails until this January of 1986, when the U.S. Post Office finally opined that it might, after all, be illegal.

Meanwhile, the OLC was helping to draft Bill 115: An Act to Amend the Ontario Lottery Corporation Act, forbidding the resale of tickets unless authorized by the OLC, or to sell such tickets at more than their face value. Conviction could result in a $50,000 fine, a year in jail, or both. Eakins never seems to have questioned the bill's legitimacy, not since he'd told the House that those thousands of complaints had been "from U.S. residents who sent money to unauthorized mail-order agencies and either didn't receive their tickets, didn't receive prizes they felt they were entitled to, or couldn't get information they required," but by November 19, he'd changed his tone if not his tune – his "thousands" had become "many."

The public – and the press – seemed content with the notion that a few sleazebags and scuzzballs operating in the shade were going to be put out of business. No one knew that an industry that had broken – as far as could be determined – no law was going to be eliminated, an industry that brought that $60 million (U.S.) a year into Ontario, that was responsible for some 1,000 jobs and some $300,000 in donations each year to hospitals (Credit Valley), young artists, young entrepreneurs, and literary publishing (including Exile Editions, my own small literary press), sports and service clubs. If Yemec had a fault through all this, it was his sense of decorum. He wrote letters, and letters, and letters. He didn't know how incurious good men could be. No one would talk to him. No one would come to see his three office floors of workers. He did, at last, get a letter from the minister, Mr. Eakins, saying that he would be able to make his case before a legislative committee once the bill got second reading. The reading was to take place early in December. But that was a piece of flim-flam, for on November 19, Yemec got an urgent call from his own representative at Queen's Park. There were to be no committee hearings; in a hasty afternoon double play, the Liberal government, eagerly supported by the NDP, was going to give Bill 115 second and third reading. The minister was going to ram the bill through. Yemec rushed to the office of Earl Rowe, the Tory lottery critic, who went with him to the Members' Lounge, the hallways, and the toilets. He pleaded for fairness, a chance to explain that he was not a boiler-room bozo, but a businessman who had done nothing wrong and was responsible for hundreds of jobs. Finally, twenty people were persuaded to stay in the House, enough to vote the bill into committee. Yemec now thought he'd be able to talk good sense to good men.

Little did he know, for matters fell into the hands of feisty little Floyd Laughren, the NDP member from Nickel Belt. As committee chairman, this tough socialist turned out to be a bit of a player himself, much to Yemec's dismay. There were headlines in the *Globe* and the *Star*. Laughren said he had been threatened just as hearings were about to open. Workers for the companies had called his office. They had left threatening names: "Cyanide" and "Slaughterhouse Corporation." Laughren assured the press he was not intimidated. Even the poor premier fell into line, suggesting that the OPP should investigate. Yemec's words to the committee on that same day, refuting the OLC's "facts," were lost in the headlines. When it later turned out that the caller was an eccentric twenty-year-old worker about to lose his job – whose actual name was Kenny Syinide and who wrote for Slaughter-house Concepts, a small publishing concern in Nova Scotia – no one seemed to be embarrassed.

As the committee met a second time, Yemec had come to understand too late what is necessary in the politics of good men, and that is, a good lawyer. Clayton Ruby explained to the committee that in his learned opinion Bill 115 was unconstitutional, that Yemec had violated no civil laws, and further – according to a learned opinion in the U.S. – he had violated no laws there either.

Then, there was a truly bizarre moment. Legal counsel for the Ontario Lottery Corporation, who categorically disagreed with Ruby's opinion, showed up with two U.S. postal officers. The legal counsel explained that Yemec, in business for ten years, had been breaking the "criminal" law.

Now here was pause for thought. With millions of dollars at stake, why hadn't the police ever laid a charge? Was the counsel, Kenneth Cancellara, suggesting the police were so incompetent in criminal matters that Bill 115 had to be enacted to protect the people from criminal activity? The argument satisfied Mel Swart, the NDP member for Welland-Thorold. He drew the counsel and the U.S. postal officers out, gently lobbing leading questions at them… emphasizing over and over again that this was criminal, criminal, criminal.

Swart: "Would you go so far as to say it might be possible that the government of Ontario could be guilty of infringements under the criminal code if this is permitted to continue?"

Cancellara: "This is something the government should consider but certainly I would have some concerns about being associated with an illegality."

Swart: "A straight question to Mr. Parrot [a U.S. postal officer]. In your view, the activities of the mail order companies, what they are sending into the United States, the ordering of tickets and the information, are illegal?"

Parrot: "Yes."

The U.S. postal officers plodded through their prepared texts and under examination made it clear that they knew nothing of Canadian law, were confused on American law, but were good sports.

The tone had been set by Laughren. On this final day of the committee hearing, Yemec had been given one hour. When he tried to explain that Winshare president Ernie Priess had the most to lose and should have an opportunity to speak, Laughren said: "Sorry. The committee has already made a decision about the time; so if you want to use it debating a decision the committee has already made, it is up to you."

Yemec: "I just want to go on record that Mr. Priess has been denied once more."

Laughren: "Fine."

Toward the end of the day, when F.J. Pierce, the Conservative from Rainy River, realized the committee was expected to question the U.S. officers *and* Cancellara, *and* heed the words of Eakins, the minister, in fourteen minutes, he asked: "Maybe the chairman could give us a better idea of what the timetable is. As I understand it, the discussion is going to cease at 5:30 so that the motion can be entertained. Does that mean we are going to do all these things that you just suggested in the next fourteen minutes?"

Laughren: "Absolutely."

Pierce: "That's great, Mr. Chairman, you are in control. Let us go."

Laughren: "OK, let's move it."

Nothing that Yemec had said was going to matter, not even a reading into the record of eloquent letters from employees pleading for their jobs. As Eakins said pointedly to the committee, "The issue is not free enterprise or employment, it is the integrity of the lottery system." Yemec had discovered how the system was working when he'd asked earlier on why the owner of one of the largest companies involved – Winshare – had not been asked to appear; Laughren said "the committee members…were attempting to have an hour for the Winshare Club of Canada, but Winshare is not appearing…"

When Winshare operator Ernie Priess showed up and declared that no invitation had been received, Laughren shrugged.

Finally, the vote was taken: three Liberals and three NDP for, and four Conservatives against. With just five minutes before the House was to rise for the day, the committee decision was rushed into the legislature and Robert Nixon, the government house leader, attempted to push Bill 115 through third reading. Nixon was stopped by Conservative House leader Michael Harris. The next day Earl Rowe and several other Tories warned the government that if Bill 115 was put forward, they would debate it clause by clause, even if it took all day and all night. With the legislature about to prorogue, a filibuster would have killed several pieces of legislation that all sides of the House considered more important. So, Bill 115 was shelved until the next session, set to begin April 28.

George Yemec stood in the hall outside the committee room, unshaken but with a strange smile on his face. He is a man of grooming, and is soft-spoken. "I had a marvellous moment in there," he said. "I realized that it didn't matter what I said, and I suddenly felt this terrific oppression, of good men oppressing me... and I could feel my father's voice inside me. It was exhilarating." He smiled again, being the son of a Ukrainian nationalist whose father had been in Stalin's jails, whose grandfather had been in the Czar's courts and jails, and he said: "It was extraordinary. I felt almost a serenity, it's so long since I heard my father's voice trying to explain to me how these things work." But it was not, I am sure, quite the moment of serenity that the good man Robert Nixon would have wished for, nor any of the other good men around him.

Toronto Life, 1987

Note: Third reading of any bill in the legislature is usually a formality, a foregone conclusion played out for the sake of procedure. On April 28, Parliament reconvened and the session got underway. In that same week, "Good Men Gone Wrong" appeared in *Toronto Life* magazine. Robert Nixon, the Ontario government house leader, read the article, or so I was told. Anyway, Nixon, a good man, rose on behalf of the Liberal government and withdrew Bill 115. He offered no explanation.

WOODCHIPS

(a prose poem)

Each day has a given name. It bobs up as a melodic motif, surfaces, seizes control, and haunts me.

Woodchips…

A truck went down the street, the wind sucked shavings from the load of lumber and swept dust by me on the breeze.

A shaving disappeared down a sliver of endless city space, but since then the day's been filled with fragrance. To me, sawdust is the quintessence of life. It's no surprise that I link the smell of green shavings to a particular coffin that stood in the granary loft stuffed with shavings, and we knocked out the knotholes. We played sailor boys in the loft, and grandfather's death didn't seem so sad: he shipped out, went down to who knows where – in his final cradle, scent of sawdust and shavings lingering in the air.

I love the spiral swirl of shavings. They conjure up dervish dancers, the bolero, cha-cha.

Shavings curlicue like tendrils of hops, conceit twirls on the tips of moustaches; and corkscrew piglet tails tend to cheer me up.

That's why I can work so hard. Because shavings reek of work. I remember the old master boatbuilder in our village. His cap, his room, and even his dog reeked of shavings.

Out on the walk, I'd watch his bit bore into a log, turning out swirls of wood, and old Miklāvs would say: Now, my boy, I'll set you a riddle: what d'you call a toddling ram that shits in toddling circles?

The smell of woodchips and smoked pilchard always blend in my mind. Huge mounds of woodchips in the factory fish yard, and we three boys, perched on a mound, snapping down cards, with the sea beyond the fence, screeching gulls in the blue, but below where they do the weighing, salting, and smoking, billows of smoke, and the watchman cursing like a trooper says he'll tan our hides. Mother smelled of woodchips and smoked pilchard, and so did grandmother; I suspect all great-grandmothers in the everlasting stroll around cowled in the smell of wood, smoke pilchard for old Peter.

Chipboard is all the current rage. What a violation, vicious. Imagine the chips of a tree lying down beside chips from another tree in a presswood sheet, alien pulp, cemented by synthetic glue in some press, this glue the only bond that binds, nothing else. Like a couple at cross-purposes, or friends who've calculated their affairs.

It's crystal clear, this glue's got a different formula. And moreover, this formula for inorganic matter is much simpler than mine. But sawdust is an organic compound. The formula for oaken sawdust hasn't been figured out, not yet. The birch shaving is my sister, both of us alive and organic. In tapping season, I recognize and respect this shaving as it is bored from the birch's living flesh. Let the shaving rot by the roots of its tree, moulder and melt into sap and rise up through the branches once more. As for panelling, who could love such pulp? A mechanical composite. Flat. And most disgusting – the glue – that seals it together, synthetic and inorganic. I like a wood strip that retains its inherent quality when torn from its tree. A woven basket has no glue, no nails…taper plaited to taper, all of the same tree. And that's beautiful!

I respect the tapers crackling and burning to ash as much as the pine tree itself.

As I loll about on a mound of woodchips, each chip breathes – breathes freely, confidently. It's just like delegates from trees in the general assembly of an alien world.

I suspect they'll each defend their own trees in sorting yards, sawmills, and the lumber mills of the United Tree Organization.

No one will be allowed to heave a larch into the river, drowning raftwood; the larch is our land's heaviest tree, the river will suck it down.

Ash won't be sold for firewood, not while so many pine spade and axe handles wobble and split. Sliver of chestnut defends the chestnut's right to mosaic leafing, little and large leaves interlocked, though birch and fir can't comprehend that sort of thing, meanwhile, tendrils of weeping birch are free to droop, which is why, if we listen to its slivers, this is the world's most beautiful birch tree.

Lolling on a mound of woodchips, I seem to be in a forest, thousands of trees around me, and so, if I were a sliver, just a naked little sliver, I'd still keep my character, since I'm the sliver of a great rooted tree.

A crow caws on a dead branch, but a sap bottle hangs from a supple bough. I watch men carrying saws, augers, and axes. They're going into the woods. Chips are flying. The world is full of sawn wood and sawdust. To me woodchips are the vital signs of life.

Imants Ziedonis, translated from
the Latvian, *Flowers of Ice*, 1987

JOHN MEREDITH

There was no painter in the country like John Meredith, no painter of such talent so isolated by temperament.

John Meredith was one of the Smith brothers from the small Ontario town of Fergus. The other brother was William Ronald (Smith), who was all confidence and, by nature, flamboyant. As a budding abstract expressionist, he fled Fergus as fast as he could, passed through Toronto, and after a stint in New York, at the important Sam Kootz Gallery, he declared – among his many declarations – "Andy Warhol paints Pop Art. I am Pop Art."

John Meredith (Smith), slim and boyish, stayed put, stayed home. His studio was in the cellar of the Smith house. From the beginning he was good at the mumbled phrase and good at drinking good whisky to bad effect, and smoking packs and packs of cigarettes until, not so many years later, he would die on a breathing machine.

He was also, for a period of years, a painter unlike any in this country, with no easily discernible influences, no Hoffman, no de Kooning, a touch of Clifford Still, or perhaps a very early Motherwell (if there was any way he could have seen Motherwell), none of the surrealists, no Kandinsky…and certainly not the local jack pine and ice floe huggers…

There was, in fact, something rough-hewn about his Fergus paintings. Little sense of emanating light. They were cellar paintings.

There was nothing seductive about his line or his fields of colour…brown, yellow, ochre, maroon, black, burnt umber, burnt sienna…primal in effect…the surfaces having the feel of something kneaded, only to be slashed by raw bright pigment out of the tube…most of this was oppressively dark but powerful and even, somehow, poignant.

When he came up out of his father's basement, he settled in Toronto in a studio flat on busy Yonge Street, just south of Wellesley. His neighbour was the third-stream (jazz-and-classic) composer Norm Symonds, known affectionately among friends as "Skull" Symonds. John thought that that was pretty funny, living beside a skull. He had, in fact, a hearty laugh, always amiable, even when he was drunk…which was a lot of the time…but, of course, he was short-spoken and often he made his brother, on the few occasions that they were together without rancour, seem to be big and blustery.

John soon had a show in Toronto of new paintings, moving in a new extraordinary direction.

He also fell in love.

He was too drunk to be on time for his marriage at City Hall on a Tuesday. So he got married on a Wednesday.

After a while, trying to show his wife, who was easily irritated and often angry, how angry he could be, he kicked a wall or a door (he was never clear to me about this) and broke his foot. He hobbled about on crutches, his foot in a cast. Which was hard to do when he was drunk.

But even when he was drunk, there was no meanness in him.

He wanted to like and be liked. He just didn't know how to say as much in so many words, in a way that wasn't the whine of a drunk or the moan of a man who couldn't understand why he was alone, even though he'd just been married.

After a while, the woman, no longer wanting to be his wife, went home to Switzerland.

A few years later, he married again, to a very small but big-hearted Japanese woman who worked with flowers. She spoke little or no English.

But then, he never spoke in what you would call a run of words.

He almost never said a word about his paintings, except that he thought they were good, maybe even great.

He was a painter who had his way of working.

He would sit in his paint room on Yonge Street that was spotlit or pot-lit because he worked a lot at night, and that was when I would visit him, to sit with him and drink whisky and watch him draw, hunched like a frail monk over small sheets of paper, squares, vertical oblongs, landscape oblongs…meticulously working with black ink and watercolours…

These were not drawings as mark making, these were not sketches meant to seize the fleeting moment, these were not whimsical gestures meant to defy morbidity, this was not drawing that had anything to do with the aesthetics of rubbing out the line – this was drawing as an investigation, the work of a man determined to go with his line to wherever his intuitions might lead him…this was a nurturing of that line…. much like Klee's idea of "taking a line for a walk," with a quite specific idea of how that walk, with its swiping and dragging, its feathering of the line, should end…in a completed image (sometimes overlaid by a grid) that was then blown up (as one might do for an outdoor billboard) as an acrylic painting that would be, in and of itself, a reproduction to scale – the scale sometimes enormous.

The result was not just a copying of the drawing.

The expansion of scale opened up – in the finished paintings – a turmoil of activity…arches, bent oblongs that had their own colouration, jagged and dangerous triangles that had their own colouration, wheels of colour within colours…the heavily articulated, calligraphic black lines defined the basic colour fields, jagged their way through those fields, and what colours they were, what combinations… He made most abstract expressionists in his town seem tepid, tentative…his colours being…magenta, carmine red, violet, orange, purple, yellows, lime green…a kind of hysterical colour sense that he held tightly under control so that the final effect was one of…not quite rest, but of a frenetic energy brought to heel.

These intense and provocative paintings, sometimes risking a baroque clutter, were unlike anything ever done in this country, and all were completed between 1963 and the late 1970s.

Sitting with him late at night during those years, particularly the late 1960s, trying to talk with him while he worked, I commissioned, from a lean, legal-envelope-sized drawing, one of those huge paintings. For a number of years I was surrounded in my writing room by Merediths, paintings and drawings.

In the early 1970s, after many nights of halting talk and easy drink, I tried to capture John's voice in a sequence of poems. I published these poems in *Exile* in 1973.

After he read the poems, he phoned me late at night and said, "Well, I don't know what to say…it's me, I guess…"

Then his paintings went soft, flaccid.

He'd got sick.

And he grew, during his last years, hopelessly paranoid (I remember sitting with him in a rented house long after he had left the Yonge Street flat, when he wouldn't come out of the kitchen because the Mafia – at that very moment, he said, the black car in front of the house, I could go and look, I'd see…they were after him, they had warned him on the phone). Sometimes, he'd call me on the phone after midnight to explain how frightened he was.

The after-midnight phone call became much of his social life.

Usually drunk.

Always amiable, yearning, always with a good bemused word for his wife.

Always smoking.

Watching movies on television. He liked movies.

Not really able to paint with any conviction.

Still managing a gallery show or two: but, with his breath laboured, he was too sickly to work with vigour; the few paintings he turned out were loose, the images were empty gestures, the colours oftentimes insipid, and on top of that, he hung a silly show of cartoonish nudes.

His wife still looked after him with great care and loyalty, no matter his infirmities, but she had to work at her flower shop most of the day.

How he bore the days alone, year after year, and not working, I have no idea.

Toward the end, he and his wife once again lived in a flat, and sometimes an acquaintance would drop by, but not often.

His brother, William Ronald, oldest of the Smith brothers from Fergus (flamboyant and still painting well, selling out of his studio to a steady stream of clients), died of massive heart failure in 1998. His children put his telephone in his casket, suggesting that he call home from time to time. I am sure that John's number was not a number that went with the phone.

John himself never had much to say to Bill.

Their view of each other had remained jaundiced. John continued to insist to the end that he was a painter, that he liked talking but that he didn't need to talk.

He was thinking, he said.

Through most of the 1980s and 1990s John drank, smoked incessantly, suffered from emphysema, sat amidst several bronchodilators, and finally, in 2000, died of pneumonia.

The Poems

1

when I am alone I think of dying.
I am most alone when I sleep.
I cannot sleep: sleep is submission to fear, so I paint.
everything I paint is not anything you
or anyone else can know: my paintings are the mystery iceberg
of my past, but there is a way of knowing the mystery
it is the future.
it would be nice to think of my paintings as my children,
as my roots, but it is not true.

I have no roots.
if I had children I would have roots. but,
I have no woman (all my women die, always, just before
Christmas): roots are the future and not the past.
my paintings are themselves. they are oriental.
they are me. I am not oriental.
they are me.
they are a hole in unconscious space, filled with stars and me.

2
I never dream. I walk in the streets. I don't
see anything. there are trees, trees, like piano
keys: white and black, thousands, and without leaves.
and more trees.
I don't feel guilty about anything.
I don't feel hatred of myself.
I don't feel that I love myself.
I live with myself, inside the forest of trees, where
there are no birds. there
is no sound, no sun, no one else. but warm (if
you cut the bone of my arm — the clean slice —
and count the rings, there are
thirty-nine, count the years. some men count their toes.
when the forest disappears I will disappear.
I do not want to live alone but I am alone.
I never dream). I take tranquilizers.

3
a U is a U and not a you.
an O is an O and not the zero of emptiness.
my signature is only a selection by someone else
of letters: — I draw my name out of a well of lines (you
will never find the beginning or end…):(

4

behind the leaves, my mother, of the lily of the valley, dead.
I had a premonition. one day
she was pinned against her chair by the sunlight. I am secretive.
I did not tell her;
she has since turned half-over in her grave watching
my other women. but, women
are not cruel. I have only been unlucky (the karate champion
who became a cop and threatened to arrest me for assault, but
left and put a parking ticket on some unknown overnight wind-
shield
by the side of the road); she was one of two snake
eyes I rolled (the other
two in her bed, then four, then six,
and a long sienna field and a cliff, and on the beach, between
the stoneface and the water, a cobra, poised. a man could
die there). but,
I didn't: de Kooning said – it is more important to be a man
than to be a painter. I am a painter, ruthlessly.
I am flesh and bone with a brush in my hand.
my mother, that afternoon in the sunlight, said: don't drink,
paint hard.
well, I am not perfect.

5

I do not dance, but only by myself in the dark,
the way some people sing in the shower: – I have no shower,
so I never sing.

6

I am a non-Protestant,
fantastically non-. I have three non-
Catholic Catholic friends: being sometimes

a clotheshorse-dandy, I have elected myself
as their Pope (one afternoon I opened my porch
window onto the tin roof square; there was
one pigeon, one broken deck-chair, and an opposite window
with the green shade drawn) non-practising.

7

I always keep cut fresh flowers: thick
heads of summer born in the glass-house: in the
radiator heat, the shag leaves collapse first,
like men hanged before their time.
I think I am someone living before
my time: watching – and when
I'm at last born into my time,
there'll only be time to say goodbye.

8

blood on my hands, pieces of eight
words: – bones, of the body, of chairs, are brittle (they
collapse like old-movie break-away furniture); I've
always been nostalgic for what never was (Bogart
and Lauren, seedy elegance, immortal
under the propeller fans of North Africa) – peace.
•

I walk: : 3 miles, seeing nothing: only
the getting to where I am going. I'm afraid of these
things (…fame
has become Barnum show biz; and Napoleon
is only Bailey seated on a celluloid horse on a celluloid hill
saying celluloid words…) the last which is not a word but a
beginning: Help.

Exile: A Literary Quarterly, 1973

MAVIS GALLANT

When I was asked to talk about Mavis Gallant, my heart sank.

I thought of a day some years ago when I received another call. It was from New York, an upstate city. I was asked to be the best man at a Mafia wedding. My heart sank then, too. A week later, in a cozy kitchen, Big Frankie the Mook told me how he and his brother had killed a drug courier from Toronto. "Yeah, we tied him up in bailing wire and burned him." He patted my cheek and said, smiling, "Little Frank, my nephew, he says not for me to worry, you we can trust."

A man can stand so much trust. I loved Little Frank, I liked Big Frankie. But I could tell that the Mook didn't really trust me. When he looked at me one of his eyes actually wandered. When it came back from its orbit, it was on me, hard.

I know Mavis trusts me. I think she trusts me. I hope she trusts me, after all, I like her, I admire her, but she can be disconcerting. She looks at you with those big steady brown eyes, and what do you see: all the virtues that seem to be long gone in our time – discretion, courtliness, a ready unsentimental compassion, a disdain for any sign of emotional incontinence.

So, the boys might say, "What's to worry? And anyway, she likes men." Several knowing men have told me she likes men better than women. "Everybody knows that," they say. But the last time I saw Mavis in Paris, it was a Sunday with that eggshell-white morning sunlight coming down, a late June morning, and I watched her come along rue de Seine, alone, unhurried, at her own pace, carrying freshly cut roses. I said to Claire, "Look, she's brought me roses." As far as I knew, Mavis had no idea that Claire, too, was in town, so I went toward Mavis, hand out, warmed by those brown eyes, by that easing smile, but the smile was there to deflect me. She strode by me and handed the roses to Claire. I stared at the eggshell sky. "Of course she likes men *and* women," I said to myself. "Everybody knows that."

Trust me! After all, we had confided a thing or two, from time to time, over the years in restaurants in Rome and Paris. Once, at lunch in La Coupole, talking about a woman we both knew but always saw separately, a woman given to drink, I told Mavis about a late night when our friend had slipped her hand down inside my trousers, taking hold of my backside, and Mavis said, "That's the trouble with her these days, always coming at things from the wrong side." I laughed out loud, who wouldn't, but there it was, that tone of hers, absolutely apt to the story, not quite acidic, touched by pathos. I am wary of anybody who talks or writes a prose like that. That's a prose that knows what it's doing. That's a prose that doesn't make mistakes.

It's not just the precision of her prose. Any mechanic can be precise. It's the controlled paring down to the precision that gives her her tone. Tone! That's the killer. You can't teach tone. Tone is in the bones. And it's in her bones to keep the mistakes, like the vermin, down by keeping her characters on a short leash. I sometimes think that it is this leash, her refusal to let her characters do anything she doesn't want them to do, that gives her prose that icy feel that some readers complain of, as if there had been an overnight frost and the sun at dawn had not yet burned the rime off the prose.

When I think of Mavis' tone, the pacing, her timing, one sentence on the heels of another, with a pause for effect if necessary, I often think of my mother. I think of a moment in my mother's life when her tone and her timing were so perfect, so bang-on, that she was a Mavis Gallant character.

It was an afternoon in our family room. We were all talking, my father was, of course, talking. I was trying to horn in on Morley sidewise, while a very ambitious, pretty lady of some cultural television presence was berating both of us. My mother sat in a corner of the sofa listening with a repose Mavis would have appreciated. Suddenly, the woman turned on my mother and said, "You're not liberated, you're not a liberated woman."

"Why not?" Loretto asked.

"Because you never say shit and fuck."

Mother looked at her, hesitating before the pounce.

"That is true," she said at last, "but I have done both."

Pure Gallant. The domestic moment, the blurted word, the timing, the tone, the deflection.

The deflection that shifts everything. What was in kilter is out of kilter, not wildly, not wackily. Like warped glass.

It is this matter of deflection that fascinates me in her stories.

An intended look gets deflected.

An intended hand gets deflected.

Even the extermination of the Jews of France gets deflected …as when a yellow star is found on a pavement in one of her stories and it is "moved aside like a wet leaf" by a woman's umbrella point…

Moved aside.

People carom without touching.

It's there in the carom where they don't touch that the mystery lies.

In that off-kilter moment, in that gap between words, in that silence between forgetting and remembering.

In that silence is the aloneness that haunts all her stories, her people so inexplicably alone.

(Sex is seldom a consolation, never redeeming.)

Aloneness.

Not loneliness, not sentimental self-regard.

A state of being, where each character is almost entire to himself or herself.

Almost, but then comes the carom, the deflection. The effect is sometimes quietly surreal, scary, as the silent unexpected shift is always scary. A shift into aloneness.

Once, in Rome, at the end of a happy garrulous supper –
some six or seven people at Sabatino's – as she was about to step
into a taxi, she kissed me on the cheek, saying, "Your father was
the least sensual man I've known," and before I could return the
kiss she was gone.

Deflection.

A provocation? Tease? Joke?

Sitting alone in her taxi, perhaps she herself did not know.

I did the only thing I could do. I laughed and went back into
Sabatino's for a last drink, pondering on this aloneness that is in
Mavis. But not an aloneness in her heart. I wouldn't presume to
say that I know anything about that.

No, it is an aloneness that I associate, in fact, with my father,
who was her old friend from the late 1940s and early 1950s in
Montréal when they had sometimes hung out together in a joint
called Slitkin's and Slotkin's, a place Big Frankie the Mook would
have loved.

Morley was a rare bird.

He was a writer.

That was it.

He lived close to penniless for years, freelancing on the razor's
edge. During the Depression years he had written short stories to
stay alive. He'd sold short stories, he'd supported a wife and two
children.

He was nothing more than a writer, which to him was everything. He was a writer on his own terms.

Mavis is a rare bird. She went to Paris. To be a writer. She lived
close to penniless. She suffered cuts on the razor's edge a couple
of times. She wrote stories, she sold short stories, she supported
herself.

She is nothing but a writer, which to her is everything. On her
own terms.

You blink when someone who has stood alone and kept to
the codes of courtesy and discretion, someone who has put so
much trust in herself, says, Yes, you can talk about me, I trust you.

You blink.

But then, as Frankie the Mook said, "What's to worry?" So I don't worry, or maybe I worry a little. Whatever. I know Mavis will take what I have said strictly on her own terms. If I have caused her disappointment, then I will say, "Sorry 'bout that." If she is pleased to know that her trust was well-placed, I'll say, "I owe you a kiss."

Either way, it will be okay. I have done both.

Celebration of Mavis Gallant, with Ms. Gallant in attendance,
International Festival of Authors, Toronto, 1993

LIFE PRESENTS A DISMAL ASPECT

They inhabit a countryside of the mind, these poets, that is all ice, snow, black boughs, and rain, the dragging for dead bodies in rivers, a hunkering down among dwarves under the roots of old trees. It's like their every day is the day before Groundhog Day. Bring these poets together, couple them up, and what do we get? Pale blood on the sheets:

>They had dragged for hours.
>The weather was like his body,
>Cold, though May. It rained.
>It had rained for three days.
>
>He built a shack on the shore
>learned to roast porcupine belly and
>wore the quills on his hatband.
>
>A crow flew over…
>a crow
>black as life, raucously calling
>to no one –
>
>Old ghost towns of coal
>mines & dinosaurs, the wood, petrified, the earth
>streakt white and brown…
>sea shells
>caught a thousand miles
>from the sea.

Dead trees in the seared meadows.
Dead roots bleaching in the swamps.

We have not learned
what lies north of the river
or past those hills that look like beasts.

He dug the soil in rows,
imposed himself with shovels.
His feet slid on the bank,
the currents took him;
he swirled with ice and trees in the
swollen water.
They retrieved the swamped body.

You must look for tunnels, animal
burrows or the cave in the sea
guarded by the stone man;
when you are down you will find
those who were once your friends
but they will be changed and dangerous.
Resist them, be careful
never eat their food.

The above is a kind of poem, marked by stark images and rhythms of menace harnessed to a sturdy horse. Yet, it is a selection from eight different poets, a selection of couplets and stanzas from: D.G. Jones, Earle Birney, John Newlove, Margaret Atwood, Al Purdy, Gwendolyn MacEwan, George Bowering, and Eli Mandel. Surely a poet searches for his own voice, his own tone and way of seeing things. These men and women, when you read them in an anthology such as the one at hand (*15 Canadian Poets*, edited by Gary Geddes and Phyllis Bruce – destined by Oxford for our high schools and colleges), sound like so many skinny cats sitting stricken on a fence in a desolate field.

And when the men come in from the bush to their women (always excepting Leonard Cohen and Irving Layton), they operate at a low throttle; their wildness is so earnest, their anguish so studied, their *billets doux* are so dismal. Here is "Study: The Bath," by Raymond Souster:

> *In the almost dim light*
> *of the bathroom a woman*
> *steps from white tub*
> *towel around her shoulders.*
> *Drops of water glisten*
> *on her body, slight buttocks,*
> *neck, tight belly,*
> *fall at intervals*
> *from the slightly plumed*
> *oval of crotch.*
> *Neck bent forward*
> *eyes collected*
> *her attention gathered*
> *at the ends of fingers*
> *as she removes dead skin from her nipples.*

Dead nipple-skin. Peeled!

These men and women, these poets are robust enough, but robust in fields of lichen on stones and dwarf pines. They buck the winter, and some have bucked a lover or two, but their emotions seem straitjacketed by a whittled-down white-bread Anglo-Saxon (here MacEwan, Margaret Avison, P.K. Page leap out as exceptions, capable of images that approach the mystical), a language that seems afraid of itself, as if these poets suspected that any spoken musicality – chant, incantation, let alone syncopation, let alone the gaiety of play – would be cheating, would be a way of fudging on the dour facts of daily life. Heavy, heavy sits the Arctic ice pack on their heads. Heavy, heavy as life looms up in all its dismal aspects.

As a relief of a kind, I offer the dark mocking laughter of a hymn – "Life Presents a Dismal Aspect" – taught to me by an actual north country clan, the Blanchard brothers, big men who worked nights on the rail line that crossed through a CPR bush town (sung to "What a Friend We Have in Jesus"):

> Life presents a dismal aspect,
> full of darkness and of gloom.
> Father has a strictured penis,
> Mother has a fallen womb...
>
> Sister Sue has just a-borted
> For the forty-second time.
> Brother Bill has been deported
> For a homo-sexual crime.
>
> Cousin Bette has chronic menstruation.
> Never laughs and seldom smiles.
> Oh life presents a dismal aspect,
> Cracking ice for father's piles.
>
> Amen!

And Alleluia.

The Telegram, 1970–1971

THE DISTEMPER
OF OUR TIMES:
PEARSON AND
DIEFENBAKER

Ottawa, during the years of Prime Minister Lester B. Pearson, was a wretched place: half froth, half venom, lies and sophistry, conscious simpering and proud sneers, and during election after election the people croaked their boredom, but John Diefenbaker went on frittering away the hours of the early 1960s in all his florid impotence, and the parliamentarians stood up and did their daily exercises: tickling, vociferating, hooting and panting at the prompter's signal, babbling in the backbenches, telling themselves that Lester Pearson was a worthy man, Pearson throned in the centre of his vague designs. There they were – the phlegmatic foe, Diefenbaker, and the timid friend, Pearson, their thoughts loitering behind them.

The Prince Albert politician, the prairie populist, John Diefenbaker, stood in session after session in the Commons and jabbed his forefinger at a whorl of imagined devils. In 1967, intending to attack Paul Hellyer's armed forces unification bill, he cut out from the herd of his own thoughts and ranted about the appointment of Liberal bagmen to the Senate, Paul Martin's reception in Paris, Benito Mussolini's entry into Rome, the Duke of York's marching men, the absence of a French guard of honour at Vimy Ridge memorial ceremonies, the CIA's alleged involvement in his 1963 defeat, and the Liberal press. On another day he rose and demanded to know who had dared to remove the lion and the unicorn from the official coat of arms appearing on Centennial medallions? Like so much else, he had done it to himself…Diefenbaker had removed the lion and the unicorn in 1957.

Lester Pearson had none of Diefenbaker's pretension or sense of persecution. He was not a politician overblown and stunned by power; he seemed to be a general always marching backwards, snatching humiliation from certain victory. Peter Newman, in his report on this time of distemper, tells a symptomatic tale: "John Diefenbaker had always kept in full view as a symbol of his power the red NORAD emergency telephone that connects the prime minister of Canada directly to the president of the United States. 'I can get Ike anytime,' he would boast to visitors. Pearson not only removed the instrument from his desk, but hid it so carelessly that one morning during the winter of 1964 when it rang, he could not find it. Paul Martin…was in the office at the time. The two men heard the NORAD phone buzzing, couldn't locate it and began to chase each other around the room like a pair of Keystone Kops. 'My God, Mike,' said Martin, 'do you realize this could mean war?' 'No,' Pearson puffed, 'they can't start a war if we don't answer that phone.'"

Behind these two men the House was a playground wreck. Serious policy matters became national jokes: Tory backbenchers departed the chamber when their leader rose to drone on through yet another pointless filibuster; cabinet ministers were deep in scandal and linked with criminals; a blowsy call girl, Gerda Munsinger, had her linen dredged up by a vindictive and petty prime minister; Walter Gordon, backing his nationalistic proposals with a ready promise to resign in the face of defeat, was defeated, watched the country fall under even more American economic control, and kept his place; it all seemed to be a mindless affair dragged on at the national expense of trust in the political order. By the end of Pearson's muddle of years, the House had turned into a stage for farce:

"Bill Lee (the Honourable Minister John Turner's executive assistant) was sitting in the Commons gallery one afternoon, bored rigid with the Tory filibuster. To amuse himself, he pulled out a three-foot-long telescopic ballpoint pen, which looked a little like the aerial of a walkie-talkie, and began to mutter into it, pretending to be relaying messages to Marcel Prud'homme…on the floor of the Commons, who had a similar pen of his own. The Tories, already suspicious that Lee was ghostwriting most of the government's unification speeches, came to life as soon as they spotted the by-play. Gordon Churchill promptly called a dinner-hour caucus to plan a protest against Lee's temerity in using an 'electronic spy device' to signal party strategy. That evening, just as Churchill was about to rise and make his motion, he noticed that two Conservative MPs…had also been given trick pens by Lee. He sank back, bewildered and speechless. The debate droned on into the stale night, with the three MPs and Lee jabbering like bad ten-year-olds into their pens…"

The depressing and flagging thing about Peter Newman's authoritative account of the Pearson years in *The Distemper of Our Times* is that you feel overrun and soiled by these antics, intrigues, mock heroics, failures of spirit and judgment and strength. The politicians, upon reflection, seem like so many creatures chasing their own tails in a bleary-eyed frenzy. When you read your way through the account, when Pearson and Diefenbaker are at last on the sidelines, replaced by men who seem to have at least some determination, some purpose, like Marchand, Mackasey, and Trudeau, and some common sense, like Stanfield, you can allow yourself some gallows humour: all those men should have worn crepe on their noses, their brains were dead.

With this as background, how does Peter Newman judge the figures of Diefenbaker as leader of the Opposition and Pearson as prime minister? After all, the book is about the decline of both men; Pearson from the promise of the Nobel Prize, and Diefenbaker from national high office.

It must be said about Newman that he is drawn forcefully to the idea of power. It is in terms of this fixed idea that he examines the nation and its leaders. He says of Canadians, for example, that: "Lacking a resident monarchy, Canadians have elevated their prime minister to a position of prestige as high as that found in any parliamentary democracy. The energies he releases, the standards he sets reveal the character of the country itself. He is the centre of gravity in the nation's political system and everything that happens in Ottawa swirls around his single powerful figure." This emphasis upon the office, its absolute place in the minds of the people and, therefore, its demand upon the holder, is, if not a fact, certainly necessary to Newman's political scheme. Myself, I think the office has none of the power he describes. This is a fractured country and the prime minister excites entirely different feelings in Québec, Newfoundland, and the Prairies. The office sets no standards and even a personality as powerful as Trudeau or Diefenbaker reveals only a little about the character of the country. The prime minister has high prestige in the governmental city of Ottawa, but the office is visited with more than a little indifference and much scorn throughout the rest of the country.

Now: Peter Newman continues in this book to describe John Diefenbaker as a "great" man (a virtue he does not allow Lester Pearson). With this idea of the PM's office in mind, one suddenly understands his sympathy for and attraction to the washed-up populist, the prairie preacher man with a vision, for he says: "In the end a politician's greatness must be judged as much by his impact on the country's conscience as by what he did or left undone... What would survive in the nation's folk memory would be the stride and stance of the man (Diefenbaker), the quality of his courage, the biblical cadence of his rhetoric. Here was a politician who filled the space around him; whatever ground he stood on was his."

Diefenbaker filled the office. But surely the question is: Filled it with what? That vision, and a rhetoric so hopeless in its avoidance of reality! This calls into question Newman's earlier study of Diefenbaker, *Renegade in Power: The Diefenbaker Years* (1963). Newman admired Diefenbaker for his purpose, his vision, his

faith. He condemned him as a traitor to that faith and, by implication, confessed that he was a disillusioned believer. And now,
though his great man has fallen, collapsed into embarrassing
incoherence, a touch of that belief hangs on.

But was Diefenbaker ever coherent? Did he ever have a grasp
of reality? He knew nothing about Québec but spoke about it at
length. Was there a sensible economist in the country who took
seriously his vision of a fifteen per cent shift of trade to England,
his vision of a fine green garden in the northland? These were the
articles of his faith. Diefenbaker garnered great attention and
appealed to a sloppy sense of nationalism, but once in office, his
influence and his political divisions quickly melted. With them
went the faith and his power, and on came the charge...renegade.
I see no way in which Diefenbaker can be thought of as a magisterial presence brought to mumbling and shame by inordinate
pride (there are moments when Newman's description of the collapse of the old fighter resembles an outline for King Lear). Pride
he had, but it was the inordinate failing of a comic figure:
bathetic, in that as a country boy he was suddenly catapulted
into a position of prestige and adulation, and then dumped,
tediously and awkwardly, to the laughter, scorn, and embarrass-
ment of all. It is a moving, sometimes awful story. But not one of
a great man. The flaw was not in Diefenbaker but in the juvenile
enthusiasm of his admirers. Yet Peter Newman, as astute an
observer as he is, continues to attach greatness to this figure. His
response to Diefenbaker makes one wary of his judgment of
Lester B. Pearson, who also was wanting while in office.

Pearson's whole style was antithetical to Newman's idea of the
effective exercise of power. He found the diplomat-negotiator "a
disengaged politician," a reserved man who avoided routine
encounters, a man who was not so much the agent of revolution
as its victim, a leader who regarded politics as the formidable
mission of trying to control chaos, to control "contingencies
which no doctrine could encompass and no grand design subju-
gate." In a word, though Lester Pearson had the knowledge, "he

did not use the power, and failed to supply a purpose." He had no faith. This is a reasonable observation, and when Newman adds that Pearson's acts were always a means rather than a source of action, he is on the button. But all this does not argue that Pearson failed the office as miserably as Newman would lead us to believe.

Newman points out, in some perplexity, that Pearson's accomplishments were remarkable: a new Canadian flag, important reforms in parliamentary rules, the foundations of a bilingual federal civil service, the redistribution of constituency boundaries, the beginnings of constitutional reform, a new bank act, a new labour code, the Canada Pension Plan, medicare legislation, the abolition of capital punishment for a five-year trial period…the list, as a matter of fact, goes on and on and is very impressive. It's hard to know how that bumbling, ineffectual, almost non-presence, Lester Pearson, could have accomplished so much in an office he seemed never to fill with any dignity. But there it is. So, what is one to say?

If nothing else, Diefenbaker, so full of country biblical rhetoric, had a sense of his own election; the moving finger had come to a halt on his forehead. But Pearson was a different kind of Calvinist. He had been born to the manse but he was dominated, so it seems, by a peculiar Presbyterian failure of faith. He was certainly convinced of his superior talents and ability, and he certainly saw himself as one of the anointed among a people damned to everlasting political and social chaos, but what seems to have been missing in him was any passionate sense of having been divinely chosen. He was always full of wry self-deprecation, as if God had set him apart…had saved him from death in the First World War, had saved him at university where he deserved to fail, had marked him, for no apparent good reason, for prestige and position…but even so, that old finger had never seemed to touch him with fervour, with passion. It was almost as if he felt his election was tentative; that if he committed one crude or bold act, the finger of faith would be withdrawn, and he would join all the lost souls, and so there was an unwillingness on his part to risk failure, an unwillingness to revolt against the established order of things. Ironically, he seems to have believed that the placing of other men in positions of power – as his ministers – would give them a sense not only of having been chosen, but also the sense of discretion and moderation that he treasured. Once in office, they would distinguish themselves from the chaos. Of course, his ministers failed him, but as Pearson had learned to forgive and, so it seems, expect his own blunders, he could not offer his ministers less. The lack of conviction, the chaos, swept in upon him. The office was a shambles but his record of legislation was not. Somehow, perhaps because he never lifted his eye above the immediate object at hand, he got legislation through. He got crucified doing it, but he did it. Such a method is difficult to admire and almost impossible to believe in, yet it was fruitful in the long run, certainly in comparison to that of the faith healer, John Diefenbaker.

Of even greater irony is the fact that this man, lacking a visible ideology, gave the country not only a flag and an anthem while managing to accommodate the violent days of quiet revolution in Québec, but he brought into his ministry two French Canadians of a calibre seldom seen in this country before: Marchand and Trudeau. And so I agree with Peter Newman that Pearson gave no sense of authority to his office, excited no sense of mission among the people and, frankly, left me feeling from a distance that he was not much more than a superior, sometimes hard-nosed civil servant. But the legislative record is there. As I have none of Newman's mystical feelings about the office of power, I cannot agree that Pearson must be presented as only a fumbling shallow legalistic figure.

The Telegram, 1968

JOHN TURNER: THE NIGHT THE BALLOONS WOULD NOT COME DOWN

Nighttime in Chinatown. Red and yellow neon signs swung in the strong wind. Pierre Elliott Trudeau was coming to an exhibition at the Toronto Art Gallery, paintings by the abstract expressionist William Ronald, of all the prime ministers. Board chairmen and sensibly dressed women clustered around the glass doors and the inner courtyard. They wanted to be close to Trudeau. "These people have been cursing him for years," the beautiful, long-legged publisher Louise Dennys said, "and look at them, gone gaga." Trudeau slipped through the crowd with that curious deferential shyness that makes him seem so self-possessed.

The paintings were "portraits" of our sixteen leaders since Confederation, men who had seized their own destinies by the scruff of the neck, all a little strange: one, who had dressed up in a bearskin and played the concertina; others, who had boiled to death in a bathtub, or sought mystical signs in shaving cream, chewed tobacco, quoted Latin, kept a mistress, or slid down banisters and pirouetted behind a queen. When Trudeau stood in the gallery courtyard to speak, he said it was the sense of wonder in the paintings that fascinated him, the astonishment at life itself.

"There is a difference," he said, resting on the podium, "between the craftsman on his trapeze and the artist who expresses life as he sees it. An artist must always be wary of trying to please, and, in that he is like some politicians, he must never seek to please." The crowd laughed and clapped, and Trudeau, musing as if he were among friends, smiled. "The bad politician," he said, "like the bad artist, seeks to please."

"Well," a local critic whispered, "I do not intend to be lectured on the nature of art by a politician." Though heavily set, he took three fluttery steps to the right.

"The artist who sees for himself," Trudeau went on, "opens up the treasure of innerness, the pleasures of wonderment, and such a man is basically a loner, but although he's a loner, if he has genius, he creates something universal…"

The crowd applauded. His security men cleared a path as he shook hands and moved slowly, talking, often touched on the arm by women, his head bobbing back, still – after all these years – a little wondering at the way women girlishly crowded around him. "That," my father said, "may be the most remarkable little off-the-cuff speech ever given by a politician in this country." The critic, seeing that the security men had suddenly changed direction, leapt nimbly around a pillar, trying to place himself in the prime minister's path.

In 1968, Trudeau and his close friends liked to say, "The style is the man himself."

In 1984, John Turner and his close friends like to say, "What you see is what you get."

Separate truths.

At the 1968 Liberal leadership convention, Trudeau, with his cropped hair and skin tight on the skull, looked like an anchorite waiting for the call. Unsullied, he stood apart, toying with a rose and, while he waited, he stripped the petals from the rose. He was a man with a special sense of himself, self-contained, seeking power with a seeming diffidence. Men who wait for the call share an arrogance, a fear of failure, and sometimes an almost maniacal conviction that their names are written in the halls of

heaven. This does not make these men mean or dangerous…
(unless, of course, they are overlooked…for after all, John Stuart
Mill – a gentle man – agreed to stand for election but only on the
condition that he make no pledge of party loyalty and give only
one election speech).

John Turner, with his own special sense of himself, is as enigmatic as Trudeau: his open face contains a coldness that gives an
edge to all ease; a man of the broad corporate world, he keeps to
narrow, rigid rituals; industrious and dominating, he seems inse-
cure and not to have done enough; on display at table twenty-
three at Winston's, he has no anecdotal life; a private man, he
has no secret life; a devout man, he seems to have no spiritual
concerns. For nine years he has appeared on the periphery of
the centre as the *eminence en attendant,* waiting for the political call.

Now that the call has come and he is out on the hustings, it is
hard to know what touches him deeply, what seizes his mind. His
tone is corporate decisiveness but by being so decisive about
everything – he is decisive about nothing. Distinctions blur. "He
bites all his words," a woman said to me. "How could I be comfortable with a man who told me to take off my clothes and but-
ter my toast in exactly the same tone?" This flatness has caused a
failed connection with crowds. It is why, as an unloved winner, he
could end up an unwanted loser.

*If you want to see the human brute at his professional worst, at
his most cunning, most self-deluding, then look to his elected
representatives.*
—Justice Oliver Wendell Holmes

The Coliseum, Ottawa. In the drab basement beneath the hall,
delegates bickered and talked about deals and dealerships,
women's rights, and travelling expenses, and sat back and read
the newspapers. A man with a loose, wet lower lip, wearing

Turner and Chrétien buttons on his lapels, said, "I'm here in the spirit of compromise."

"Between those two?"

"Right."

"But what about Munro, Roberts…?"

"Them," he said, straightening his lapels. "They're like all the other languages in the country, they're there but they don't count, not officially. They just make speeches." He turned toward the hollow sound of cheering and squealing coming from a tunnel. Cameramen switched on their lights. Mark MacGuigan, the Minister of Justice, marched out of the shadows, grinning. No one got up, but the cameras were there, so he spun around to his supporters – among them, a dusky man wearing a turban and a squad of girls. He shook their hands, the fixed smile of feckless amiability and fierce ambition on his face.

"Any deals?" a reporter cried.

"No deals," MacGuigan said.

"Who will you support?"

"I haven't initiated any discussions."

(I'd been told, however, that on Tuesday he had offered to pull out, but the Turner people had suggested it was too late, certain they had most of his votes on a second ballot.) MacGuigan went to the podium and told the delegates he had been going to conventions since he was a child. Many did not look up from their newspapers. "Has he made a deal?" I asked a man in the Turner camp.

"Never mind him. I'll tell you who's done a deal. MacEachen."

"MacEachen! You're kidding."

"Nope, it's for sure."

"But Turner carved up his budget."

"So?"

"So what about Trudeau?"

"He'll be all right."

"That's not what I mean."

"Look, MacEachen's the shrewdest sonofabitch in the country."

"But it'll be absolutely shameless."

"There's no place for shame in politics."

"There's no place for pride, either."

"You know how you get pride?" he said, taking me by the arm. "You learn how to swallow, how to swallow hard."

The next night, MacGuigan – with his cheering section on the floor led by a testy woman on crutches who had one leg – delivered a flat, inane speech. His important supporter was Lawrence Decore – the popular mayor of Edmonton. As Minister of Justice, MacGuigan had appointed Decore's brother to the bench (the brother had quit in eight months, bored by the job), but on Saturday, more than an hour before the first ballot results were announced, Decore – with shameless haste – plunked himself down in the Turner section. The vote: MacGuigan, a paltry 135.

"How do you feel about this kind of humiliation?" he was asked. He walked to Turner, kissed the hand of Turner's wife, sat down, and hovered at Turner's shoulder, that feckless smile on his ashen face. At the end of the day, as the losing candidates were introduced to cheers, MacGuigan was booed. He smiled wanly and later said, "I think I came out of it with greatly enhanced stature."

Hell no, let's go first-class, let's take the whole bag, on y va en *Cadillac.*

—Pierre Trudeau

Trudeau sat between his sons and his sister as the crowd celebrated his years in office, his coming and his going. It has always been that way since he showed up in the pinstriped world of politics wearing sandals and a turtleneck sweater: split feelings that were reflected in his face and on his signs at the 1968 convention – one side in empty outline; the other, half-hidden in shadow. A man of inexplicable contradictions who caused contradictions.

But now it was time for nostalgia and praise and home movies in the huge hall: film clips, moments of incredible grace, charm, quick contempt, a man so measured and so mercurial, so much a star and so star-struck. As the crowd chanted *Trudeau, Trudeau,* I remembered the night in 1968, the night of the LaFontaine Park riot, when snarling people chanted *Trudeau aux poteaux* (Trudeau to the gallows), and then bottle throwers broke through the barricades and, while other politicians fled, Trudeau – brushing his bodyguards aside – shook his fist, alone…

Rich Little, the comic impersonator, a man symbolic of another generation, a man with everyone's voice but his own, reminded the crowd of what a cuckoo's nest parliament had been in the early 1960s, and then Paul Anka, with his bobbed nose and margarine manner, sang some homemade words about Trudeau to the melody of "My Way":

> *For what is a land,*
> *What has it got,*
> *If no such men – then not a lot?*
> *For sixteen years, you will admit,*
> *He stood up tall against the split,*
> *Stuck out his neck*
> *And told Lévesque,*
> *The answer's No Way.*

I remembered another sunlit day in 1968, out on the west Coast, when a small-town grandmother named Vera Johnson belted out the same kind of lyrics as she stood beside Trudeau on a crude wooden platform:

> *Pierre Trudeau, he comes from Québec,*
> *But doesn't think like René Lévesque;*
> *He wants to see our Canada grow*
> *Both strong and free, Pierre Trudeau.*

And then, the cluster of townspeople, reading from mimeographed sheets, sang along:

> *Pierre Trudeau, il parle bien,*
> *Avec candeur, sans peur de rien;*
> *'Les Liberaux; ils son idiots;'*
> *Il dit cela, Pierre Trudeau.*

Trudeau had given the woman an unsure, awkward kiss, but now – in the convention hall – as the farewell songs, sentiment and jokes went on, he smiled easily, stoic about betrayals and enemies.

Then, Marc Lalonde – looking for all the world like a maître d' in his white dinner jacket – ushered him on stage to a huge, happy ovation. He had no notes, no podium, no prop other than the rose in his lapel.

"I relived tonight," he said, "in a certain sense, my whole youth…" He made that strange nervous motion of his, a halting handshake into the empty air, and quoted lines of poetry:

> *I wandered off with my hands in my pockets,*
> *I went out under the sky and stared,*
> *And oh, I dreamed of such splendid love…*

"Yes, we have dreamed of splendid love," he said, "for ourselves, for our country. We rebuilt this country, the country we carry within ourselves…" (And there he touched the core of what seemed to separate Trudeau and Turner: one exploring "the treasure of innerness" – "the country we carry within ourselves," trying out of aloneness to create something universal…and the other, "I think that what you see is what you get… I tend to think that the shortest distance between two points is a straight line. I'm reputed to be one of the best organizers of time in the country. I listen… I consult widely before making my decision, and once it's made I stick with it."

Trudeau, sometimes with a real flash of feeling, went through a litany of Liberal accomplishments: bilingualism, the constitution, the extraordinary extension of offshore limits, and then – having spoken lucidly and without text for almost an hour – he suddenly cried, "Oh la la...such splendid loves I dreamed of... hopes are high, our faith in the people is great, our courage is strong, and our dreams for this beautiful country will never die."

There was sustained applause from those who loved him, those who admired him, and those glad to be rid of him. When there was a lull, he suddenly called out a line from the "Marseillaise," calling for his children: "*Allons, enfants de la patrie...*come on, kids." The children doffed their house painter's caps, and Trudeau waved and waved and went off stage, and then came back for one moment of whimsical and wonderful childishness, mocking his own emotion and the seriousness inherent in such a celebration, pirouetting for the last time, as he had done behind the back of a queen.

As a gift, the Party gave him a painting by Charles Pachter – a painting of the flag ravelled in the wind, and the flag is seen in a background that is all black, and even the frame is black. A red and white flag in the colours of the resurrection, set in the funereal air.

Late evening. The convention, after the rally and closing in on the midnight hour, clearly had no sensual feel: the delegates were either determined and busy or listless and bored. Even at the Jean Chrétien tent downtown, where Rompin' Ronnie Hawkins cranked up his rock-and-roll band in the late night hours, there was very little drunkenness and little dancing. People were having a good, sensible time. At the Turner tent, it was hard to feel good in the dimly lit park; someone had put canary-yellow Johnny-on-the-Spots beside the bandstand. There was a scent of urine on the midnight wind.

Friday: In the hospitality tents outside the Civic Centre, there were long folding tables, plastic horns, and hats stacked on tubular chairs, listless delegates drinking beer, a pickup band playing "Flip Flop and Fly" for a lone old man seated on a folding chair who was doing a crossword puzzle. Mitchell Sharp, his letterbox mouth open a little, paused and looked at the sky – a single bird, a single cloud. Small girls carrying red and yellow Turner signs let him pass. One trilled and trilled on a red plastic whistle. A Whelan delegate, a man wearing knuckleduster rings and smelling of Old Spice, said, "See all them Turner signs in big yellow letters…? Yellow's the colour of caution and piss. That guy's got so he wears two sets of shorts."

Soft clouds gathered and then shifted apart in the strong wind. Three Munro delegates were speaking into walkie-talkies, staring straight ahead like submarine commanders in the movies. "I wonder about Turner," a senator said to me. "I wonder about a man who eats the same meal all the time at the same table, the same sliced tomatoes…" At the back of the lot there was a decorative but decaying old building, with carved swagging over the windows and hammered metal on the walls. Two signs read:

SHEEP AND SWINE
CANDIDATE CITY

Beside an ice cream truck, a stoop-shouldered man said to a blond woman, "Who tinks de accent of Chrétien is too bad for de people should watch out for demselves… It could be de Jews are next, and you are German, de German people could be next…" A Turner delegate thrust a sign into her hands. She stepped back, shaking her head. "No, no, I'm committed."

"Who to?"

"Never mind. And your man," she said angrily, "he should be committed, for lying."

She crossed her arms. An elderly woman wearing a cardigan covered with buttons was talking intently into a walkie-talkie.

"Who do you think she's talking to?"

"How do I know?"

"Maybe she's talking to nobody."

Friday night: the key speeches. Turner was in the tunnel under the stands. Children shouldered long aluminium crosses, the attached banners furled in their arms. As Turner stood open-mouthed beside his wife, beaming, a cop said, "What a set of clackers." Turner flicked his tongue, flicked it again, jabbed it around the inside of his upper lip. Instead of jogging at the starting blocks, he was giving his mouth a workout, a nervous loosening up. Peabody, an ebullient black photographer, suddenly called out, "Hey, Mr. T... Keep the faith." Turner broke toward him, stumbling, wide-eyed, a false start. One of his floor-men screamed into a walkie-talkie, "Wait, wait...wait as long as we can, let them wonder when he's coming."

Then he strode into the crowd, crossing the floor in a flow of banners to the platform. "He's got to be great," one of his advisers said to me. "We're stalled, if it goes to three ballots we could lose. He hasn't made the connection, he hasn't hit the right chord." Turner, with that abrupt clipping of words that would be abrasive if he weren't smiling, looked up to Trudeau. "I have said on several occasions, but never face to face to him, that he has surely been the most remarkable Canadian of his generation." Turner bobbed his head eagerly. The crowd cheered. Slumped in his seat, Trudeau nodded. "Holy Christ, if he can say that he can say anything," a Chrétien supporter said. "I can't believe it." Then Turner, despite his declared determination to cut the deficit, spoke like a reformer, saying economic recovery would never be at the expense of the aged, the sick, the poor, or the unemployed. He endorsed the family farm, women, compassion, clean air and clean water. Crisp and convincing, he left the stage to roaring approval, and a tall, bony woman with peculiar fat hands, as if her fingers were swollen with water, said: "Now that's a prime minister."

"He's a winner. You're looking at a winner," another woman cried.

For a party led by an intellectual for sixteen years, the absolute lack of concern for any cultural subject by any candidate on any occasion was appalling. There wasn't even any lip service to the arts. Spiritually, the party seemed to be sucking wind, with all the candidates saying Liberals were different because they had compassion. The middle-class crowd was full of approval, co-opting compassion in the same way middle-class women have co-opted the problems of the poor, such as abortion.

Jean Chrétien mounted the stage to the music from *Chariots of Fire* – the melody of the runner's loneliness. He looked drawn, dour, grey-faced, the raw man who wore his heart on his sleeve. *"Il est un dure qui ne rait pas mal à une mouche,"* one man said. But he hurt himself: *le petit tough*, trying to be prime ministerial, read from a prepared speech, tying himself to the rhythms of calculated incantation. It was a mistake: the emotion was truncated, trussed. Still, men and women wept. He pounded the air with his fist and mocked Mulroney and mocked Turner – a man who felt betrayed by his confrères, Ouellet, Joyal, and Bégin – but every time he rose on the reverberation from the crowd, he looked down and returned to his text. At last, he cried, *"Vive le Canada."* Marc Lalonde, with the smile of a benevolent man bemused by the foibles of ambition, clapped warmly. Chrétien strode across the stage, punching the air to the roar of affection. He criss-crossed back and forth and held the empty stage. It was a farewell, not a promise of support.

As the hall cleared, the woman with the swollen hands sat in the shadows of the tunnel under the stands, little beads of sweat on her upper lip. "Oh, I think Turner's got it," she said, "I think we've got it."

"Are you going downtown to the tents?"

"Oh no," she said. "No, I've got delegates to talk to." She stood up and licked her lip. "My goodness, I'm sweating," she said and took a small linen handkerchief from the breast pocket of her blouse. We walked up the stairs, and there was Peter Newman talking to Jerry Grafstein, and Jim Coutts talking to Senator Peter Stollery. "You know what?" she said. "You know what I like? This is power. It's clean, you never have to worry about sex."

Liberalism is essentially revolutionary. Facts must yield to ideas. Peaceably and patiently if possible. Violently if not.
—Lord Acton

There was a hollow at the core of the convention. Chrétien had promised emotional authenticity and Turner had argued that the plausible was possible: in other words, neither had said much of anything. Turner, after ten years of gearing up, had conducted a confused, sometimes amateurish campaign; his workers were often inept (at one point, financial contributors couldn't find out where to send their money), and for all their tactical energy they had no strategy other than wanting to win. That was the word. Turner was a winner. That was why Ouellet and Bégin abandoned Chrétien (once Turner had won, they were startled by Chrétien's fierce animosity): winning was the game, and at times the convention had the feel of a television game show. But a winner of what, other than the power game? A rich, political power-player, such as Torontonian Hal Jackman, had put the matter perfectly: born a Tory, he can't imagine being anything else, but it's not a matter, he says, of embracing a set of ideals – "I don't have an ideology. I could have been a Liberal; but if you play the game you have to be on one of the teams." It is a team exercise, such as the war games he says he plays in his house with his valuable collection of antique toy soldiers. Turner, too, is a wealthy man good at games. He knows how to play and, in terms of tactical positions, he might just as easily be a Conservative. But the question remains: Is it better to know where to go and not know how, or how to go and not know where?

Trudeau was responsible for something splendid. It is now taken for granted, in even the smallest towns across the country, that a child would be better off if he or she could speak and think in two tongues. It is the gift of a larger world, and at the convention, lost in the placard-waving, speeches, and shouting, two women stood side by side on a small stand, attentive to the speakers, making signs for the deaf and dumb, signs televised in simultaneous translation: bilingualism had broken the sound barrier, and while Chrétien spoke, as his rhetoric became florid, the motions of the two women took on the temper of the two cultures, one angular and excited, the other sensual and sweeping, sending a gift of silent tongues, a gift appropriately silent in all the noise of hollow notes.

> *I don't want to be prime minister in the future, in 1984.*
> —John Turner, at the 1968 Convention

Supporters on the floor were melancholy about Chrétien's speech. Patrick Lavelle, one of his advisers, was frank: "It didn't work, I don't think we have the numbers." He had spoken to MacEachen but could not get a commitment. "I knew then," he said later, "that the fix was in." Delegates stood in small clusters, bent toward each other in moments of quiet persuasion. Senator Keith Davey, with that amiable hunch that comes to a big man who's held too many canapés, said, "I think it'll be one ballot, he'll win on the first ballot... Hello, hello, how are you..."

As voting was about to begin, there was a sudden rush around MacEachen. The old bachelor, self-enclosed, shrewd – a public servant now serving himself – moved across the floor and up the stairs to Turner's seats. Someone had slapped a Turner sticker to his back between the shoulder blades, but the blow was felt in the

Chrétien camp. "*Maintenant,*" a man wearing a Chrétien scarf knotted at his throat said, "*tous les poissons sont dans le met. Le problème avec les mets c'est qu'ils ramassent aussi les vieux pneus et les capotes usagées.*" (To get the thrust of this insult, one should know that the full slang phrase for "safe" – as in prophylactic – is "*capote anglaise.*") MacEachen was embraced by Turner. The Turner supporters were ecstatic. Others were astonished: "What a scummy thing to do," a man said. As the delegates lined up to vote, I discovered, running into advisers and old pros, that if they asked me a question and I gave them a meditative pause, they were gone when I looked up. They wanted only quick answers, and answers that agreed with the data they already had.

The night before, Jerry Goodis, working on computer projections, had told me the Turner vote would be 1,600: it was announced at 1,592 – he was short by eight. It was over: the elected delegates had played their part, but a majority of ex-officio delegates – all those ex-privy councillors and riding presidents and Liberals who had once run and lost, the shufflers of back-room dreams – had given Turner an edge, and though Turner had said he would shed the old power players, he had come in from the cold as the old network candidate, advised by all those faceless backroom names – Bill Lee, Swift, Hunter, and Payne – better connected than Lester Pearson ever had been.

Iona Campagnolo asked the prime minister and all the candidates to come on stage. Trudeau stood by the backdrop, disdainful and a little defensive, his strange, shy grin sealing into a waxen mask. He and the losers shook hands. He held Chrétien by both arms. Then MacGuigan, as he mounted the stage, was booed. They waited but there was no Turner. "What kind of Party is this?" Campagnolo asked. "We've got a new leader and we can't find him." Men were talking into their walkie-talkies. Turner bounded onto the stage, double-clutching Chrétien's hand, smiling like a beamish boy, getting into line beside his wife and children. Campagnolo was candid. She introduced Chrétien as "the man who fought so hard and came second –

but first in our hearts." Turner blinked, and then he broke from the line for the front of the stage. Someone handed him a maroon folder.

Chrétien looked heart-weary. The crowd chanted his name, and with a pained longing, as if it could never end this way, he pumped his arms and punched the air and talked a long time, for a loser. It was touching.

> Worshipped and loved, their favourite visitor,
> a country uncle with sunflower seeds in his pockets,
> full of wonderful moods, tricks, imitative talk,
> he is their idol, like themselves, not handsome,
> not of the Grande Allée! Un Homme!
> Intimate, informal, he makes bear's compliments
> to the ladies; is gallant and grins;
> goes for the balloon, his opposition, with pins;
> jokes also on himself, speaks of himself
> in the third person, slings slang, and winks with folklore; and
> he knows that he has them…
>
> —A.M. Klein

But only in the heart, not in the ballot box, and at last he raised his arms for Turner and stepped back from the podium, and then he clapped for Turner. All the candidates were clapping. Turner stood there clapping for himself. Turner strode to the podium and opened the maroon folder. If ever a moment in a man's life called for spontaneity, this was it, but he had a prepared speech. The moment of triumph suddenly took on the tone of an after-dinner talk. The speech was all wrong, full of plain old planks and tactical bric-a-brac. He was running for election when he had just been elected…pitching to the people who had just given him their hopes, and their failures. He bit his words, he looked firm, decisive, but what he was saying, unless you were a by-election junkie, was irrelevant to the scene. Women shuffled, exchanged buttons, whispered, talked out loud. Though there was excitement, even zeal in Turner's eyes, the bonding moment was lost...

No storyteller believes what Turner has said about himself: that what you see is what you get. It's a slogan about the surface of things, and no man, particularly a man so primed for a place in history, believes he is only superficial – only a man who gets things done, a glorified form of fetching and carrying. Yet, Turner has said that his hero is C.D. Howe. Of all people! C.D. Howe. (Just after World War II, Paul Martin asked my father to come to Ottawa and talk to the men in government who were making policy. "Oh," my father said, "that'll be C.D. Howe and..."

"Heavens no," Martin growled, "Howe doesn't get involved in the philosophy of the Party, he isn't much interested, he's a practical man...")

If Trudeau was disappointing and puzzling, it is because – as a man who knew where he wanted to go – he quickly gave himself over to practical men, gadget minds, onstream advisers, jargon-junkies, flow-chart collegiality...and, not surprisingly, within a short while, he was reduced to a losing slogan: The Land Is Strong. How he ended up in the hands of sloganeers is the riddle at the heart of his enigma.

This is the interesting thing about watching a winner, whether in a lottery or politics: the question is, what will the winner do, what will he become after he crosses the finish line? John Turner is a winner. He can savour that, and he has the power to match his big cigar. But will he limit himself to an energetic zeal that always leaves a question: Zeal about what? Will he learn that a speech to a crowd is like a private word to a person, something singular, and the singularity is what touches the heart? And because anything is possible for him now, will he discover an innerness, a country that he carries around inside himself, and will he – out of his own aloneness – try to reach out and create something universal, or will he only seek to please? As he stood there, at the fullest moment of his political life, life drained out of the crowd. The words fell flat. Turner went to Trudeau and then to Chrétien. They were wearing their game smiles, and then Chrétien caught Trudeau's eye, a bond between them. Turner went to the left, lost; his family was on the right. The man was now conjecture: maybe his friends didn't know where he would go, what he would do? Maybe he didn't know? It would all be a discovery. The music blared. There were huge clear sacks tied to the ceiling, filled with coloured balloons, signals of buoyancy and dreams. Two men pulled the strings but the strings broke. Someone cheered. Chrétien punched the air, Turner clapped a man on the shoulder. The sacks shuddered. People stood and stared, waiting, waiting for the air to fill with balloons, but the balloons would not come down to join the party.

Toronto Life, 1984

HE SAT DOWN
AND THE MIRROR
STOOD UP

Q: What is the poet's loneliness?
A: A circus act not included in the program.
—PAUL CELAN

Cahoun's Hollow, Wellfleet, Cape Cod: alone on the shore he is easing a black kite up into the wind, up toward the dunes, a hundred feet into the wind away from the water, standing with his back to the water, playing the long drift-line of a dream high on the wind, pulling his dream inland from over the water

the kite falling like a black bird into the water

(can a kite be an omen?)

(of?)

"You have to play the line," he says, "it's all in your fingertips, you've got your hand on the wind."

In the Saltbox house on Long Pond Road: William Ronald the painter is settled in his chair. The ocean breeze through the open windows: smell of the burning dune sand...sweet pine. Salt. He has been alone for hours listening to *Bitches Brew* by Miles Davis and to Boston talk shows, an undertone of black-baiting in the Beantown brogue...endless nattering arguments, endless bickering: the higher mathematics of $3 + 2$ always = an opinion of 6, or 4, or *how's your ass, knucklehead*?

"How're your friends?" I ask.

337

"Who?"

"Them motormouths in Boston with the cleft minds."

He laughs and turns off the radio.

"They're fine. Boston hates Muhammad Ali. How're you?"

"Good. I was talking to Edmund Wilson last night. He told me a funny story, about the woman who owns the old hotel down our road here, you know, Eulalia Price. Her carpenter husband had got the place half-built, the hotel part, but then they had to put him away. He kept taking guests on private tours of the third floor, up to the unfinished wing, and he kept opening doors for them, gone out into nowhere…"

"Eu-lalia," Bill says.

"Eu-lalia."

We chant her name, like *the bells, bells, bells…* Eu-lalia…

Then, a moment's silence, a pause in the clock.

He is sitting very straight, his sore legs and feet in silver cowboy boots (tendonitis) set squarely to the floor. His cane, which is my dead grandfather Tom's hawthorn walking stick, lies on the floor at his feet.

"Why don't we go and see Wilson tomorrow?"

"Okay."

"But I can't go through that routine of yours again," I tell him, "like when you went with me to meet Marie-Claire Blais."

"What's that?"

"The original quick-change artist…"

That day he'd dressed in green slacks and a green Cardin shirt, and then he'd changed, to the same shirt and white slacks, and then the white slacks and a vermillion shirt, and at last, all white, even his boots. He was ready, he was in his stride with his cane. We'd gone down a back road between pine trees on a hot summer afternoon to have a glass of cranberry juice mixed with soda water and gin.

Marie-Claire and her friend, Mary Meigs, were waiting, Marie-Claire in her usual loose sweater over her large breasts (in the fall, it'll be loose sweater over loose sweater), with her long dark hair blown a little awry by the wind. Pale, pale cheeks. Dark eyeliner. Small and delicate. Mary, a Philadelphia-born painter, moneyed, once a WAC during the war, elegant in her leanness, she did most of the talking, about ink drawings she was working on for Marie-Claire's new novel, *Pauline Archange.* Bill said little. He was polite but didn't pay much attention to Mary Meigs. He sat with his arms folded across his chest, self-enclosed, protective, all in white, his bush of black hair, his eyes hidden behind black glasses. We did not stay long and Bill walked ahead as we left, and Marie-Claire said, "So quiet, that man, and his black mane of hair, like a sullen horse, a little nervous."

As we drove home Bill said, "She's shy, isn't she? And that Mary Meigs, too." I agreed, yes they were shy, or perhaps with Mary it was more a matter of reserve. "But," I said, "she has her own shrewd eye."

"I wonder what painters she likes, I should have asked her."

"She told me once. Blake!"

"I dunno. Maybe because Blake's men are all so androgynous, like angels."

"No angel lives here."

⤖✦⤕

I remind Bill of that afternoon. He laughs at himself as the little Ojibwa girl who is his adopted daughter comes into the room and demands, "Me paint, Pop."

"Only old horses are called Paint," he says but she is too young to understand and get the joke, so she stares at him, shaking her head. She scoops his coloured pens up from the table and marches out of the room. Bill calls out, "Diana…" She comes back and sticks out her tongue. He claps his hands. "What a performer…"

339

"Runs in the family," I say.

"I hope so."

"What the hell were you after, that day with Marie-Claire, ending up all in white?"

"Nothing…"

"Like you were a big white Minoan bull…"

"I feel better if my colours are in the same space as my mind. Look, it's part of my nature. I perform on the canvas. That's more or less the way I go through life. When you perform you take an awful lot of chances. Some people don't want to take chances. Play it close to the vest, carve out a safe career. Never gamble. I love ludicrous relationships in all walks of life and in all situations, even in my paintings. I like to have something bother you. That's when I'm at my best. I don't make many rules but every painting should have some sore point. When I get too pretty I start to worry, I'm not getting there. I should be a little uglier than I am, a little more brutal. I do these performances…like with that girl who used to be a stripper, when she was dancing nude around me, and that jazz/rock band out in Brandon, of all places, to be able to do that, well, it's myself enjoying, not exactly a death wish, but, Jesus, if I make a mistake, the whole thing turns to mud on the canvas. But those paintings have an electricity about them I can't equal any other way. I even once hired a band to come up to my studio. But it didn't work. I wasn't loose, not like when I was there in Brandon that day at twenty-four below zero in a white suit on the stage doing a painting in front of three hundred hostile people. It was beautiful. I like paradoxes. I like pressure. I like strippers."

⤛✦⤜

An early evening at Edmund Wilson's Wellfleet House: Wilson has been swimming in the ocean. He is wearing a black paisley dressing gown, but when he sees Bill, he goes back to his rooms to change into a broadcloth shirt and slacks. Elena, his wife, entirely at ease, remains in her black bathing suit, crossing her long legs on the couch and pointing to the paintings on the walls.

"Well, we'll see how good you are, Mr. Ronald. Who painted these?"

He is taken aback by her directness. He doesn't really look at the paintings and shrugs. When she says that one is a Tschelishev that she retreived from a waste-basket in an editorial office in New York years ago, he looks and says, "I don't really know his work but it's very good." Elena is pleased. Edmund has returned and is pouring drinks.

He begins the conversation by setting up his usual game of double solitaire on the coffee table before him, methodically laying out the cards, talking about Marie-Claire and how her recent work is not, he thinks, so good because she's unable to criticize her own work. Bill, who's been sitting as if locked into his chair, breaks in, "The really fine talent is always able to edit his own work. The critic is the last one capable of telling an artist what should be left out. The writer's no different from the painter. The painter has to know when to quit, when to erase, and only the great painter can be sure when that moment is. Everyone else is wrong."

It is a curious moment, these two together; Wilson, so famous and feared for his blunt abruptness, yet personally so amiable in his self-assuredness, a little awkwardly so, with a saving, almost boyish air of reluctance, as if he must say what he thinks and cannot allow himself to care if someone is offended, but always hoping they will not be offended. Wilson warms to him immediately.

"But isn't this whole Pop Art thing," Wilson says, "a concoction...aren't they all just capitalizing on a sudden burst of bad taste?"

"I don't think so. They're astonished at their success. Besides, most of them aren't doing that well, it's the buggers who run the galleries who're doing well..."

"Yes, yes, I know something of the French situation and the French dealers are impossible, ruthless… I saw recently a Matisse show. He seems to me not of the first order, a colourist."

"I don't agree at all."

"And Picasso's much overrated. I'll tell you a story about that. Years ago Mary McCarthy, my wife then, wanted me to buy the Picasso of the bull and the little girl and Clement Greenburg recommended she not buy it, that I'd get tired of it…"

"Greenburg, I knew him. He'd call Picasso a windbag…"

"A windbag? What in the world would he mean by that? Anyway, I told her to buy it and within a month I was tired of it and gave it away."

"Maybe Greenburg put the idea into your head?"

Wilson is startled. It has never, I think, occurred to him that anyone has ever put anything into his head. He snorts with a little laughter and says, "No…no…quite certain."

Two small girls in white nightdresses appear at the door, Wilson's grandchildren. He says, reaching out for our hands, "Well… I've got to read the girls their bedtime stories…goodbye…finish your drinks…goodbye."

We go home. Bill is persuaded that a man who has never drawn or painted cannot say anything important about painting, but it was, he allows, a pleasant visit.

The next day I meet Bill on the way to the beach. I tell him I've been talking to Wilson.

"Oh yeah, what'd he have to say?"

"He asked me what kind of painter you were."

"Yeah."

"Abstract expressionism," I said.

"What'd he say?"

"'Too bad,' he said. Otherwise, he thought you were a very nice man."

The Sheik of Araby: Where we are just south of Provincetown, the dunes roll and dip down to the ocean. The sand is rippled by the wind, creamy-white in the sun at noon. There are small clusters of crippled pine trees, hunchbacked by the winter winds, and scrub grass, but then, along one high ridge the pines are tall and thick. We are on horseback and have to duck our heads to get through these trees. The horses are sweating in the heat. Bill uses his crop to keep his horse going. He is erect in the saddle, big in the saddle, almost barrel-chested and over six feet and two hundred-and-twenty-some pounds. He cares about how he rides his horse. It's a discipline he's worked hard at, that he takes pleasure in…a little dressage on the dunes, keeping his horse at the right pace in the soft sand, the reins just taut enough so that the horse's head is up into the salt-wind, and then, abruptly, as he yells out, "You know, this is where Rudolph Valentino rode," we drop down into a gully, a wide bowl of sand, the sides higher than our heads, which we slowly climb back up, to a long flat run by the water, a brilliant cerulean blue, and the sun playing as if there were sequins on the water. Before we break into a gallop, I look back…our trails hook like question marks back into the trees.

After the run we walk the horses.

There is a constant tension (a contradiction?) in Bill…his love of and respect for discipline, and his love of the ludicrous: he so often seems to be at odds with himself – sometimes ingrown and reticent, whining and selfish, and then, wide open, vulnerable, generous to a fault, and courteous…that generosity…not only his giving away of things, but the ready giving of his time and his compassion to men and women who he knows will only disappoint him. It's as if his generosity is rooted in a despair: aware that there is so little generosity on the loose in his world, it's as if he feels he has to prove generosity's existence…by giving, and giving again…expecting nothing in return; and yet he insists on dominating most situations…he insists on having his presence, his style, his regalia not only felt but applauded…yet with a straight face he is able to agonize over having no money as he stands dressed in that regalia, a satin-lined cape and a beautifully hand-stitched brocade suit and shirt with lace cuffs; the cape, of course, signals a radical departure from the norm, yet he is openly contemptuous of know-nothing radicals and mind wreckers…but not because he is conservative (which to a large degree he is), but because he wants these others to be more dangerous, more expert, more disciplined in their destructiveness so that he can be astonished, so that he can be forced to respect them enough to really despise them; and so, the end effect of all this carrying on is that he often seems to have no centre even while he tenaciously holds on to his centre, his family, to his wife (even if estranged), his children, and the few women with whom he has been especially intimate…he gathers all of these around him, as if it were possible to patiently organize not only his emotions but the emotions of others; which is another way of saying that while he is outrageously public and always on stage, he is enormously private – with only two or three close friends (the Toronto island priest he had loved – whose chapel he had painted – now dead, a thorn of loss), supportive friends whom he seldom sees, which causes him pain. About pain he knows: he lives in constant physical pain, sometimes unable to walk, strung out on painkillers or ecstasy, work, rage, pinballing his pills inside his brain, uppers, downers… MAINTAIN A STANDARD OF CHAOS, he says, and has the pleasure of contemplating the organization of his own distress.

We are talking about his image of himself. "You see," he says, "image is much more important than ego, the image you have of yourself, but it's not show business. It's a completely surrealistic Pop Art thing. When I perform on television it's more Pop Art than Andy Warhol because I really get out there and do the thing and come out of that box into your living room, for real, except I'm not for real, I'm Ronald all dressed up as Ronald, pure Pop Art. When I was with Duchamp he said, 'Pop Art just popped up,' and so I tell you there I am, the theatre of myself…"

"But the problem, I mean, you've got this theatrical sense of yourself…"

"Yeah…"

"And you're able to maintain a certain intellectual and comic distance from yourself, which is maybe a French kind of wisdom."

"That's right."

"And people in your own country don't go in for that."

"WASPs and people who have their heads in WASP space, that's the country's sore spot."

"And they get sore because they see your theatrical thing as showboating…they're embarrassed for you, embarrassed for themselves…"

"Which is why there's no Canadian Fellini."

⤞✦⤝

His face is white, his speech slurred. There are three Cokes at his feet, half full. "It's just been endless bullshit," he cries. He's listening to the blues on the old record player:

> *I'm a stranger here*
> *Just blowed in your town…*

He is sick. Shaking. Cornered by uncertainties. His blood pressure falling…he's doped up on pills, and yesterday he collapsed, falling head first into one of his wet canvases. Nose into the paint. Now he's hysterical about his hysteria. His recent paintings…so many of them…he's been working all through the nights…4x6, 5x7, 6x9…the images have opened up, come apart since his *Homage to Angela Davis,* they are more daring…words and letters, graffiti-like hieroglyphics…parts of a name, his own, those he loves…or hates, having a curious effect…they suggest broken rituals or fractured mysteries…painful yet joyous… I can only put it this way: with a narrative painter like Kurelek, wanting to have each painting tell a story, so didactic, so almost boastful about the success of his faith…his agony before God is authentic, but his paintings that attempt joy, they appear contrived, cartoonish, unfelt, all earnest hokum – a joy that is joyless, a mirthless laughter.

But in some of Ronald's recent paintings, there is the agony inherent in celebration, there is celebration in the pain…this tension, painted within fields of whiteness that are new for him, approaches, for me, a religious experience…(Marteau, the alchemist French poet, says white is the colour of God's mind)… I don't know what Bill would think of this. I've never spoken to him about such experience (except for one painting, *Resurrection,* which hangs in his hall at home, which he refuses to sell to me – a painting that exudes, as I've told him, a Botticelli tomb-light, whatever that image may convey to anyone but me).

As he calms down, we sit and talk about writing, his writing: "It's peculiar, even Beckett I find a performer, and yet he's the most unperformer performer – stillness, silence, sucks up all the light – I see Beckett on the stage all the bloody time. The greatest play I've ever seen was Bert Lahr and E.G. Marshall in New York in *Waiting for Godot,* and I never laughed so hard in my life. It was the goddamndest thing I'd ever seen and I could see Beckett all over the stage. Anyway…my point is, I don't want to be, I never will be a writer, but I continue to write. I don't want to learn anything about writing, yet it puts me at ease with myself, I can see things much more clearly. You know, there're a lot of advantages to getting older… It's beautiful to get to feel that you have a tradition within yourself to draw upon, a vocabulary of neuroticisms that are you. This is me. I'd like you to read it. On one hand, it's contrived surrealism, but on the other, it's a complete confession…"

There is a wide crack in the wall. That's what they get for overbreeding. Passion leaves its mark. A perishing corner. No. Don't blow the light out. Let me tell you a story:

Rosie stood in front of the mirror. Rosie was standing but the mirror sat down. She started to cry and I said, "Rosie, come here." But she began to put on more clothes. She kept dressing. She put on everything she owned. Now she wore three wool coats and a fur cap. Numerous stockings. My shoes over her own.

"Rosie," I said, "you look stunning."

"I've never been so goddamn hot in my life," said Rosie.

She was winding her way through the bedding.

By the third day I saw that the bed sheet around her neck was wet. She was crying.

"What the hell," I kept saying. "What's gotten into Rosie?"

I went for a doctor.

When we came back she was lying in a heap in the living room, dead, smothered in the dining room drapes. The doctor took off both his overcoats, knelt down.

He began to get dressed in her clothes, to put on her coats, her dresses, her shoes, her bed sheets. He put on everything.

Then he sat down and the mirror stood up. There was Rosie, naked in the mirror.

We sit saying nothing. Quietude? (Why that word?)

"I wouldn't know what to say," I tell him.

"I don't want you to say anything. I just wanted you to read it, to know that story."

Young children are coming back along Long Pond Road, back from the beach, their radio blaring rock. The curtains lift with the wind.

"I think maybe it's going to rain," Bill says. "Remember that summer here when it rained all month? There's been nothing like it on the Cape…when all we did, all of us, was paint and draw and paint and draw…such rains, and I've been coming here for years."

"You know, I was thinking about you yesterday when we were down at the beach, you flying your kite. Here we are by the water. But you never go in the water."

"I can't swim."

"But you even stand with your back to the water."

"I never noticed. I guess that may be true, but the wind's always coming up off the water, over the dunes. For the kites."

"Peculiar, I mean, coming all the way down here like we do to get a little peace, the water, but you…"

"I don't have that much peace here… The kite, yes, the way it rides the wind, a kind of freedom for a few moments, sometimes if you're lucky, for an hour. I've had that kite up there for hours on a good day… Like I told you, you're playing the wind, it's all there, in your fingertips."

1994

HOGG ON 96 POINT 6

On a plain chair
he sat down drunk with one eye
open trying to locate the lame
pallbearer who had been dogging him

as he sat down
on a plain chair and crossed
a short right leg over what felt like his long left
trying to find ground zero, his toes

as he sat down
on a plain chair, mirthless no matter
how loud he laughed, and cried,
"Don't worry 'bout the horse being blind,"

as he sat down
on a plain chair, "just load up the wagon,"
feeling as empty from the dry heaves
as the hat he held on to in his lap

as he sat down
on a plain chair and teetering saw that he
could no longer see and fell asleep before
hitting the floor, still wary, with one eye open.

Note: In Russia, when ordering cheap vodka, many ask for a bottle of 96 point 6, indicating proof.

Hogg, The Seven Last Words, 2001

SOUTH AFRICA: THEY PLENNY ZIMS

South Africa is the homeland of exile.
—BREYTEN BREYTENBACH

MIDNIGHT MIRROR

Johannesburg: – a bar on Twist Street, it is clean and quiet and dimly lit, it is dispiriting, the barstools are chained to the floor. A pert young white woman, a federal worker for Internal Affairs, was reticent and tight-lipped. I told her I knew that she also worked for the police. She stared at me, unblinking. I was reading the work of a poet who was in prison. "That poet," she said softly, "is a traitor." He was the Afrikaner Breyten Breytenbach: *Looking into South Africa is like looking into the mirror at midnight when you have pulled a face and a train blew its whistle and your image stayed there, fixed for all eternity. A horrible face, but your own.*

PRIME CUTS

Old Potash Road. Private Road. Private meant no whites without a permit. I didn't have a permit. Cinder-block houses, rows and rows of block houses, corrugated asbestos roofs. There were utility poles along the road, a cross-hatch of overhead wiring, and street lamps, but there were almost no lines from the poles into the houses, no lights at night, no wiring in the rooms, no electric kettles, toasters, stoves, brooms, clocks, heaters – none of the equipment of domestic comfort, only cold tap plumbing, cardboard ceilings, mud floors, no pavement, one movie house, no hotels, no bars, desultory garbage collection, outhouse shacks set over septic holes in the backyard...mushroom brown soot, the sour smell of coal stoves and nicotine-coloured smoke clouding the sun, clouding the old man, a coal merchant, who was butchering his horse, a worn-out nag that had dropped dead in the street a half-hour earlier. Women lined up to buy the meat-cuts. Pariah dogs darted among the women, baring their teeth, aroused by the blood.

TSOTSI TOWN

One million black men, women, and children cordoned off eighteen miles from Jo-burg – half officially unknown, half officially nowhere – "one half of nothing is nothing except we are everywhere" – sometimes living sixteen to a block house in Soweto, a name that isn't a name, only a euphonious abbreviation for South Western Townships – something some clerk thought up in 1963 to describe eighty-five square kilometres, the fifth largest city south of the Sahara, a brutal bunkhouse for black Johannesburg workers (it is the nature of this mining city that everything is abbreviated – Soweto, Jo-burg, life in a passbook, a dwarfed childhood, marriages stunted, broken). If you are a black man you have, on average, forty years to live, bleary years of desperate nights, and one jump-up-for-Jesus joy-day on Sunday in one of the hundreds of holyroller churches, or – bearing ripe tribal scars on his cheek – a man who sits outside his small square block house on a kitchen chair and hoses down the mud, the hose like a lariat around his feet, a man who gets drunk on laurentina in a shebeen, more afraid of night-prowling *tokoloshe* than the cops with their shotguns, and maybe he's already done a deal with a *skollie* for a finger of *sol* and he's ended up with a shebeen queen – her *makapulan* tight around her hips – which his wife won't complain about because she is afraid of divorce because divorced women have almost no rights and can be sent off into nowhere,

to one of the reserves, unless, of course, she has an inside track
to a *sangoma,* a witch doctor, who might give her a potion that
she will give to her husband so that nowhere will bloom inside
his head...but then, he might not ease off into a lethargic
nowhere, he might go totally crazy instead of the half crazy that
he already is:

> *if I pour petrol on a white child's face*
> *and give flames the taste of his flesh*
> *it won't be a new thing*
> *I wonder how I will feel when his eyes pop*
> *and when my nostrils sip the smell of his flesh*
> *and his scream touches my heart*
> *I wonder if I will be able to sleep...*

Three murders a day in Soweto (as of this month, July 1976,
South Africa averages 5,700 killings each year, and through the
past two decades 220,000 men have borne approximately
1,220,000 strokes of the lash; over five years in the 1960s, 508 persons were executed, almost half the world's reported total of
1,033).

They plenny zims, you watch out for zims...

Every day a quarter of a million people travel in and out of
Soweto to work in Jo-burg, by car, taxi, bicycle – listening to
American race records from the 1950s, rhythm and blues, Amos
Milbourn singing, "One Scotch, one bourbon, one beer..." but
most of them are sardined into the long brown trains that leave
every two and a half minutes at peak periods, travellers terror-
ized every payday by *tsotsis,* the young thugs who stab workers
in the back with sharpened bicycle spokes, hitting directly into
the heart or above the coccyx: instant paralysis, the dead
jammed upright in the crowded cars doing the dead man's stare
through windows at a pale blue sky the colour of airmail writing paper whose bottom end has been dipped in mud, the sun
sitting in the mud...

Lord come to our help Yourself, send not your Son, for this is not the time for children.
                    —Field Marshal Jan Christiaan Smuts

Least protected under apartheid are the women: houses allocated under the Bantu (Urban Areas) Consolidation Act are awarded to men who qualify under Section 10 (1), (a) or (b), that is, those born in Jo-burg, those who have lived in Soweto for fifteen years or have been employed by one baas for ten years. If a husband dies and a widow is left with minor children, and qualifies for the allotted house, she still has to find a man to marry her who is also qualified under Section 10 (1), (a) or (b). If not, she and her children are out, removed, or go into hiding, scavenging for a corner to lie down in.

A zim is a Xhosa cannibal creature from the Transkei. He is born with one bitter leg and one sweet leg. At birth, the parents pounce on the child and eat the infant's sweet leg. Nonetheless, the grown zim moves with great speed, a cannibal running on one bitter leg.

VULTURE CULTURE
A sprawling city dump of sloping slag hills, slag from the gold mines, a luminous honey-cyanide sheen in the sunlight, crusted and polished by the wind and rain, steep angles, perfect curves to the slag hills – and children run up and down the slag and some pop through the crust in the sunlight and disappear into the soft dust and suffocate, and others come down off the hills and rest inside cannibalized cars that are littered all over the surrounding fields, cars stripped clean, eruptions of shaped steel. Nothing goes to waste and everything is waste – the logic of Vulture Culture: Breytenbach said, "Apartheid is the White man's night, the darkness which blurs his consciousness and his conscience. What one doesn't see doesn't exist... In the name of the state – the daughter of apartheid – all dissidence is suppressed. White workers, too,

sacrifice their legitimate claims on behalf of apartheid. It is fascist. Totalitarian. Apartheid is alienation. Schizophrenic – a mental disease marked by disconnection between thoughts, feelings and actions. It is paranoiac. Apartheid is White culture. The culture of the Whites is Saint Albino – this condition of whiteness, the prison of laws and taboos – negates all political consciousness. Apartheid justifies itself in the name of Western civilization, in the name of the Afrikaans culture."

UMGUNDLOVU

Natal, 1837: – Francis Owen, a proper parson of the English Church Missionary Society, settled with his wife to the east of the Drakensberg mountains, land controlled by the Zulu king, Dingaan, whose large royal town – fenced around by thornbush – was called Umgundlovu…a palace enclosure of

four cattle kraals

an enormous harem

and several thousand beehive huts.

Dingaan had a cheerful demeanour and a grisly sense of humour. He allowed the Reverend Owen and his placid practical wife to live close to Umgundlovu…along with a white maid and an interpreter, in a home that faced a hill called kwaMatiwane. It was a killing hill. A stained hill. Men were killed there every morning, hammered to death with clubs. Or impaled. After watching these executions, Owen was allowed to preach to the king from the king's palace floor – through his interpreter – a floor that seemed to be made of marble, but it was a floor made of mud and dung polished to a high sheen with increases of blood and fat. In the evening, to ease his mind, Owen drank tea as he faced the darkened hill.

One day, Owen wrote in his diary that a party of Boers (*boer* is *farmer* in Afrikaanse) led by a man called Piet Retief had come on horseback to Umgundlovu. Retief, hoping to negotiate passage and land rights with Dingaan, kept a diary, too, in the form of letters that he sent sporadically to the *Grahamstown Journal.* Both diarists found Dingaan impressive: tall, very black, entirely hairless (his whole body was shaved every day), enormously fat, oiled, and indolent. Surrounded by three hundred concubines but no known children, he looked a sedentary hump of black suet but actually was nimble on his feet, a dancer and composer of songs,

a designer of harem dresses

a choreographer...

and – to Owen's astonishment – a natural watercolourist who worked eagerly with Owen's badger hair brushes and paints...

and no matter what he did, or where – he was accompanied at all times

by a dancing dog, Makwilana.

Piet Retief, the white warrior, was received by the king and 2,000 black warriors dressed in kilts of cattails, beads, feather headdresses, and ox-hair anklets – and as they drummed on ox-hide shields, two hundred hornless oxen moved in twos and threes in a slow march, followed by the king's elite oxen – "all alike, red with white backs" – numbering 2,424.

Dingaan asked his court advisers if Retief was a wizard, a ghost who had come in the guise of a man. They said, Yes. *They plenny zims.* Among the Zulus, wizards were put to death, so the cunningly cheerful Dingaan staged another massive parade of cattle, featuring a herd of pure white beasts. The Boers – jaunty and brash – were given great cups of sorghum beer and milk until Dingaan cried, "*Babulalebai abathakathi* – kill the wizards." The Boers were swarmed and bound with leather thongs and dragged to kwaMatiwane, where their skulls were cracked open. Then they were gutted. Retief's heart and liver were presented to Dingaan. His dog danced. The rest of the Boers were spitted by the anus on impaling stakes. Through his telescope, the Reverend Owen watched as the king's several impi divisions set out for Retief's Boer camp in the north, running full tilt through a day and night into a valley the Boers now call Weenen – Weeping –

355

where they hacked 530 men, women and children to death, disembowelling the men.

Then Dingaan, for no known reason, faltered, stewing in his own suet. His troops fell back.

Days passed.

He painted. Pale watercolours.

PELINDABA

Esther, the young woman worker for Internal Affairs and the police, was listening to *boerersiele* polkas on the car radio. She said she liked country polkas, "And I used to like playing the piano, I was a little girl on the farm. But not anymore. I used to like our blacks, too, but not anymore..."

"Why?"

"No one talks about how they kill us but also they kill each other."

"You trusted them?"

"Yes. As long as we could look after them like children."

"And now?"

"Everything is ruined once we spare the rod."

We turned toward Pelindaba. She was taking me there, and I didn't know why or how she had got permission to do so. The name means: *This is not talked about* – and what is not talked about is an enormous concrete bunker, a research reactor, SAFARI-1 – the site, so it is believed in intelligence circles, of a developing nuclear military capacity – with links to the Israelis (these links are not talked about either, though it is known that there are Israeli advisers in the country...a relationship marked by its own dark ironies, in that Rafael Eitan, chief of the Israeli Defense Force, not so long ago told students in Tel Aviv that blacks in South Africa "want to gain control over the white minority just like the Arabs here want to gain control over us. And we, too, like the white minority in South Africa, must act to prevent them from taking us over...") – links certainly not to be talked about in the Pelindaba bunker with a young man wearing a white smock who has been appointed to walk on point with me down long halls that lead to a nowhere of other long halls, encouraging me to look into more all-white rooms that show me more of nothing: "One of the things built for this reactor," he said, "is a cryogenic loop that we use for radiation damage studies… and there's a most-up-to-date neutron diffractometer…and within another complex, in another part of the building, if you're interested in physics, a 3 MV Van de Graaf accelerator, it produces a pulsed neutron beam…" We shook hands and he said, as if musing to himself, "…enriched uranium, fuel you see…" and turned away.

Babulalebai abathakathi…

TOADS

The black man had one arm. He had tucked a loaf of bread and a small carpet for sleeping under this arm. He was rolling a cigarette with his one hand: "Oll the time I tink mebbe they get free from us, maar mos white mens they tink how to be baas inne blek land but make sure the bleks be nobuddy. They plenny of police and they part of us here and white mens dere. The wishbone don break for nobuddy, we bleks en white mens locked hold like toads. Toads thet are fucking en canno let go, sometimes die that way, so Soweto like a toad locked on white mens for death, mebbe. You go see the blek toad inne Soweto, maar you need a permit to go inne Soweto."

"I've been."

"The police mens know?"

"No."

"You tink they don know, maar you mos fool, they know."

TREKKING

South Africa is, on the whole, arid and infertile soil. In the early nineteenth century, many Boers, feeling contained and constrained by English settlers, set out on a singular "errand into the wilderness" – leaving the Cape to drive their cattle beasts northeast through wilderness grass so acidic the herds would not eat; migrating antelope moving ahead of these cattle drained the water holes; locusts moving ahead of the antelope in dense clouds died in the millions but more swarms of locusts laid down bridges of their dead so that other swarms could cross the rivers. The Boers followed the locusts, trekking farther and farther away from anyone who was English, encroaching on Zulu country.

Then, in 1814, after the Napoleonic Wars, the British formally occupied the Cape and got directly into the craw of those Boers who were still settled there. The English hired blacks as policemen and they set up a circuit court to hear Hottentot slave complaints against Boer masters, and they brought out Scottish Calvinist ministers to pastor in Dutch Reformed Calvinist Churches. In 1815, the Cape Boers balked and then rebelled and five were hanged in front of their families, and when the gallows broke they were hanged again. *The crowds stood on one bitter leg.* Then, in 1838, the English abolished slavery and this led to the ruin of Cape Boer farms, and the Boers rose up in righteousness and mounted their ox-drawn wagons and crossed what is now the Orange River – going east and north – pursued – as they interpreted it through the celestial Words of the Book – by the Pharaoh (the English) while being harassed by the Canaanites (the blacks) as they trekked in wagon lines toward what would be called Blood River.

BLOOD RIVER

Under the command of Andries Pretorius, the Boers – knowing they had to defend themselves from Dingaan's troops – moved to the leeside of the Ncome River and gathered their ox-wagons into a circle – making a *laager*, sixty-four wagons lashed together in a circle with ropes and trek-chains – and they waited for Dingaan's impi divisions, confident because they had a protective hippo pool in the Ncome River to the right and a deep donga, or gully, behind. "Then Andries Pretorius…fought the memorable battle of Blood River on December 16, 1838." Five hundred Boers faced a Zulu impi army of 10,000 to 15,000 led by their two great generals, Ndlela and Dambuza. When the battle was over, the Boers had shot and killed 3,000 warriors. Inside their *laager*, they had not lost a man.

Furujani took up a pail of paraffin, he also took him some fire en he poured the paraffin, so that the hair of the zim was on fire.

The zim said, "Demazana, Demazana, what that always going Zzzzzzzzz?"

Demazana said, "Grandfather, it just clouds gathering up."

The zim ate, en he ate. Its hair go on burning, maar the girl say only that the clouds were gathering up, while the hair of the zim still burning, close up to the skin of the zim's head.

The zim said, "Demazana, what that always going Zzzzzzzzz?"

Demazana said, "Grandfather, eat the meat, eat, the clouds are just gathering up."

The zim felt its head-skin burning. It ran, it ran on its bitter leg en threw itself inne marsh, its backside stuck inne air, its head disappearing inne marsh.

KITCHENER'S CAMPS

With their broad-brimmed hats and poke bonnets the Boers – emboldened by their God and as dour as their cattle – were quite different from the Cape English, who were civil servants, tradesmen, shopkeepers, and mining speculators. All of whom expected to be protected by a caste of professional soldiers. The self-reliant Boers, on the other hand, thought that they had managed to disappear north into open spaces where they would be able to commune with the dream they had of themselves as the Chosen of their God. They herded sheep and cattle in a "free republic," the Transvaal, but unbeknownst to them, and tragically, too, for them, the republic contained the richest gold deposit in the world, the Rand. The British Governor, Sir Alfred Milner, told the Boers that the British – with the Cape nicely under their protection – were not only coming to get the gold; he promised to "humiliate them and crush them into dust." The stiff-necked Boers chose to fight the foremost imperial power in the world.

It was 1899. The Boers were sharpshooters and acrobatic horsemen. They "could leap in the saddle," they knew how to flank and out-flank, to cut, slash, and run. They formed into commandos. The British sent 450,000 disciplined troops to the field via the Cape – the largest army ever assembled. The Afrikaner commandos were never able to muster more than 40,000. The English generals and their officers waged an incompetent, plodding campaign. The commandos slashed at their flanks and disappeared, taking to the high hills. So it went: "Say, colonel," inquired an American observer as he watched an English battalion prepare for another frontal assault on another impregnable hill, "isn't there a way around that hill?" No, he was told, there was not. Attack had its own principles. Frustrated English officers retired at the end of day to railroad restaurant cars, where they sang the words that would become Edward Elgar's Opus 5, No. 1 – *fieramente* – :

> *Hear the whizz of the shot as it flies,*
> *Hear the rush of the shell in the skies,*
> *Hear the bayonet's dash, ringing bright,*
> *See the flash of the steel as they fight,*
> *Hear the conqueror's shout*
> *As the foe's put to rout…!*
> *Ah!*
> *Glory or death, for true hearts and brave,*
> *Honour in life, or rest in a grave.*

For the English, the war soon entailed too many graves, too little honour. The bibulous general, Sir Redvers Buller – belittled as "Sir Reverse" by his troops because he had led them across the river Tugola, and then he had led them back, surrendering the riverbank – only to retake it, and then surrender it – the bibulous man was retired from the field. His soldiers sang:

Cheer up, Buller my lad,
Don't say die.
You've done your best for England,
And England won't forget.
Cheer up, Buller my lad,
You're not dead yet.

Lord Kitchener, affectionately and admiringly known as Butcher Kitchener, was summoned from Khartoum. A methodical man (as the Romans had been methodical when they had decided to commit a year to the building of a containing wall through and over the Dead Sea's desert hills that surrounded Masada so that no Jewish Zealots could ever escape from their hilltop fortress), he had the English army engineers build a block house every thousand yards along the railroad lines, for miles and miles, and then Kitchener installed 8,000 soldiers and telephones in the houses and ordered 9,000 more soldiers to march in a beaters line that was fifty-four miles long – slowly beating
      beating
         beating
            the bush for Boers...at twenty miles a day. Kitchener scornfully complained that the Boers lacked the dignity of the Sudanese, "who had stood up to a fair fight" so that they could be shot down like dogs. With no standing-still target to shoot at, Kitchener, in consternation, scorched the earth, setting crops on fire, blowing up 40,000 farm houses, killing 200,000 sheep, boxing up in open railroad cars the homeless Boer women and children, locking them up in forty-four camps behind barbed wire, leaving them to starve, to grow sick, to die.

Kitchener's contribution to military tactics, the concentration camp, caused the Boer guerrilla fighters to surrender.

Once a peace had been struck, thousands of Boer farms lay burnt and blackened to their roots, thousands of Boer sheep and cattle lay in the open fields as hoops and cradles of charred but slowly whitening bone. Only 5,000 Boer men had died on the field, but 26,370 women and children had died in English concentration camps. The Boer farm economy had been ruined, their independent republics were lost, and a huge class of bitter Afrikaans-speaking whites had been created. The Blood River covenant had been sealed. Rudyard Kipling predicted the rise of Afrikaner nationalism: "We put them into a position to uphold and expand their primitive lust for racial domination." They became – in the land of *zims* – the white tribe, the *laager*, the embattled Children of God, burdened by the Pharaoh and circled round by the children of Ham. Everything in their lives became a sign of their apartness – their colour, their language, their faith, their customs, their dress – all took on sacred Afrikaner significance, their signs of tribal singularity.

JE ME SOUVIENS
F.A. van Jaarsveld, the Boer historian, amiable and bookish, had a good steady eye and a forthright easy tone.

"Is it fair," I asked, "to say that Afrikaner nationalism, from its inception, was essentially defensive?"

"Well, in the Cape, the English – through their language laws – made English the only official language and, like French Canadians, Cape Afrikaners felt very strongly about Dutch as their language. They felt themselves threatened on the cultural front…"

"The books behind you in your bookcase, the shelves, are packed with Afrikaner history – with one exception: books about the Québécois. What's the bond?"

"Well, if an Afrikaner looks out into the world for a people that shares his experience, he finally finds the French Canadians

...their sense of defeat and oppression at the hands of the English, the conviction that they are a tribe alone on an alien continent that nonetheless is theirs...after all, they are Catholics among Protestants, determined to not only survive but to preserve their faith, their language, and their culture. You can find among French-Canadian soldiers who fought for the British in the Boer War a curious, but to me, a totally understandable confusion, because they came to feel that they had fought on the wrong side, that they were more akin to us than they were to the British..."[1]

THE RED FLAG

Poor white Afrikaners, driven off the platteland by war and soil erosion, trekked into the cities, taking the unskilled jobs that they despised, jobs fit only for kaffirs. Seldom able to scrawl more than their names, and certainly unable to write in English, they were the scorned and laughed at: "big fellows with long limbs, awkward gestures, constrained deportment, physiognomies that bespoke nothing." Then, at the end of the First World War, the

---

[1] The Québécois novelist Jacques Ferron, hearing of van Jaarsveld's comments, alerted me to a forgotten post-Boer War novel, *Allie*, by a Joseph Lallier, a Québécois who had fought as a Canadian soldier for the British. The hero of his novel, one Olivier Reillal, decided during the war that the Boers, like the French in Canada, were victims of an imperial power. *"Ce n'était pas le Canada qui était en guerre! Et cette guerre ne pouvait être faite que dans un but de conquete! C'étaient les mines d'or et de diamants que convoitaient les Anglais. J'avais encore frais a la memoire le recit des incendies commandes par eux, le long du Saint-Laurent, lors de la conquête du Canada... Quelle affaire avait un Canadien-Français à aller répeter la-bas ces exploits sanguinaires et incendiaires don't l'histoire coloniale d'Albion est remplie?"... "Était-ce que je voyais, dans cette armée de Boers, luttant bravement pour conserver leur liberté, les regiments de Montcalm, succombant dans un combat heroique sur les Plaines d'Abraham, on the brapeau français dut se replier pour repasser les mers, disant adieu pour toujours au grand fleuve..."* Olivier returns to French Canada after the defeat of the Boers determined to reaffirm the "old" Québec ways – the church and the rural life of the habitant. He marries his childhood sweetheart – a child of *la terre* – and centres the defence of his culture in a defence of his language, as Afrikaners did and, like the Québécois, as Afrikaners still do.

price of gold fell. A boom had gone bust. The English mine owners said that they had to cut labour costs. They fired the white workers and hired more cheap black labour, which enraged the poor whites. At the same time, the owners of the coal mines announced a wage cut. The coal workers called a strike. The gold miners joined the coal strikers, and by January 1922, 20,000 whites (and 180,000 blacks) were pounding the pavements and the dirt roads: "Workers Of The World Unite For A White South Africa." The workers declared a Red Republic, and white workers seized part of the Rand. The British army, called out by the government, bombed, shelled, and machine-gunned the strikers into submission. Eighty died. Four leaders went to the gallows singing the *Red Flag.*

It is said that the zim often hides who he is by becoming the hangman.

I am no dove to be beaten, kantikintikintiki!
I am no dove to be beaten, kantikintikintiki!
His sister is being eaten, kantikintikintiki!
By an old zim, kantikintikintiki!
Bone by bone, kantikintikintiki!

OB (The Ox-wagon Sentinel)
By 1938, as Afrikaners celebrated the anniversary of the Great Trek into Dingaan country, they were no longer just straggling country folk from the outback. They now appeared at monuments and at festivals in the garb of *volk* – ox-carts and wagons, black hats and bonnets and high-top heavy boots – but they had become play-actors in their own rituals, pragmatic farmers and pallid city-faced civil servants who sported pencil moustaches and belonged to secret societies like the Ossewa-Brandwag, paramilitary commandos who paraded in slightly comic pioneer uniforms – two million men bound by secret

oath to a commandant-general – a blood bond that was viru-
lently paranoid – anti-British, anti-Semitic, and anti-Communist.

England entered the Second World War. There were Nazi
sympathizers among the Afrikaners who believed in racial
purity but, more to the point – as with large numbers of Irish
and Québécois at the time – Afrikaners supported Germany
because Germany was England's enemy. It shocked Afrikaners
when their parliament, by a small majority, voted to enter the
war in support of England (the same profound shock a large
number of Québécois felt when conscription was imposed in
Canada).

THE HANDLE

Every night in Jo-berg I thought I heard whistling outside the
hotel bedroom window. A sharp whistle. I was on the eighth
floor. The housemaid told me not to be troubled, it was night
birds, or maybe, she said, it was *zims*.

One night I could feel someone breathing on the other side
of the door. I opened the door and there was a man staring at me,
as if he'd been staring all night at the door.

He hurried out the emergency exit and ran down the stairs.

I watched for him in the street.

He didn't appear.

I heard loud keening, a woman, a hurt animal's cry. She
lurched from corner to corner, a Hillbrow woman, a poor white
Afrikaner holding her high-heel pumps in her hands.

No one was molesting her, or even talking to her.

But she was keening.

Blacks huddled against the walls with wool hats pulled down
over their faces against the night wind. She was running her own
cat's cradle path from curb to curb, crying – *Wat soek julle in die
straat die tyd?* – crying out, but not to a small black man on his
coal wagon, a wagon with heavy rubber wheels, noiseless, the
wagon drawn by a clopping bony horse.

He drove past her. To him, she was not there. She fell to her knees. He was wearing a jacket cut from an old khaki canvas duffle bag; armholes had been sliced into the sides and he had split the bag up the front, so that the clear plastic handle of the duffle bag sat on his back between his shoulder blades.

ERAHUTINI

Industrialized during the wartime forties, built up as a repair and restocking post for the Allies, the country entered into a wartime economic boom. White men were sent to the theatre of war. Blacks crowded into the towns (in Xhosa, the word for cities is *Erahutini* – where the gold is) to work at jobs that had never been open to them. Between 1936 and 1946, blacks in urban areas increased by about 500,000, or some fifty per cent, and by the end of the war, town blacks and whites were almost equal in number.

After the war, white country boys, many of them returning soldiers, had to compete for skilled work with the trained children of Ham. The National Party articulated an Afrikaner formula for a political victory that would contain this "black eruption" in the election of 1948. "The policy of our country should encourage total apartheid as the ultimate goal for a national process of separate development...to ensure the safety of the white race and of Christian civilization."

The two races had become copulating toads.

THE DEEP

In a dank little bar, the Deep, a Portuguese man told me that he pumped iron every morning. As he pumped he asked Our Lady of Fatima to send him to Rhodesia. He had been a paratrooper in Angola. Now, he wanted to go to Rhodesia to kill *haut-kops*, nigger-knuckle-heads. I asked him if he ever thought about evil when he was praying to Our Lady? He laughed. He wanted to know if I was a *kafferboetie*, a nigger-lover. He showed me the clear plastic cylinder that contained tar in his stubby cigarette holder. The black tar, he said, was evil. "It is the blacks. They're there with every breath I take, they're always there, like death."

THE WILDERNESS ERRAND

Apartheid as a theory was developed in 1947 by professors at Stellenbosch University (these academics, looking for a model, had noted that Canada had isolated – politically and culturally – its Aboriginal tribes on pockets of waste and scrub lands, and these homelands, so to speak, were called reserves). The Stellenbosch balkanization of blacks created Bantustans (reserves), far-flung tribal groups (as in Canada) surrounded by whites (as in Canada) separated from each other by great distances (as in Canada)...impotent tribal families unable to support themselves in any significant way (as in Canada) or unite into any kind of opposition...but unlike the Canadian reserves (where the natives were by and large abandoned to their own "governance" over economic destitution and idleness and the consequent drug use and drunkenness), the "homelands" in South Africa were set up as tribal labour depots that were not just dependent on the white economy but fundamental to the white economy. Which meant that the blacks had to be kept working (the owners of the diamond mines quickly understood the advantage that apartheid would be to their international business), but under strict control – orderly when outside a burgeoning place like Soweto (passbooks), and contained in a state of relative calmness when inside on their depot streets (laws laws laws laws). To Afrikaner voters – and substantial English liberal (so-called) voters – apartheid was the solution to that existential and necessary evil, the black peril.[1]

---

[1] The first public use of the term "apartheid" by Dr. C.R. Kotze in 1941 referred to the necessary separation between "the Boer people" and "the English," not between black and white. Kotze described the children of mixed marriages between Afrikaners and the English as "monstrosities."

BAAS LAW
The hand of Afrikanerdom, a closed fist.

The Minister of Justice, under the Suppression of Communism Act, was given the power to act against persons or organizations deemed to be subversive (Communism was and still is a catchall word; even a jaywalker can be arrested as a possible threat to the state). Under the Act, there were neither trials nor rights of appeal against the Minister's decisions. Journals were shut down, and anyone whose words in favour of racial equality could be interpreted as a threat to security was banned – which meant he could be restricted to the locale in which he lived; he could lose the right to speak at public meetings or write for newspapers or publish anything; he could be prohibited from entering any building where educational material was being prepared, prohibited from entering any building where a trade union was registered, prohibited from entering any area prohibited to him, like an African township; in his own home, he could be prohibited from seeing more than one individual at a time; he was allowed to go to church but not to speak to more than one person at a time. And anyone quoting the words of such a banned person could be guilty of a punishable offence.

By 1961, as South Africa abandoned the Commonwealth and became a Voortrekker Republic, repressive laws read like a litany: the Unlawful Organizations Act, the Public Safety Act, the Criminal Procedure Act, the Criminal Law Amendment Act, the Group Areas Act, the Bantu Authorities Act, the Suppression of Communism Act, the Sabotage Act, the Terrorism Act, the Official Secrets Act. The police could detain people suspected of possession of information about subversion without trial for 180 days. *Habeas corpus* was suspended and the police could arrest a man and not have to tell anyone they had him in the *boop* for 180 days. The security police were given special powers of interrogation in certain circumstances and, if necessary, some men did not have to be dealt with in public at all, because the prime minister – (or his nominee, whoever he might be) – was given the power (under Baas Law) to prevent the courts from considering any matter which the prime minister – (or his nominee) – thought affected the interests of the state. Public security had become the endgame to the Boer "errand into the wilderness."

FREEDOM'S SCOPE: J.F. MARAIS, ELDER JUSTICE OF THE SUPREME COURT

He was light on his feet, full of throaty laughter, a lascivious little glint in the eye. He had been married more than a few times, he said, as he poured tea and then plunked his lean body into a well-padded sofa. "Now, as for World War II, it was Smuts who decided we should fight with Britain against Germany. This led to a huge protest meeting in Pretoria in September 1939, where 80,000 to 90,000 people congregated to protest against the declaration of war. It was not that we were pro-German or pro-Nazi, or anti-Jewish, we simply said that we should have stayed out of the war, and I and thousands of others, more than 200,000 Afrikaners, formed the Ossewa-Brandwag and resisted the government. We embarked on subversive schemes. We were caught, and we were interned, and we were kept in internment during the entire course of the war."

"Was the government right, putting you in prison?"

"Oh yes," he said, "they put me in detention without trial, but they were fully justified in doing so. If they had not done so, the results would have been very bad indeed for the government of the day."

"You mean revolution?"

"We were bent on revolution, no doubt about it. We were waiting for the time when Britain would be conquered, be invaded, and would lose the war. We would call for a republic in South Africa, divest ourselves completely from the bonds of the British Empire."

"You must have a peculiar feeling for the law," I said, "sitting now, in judgment on subversives."

"There is a sort of poetic irony involved in the matter."

"When a man is now charged under the Suppression of Communism Act, yet he is clearly not a Communist – certainly it is clear to you – how do you convict him?"

"The anti-Communist legislation is not designed to fight an ideology. What's it designed for? It is designed to fight subversion, acts that might endanger the safety of the state."

"But isn't the anti-Communism law, in its refusal to define what Communism is, a form of intimidation?"

"That is exactly what Parliament intended it to be."

"What?"

"An act of intimidation to scare anybody who might toy with the idea of tactics that might subvert the state."

"But that's exactly the reverse of what's intended in British Common Law…the intention is to define…be specific…"

"Yes."

"But here it is intimidation rooted in uncertainty."

"Yes."

"This is crippling."

"The point is, and this is healthy, you are inhibited from doing certain things, inhibited because you never know the exact scope of your freedom."

BOY-BOY

Boy-Boy, the son of Esther, the prostitute and shebeen-keeper, was born crippled in the left leg but when he was ten years old he was already earning his living. He sold newspapers in town. He hoarded his money like a miser and a year later he was able to buy himself a pair of long pants and a colourful windbreaker. He felt like a man as he hobbled around on one crutch in his long pants and windbreaker.

"Ma?"

"Yes, my boy?"

"You know those steps at Johannesburg Station that walk?"

"Yes, they call them escalators," said Esther, wondering which of her many lovers had told her that word. Probably that matric student with the hairy chest, she thought to herself.

"Those steps are always walking up. Why don't they walk down?"

"There are others that walk down."

"But those are always walking up. Can I walk down on them while they are walking up?"

"I don't know."

"Have you tried it?"

"No."

"Has anybody tried it?"

"I DON'T KNOW. PLEASE SHUT UP!"

"I'm going to try it."

Boy-Boy did try it and he was pleased when he realized that it was possible to go down an escalator while it was moving up.

"Ma, why do we have policemen?"

"To arrest people."

"I'm going to be a policeman."

Boy-Boy managed to get himself a pair of handcuffs and a police whistle. He loved blowing that whistle! And it got on Esther's nerves!

"I'm a policeman. I'm going to arrest one of those people drinking skokiaan in the kitchen," Boy-Boy told Esther with the light of justice shining in his eyes.

"I'm arresting you," Boy-Boy said to one greyhead who had just taken a sip out of his tin.

"Owright, arrest me," said the greyhead, trying to humour the boy. He thrust out his hands.

Kraang, kraang, went the handcuffs.

Two hours later the greyhead was still pleading with Boy-Boy to remove the handcuffs. But Boy-Boy demanded five shillings first.

"Five," he said for the umpteenth time.

The greyhead was furious.

"If you don't take them off I'm going to kick your bloody…"

Boy-Boy hit him over the head with his crutch before he could say another word.

"ESTHER!" The greyhead was in tears. There was blood on his head.

Esther paid the greyhead's fine and the handcuffs came off.

"I'm a policeman," shouted Boy-Boy as he hobbled out of the house into the street.

OOM BEY

I had made contact with Beyers Naude through messengers (phones, of course, could not be trusted). The messengers called him Oom Bey – Uncle Bey – and one said, "Maar, he mos alone." Naude had been a prominent leader of the Dutch Reformed Church, he had been a member of the Broederbond (his father was one of the founders) – he had been because he was now banned…he was an outcast, he was shunned as a traitor was shunned – by his church, by the Afrikaner press – he was forbidden to speak publicly, to attend meetings, to be with more than one person in his home…banned, he was being ritually humiliated every day. He agreed to meet me outside my country motel room at 5:30 in the morning ("Those watching you will still be asleep at that hour"): he would, he said, be sitting in his car at the bottom of the motel parking lot, "And you should join me there."

I did, at an hour when the moon had paled but it was not yet dawn. He was wearing a double-breasted suit, a shirt and tie, and his hair was combed straight back from his forehead. There was no flinch in his blue eyes. No light of sourness or self-pity. A wide mouth, open in easy, quiet, welcoming laughter. I sat with him in the front seat of his car. We were facing a wall, he was watching the parking lot in the rearview mirror. He looked expectant, fresh, he sounded eager and unswerving. He spoke rapidly, wanting me to know that the injustice of apartheid had to be explained to the outside world, not so much to name and punish perpetrators for their crimes – though criminals would have to be punished – but to discredit and end the regime and relieve – if not redeem – the Afrikaners from the evil curse they had imposed on themselves and on the blacks. He did not want to talk about his own plight, the difficulties of being banned. It was true, he had spoken out, but his having spoken out was "a matter of not swallowing your own silence, of not choking to death on your own silence." He took and held me by the wrist. "Be careful," he said. "Be careful." It was a warning, but it also was a comforting gesture – a pastor's gesture – in evil times. After twenty minutes with Oom Bey, I stood alone in the parking lot, shivering in the dampness, the mist, and watched him drive away.

WHITE BEETLE

"The first thing to point out," Breyten Breytenbach said before he was led off to his cell, "is that apartheid works. It may not function administratively; its justifications and claims are absurd and it certainly has not succeeded in dehumanizing – entirely – the Africans, the Coloureds or the Indians. But it has effectively managed to isolate the White man. He is becoming conditioned by his lack of contact with the people of the country, his lack of contact with the South African inside himself. Even though he has become a mental Special Branch, a BOSS of darkness, he doesn't know what's going on – since he can relate only to the syndrome of his isolation. His windows are painted white to keep the night in."

Anyone here ever seen a white beetle?
Neither have I
But it's a terrible creature
Like a missionary in Africa
With helmet and dark glasses

White beetles live in bright rooms: camouflage
Scampering lumps of sunlight on the wall
Beware the white beetle with its sting, its poison flask

Keep your eye peeled, be sure
To look carefully under your bed at night

The white beetle's night has its own sting – a woman who is a white beetle, who is half asleep, stirs…stirs and hears…yes, her door is locked but she hears…the door being unlatched – she is a white beetle in a story by Nadine Gordimer…a white beetle in her bed, her lover gone, the night wind pressing against the walls and windows, a pressure in her ears and a door bangs in the story, the latch is loose.

Her thoughts cohered around the sound.

He's left the door open. She

> saw it; saw the gaping door, and wind bellying the long curtains and sending papers skimming about the room, the leaves sailing in and slithering across the floors. The whole house was filling up with wind. There had been burglaries in the suburb lately. This was one of the few houses without an alarm system – she had refused to imprison herself in the white man's fear of attack on himself and his possessions. Yet now the door was open like the door of a deserted house and she found herself believing, like any other suburban matron, that someone must enter. They would come in unheard, with the wind, and approach through the house, black men with knives in their hands. She, who had never submitted to this sort of fear in her life, could hear them coming, hear them breathe under their dirty rag masks and their tsotsi caps… She was empty, unable to summon anything but this stale fantasy, shared with the whole town, the whole white population. She lay there possessed by it, and she thought, she violently longed – they will come straight into the room and stick a knife in me. No time to cry out. Quick. Deep. Over.

...a beetle's stale death wish...in a system that works because the laws are like twisted glass – what is, is never what it seems:

> Removal of Bantu who unlawfully remain in prescribed areas – (1) a Bantu who has been convicted under sub-section (4) of section ten or sub-section (2) of section twelve or has been introduced by a person into any prescribed area contrary to the provisions of sub-section (1) of section eleven or whose employer has been convicted under sub-section (9) of section twenty-one of the Bantu labour Regulation Act, 1911 (Act No. 15 of 1911), and with due regard to his family ties or other obligations or commitments, be removed, together with his dependants, under a warrant issued by the court convicting him or such person or employer or by a Bantu Affairs Commissioner and addressed to a member of the South Africa Police, to his home or his last place of residence or to a rural village, settlement rehabilitation scheme, institution or other place indicated by the Secretary, either generally or specially, within a scheduled Bantu area or a released area as defined in the Bantu Trust and Land Act, 1936 (Act No. 18 of 1936), or in the case of a Bantu referred to in section twelve, to the country or territory from which he entered the Republic or the nearest point in the Republic to the district of his origin.

OOPS, A DUPE

I had been told by David Goldblatt, the photographer, to call Nadine Gordimer. Her husband, a wealthy man, invited me to their comfortable house for cocktails – the rooms smaller than I had expected, or perhaps they seemed smaller because there were so many people in the house, guests at a late afternoon party. Gordimer was abrupt, perfunctory; she was busy encouraging an avuncular old man, a family friend or favourite uncle who was given to telling stories about himself, which were amiably amusing but pointless and boring to an outsider, and so I sat alone, drinking whisky, trying to listen to the bluff old man until finally, with a sudden sigh – out of stories, out of breath – he stood up and left a room that radiated affection for him.

"What are you doing here, my husband says you're making a film?" Gordimer asked.

"I'm a friend of David Goldblatt's. I think he's a wonderful photographer," I said.

"I wrote an introduction for his book on the mines."

"Yes."

"And you're making a film about Afrikaners," she said.

"Yes."

"You're making a film about the Afrikaners, I don't understand that. You've just come over and you're making a film?"

"And it's going to be something," I said.

"In what way?"

"Well, I've got them talking, quite openly."

She scoffed, full of suspicion. She was looking at me like the young woman from Internal Affairs looked at me. I wished that I had said nothing. But instead of keeping quiet, I said, "Yes, they're singing like canaries…explaining who they are. Almost guile-less…"

"Do you know the BBC has been trying for two years to get into the country to make a film about me, and the government won't let them in…"

"Maybe so. It took me two years to get in, too."

"The BBC…they can't get in to film me, and you're here, and they're telling you exactly who they are…"

"Yes."

"They don't tell anybody who they are. They tell you what they want you to hear, and they listen. They're probably listening to us, now, in this house…"

"Maybe."

"If they're making a film with you, you're either one of them or you're a dupe."

I was sitting, she was standing. I wished there was ice in my whisky. I wanted to chew on ice.

"I hardly think," I said, "your friend Goldblatt is dumb enough to send a dupe around to meet you."

No one said anything.

Her husband looked embarrassed.

She was not embarrassed.

"I'm no dupe," I said, "and I'm not stupid either. Time for me to go."

Her son drove me to my hotel. White beetles were crawling, the night birds were whistling.

Zims.

They moss plenny zims.

ON THE BRINK

At Port Elizabeth, André Brink, the Afrikaner novelist, stood in the open doorway of his house. "One hates to turn off the Mozart," he said. "They may be recording us." Self-assured and used to close police surveillance, his tone was measured. His conversation, a studied spontaneity, studied out of necessity. No untoward word. An ease, but the ease of honed emotion: "The poet and writer still exercise a quite exceptional influence in this society. I'd like to read you the poem Breytenbach wrote and gave to me immediately after he was sentenced to nine years imprisonment, just before he was led off to the cells, a poem I've translated:

> *May the trees remain green*
> *and stars white*
> *and may there always be men*
> *able to look one another in the eye*
> *without shame*

for life is long as a single breath
and the stars of that other place
are dark.

"Here is a very definite sense of the schizophrenia that is in the Afrikaner's world. He has to try to equate what he believes in with what is actually happening. One finds it all the time with government policies. Almost ninety per cent of the work in the building profession will be done by coloured and black artisans – who don't exist. Officially, they're simply not there. This unreality pervades the whole South African atmosphere; it makes it easier for the government, or for any person in an official position, to get something done if he needn't say that he is actually doing it or, in fact, is pretending to do the opposite.

"One discovers saddening and unsettling parallels between the South African situation and some of the things revealed by Solzhenitsyn, especially in *The Gulag Archipelago*. The way in which a people can, for the sake of an ideology, distort reality and do the most terrible things, things society would be horrified to look upon: South Africa has the highest murder rate, the highest rate of violent crimes in the Free World, the highest prison population in the Free World, the highest divorce rates, the highest road accident rates, symptoms of an essentially violent society. Apartheid is the legalizing, the legitimizing, of violence in an institutionalized form. Everything relies on violence, violent forces that may assert themselves in one hell of an explosion."[1]

BUTCHER BOY

Breyten Breytenbach wrote an open letter from prison to Prime Minister Balthazar John Vorster:

---

[1] This conversation, all these conversations, took place only a few weeks before the eruption of violence and resistance in Soweto in September of 1976, a spreading resistance among schoolchildren that led to the collapse of apartheid and the release of Nelson Mandela from Robin Island.

trying to scream light in the dusk
with electrodes tied to my testicles
I'm writing slogans in crimson urine
across my skin across the floor
I'm keeping watch
smothered by the ropes of my entrails
slipping on a bar of soap I break my bones
I kill myself with the evening paper
and tumble from the tenth sphere of heaven
in search of redemption in a street surrounded by people

and you, butcher
you burdened with the security of your state
what are your thoughts when night begins to bare her bones
when the first babbling scream is forced
from the prisoner
like the sound of birth…

WHO GOES THERE

Salt flats near Port Elizabeth, pea-green foothills, a small-gauge railroad track running inland, staggered mountain slopes in the distance (range pressed against range, the way a child lays down staggered layers of construction paper), a line of young black boys prancing along the shoulder of the road, dressed like birds, dyed feathers, bracelets hung with small drums, whistles, bangers…click-singing Xhosa, driving a single cow through the Kei Valley toward Transkei…driving toward the pitch-dark and cold until it was nine o'clock at night outside the town of Umtata, a police roadblock, black police (their uniforms never fit), who said they were searching for drunk drivers, but after taking note of my name in my passport they passed the passport from hand-to-hand, and then they let me go, waved me on…smirking, jocular…

Then the ox was cooked.

The boy was given some meat, but he did not eat it. He went about picking up bones, he gathered them together. Then the meat was finished. He took the skin and put it into the kraal. He took the offal and poured it inside. Then he took the bones and put them inside. He collected the skin. Then the zims left to gather firewood.

The boy said,
Get up, Ndololwani, hurry!
Get up, Ndololwani, hurry!
Don't you see we'll be killed,
Ndololwani? Hurry!

UMTATA

Umtata, a sullen scrub town in the Transkei, with low-slung houses, a few flickering neon tubes in the night, and a drive-in short-order grill at the crossroads gas station: on a dimly lit street a drunken black soldier, in a flapping greatcoat and one sole slapping loose on his boot, whistled and hooted after passing cars. At the Savoy, a four-floor hotel, there were two white women at the desk, and one wore her hair in a bun; it held four yellow pencils. Both were brusque: "Coffee in the morning, 6:30…room service quits at 6:45, you're on your own after that… No, no calls, we close down the phones at evening, getting lines out of Umtata's too much trouble. Don't know about trains neither, it'd take maybe two days to the Cape, can't say, it's years since I travelled…"

There was a semi-spiral staircase to the musty second floor; battleship grey walls, doors ajar with single men sitting backs-to-the-wall, staring out; the room numbers made no sense… 209, 222, 290, 201, 216… My room had a steel-frame single bed with wire springs and a thin mattress, threadbare rugs, a broken wooden seat on the toilet bowl.

I took off my clothes and propped two pillows behind my head and began to read André Brink's banned novel, *Looking on*

Darkness: "…sometimes of an evening I take off my clothes and stand with my back pressed against the wall of my cell, or lie down on the narrow bunk, studying and touching this body, strange and familiar as that of a beloved. Even when I know they are watching me through the peephole in the door it doesn't upset me…" I heard footsteps in the hall, a whisper, then a knock in the night.

"Who's that?"

"The police. Come to the door."

Naked, I opened the door. Two men offered no identification. They were in their thirties, casually dressed. The one with a moustache and a pouch belly hung back, as if his presence were a mistake. The other, self-assured, taut, wearing a mustard-green pullover, dust-pink jeans, loafers, and tinted glasses, spoke as if his jaw were locked at the latch. He made no accusations or explanations, he only wanted my passport and said, "We'll be back." I got into bed, yielding to a dread that had been with me all day, yet suddenly too tired to worry, and when they knocked again and came in and the cop in the pink jeans said sardonically, "Did you have a little sleep?" I sat cross-legged, naked on the bed, and smiled, a wan smile, but a smile, waiting.

"You're under arrest."

"You're kidding." I got up, staring at them in the dingy sixty-watt light, certain for some reason that by not covering myself I would make them so self-conscious they might shy away. "I did have a little sleep," I lied, feeling the pit of my stomach go hollow.

"Get dressed, put your clothes on, get your bags together."

"What for?"

"I just told you. Put your clothes on."

"You mean I'm going to jail?"

"Yes."

"Why not leave the bags here?"

"Jail's in East London."

"What?"

"Get dressed."

"But I just came from there, that's three hours, it's midnight, for God's sake…"

The bags were put in a Land Rover. I got up into the cab with the cop in the pink jeans, who told me he was a captain.

He said, "If you have to fart open the window."

Baas Boy-Boy

"There are too many flies in this house," Boy-Boy, the policeman, said to his mother. She did not reply. She just shook her head sadly.

A few minutes later Boy-Boy came to her carrying a dozen boxes of matches. He sat on a bench, opened one box, and pulled out one stick.

He struck it and laughed as it burst into flame. He did this until the box was empty. Then he reached out for a second one. After some time, all the twelve boxes were empty.

"Now I've got twelve coffins," Boy-Boy said, eyeing the twelve boxes of matches gleefully. "I'm going to kill and bury twelve flies today."

Twelve flies were buried that day.

The next day Esther found her son busy at work with pieces of plank and nails. He looked in such a happy mood that Esther, although she was never too keen to engage her son in conversation, could not help asking what he was doing.

"I'm building a coffin for Topsy."

Topsy was the family pet dog.

"But Topsy's not dead!" Esther was shocked beyond words.

"I dreamt he was dead last night."

She felt relieved. "Well, it was a bad dream. He is not dead."

Tap, tap, tap, went the hammer.

"Then I'm going to kill him. I must bury him in his coffin."

Esther went out in search of the dog. "Topsy, Topsy, TOPSY-Y-Y!"

When she got hold of the dog she took it by taxi to the safety of her uncle's place in Alexandra.

It was about nine o'clock at night when she came back. The door was locked. She knocked.

"This is my house. Go away," Boy-Boy shouted through the window. "My mother is not born yet. Go away! Go away!"

At the police station in East London, crowded at four in the morning, the captain in the pink jeans said to the desk sergeant, "Do what you want with him." After a pat-pat search, the desk sergeant said, "You've got all that cash, two thousand, you take it into the cell, we're not risking responsibility for that…" and they led me into a dank, damp yard, a high plastered brick wall with long doors like open coffins upended in the flood-lit wall. We went through a mesh door and a solid steel double door into a cell's courtyard, thirty-foot walls of concrete. There was a second set of mesh and steel doors into the cell itself. The six-by-eight cell had two windows, one to the courtyard, the other facing onto a blank wall. The damp coldness clung to the skin, like a fungus; I had the strange feeling that I was about to lie down where mushrooms grew; the cell was, in effect, an open room, the windows creating a wind current, the concrete holding the coldness. I felt strength ebbing out of me, a kind of surrender by my body, a weeping by my bones…the white cells in my body beginning to attack the arthritic joints. I knew that the long night drive, this cold cell…it was all intended to exhaust me as quickly as possible, to break down my morale; demoralization, standard procedures.

They plenny zims, you watch out for zims.

The mattress on the cement floor was three inches of foam rubber covered by a zip-on soiled bed sheet. There was a charcoal-grey blanket made of fine mesh (impossible to rip in strips, to use in a suicide). The walls were painted black, to gloom the prisoner down. Lying on my side, knees tucked up into my armpits to cradle my own body warmth, I smelled sweat in the stiff bed sheet, the sour sweat and puke of frightened men, and shit on the wind from the open filthy toilet, sour shit, piss, puke, black walls…the overhead light, a bare bulb, always on, the freezing floor, body aching with exhaustion yet aware of everything at the tips of the nerves…except for moments when my mind reeled off into blackness, a dislocation from the self, almost like drifting under water, eyes closed, lost in the peace of unknowingness, and then BOAM BOAM… Every half-hour there was a cell check; the double steel doors opened and slammed, BOAM, sleep was impossible. Rest was impossible. At 6:30 a young cop with a line of little pimples along his left jaw came to the cell door and called out, "Graze time…" and I asked, "What's that?" and he said, shoving me toward the door, "You know, like animals, you graze…" He had put a tin plate of stale brown bread and a tin cup of coffee and a tin cup of fish bones and a fish head in a rancid gruel on the open courtyard floor.

"Why was I arrested?"

"Kneel and eat."

"Why?"

"Someone'll tell you. They'll tell you. You're not eating."

He was narrow through the shoulders, he had a slouching animosity, his uniform didn't fit, he looked like he wanted to hit me…a litany ran through my mind: the Criminal Procedure Act, the Immorality Act, the Abolition of Passes Act, the Sabotage Act, the Terrorism Act, the Suppression of Communism Act… BOAM BOAM…the pain now dull because it was everywhere as I knelt down and tasted the gruel and wanted to vomit, tried to vomit, a surge of nausea…

At noon, they took me for interrogation…passing up a caged staircase, wire mesh with floor-to-ceiling bars on the landing, and another cage that enclosed an inner office. There were two men inside the cages; one old, about sixty-five, pasty skin, compassionate eyes, a bemused smile; the other, the colonel, who was wearing smoked glasses and had fine even teeth, olive skin tight on the bone, skin like a polished gourd. "I am the colonel," he said, "and, Professor Callaghan, you have the right to say nothing; but if you speak, your words will be written down by my associate."

"Okay."

"And no need to be afraid, my associate, too, has been in prison."

The old man smiled.

"What would you like to know?" I asked.

"Tell us why you are here."

The old man, a clipboard on his knee, began writing, nodded, and then stopped as I told them about the woman from Internal Affairs and my meetings with Judge Marais of the Supreme Court, van Jaarsveld, the established historian, my visit to Pelindaba the nuclear plant…and how the woman had nearly always been with me – except when I'd met the novelist André Brink …and as for the captain in the pink pants who had arrested me…"All unnecessary," I said. "They knew I was in the country to talk to Afrikaners…the ministry, the minister himself, arranged the meetings." The colonel was flustered, he apologized. He looked for help to the old man. I realized that the questioning, this talk with the colonel, was taking place because he had no idea why he had me in his prison; no one in Pretoria had given him an explanation; he was interrogating me because he wanted me to tell him why I had been arrested.

"Will you have tea?" asked the old man.

"And," said the colonel, "…you say you were going to the Cape… You want to fly, we'll book you on the late afternoon flight." The old man served tea and biscuits. He looked mournful, his hands blotchy with liver spots.

"I speak six languages, you know," the old man said.

"No kidding."

He stared at me, unblinking, and said in a curiously flat tone: *"Ich will mit dem herrn Kommandanten sprechen…"* I felt a chill, and then was sure that he wanted me to feel that I had been unfair to him, not forthcoming enough and appreciative enough now that my arrest had been resolved and he had given me tea.

Two hours passed. The colonel had locked the cage doors to his office. He had locked himself in and would not come out.

The tea in the pot was cold. I looked at the clock on the wall. The plane for the Cape was taking off. A tall thin man came into the office. His skin was mottled, as if dappled with peroxide. Apparently, he had flown from Pretoria, he had papers. The old man stood up and put on his tie and suit jacket. He stood aside, at attention. "Please sign this paper," the mottled man said.

"What is it?"

"Sign, please."

"Can I read it?"

"No."

"Can I read it after I sign?"

"Yes," he said, a tired man with scuffed shoes, his face and body all pouches, carrying a pouch of papers: *Under Section 8 (2) of the Aliens Act No. 1 of 1937 and in terms of Section 5 (1) of the said Act, you are required to leave the country within twenty-four hours, otherwise you will be liable to prosecution under the said Act.*

"But what did I do?"

"That's a matter for them to explain…"

"When's the plane to Jo-burg?"

"Six. There's a plane out of Jo-burg tomorrow at six, for London. You'd best be on it."

The old man walked me down the caged staircase, past the sullen, grumbling policemen, to a car parked in the lot on the other side of the police station. As we approached the corner of the brick station house, he said, "Pay attention." Then, as we were at the corner, his hand touched mine. "This is the only place we cannot be seen. I've just given you a piece of paper, it has a private number…phone that man, that number. This is all wrong, he will do something."

I drove to the East London airport, where I read the note. It was a phone number, it was Connie Mulder's home number. He was the Minister of Information, who was also the Minister of the Interior – so – it was Mulder of the Interior who had ordered the Mulder of Information to have me arrested. This was the Mulder

of Information who had let me into the country who was Mulder
of the Interior who was expelling me from the country.

They moss plenny zims, mon.

The mottled man appeared. He was very polite and said quietly, almost pleadingly, as I picked up my bag to board the plane,
"You have to understand, the laws have to be followed, they made
an oversight perhaps…but you have to understand, too, the old
man, his wife's sick, you know, a good man…he's a good man.
Problems, you know…they…"

"But what did I do?"

"That's a matter for them to explain."

> *Travel on, Ndololwani, hurry!*
> *Travel on, Ndololwani, hurry!*

The plane was almost empty, except for two men I'd seen at
the police station. They were wearing blue suits and brown shoes.
They had pencil moustaches.

The plane rolled down the runway.

> *Don't you see we'll be killed,*
> *Ndololwani? Hurry!*
> *Ndolowani hurried out of the kraal.*
> *Hakiiiiiiiiiiii!*

The steward delivered a brown paper bag. My name was written on the paper bag. Blue ballpoint pen. Inside was a bottle of
South African brandy, reserve stock.

A parting gift from a white beetle.

*Zims appeared here! They appeared there! Appeared here! And
there! The zims were at home everywhere.*

2011

LONG AFTER MIDNIGHT: BURGESS AND ME AND MORLEY MAKES THREE

Through the last half of his long life my father and I talked to each other by phone late at night, two or three times a week. Long after the Tonight Show, long after midnight, when all the lights were out on his street in Rosedale, and most of the lights were out on my street in Chinatown – he would phone, or I would phone. We talked about what we'd done that day. We talked about the local newspapers and television, too, the Blue Jays baseball games and NFL football, and the news channels. Sometimes we would talk for an hour.

It was crackerbarrel talk, two old hands at anecdote and comeuppance sitting in the half-dark, holding forth on the beauty of Dave Steib's curve ball or the strength of Joe Montana's arm when he threw into the flat, or Bob Hope's quick feet as a vaudeville hoofer, distressed by the distemper of the times but taking special delight in the plight of those politicians we most despised…running the reputations of the local punditi and literati up and down the flagpole…perplexed by the serious attention accorded to hothouse talents like Donald Barthelme and perplexed by great talents, like Norman Mailer, the whole of his work never seeming to be worthy of its parts (we unabashedly admired *The Executioner's Song*), and finding it somehow significant (but only to ourselves, father and son seeking moments of synchronicity) that during the Vietnam War years I'd sat alone for two hours talking with Muhammad Ali in a sad-ass hotel room in New York shortly after he had been stripped of his title, a time when he was shuffling and singing on Broadway, trying to keep his family alive – and the fact that Morley had sat alone with Ali for two hours in a posh hotel room in New York after he'd come back from the Thrilla in Manila, talking about having resurrected himself from the dead, and amidst all of this schmoozing through memories, at least once a month, he would say (as if he'd never said it before), "I've been reading Robertson Davies…there are some extraordinary tricks he's trying. I mean, as a writer you should be interested…"

"Why do you care?" I would say sharply. "All that arcane, artificial intellectual clap-trap – his trilogy sold nothing in England, his international reputation is all a hometown fake…"

Morley knew, of course, that I could not bear to talk about the Davies' novels. I felt only boredom with the work, and a brackish distaste for the man that went back to a stupid, dismissive review he had written for the *New York Times* in which he had snooted the young Marie-Claire Blais' novel *A Season in the Life of Emmanuel*…and even further back to my graduate school days when Davies, as master of Massey College, had an earned reputation among many doctoral students for being a cruel, mean-spirited examiner…

"Look at it this way," Morley said, "he's trying to write—"

"You tell me," I interrupted, "how weak is the chin hiding under that beard…?"

"He is, after all, a writer," Morley insisted, "who tries to bring off a certain kind of intellectual tone quite unlike anybody else in this country, who…"

"Did I tell you that late one night Yehuda Amichai called me from Washington – he never ever called me late at night – because he'd found himself seated for hours at this official supper for writers beside a man he'd never heard of who had a big air about himself to go with this big beard and an accent Yehuda could hardly understand, and Amichai is laughing out loud – and he never laughed out loud – asking me, Who is this Davies person, is he any good as a writer? and I told him like I'm telling you…"

I was, by then, yelling at Morley over the phone.

I heard him chuckling.

He had done it to me again.

I fell into silence.

"Well," he said at last, "I got a note from Pierre Trudeau today…"

"Trudeau. What? You did not. You'da told me right off the bat."

"Well, no. I did not. But then I thought I might write him a note, suggesting that maybe he should hire you as a cultural liaison to…"

"Never mind," I said as tonelessly, as menacingly, as I could. "Cut it out."

Morley – I could see him seated on the little telephone chair in the shadows of the stairwell of his house, wearing his old shawl-collar cardigan and baggy corduroy trousers…cradling the phone to his shoulder with one hand, holding his pipe with a hole chewed in the stem in the other…and he was laughing so hard while trying to make no sound that he gave himself what he called "a stitch" in his side, and for a minute all I heard from his end of the line was a muffled "Ow, oh, ow…"

Three or four weeks later, he phoned, not after midnight but in the mid-morning, at the hour of his poached egg on whole wheat toast and mail delivery.

"What're we going to do?"

"What d'you mean, about what?"

"Haven't you got your invitation?"

"I haven't opened the mail."

"Davies, and Anthony Burgess."

"What?"

"Gatenby's having a big special reading, just the two of them, it's a big deal for Greg, at the Elgin Theatre. Good heavens – I will not sit through an hour listening to that windbag."

"Who?"

"Davies."

"Your guy!"

"This is serious. That Burgess has been out telling the world that Davies should get the Nobel Prize. Heavens above, Greg will never forgive us if we don't show up, this is a big night for him…"

"So, we'll show up."

"I cannot sit and listen to Davies…"

"I tell you what," I said. "Look at it this way. If it starts at eight, Greg'll take for about ten minutes to introduce them. Burgess will read and keep to the half-hour, a twenty-minute break, and we can figure that Davies will close by going over the time, maybe forty-five minutes. So what we will do is do the arithmetic and take a cab and show up just when everybody's coming out…it'll be a big sold-out crowd and we'll step right in with the crowd and go to the reception, like we were there the whole time. And no one will know the difference."

"You think that'll work?"

"Why not?"

"Good," and never easy with a dollar, he said, "You pay the cab because we'll need to move fast."

At the calculated hour, we stepped onto the curb from the taxi, and under rippling marquee lights threaded our way into the crowd coming out of the theatre, and slipped easily between friends. "Wasn't that wonderful?" someone called out, and Morley said "Uumm" as he chewed on his pipe, and then he said, "Uumm" again and, so that many would hear him, "Isn't this great for Greg? He really deserves this kind of success." He put his pipe, dead ashes still in the bowl, in his jacket pocket as we walked into a reception room where wine and canapés were being served by tall men wearing red jackets of a military cut, a room of clustered literati, many of whom were old old friends.

"You're gonna get ashes in your pocket," I said. "Your thumb is already black."

"Good heavens, there's Burgess," Morley said. "I think he's heading right for us."

Burgess, with the cheerful eagerness of a man much at ease with drink, held out his hand, saying, "Morley Callaghan, what a pleasure to say hello to you..."

"And to you, too," Morley said, trying for a ready affability.

"And this is my son, Barry."

"Morley, I can tell you, I have always admired your stories deeply, a deftness... I can remember the three volumes being sent to me when they came out in London..."

"Two..." I said under my breath.

"The understated way you have of saying something big..."

"Yes," Morley answered, beaming a little at this unexpected compliment.

"And so," Burgess said, "what do you make of Davies?"

"Make?" Morley asked, taken aback. "What do you mean make?"

"What do you think of him as a writer?"

Morley, with a wan smile, said, "Well..." and then, giving an impish toss of his head, he suddenly assumed the confiding tone of one old gent talking to another old gent and said, "Look here, Anthony, it doesn't really matter what an older writer like myself thinks about Davies' work, what matters is what a young writer would think of him, so you should ask my son, Barry..."

Morley edged a little closer to Burgess, who said, "Quite so, quite so. Barry?"

Set up by my father, who looked like he was about to suffer another attack of "stitches" to his side, I thought, *Okay, you wise old guys, I'm not going to fool around and play the patsy.*

"Robertson Davies," I said, "is Anthony Trollope...in Jungian drag."

Burgess burst into laughter, taking me and Morley by surprise.

"Good, that's good," he said, and he laughed approvingly again. But then he put up his hand: "Good, yes, but not quite right. Trollope was actually a good writer. No, not Trollope, I think more like… Thackeray…in Jungian drag."

Giggling, almost gleeful, saying, "Great pleasure, great…" he turned back into the crowd.

Morley and I stood on our heels, astonished.

"What in the world?" Morley said, taking his pipe from his pocket, spilling ash on his camel hair lapel.

"I've nothing to say," I said.

"God," Morley sighed, "think of poor Davies, not knowing… And my goodness, who knows what Burgess really thinks about my stories?"

"He's probably telling your friends that you should get the Nobel Prize."

Greg Gatenby, who was passing nearby, called out happily, "Great you're here."

"Great," Morley cried.

Another man of military cut approached carrying canapés.

"Come on," I said to Morley, "let's send you home in a taxi. I'll call you after midnight. We'll talk."

2011

VENI, VIDI, VENEZIA

Venice, city of canals, where people walk on the water, or so it seems. So much of Venice is seeming: from afar, it floats, anchored to some 400,000 Siberian larch wood logs, an iron wood brought over the course of 400 years from the Angara River and made into piles driven down into the heavy salt-marsh slime and clay; underfoot, close to hand, it is a hallucinatory city of grey trachyte paving stones, of sludge-stained stucco walls, *sgueros* (boatyards), lacework cornices, ink-white marble stairs, chapels the size of huge closets, an ivory bridge, balustrades and parapets, clusters of cupolas and domes, rotted wooden doors, mooring posts, docking jetties, vaporetti and gondoliers, churches upon churches upon churches, disconsolate cats in estrus, stalls of cascading flowers, rusted iron burglar bars, the candy-floss-pink walls of the Palace of the Doges, a reliquary of the Blood of Christ (one of seven such vials in continental Europe), handkerchief-glass vases of scarlet red and peppermint green, roof tiles slipping, *altanas* (wooden balconies built on short stilts above roofs), lines and lines of household washing...

This is not an ethereal beauty. It is all too cluttered, too human, the beauty of decay – women and men out walking the waters, hurrying down *sotoportegas* (elbow-wide alleys), under small shuttered windows, closed. A man tells me that if I want to truly savour and absorb the inwardness of this island people, I should always order at a local bar, known as Bacari, deep-fried stuffed olives.

⤜✦⤛

Cassiodorus, chancellor for the Constantinople Empire, wrote: "Where you live, the movement of the tide in turn reveals and conceals the surface of the fields. Your houses are like the nests of sea birds, which sometimes seem bound to the earth, and sometimes float over the waves… You use interwoven rushes to secure the land and fearlessly offer this fragile barrier to the sea. One could believe that your boats glide over fields; their hulls can barely be seen." The Venetians chose one man to govern this fragile world of flux. The duce, called in the local dialect, the doge.

This man, despite his eventual reputation abroad as an absolute power, was more like a chairman of the board. The board members were rich merchants. Two hundred of them. A Family Compact whose names, beginning in 1197, were entered in the "Golden Book." These Worthy Ones, as they called themselves, made the laws and controlled commerce in a world of formality, power, and deception. They were middlemen; they got fabulously rich and though, like brokers everywhere, they had no particular talent, they became fabulously powerful. The doge seemed the most powerful of all. In fact, and true to the nature of the city, the less power the doge had, the more he was revered.

⤜✦⤛

The Venetian mind is not just crowded but is cluttered with images and icons of sheer playfulness, pure mercantile power, ascetic faith, and a faith of flamboyance and flair…and at the centre is the body of a winged lion…symbol of the citizens' patron, their saint, Mark, whose bones – after a *furta sacra*, a holy theft – were brought in a basket out of Alexandria and across the desert wrapped in raw pork and white fat to disgust and deceive Arab customs men.

Those bones lie in a Basilica of five russet and yellow domes, lie surrounded by swarms of saints, a celestial aristocracy swathed in gold; they lie amidst marble mosaic floors shaped into the heaves and swells of a sea becalmed before a storm under ceilings made of thousands of enamelled cubes of glass that tell allegorical anecdotes of naked flesh – the daydreams of pious men cloistered in darkness – men staring into a future that wears the masks of its own decay. And mounted at the head of all this, the pure pagan power of four huge gilded bronze horses – horses high-stepping off the outside loggia into nowhere.

Petrarch said he dreamed of the horses of San Marco, horses in a city where *Coltivare el mare e lasciare la terra* is a catchword: *Cultivate the sea and leave the land alone.* It seems that they are horses of the air, if not the sea. Petrarch said he could hear the rasp of the breathing of the horses. I, too, hear horses and dream of the Celtic goddess Epona in her full stride: I hear her moaning and hard breathing because – like all of us who seek the ecstasy of a higher intoxication – she is, without her wings, in pain. The men who sit astride Epona are the closest she has ever got to her dream of wings. Not surprisingly, the look in her eye, which is not a horse's eye, seems human.

When I first went to Venice I, of course, found myself standing on the edge of the Piazza San Marco. It was early morning. I was staring across the great square at the Basilica. It is a strange sight. Mark Twain said the Basilica looks, with its domes and humps upon humps, like a bug with warts that is out for a stroll. Bug or not, over the entrance there were the four horses. Their heads were into the wind. Steeds of the aristocrats, the chevaliers, like the general who is saddled up close by, in front of the Scuola Grande di San Marco.

Leonardo da Vinci's teacher, Andrea del Verrocchio, had been commissioned to create the finest horse after antiquity, and just before he died, he did: the equestrian statue of Bartolomeo Colleoni. A mercenary general, he was the commander of Venice's army. His name, Colleoni, means "testicles" in the Latin vulgate, and is *coglioni* in modern Italian. He boasted that he had three.

What else could a military man clanking around in Venice do or say? – this commander of foot soldiers and field troops bivouacked in a city of no land, sinking campanile, and stinking canals. He had to somehow steal into the imaginations of men: three testicles, his "fierce cutting eyes," his great horse in full stride, companion to the moaning horses of Petrarch's dreams.

Those horses on the loggia are in fact a stolen dream…stolen in 1204 from Constantinople by warring Crusaders. Since then, their muscled flanks have been longingly stroked by Goethe, Mann, Schlegel, Ruskin, Pound, Monet, Browning…all staring at the only prancing quadriga to have survived from the classical era, staring into the eyes of horses full of the potency and thrust of real power. Yet, there is something touching about their thin tilted luminous muzzles with their networks of veins, the dilated nostrils, the cropped manes, the forelocks tied together between the pointing ears…the articulated hair inside the ears, mouths half open, as if drawn by iron bits, the precise teeth…something touching about the tips of their tongues so delicately curled upwards…

They seem to be noble brutes. And yet the eyes…there is something strange in the eyes that are set so deeply in the sockets under arched eyebrows…strange because horses have horizontally elongated pupils, but these are round, and brought to life by the lunula, the incised half-moon shape that fills the human eye with light, and the deeper and darker the incision the brighter the light seems. On the loggia, suspended over the great square, the horses have the vivid, penetrating, and terrifying eyes of a woman who is in mid-stride in a race, not against the wind but – because of those eyes, those mortal eyes socketed in a horse's skull – a race against death.

Leisureways, 1983

FATTENING FROGS
FOR SNAKES

Sunnyland Slim, greying hair cropped to his skull, let out a high nasal moan…*uun uun uun uun uun, you know the devil's got the best o' me, Muddy, it's too late for me to try to pray* ("thas a Tin Pan Alley bloodletting," he later told me) as he church-rolled the blues on the piano…

"Well, I like that," Willie Dixon, the Big-Pappy bassist who had once been heavyweight boxing champion of Illinois, said in a meditative drawl. "I remember down south, we used to be out on plantations, and you would meet a guy who'd got up early in the morning, and unconsciously he would just be thinking, and he's thinking about his condition and if he was in some other place, or if he was up the road, because you know down in the southern states, they always felt like the northern states would be a place where he could really enjoy and relax and be himself. And maybe he'd worked all day, and unconsciously he's thinking, that's the way the blues are. Unconsciously you think about the things that you would desire, and in mind you go gradually to singing them. That's why early in the morning you'd hear a guy going out to catch his mules or to pick cotton and he'd come up singing about

> *one of these days*
> *an' it won't be long*

you're gonna look for me, Captain
an' I'll be gone"

Muddy Waters, who is a tall-enough man but was sitting small beside the standing Willie, said – with a hurrying hitch to his words – "My version…was this… I would do the same thing as what you're talking about…and I would sing,

If time don't get no better
up the road I'm going"

Otis Spann, a man of almost guileless ease, said to Muddy in a testifying-sounding way, "The blues is like a doctor… He can heal you, and he can pull you down."

"But last night," I said to Otis when we were at the piano, "you said to me, 'The blues is ugliness.' What'd you mean by that?"

"What I mean is no one never saw the blues…but we always feel the blues…"

"That's right," Muddy said. "You cain't see 'em, but you can definitely feel 'em."

"Everybody have the blues," Willie said, laying down a confirmation, "there's no doubt about it. Everybody have 'em. But, everybody's blues aren't exactly the same. And everybody don't express it the same way. They express it according to the type of the raising or the surroundings that they had been around."

⤞✦⤝

At three o'clock in the morning in a downtown Toronto hotel room, the Frontenac Arms on Jarvis Street, Muddy and his sidemen were sitting around sipping cash bar bourbon and quipping back and forth about who was Bad-Bad as Jesse James, and who had got 'cused of forgery though he couldn't write his name, who had a hand full of gimme and who had a mouth full of much obliged. Muddy, his hair conked into a small pompadour, was holding a bottle of Chivas Regal. "Thas my drink. I drink Chivas when I can, an' I'm still regal when I cain't." Born in Mississippi in Rolling Fork, and raised on the Stovall Plantation where he had lived in a one-room log hut and held his first guitar strings together with a hairpin. He went on to tell about Lil Son Jackson, who had carried a black cat bone in his pocket for protection against evil.

"And he die, too, one day," Otis said.

"Seven stab wounds in his back," Muddy said.

Also in the room were blind Sonny Terry, baptized Saunders Terrell, harp player born in Georgia but raised mostly in the Carolinas, and Brownie McGhee, hobble-legged guitar-singer from Kingsport, Tennessee, where, at the age of four, he'd contracted polio. The boys in the Waters band – Pee Wee Madison, Samuel Lawhorn, Otis Spann, and James Cotton – were making a coy little show of shunning Sonny and Brownie ("They gone uptown up the hill, man, with Belafonte in them concert halls and palladiums"), sniping at Brownie, telling him he hadn't kept the faith. In fact, Brownie had just shaved his head clean – "to keep the faith" – that's what he'd told me – to answer the call of the preacher-man-politician Adam Clayton Powell, who – on the crest of freedom marching – had testified from his Greater Abyssinian Baptist gospel pulpit in Newark, "Black is beautiful, black is beautiful."

There in the hotel room, with a pugnacious thrust of his chin, Brownie stood his guitar upright at rest on the toe of his highly polished oxblood boot and faced the band. One of the boys, Pee Wee, from behind an open newspaper that he pretended to be reading, said quietly but as a challenge, "Man, I'd never go up no ofay hill to lose my talent..." Muddy said sternly (quoting from one of the band's seminal songs), "Man, you cain't lose what you ain't never had." Brownie, too smart to be offended, said, "All I want to say to you about singing with Harry Belafonte my father already said to me...*the grave holds secrets, son, that'll never be told...*"

Brownie then swung his guitar under his arm and started to sing his song of the sayings he had gathered down through the years from his sharecropper father, Huff, operator of a backwoods still and a Saturday night fish fry player himself. Brownie sang about how it took rocks and gravels to make a solid road and how with every rose there are some thorns, too, and how those graveyards hold old secrets and how the way to love love is to never let your right hand know what your left hand is doing. The boys had gone quiet. Muddy sat presiding with the knowing look of a ripe old church warden listening to the cryptic gospel of the tobacco road, the cotton field, and the prison farm. When Brownie stomped his boot, singing out, "The blacker the berries the sweeter the juice," the boys hollered in approval. Brownie smiled, trying for expansiveness (he had once faked being a preacher). "If I ever get lucky," he intoned, "and go to heaven, I'm gonna sit down in St. Peter's chair and say to Peter, man – I'll have some of this good drinking whisky you got up here." He reached and took a swallow from Sonny's bottle. Muddy poured himself two fingers of Chivas Regal.

"I can remember…" Sunnyland said to Muddy, "Big Poppa Snowball was singing a song, a song with Silas Green, Rabbit Foot, in Sugarfoot Greene's Minstrel Show, and he sang a little song… I'm gonna sing it just like he sung it:

> *They say the white man went to the river*
> *He sat out on the bank*

"You know he's tall…and Sugarfoot lifted his hand up over his head, singing,

> *The white man went to the river,*
> *sat out on the bank,*

got to thinking about his good girl,
jumped overboard and drowned.
But the black man went to the same river,
sat out on the bank.
The black man went to the same river,
sat out on the bank.
He got to thinking about his good girl
and just curved on back uptown.

"And that's the truth," Sunnyland said.

"Really," Muddy said with wry approval, "where we get all our blues from mostly is our beautiful ladies."

"Amen," Otis called out.

"You know," Willie said, "even in history, way back in history …in biblical days, even Adam was supposed to have been blue and lonesome."

"Alone," Muddy said with finality.

"Yeah," Willie said, "but when he got a woman, he's still the same thing. He's still got the blues."

TWO YEARS EARLIER:

All through the night, a drumming rain. At five in the morning the rain cleared and in that milk-white hour, in a lean side-alley to a closed restaurant under a folded steel fire escape, Sonny, his wide-brimmed fedora square on his head, shuffled along the cement, rapping his blind man's cane against the brick wall. Several paces behind, riding up and down in a hobble-step, was Brownie.

On this morning, Brownie and Sonny were alert and laughing though we had been quick on two bottles of Johnnie Walker Red all night in an apartment over the restaurant. Brownie held his guitar under his arm. He called out, "Walk on, Baby. Break clean, come out fighting," and he swung the guitar across his paunch, singing out as we came into the ordered emptiness of College Street on a Sunday morning.

I'm a stranger here,
Just blowed in your town
If I ask you for a favor
Please don't turn me down…

A streetcar clattered by, pale Mass-bound faces in the windows staring sleepily at two black men, one burly and blind, the other crippled, singing their way out of a dead-end alley, followed by an ofay with his shades on. Sonny hollered, "Man, you see me do a buck and wing? You see me do that? Hold my cane."

"Watch that drainpipe, man."

"Watch your worried mind."

Sonny moved his feet in a sand dancer's shuffle, staring straight ahead, a white film over one eye behind glasses. He had a boyish smile and spoke with a country slur sometimes so thick that not everyone could understand him, and there he was, doing a buck and wing, big feet slipping back and forth and up and down, snapping his heels, and then he leapt into the air, crossed his legs and smacked his heels with his hands. Taking his cane back, he said, "Man, I could do that the whole time 'fore I got the gout. Can't do nothing with the gout. Got me pills from a doctor in Washington, they hardly do nothing."

Sonny, Brownie, and I stood under the fluttering dying neon of the closed restaurant. It was too early for Brownie to go to his hotel, a flop for rummies and roach peddlers on Jarvis Street, the Hotel California, where the deskman padlocked and chained the doors at two in the morning – despite fire regulations – and didn't open again until seven, trapping anyone asleep inside, but, "Never mind, a man should have an official room to rest his head," Brownie said, "and I surely do." He thrust out his chin, and stepping back, aimed his "freedom" guitar at me "Mother, when the great day comes…"

Sonny tapped his cane. "What's happenen, man, what's going on?"

⤙✦⤚

"Sonny, you think you should, in your songs, sing about social questions?"

"Do I think I should?"

"Yeah."

"I don't say I should, but I could."

"Why don't you?"

"Because I don't feel like doing it."

"You see, Sonny, I think that Brownie has, oh, four or five songs that are really social songs."

"What do you mean?"

"Protest songs."

"I don't do that, man. I don't do none of them kind of songs."

"Why is that?"

"I just don't do it. I don't know why. I don't know none of them. I can't write no song like that because I don't know about those songs."

"What do you think about those folks who are making such a storm about civil rights?"

"I won't say too much about that. I would say they're right. Everybody wants equal rights. A man is a man. He wants to live where he wants to live. And, I think he should live where he wants to live. I ain't been to no march or nothing. I couldn't say what I would do if I could see. I'd go, I guess, would be the truth. But my being out there now, it might be I'd be getting hurt. We need somebody who can see what's going on, you know. Them boys can throw a brick or something. If you can see it coming, you can dodge. But I couldn't go out. I'd be a target for it, somebody'd throw a brick at me."

⤙✦⤚

I said to Muddy, who was looking thoughtful, expectant, "I once asked Brownie what the blues are? And, you know Brownie, an eloquent man of many words, he said, 'I'm just going to tell you one thing about the blues, and no more. I'm just going to give you one sentence, and it's all you'll have to know about the blues from me, and the blues is my colour.'"

"Well, I doubt it," Muddy insisted, shaking his head "I doubt it. I doubt it. I doubt that."

"I doubt that, myself," Otis agreed.

"It don't have to be…" Muddy was wanting to avoid the issue of colour "It's the feeling that's the blues. The blues is feeling. And we don't have to be the only ones that's had some hard days."

"No, Lord," Sunnyland intoned.

"And hard days," Willie pronounced, "don't make the blues."

"Hard days make the blues…" Muddy said, laying a decisive rap of his knuckles on the apron of his guitar. "Lovesick and hard days."

Willie, whenever Muddy disagreed with him, had a habit of turning his head away, a bemused, biding-of-time look in his eye (or perhaps the look of the man who not only believed he had insight into who Muddy was but had parlayed that insight, having written Muddy's signature song, "Hoochie Coochie Man"…). "Two things," Muddy said decisively, "give a man the blues: he got no bread, and…lovesick."

"But I think," I said, "what Brownie was telling me is that the feelings you have are really dependent on the fact that you were born black, born in the south, born in a situation in which you had to erect the blues as a kind of defence."

"That's beautiful…" Muddy said.

"He told you the truth," Otis agreed, always trying to be agreeable, nearly always amiably on the drink.

"Well, all right, then." I asked, "Are the blues the colour of your skin?"

"No, no," Otis said, to my surprise, emphatic.

"No, and I wanna tell you why," Willie said, "because, to start with, the reason the majority of us have blues is just as was stated, because of a condition from the beginning. Many generations, you know, many generations of our people had been poverty-stricken in many ways, and this is where it first comes from. That's why Brownie says a thing like he did, because it's the ABCs of the blues."

"In most of the cities you go to," Muddy added strongly, "in every town there's a skid row, you know? You go down and see how those peoples is living, and sleeping in hallways, and don't have fifteen cents for a bowl of beans. He can be your colour, my colour, anybody's colour. Ask him, does he have the blues the one day you catch him not drunk?" A sour edge had come into Muddy's tone. "I can say," he went on, "'Do you have the blues?' He'll tell you, 'Yeah.' If he ain't got fifteen cents for a bowl of beans...an' if he ain't got the blues then... I don't know when he's gonna have 'em. That's the two things. Hard times. And when you're in love with a lady and she cuts loose...if you ain't got the blues, when you gonna have 'em?"

"I've still got a problem, Muddy," I said. "What you're saying is that when Brownie says that the blues are the colour of his skin, historically he's right, that the blues come out of those years...would you say, closest to emancipation?"

"That's right," Muddy said.

"Right, so I want to ask you a question, then. Why is it that... most of you, I suppose, came off sharecropper farms in the south?

"Yeah."

"Why is it that the white sharecropper doesn't sing the blues?"

"Well," and Muddy rapped his guitar again, "he has his type. He has the blues, but he can't express them like one of us. You have to learn this from the coloured man. He has 'em. We was born with it."

At Gerde's Folk City in New York's Village, Brownie shouldered his way through the swinging kitchen doors and sidestepped, with surprising deftness, given his limp, several straddlers sprawled on their bar stools. Sonny followed with his hand heavy on the small of Brownie's back, and when they were on stage Brownie, laughing, assumed the expository tones of a corn-pone barrister.

He thrust his jaw into the spotlight, the tendons in his neck and forearms catching that light, and there was a slight curl at the corner of his lip, a claw track of anger under his haughty yet seemingly available air, and he turned to Sonny, who was sitting beside him on a stool staring unperturbed into the glare of the spotlight, and Brownie asked, "River, what you doing?"

Sonny replied, "Just relaxin' my mind, man, just relaxin' my mind."

"How you relax your mind?"

"Fattening frogs for snakes."

Brownie settled on his stool, his hobble-boot hooked on a rung, and he eased right into a talking blues, a song full of comic innuendo, showing – with his command of phrasing (a kind of heartier Josh White) – that he was no mumbling country boy – he knew how to deliver each articulated syllable in each word for a bending, a flattening, and tongue-in-cheek effect: "…only one town in the world can afford this song. I want you to know what town it is. That's New York City. I'm not a New Yorker anymore. I'm a Californian. But, to be exact and truthful about it, I happened to be in New York about two weeks ago. I was walking down 42nd Street between 7th Avenue and Broadway, and all the New Yorkers call that spot 'the Crossroads of the World' because there's so many colours and kinds and different nationalities. Old unlucky me, a country boy from California, happened to be in the crowd that day, and I heard somebody whistling. Being curious and country, I looked back, and it was a lady cab driver. Her cab had stopped. She was beckoning her hand, and I walked over, as any other gentleman would have done. She said, 'Yes, you'll do. Do you know anything about a car?' I says, 'A little, ma'am, I used to own one back in the Thirties, when things were tough, and they were tough enough. She says, 'I've been here half a day and I can't get this cab to move. Would you lend me a helping hand?' 'That's an agreement.' Well, I got inside, stepped on the starter, but nothing happened. Put it in low and tried again. Bad condition. I'd never seen a car in that shape in my life. 'Try the ignition key, lady. It don't have to be in. It don't have to be on.' Oh my, not a spark. 'Only one thing I know to do.' She said, 'What's that?' 'Got to look up under your hood':

That's no way to take care of a car, ma'am.
You've got to put antifreeze in the wintertime
so it won't freeze up and bust on you.
Change the oil every thousand miles
and grease it sometimes, too.
Your old man ain't around to grease it,
grease it anyway. Ain't no harm in it.
Makes it run better.
and you'll get more mileage.

Try better gas next time."

A very small white woman with cropped hair had followed Brownie and Sonny out of the kitchen and she was standing in the shadows at the end of the bar, four coloured felt pens and a wire-ring pad in her hand. As Brownie and then Sonny sang, she sketched. Her name was Laura. She was so small and she worked with so little flair that no one noticed her. She sang along as she sketched. She worked very fast. I held her little pads for her. She

408

tore drawings out of the books and gave them to people. "It's a gift of a gift," she said. "I got a gift and now you got a gift. Me to you, man."

After the set, when Brownie and Sonny were closeted again in their cramped dressing room downstairs below the kitchen, she appeared with a string-bean black boy of about nineteen. He had a straggly beard and wore a patterned skullcap. She said, "Meet a friend, Sonny. He be from Chicago." Sonny jabbed his hand into a blind man's nowhere space and the boy grasped it. She added, "He also be a artist." Sonny shook his hand again. After banter about Chicago, the boy departed. She said, "He be coming apart, bad…he be like me, man, messed up, man."

A year before, Laura Brown had showed up alone at the dressing room. Since then she had looked after Sonny whenever he was in New York playing in the club. Sitting with her in a corner of the tiny room, sharing bar Scotch in a paper Dixie cup, she told me that at sixteen she had received a Guggenheim Fellowship and had gone to study in Paris. Returning to New York, she "was sickened – man. Really, I be so sickened of this town where the peo-

ple be more like the roaches they trying to kill. It be a sewer town, man. Happy time in rat town." She married, continued to paint, made no effort to sell her work, and each evening moved nimbly after Sonny, guiding him up narrow stairways, taking him home to his very ill wife, sometimes helping Sonny's wife sew Sonny's clothes. Her sketch pads were filled with portraits, in brown, black, green, and yellow, of Sonny.

Of an early evening, I went to have supper at Sonny's. He had just moved to 85th Street, west of Central Park, a brownstone full of boosters and bootleggers. He had lived with his wife, Roxanne, for more than twenty years in a two-room Harlem flat at 110 West 125th Street; but after the Harlem rent riots and all the junkie killings, no one – not even Brownie – would go into Harlem for a drink and supper with Sonny. Harlem, certainly Sonny's old neighbourhood, reeked of decay and dying and rats played hop-scotch in the gutters. Stores, the Jewish delicatessens, were boarded up, the broken glass of the looted windows catching the pale sun of the early winter days.

The afternoon that Sonny left Harlem, four young boys from a nearby building were struggling along the sidewalk with a mat-tress, trying to carry it home without it flopping over, but then, out of exasperation, they just dropped it and left it on the side-walk, the vermin inside scurrying for cover in the torn quilting. The music Sonny could hear as he stood in the street not far from the mattress, the music from inside the Pabst Blue Ribbon bars and the open piss-smelling doorways, the music was grinding electric blues, "E-lectric, in my brain, man."

Street singers like himself had left Harlem years ago. In the old days, in the 1940s and early 1950s, they had come straggling up out of the south "where the water tastes like cherry wine," and they had moved from corner to corner singing for nickels and dimes and there had been laughter and shared whisky, but none of those singers was ever out on the street anymore ("where the water tastes like turpentine") – where some strung-out dude could cut you with a razor, not only for your nickels but for your guitar, rings, anything that might fetch a few dollars at the pawnshops.

So, Sonny had moved to West 85th Street, into big rooms down a dimly lit long hall that stank of pork and cabbage, a bleak light at the top of the stairs from a bare bulb in the ceiling. Sonny had brought a young man and his wife out of Harlem. They had an agreement. The rent would be free for them and Sonny would teach the young man to play the mouth harp if the girl cooked, swept up, and helped Sonny's wife around the house while Sonny was singing on the road.

The girl, dark and shy and delicately boned, seemed to enjoy deep-frying the chicken and making rice and collard greens for our supper. It was Sunday, and Sonny was full of the expansiveness of a man comfortable in his home. He sent the boy downstairs to bang on the door of one of the house bootleggers to get more Johnnie Walker Red. After supper, Sonny stomped his feet on the hardwood floor and flapped his hands across his harp as he sang, *I got my eye on you, woman, there ain't nothing in the world you can do.* He reached out, his unseeing eyes wide open, beckoning.

His wife, Roxanne, emaciated, her skin looking as if it had been brushed with wood ash, deep lines around her mouth – dying of cancer – began to hum, watching to see if Sonny would encourage her, and Sonny said, "Yeah," and then he told me that she had been churched as a child and had once sung gospel at Town Hall. Uncertain of the words, she started, "Didn't it rain children" – but lost the rhythm, and Sonny spoke gruffly to her. He stomped out the beat, making sure she got it, and she swung in, her haggard voice husky from sickness but sensual as she threw her head back and tried to roar – *See them coming in, two by two...* her thin arms, the flesh hanging loose under her arms, lifted. And as she pet-patted with her feet – her felt slippers flapping against the floor – her memory failed, she lost the words. We clapped, and Sonny let out a fox-call *whoop* and again spoke about the night she had sung at Town Hall, while Laura Brown took Sonny's bony and rangy wife by the elbow and helped her to her sickbed, a narrow cot under a window, under burglar bars in the window.

⤜✦⤛

"The gout's got me, man," Sonny said, "the gout's got me good, an' thas bad. The doctor says thas too bad for me if I don't stop drinking."

"So, stop drinking, man."

"You see my whisky?"

"Yeah."

"Gimme a drink."

⪪✦⪫

Sonny and Brownie were back in town, playing at the Riverboat in Yorkville. While Sonny was changing to a street shirt in their dressing room, he said, "Man, you remember that white girl what painted – Laura? Well, she's dead. It was at Christmas and I call her home and her husband answers and he says, 'Sonny – she killed herself. She took her life. She killed herself,' and I had to hang up on that crying man."

Sonny, putting harmonicas into a small leather travelling case, said, "And that kid, you know – the one I was helping out – that mother what was in my home? He stole everything I had, man, stole it, and he busted his wife in the face so's she wouldn't tell, but she tole me anyways."

Brownie, fingerpicking on his axe as a counter to Sonny's anger, said, "I come over from Brooklyn and I open the door and Sonny's sitting there with a gun, waiting on the little mothefucka to come on through the door."

"Yeah, I sat down and wait for him," Sonny said. "He come an' knocked on the door. I said, 'Man, you don't come in here. I'll kill you and everybody else. Don't come in my house.' That's when Brownie walked up and come in my room, and the boy kept on knocking on the door, ringing the bell. I took the door and put it wide open, slammed it, opened it, and said, 'Let him walk in now, okay, but I'll kill him dead if he come in here.

"People," Sonny went on, "didn't believe I could see a man to shoot at, but when I was coming up singing in a tobacco town, Durham – in the Thirties – a great big restaurant guy, he didn't pay what he was owing to me and I asked the man for my pay and he say, 'Go away, boy,' so I went to where I was living – with a

412

Jewish drummer and his wife – and I got the drummer's gun, a
.38. I went on back round to that place and said, 'Gimme my
money,' and that man knocked me on the table. But, you know,
I had that .38. I can make out some black and white outta one eye
and he was wearing white pants. And I shot him, man, I shot him
in those white pants. His wife had a shoe, almost beat me in the
head with her shoe heel. So, I knocked her back, and he kept on
trying to come to me, so that's when I shot at him six times, hit
him three times. In those white pants."

"You kill him?"

"Naw. He live. I put him in the hospital. He stayed in the hospital six months. The woman, she's still screaming, 'Get me outta
here, this blind man's gonna kill us all. He's gonna kill ever'body.'"

"Everybody," Brownie said, tapping his fingers on his guitar
neck, "wants to go to heaven but nobody wants to die."

"Hell, no, man. I don't want to die."

"You'd a shot that boy?" I asked.

"The one in my home?"

"Yes."

"Yeah, I shoot him."

"You'd have gone to jail, maybe die."

"Yeah, I would have gone."

>—+—<

"River," Brownie called to Sonny, because that's how they sometimes spoke out to each other on stage, "River" to "River," and
Sonny answered, "Yeah, what you want?"

"Rivers don't die," Brownie said with his sweet beamish smile.

"I can't swim," Sonny said and laughed.

>—+—<

Brownie and Sonny met in 1939 in Burlington, North Carolina,
busking outside baccarat houses, the gin mills, and the textile

mills. Sonny had been playing with the guitarist Blind Boy Fuller, but Fuller was in the last stages of kidney disease.

"Me and Fuller were together," Sonny said, "until Brownie met Blind Boy. Fuller asked Brownie to play him a piece, you know. Brownie couldn't play guitar as good as he plays now. But, he played, and he was doing good. But, as he was playing, Fuller told me to say to the man, 'You can sing and all that, but you can't play no guitar.' That made Brownie go back outside when Fuller told him that, and start fighting like a angry bear, you know, to learn how to play better. So, he did, still playing his same style, but he went home, and then to Texas for a while, and perfected it."

⋙✦⋘

Just before Fuller's death in 1941, Brownie and Sonny had latched on to each other, eventually moving to Harlem, with Brownie always talking the necessary street talk while Sonny settled wherever he found himself into a quietude. Brownie was amiable but suspicious, and sometimes he could be prickly and even abrasive – a man with a magisterial head who had a hobble that he hated; year after year he kept a journal – misspelt memories, sayings, and poems – aware of his own pain and anger, and aware how chameleon his love could be: he had a smile that could kill. He was slow to trust anybody. Sonny had to be trusting, he was compelled to be trusting. He was not only blind, he didn't "know his letters and numbers" and instead of trying to write his name he carried an ink pad and a stamp: SONNY TERRY. He was all pockets – for his harps, his keys, his papers, his money. Strangers separated his money for him into those pockets…ones, fives, tens, but from time to time people lied to him, took money from his open palm, shortchanged him.

⋙✦⋘

SONNY TERRY

❦

"You know," I said, "I sometimes think the blues has got this very private language that no white person would be aware of."

"How come," Sunnyland, liking the idea, asked us, "Blind John Davis said 'blues jumped the rabbit?'"

"That's before my time," Muddy said, laughing. "I thought he said blues jumped the dog. I thought it was a dog."

"You gotta tell me, man," I said, "what does 'blues jumped the rabbit' mean?"

"Well, I can tell you what it means," Willie Dixon said. "When they say 'blues jumped the rabbit,' it goes back to how Brownie was telling you...relating to coloured people as the blues. Now by the blues, we mean, under the conditions this guy was in, who-ever he was," and Willie started laughing, "he jumped the rabbit and he ran it for a solid mile. He ran until he lay down and cried. That's what it means, 'blues jumped the rabbit.'"

"I'll tell you..." Muddy said, liking the joke he was about to tell on himself, "see, I thought it meant that he had a very good rabbit dog, you know, a hound dog or whatever you want to call it, and his name was Old Blue."

We all laughed.

"Well, if you can't understand what it means," I said, "how do you expect me to understand?"

"I'll ask you another question," Otis said.

"Yeah."

"I was thinking just about how the blues come through Texas loping like a mule."

"I don't think I know about that," Muddy said.

"Me neither," Otis said.

"Do you understand it? I don't," I said.

"Well, I got news for you," Willie said. "There are a lot of places in Texas, if you don't go through there loping like a mule, you done messed up."

We all broke into laughter again, this time a knowing laughter.

⌐✦⌐

James Cotton sat hunched at the end of the sofa with Sonny sitting up close to him on a stool. Cotton sang out:

> O they 'cused me of murder and
> I haven't harmed a man.
> Lord they 'cused me of forgery –
> I can't write my name.

Cotton, intent on signifying before Sonny, blew his harp.

Sonny listened, seemingly impassive (in my mind's eye I heard him singing, *I got my eye on you, ain't nothing in the world you can do*). Sonny, who always acted deadpan about his blindness, was always so matter-of-fact about his having been rendered blind when he was an eleven-year-old boy: a piece of stick had flown into his left eye, and then at sixteen an iron pipe that had been thrown into the air by a child had come down and caught his right eye…and, to leave him even more vulnerable, a year later a white truck driver sideswiped his father's wagon into a ditch, killing his father and two mules. Once he'd got to be a grown man of twenty-three, he began travelling to Raleigh and Durham, North Carolina, where, as I've said, he met Blind Boy Fuller. Sonny told me he "was trying to get to some of everywhere" by blowing his small Hohner harp outside gas stations, mills, tobacco auctions. Once, for a week he even worked outside a whorehouse with a boy who played a didley.

Brownie, alert to the undercurrent of justifications in the room – his smiling gaiety always cross-wired to defiance – jabbed the neck of his guitar straight up in the air and smacked the apron with the palm of his hands, saying – as if a hard-times-on-the-road anecdote would stand against Cotton's strongest note, "The night JFK was shot and killed, I pulled into a gasoline station and the gasman leans his head in my window and he says, 'I don't serve no black gas'…and ever since I wonder why people drinks their coffee black."

Sonny had slipped his C harp from one of the pockets sewn across the front of his shirt, and he cupped the harp in his ham-fist. He let out a wail that contained a chugging sound, the call of a country train-in-the-night, and then he gave a hound dog, fox-chase *whoop* and Brownie sang, complementary to the grain of loneliness, "…*if I didn't have bad luck I'd have no luck at all.*"

Cotton grinned impishly at Sonny, forgetting that Sonny couldn't see his grin. He took up his harp again and blew hard, and harder. He was used to having a microphone. Sonny said, "You playing in my face, man?"

"I'm doing my thang, Sonny."

Sonny let out another *whoop*. He didn't need a microphone.

He blew *fox chase*, his harp behind the flutter and warp of his hands, calling out – as a mewling child, a lost hound, a fretting woman, a slow freight… Cotton put his harp into his pocket and said, "You going to blow my tree down, man."

Sonny shot his hand out, saying, "Seeing is believing, that what they say, man…"

Sammy Lawhorn, his hair processed, cried, looking at me, "Man, I'm a barber, I'd like to barber in Toronto. Ain't no Jim Crow here, don't see no discrimination. Where's the coloured section in Toronto, where the coloured folks live?"

"No coloured section here, man."

"I hear there's a coloured section in Montréal. I'll get myself there."

"You can't get yourself to the toilet," Muddy said, somehow managing to sound not nasty but impishly paternal.

Otis, sitting huddled beside the air-conditioning box in the window, downing his glass of whisky, stood up and began to fret and pace.

"Otis, when we going to get you a suit that fits?" Muddy asked.

"Women try to find me inside my suit," he said.

"I could do with some pink bootie," Cotton laughed. They began to kid each other about who got "any kinda lovin'" on the road. They were lonely men. Then they asked me who I guessed had got any women lately and I said, "Sonny..."

"The blind man!"

Sonny, with a happy little hoot, asked if I would take him down the hall to his room.

Brownie said he was going to his hotel on Charles Street to cook himself some breakfast eggs and chitlins, and Muddy said he wished he could come along but all things considered, he couldn't. He didn't tell us what the "all things" were. Sonny rose up behind Brownie, placing his left hand on the small of Brownie's back, as he did when their set was done and Brownie led Sonny off stage (on one level this was always a moving moment: on another, it was hokum) and down between tables to their dressing room...

⤞✦⤝

Sonny (the morning *Globe and Mail* had been left like news flags on the floor at the base of each room's door) said in the hallway: "Man, gotta tell you, I just lost my wife. She died. I got back and they tried to put a derby hat on my head for the funeral, but I said that that derby hat was slavery times, and the undertaker, he said he had a plot for me, too, and I said fill it over, man, 'cause I ain't about to die, and when I do you can toss me in the river. I don't care."

I said I was sorry about Roxanne, but I had to laugh at the undertaker trying to hustle Sonny for a burial plot. We walked Sonny down the hall to his room. Brownie waited by the open door while I led Sonny to his bed. As Brownie and I came out of the hotel into the early morning street, Brownie, stepping a little ahead of me, started in on a talking whisper:

> *I can walk by myself, stay by myself,*
> *I don't even have to bother you.*

>—◆—<

A HOUSE ON POPLAR PLAINS ROAD:

A line of sweat ran down Otis's cheek and shone like scar tissue in the light from a table lamp. He sang:

> *one of these days I'm going crazy*
> *buy me a shotgun and kill my baby*
> *ain't no body's business if I do*

Shoulders slumped inside a tuxedo jacket two sizes too big, the sleeves too long, almost covering the backs of his hands to the knuckles, Otis talked in a whisky drawl about botherations on his mind as he shuffled around the house and through people, and picked up small things as they caught his eye, putting them in his pockets. I didn't say anything but took them out of his pockets. He smiled sheepishly and explained, as if surprised that any explanation were necessary, "I'm not stealing, I'm visiting." He slipped a cherrywood church warden's long-stemmed pipe into his suitcoat side pocket. The owner of the pipe whose house we were in, let him be, let the pocketing pass, while Sunnyland Slim, lean and bony, laughed, showing a big front tooth gone, a dark gap. (Sunnyland was not his name, not his real name, and neither was Slim, his real name being Albert Luandrew: "I got a sunshine name," he said, "that's named after something evil, and what was evil was a train…it run its route between Memphis to St. Louis, and it would come through the night so you could hear that train, lonesome, and you could smell that train in the dark, the Sunnyland, it was called.

> *OO-ow-oh-oh, seems like I heard*
> *That ole lowdown Sunnyland blow…*

It blew through the night, and there was one night when the Sunnyland blew down and killed two families – "…a black share-cropper and his children, and a poor white and his family who were trying to push a wagon across the crossing tracks and all the poe-lice found were broken wheels and bodies in the long grass." So Albert Luandrew took his name from the killer train and sang his sunshine songs in the juke joints, blues that he "churched" with a gospel roll, nasal cries about death in the alley, first singing by himself in the 1920s until he started playing piano in Ma Rainey's travelling show, becoming a travelling man, with the long legs for it, and when I first met him he said he was just pass-ing on through untroubled, but most recently he had got himself stabbed in a Detroit whorehouse, "Where I weren't whoring, I was just handling the honky-tonk.") He smiled down at Otis, younger than Sunnyland…Otis, who poured himself several fin-gers of whisky in a glass and sat at the kitchen table, saying, "You can't understand me 'cause you don't know nothing about me, but I'll tell you something you never would know unless I told you." (… Otis, who had come up out of the Delta to play piano with Muddy Waters in South Side Chicago, always eased in his mind by whimsy and a little drink, not denying the story that he was Muddy's half-brother, though the story wasn't true), and I said to him what I had heard Muddy tell him the night before, "Do you know, you is one of the greatest blues pianists in this world, an' this is a big world."

"Thas right, this *is* a *big* world…" (He liked to dream-talk about his daddy, saying he was a white man, a lumber king in the

Delta who was going to leave him all his money and his name –
to which Sunnyland gave him a gap-toothed scoff: "You ain't got
no white nothing, you poor as dirt.")

Otis took hold of a white woman's hand. Her lips were wet:

gonna buy me a shotgun and kill my baby…
ain't no body's business if I do

"Man," Otis said, "Charlie don't give a damn how I live,
Charlie can't care how I die… So I tell you, you don't care how I
love, you can't care how I kill, I don't want none of your business,
you can't have none of mine." He tucked his head to the side, with
a shy sweet smile, as if there was no spider working in his mind.
Otis lifted the woman's hand and tasted the soft flesh between her
fingers, tonguing the little web of flesh, holding my eye with his
eye, and then he said, "You don't understand, man… I am the resurrection of the dead."

⤙✳⤚

Brownie, as a boy coming up, was a boy on polio crutches. He had
gone to school a little and had worked his father's backwoods still
a lot…*moonshine, you're white lightning in a water glass, through
a white light you're a knockout blas', moonshine, you ain't no friend
of mine…*

His father had given him a guitar, telling him, "You going to
play the guitar, you best learn to pick. Otherwise you'll strum all
your life." When full grown, handsome, and muscular through
the shoulders, Brownie took to the road, heading to tobacco auctions, juke joints, honky-tonks, and the New York streets and
bawdy houses ("I really learned about white men and cold cash
from Wall Street…when things were tough, and they were
tough enough… There was a black woman, she could squat
down and pick up folded dollar bills that these white men laid
on the floor with her bootie and one day she picked her drunk

421

self up and walked out of there into the traffic, stone blind on booze, and got herself killed on the street"), his New York, then, being Manhattan, where he and Sonny lived for a year, between 1940 and 1941, in a nine-room house at Sixth Avenue and Lennox Street…twenty-five people, street singers and their wives and lovers… Pete Seeger, Woody Guthrie, Cisco Houston, Brother Montgomery, and Sis Cunningham – the white girl who played accordion – and then there was Leadbelly, and the sweet singer, Josh White, who could make an old country song sound chamber erudite, living not far away – all of them shuffling and scuffling the streets for nickels and quarters… Brownie and Sonny left the streets after a man, who had weaselled on their fee for playing a private party, threw a jug at them from a window, and broke the brim of Brownie's straw hat, nearly breaking his head. And they quit the streets for good when they were hired in 1946 to play in the Broadway show *Finian's Rainbow*, for two and a half years. Then Brownie and Sonny were hired in 1955 to sit and play in the wings of another Broadway theatre during the long run of Tennessee Williams' *Cat on a Hot Tin Roof*. Brownie picked and Sonny *whoop*ed and hollered into the Big Daddy night, each for $350 a week.

⌐※⌐

"Man," I said to Sonny, trying to provoke him a little, "you caught a lot of women in your life."

"What you mean by that, man?"

"I mean you've got your 'Hooray, hooray, these women is killin' me' song."

"And they 'bout do it, too, but not quite, no. I'm getting old but, like I say, they ain't killed me yet."

"You must have caught an awful lot of those women."

"No, I ain't cut 'em," he said, mishearing me, "but I loved 'em. I loved the women."

⌖

"For twenty-eight years," Brownie said, "I've been with Sonny. That's a long time to last with any man. Especially two men who've been living the blues. Some years ago, I found old letters my father wrote my mother when he was in jail, and he told her to get out and leave the kids behind and if, when he got out, she was still there, he'd kill her.

"I hadn't seen my father in about twelve years. And the thing is, he used to talk to me when I was ten and twelve; I couldn't understand him. At the age of forty, I figured now was the time to ask him – what was he talking to me about.

"He said: 'Well, son, sit down. I'll lay my cards on the table and I'll tell you. I've got four kids and, you know,' he says, 'I'll see if you're able to understand.'

"So, I jotted it all down, and called it 'My Father's Words.'"

"How old was he then?"

"Around seventy, seventy-one."

"And where's he living now?'

"He's living with me in California. At the age of seventy-five, he's dancing and having a good time. Unfortunately, he can't play anymore. He still sings a lot and has a good ole ball. I learned guitar from him, but he didn't have time to teach me. He was trying to make them bread and beans. I thought that was lovely:

> *My father, my father, said these words,*
> *followed me down through the years…*
> *Yes, yes, yes,*
> *believe half you see, son, and nothing that you hear,*
> *there's a many broken heart*
> *that never sheds no tears.*
> *It takes rocks, takes rocks and gravels*
> *to make, to make a solid road.*
> *Everything that shines, boy,*

I declare, it can't be gold.
Well, the grave holds secrets, son,
that will never be told.
He said, the longer, longer the road,
the short, short, shorter the turns.
Yes, yes, yes…
Listen my son, you'll never grow too old to learn—
I said why?—
Because old coals will kindle,
Light up and begin to burn…"

One afternoon, while talking to Sonny, I asked about Harry Belafonte, and he said, "Harry Belafonte did a favour for me and Brownie McGhee, and I thank him for that."

"What do you think of the way Harry sings the blues?"

"Sings the blues?"

"Yeah."

"He sings it the way he wants to sing it. He can't sing it the way we sing it."

"Why is that?"

"Well… Why are you asking me that?"

"I'm curious."

"He can't sing the blues like we sing it. He doesn't know it. He doesn't have soul. He can't sing it like we sing it."

"You mean, he hasn't had the same experience?"

"I don't know, I don't know about that. The blues can be hard to understand."

He let out a kind of field holler moan. "Harry couldn't do that," he said. And then, "See, if I get to singing a sad blues, 'I love you, baby, baby, please don't go,' and 'I'm a lonely man,' I ain't blue all the time I'm singing that. There's happy blues and sad blues. If I had to be sad every night I play, I might go out of my mind. I ain't sad every time I do that.

"But, still blues comes from way back in the slaves and every-thing. You know, like, you would hear people singing in slavery time. You'd hear them old coloured people, I'd get my mother talking about it, 'Oh, I'ma gonna tell God how you treat me.' So, now this poor man, my father, he'd come out and listen. She's singing, talking about him. 'I'ma tell God how you treat me.'"

"Your mother was born a slave?"

"No, my mother wasn't. She wasn't old enough. My grand-mother and grandfather was."

"And your mother learned these songs from her mother and father?"

"Oh, yeah. Uh-huh."

"What one hears about blues singers is that they've lived lives that were really tough, a lot of hard treatment."

"I didn't have too much bad treatment, to tell the truth, because I always carried myself in a way that I'd get along with anybody. I'd be walking along this road playing my harmonica. White people would stop and put me in their car and ask me where I'm going, and if I was going into town they'd give me a ride, you know. They'd say, 'Come on, play us a piece.' And I'd play them a piece they liked, you know. I wouldn't get mad or noth-ing, because they treat me right. They weren't mad at me. I played to get a ride. Because there in the country like that, you were walking five or ten miles to go to town, you know."

"You seem to me, you know, kind of satisfied with the way things turned out for you."

"Oh, yeah, turned out fine. I told you about the restaurant guy with the white pants who took my money. Now, he's dead and gone. For years he's been dead. And, I'm still living."

⌁⧓⌁

If there was no after-hours booze can open where we could drink whisky at two o'clock in the morning after the last show at the Riverboat, I would drive Sonny to Fran's all-night restaurant on College Street. We would stand in the takeout serving bay beside the horseshoe-shaped Arborite bar and order Banquet Burgers (the room was always crowded with pimps, grifters, transvestites, druggies, and stalkers), and Sonny would holler, "Yea, yea, man, do me right," shuffling forward (his speed of foot dependent on the condition of his gout – stabbing his collapsible sectioned white cane at the floor, waiting for his burger on a bun with onions and bacon and cheddar cheese, with a side clump of Mrs. Fran Deck's sliced bread-and-butter pickles. He insisted on paying for the cheque at the front counter, in the way that he paid wherever he went: first asking the cost, and then taking the bills from the separate specially sewn pockets across the belly of his street shirts (a variation on his showtime shirts with their several pockets for his Hohner harmonicas)…ones, fives, tens…crying out, with a grin, "I cotch you, man, I cotch you…" but trusting that honest change was going to be put into the open palm he held out in the direction of the whirr of the cash register.

◈―◇

In his Carriage House Hotel room on Jarvis Street (in earlier years, it had been called the Frontenac Arms), we would sit at a small kidney-shaped table and unwrap the wax paper bundling from around the burgers, pour two half-glasses of whisky, and eat, he with a two-handed grip on the bun, chawing it down without a word.

After one more "taste" of "sky" he would give me a handful of cash to sort through and put in his special pockets to get him into and through the next day. One night he said, "I'm gonna give you one of my harmonicas but watch out, they got ghosts. Watch out for ghosts. They bite." He let out his fox-chase *whoop*. As I was leaving the room he said he didn't feel like he was gonna be so left alone like he often said he felt. He believed that he was going to get a morning visit from his regular German lady friend, one of the hotel housekeepers.

"She change my sheets, man."

She'd been changing his sheets whenever he came into town for over two years.

Her name was Gretel, which I thought was very funny, thinking of Sonny as Hansel, who in the old story had by moonlight followed a trail of white pebbles out of a dark forest.

"You ever hear the kid's story of Hansel and Gretel?"

"Naw."

"It's just about these two kids in a forest trying to get away from a witch who's a cannibal. She likes to keep kids and eat kids."

"My daddy used to fatten frogs for snakes. He kept snakes."

"Why'd he do that?"

"To sell to poor white folk. Peoples who churched themselves for Jesus by using snakes."

At noon the next day, the lock was off his door so I walked right in and there was Gretel, a small somewhat-drawn bony woman in her middle years, sitting naked on top of Sonny, still wearing her housekeeper's cap. She was too at ease in her pleasure to get off his body and cover herself (which was of no immediate matter: I had seen her undressed several times in his room; narrow-hipped, small-breasted). Sonny, lying back, staring blind straight up, said, "You cotch me, man, you cotch me," and he laughed, a big haroop from his belly, so she swung off his hips and put on a pair of plain canvas waitress shoes with laced-up ankle supports, white panties, and a black brassiere, and then she reached down to Sonny and stroked him, something wistful in the parting stroke, saying with a smirk, "Zis…"

He pulled on a plain white T-shirt, his body having the heft of thickness and weight, not muscled, but a slab-like solidity through the shoulders and chest.

"Get dressed, Sonny," she said smiling broadly. "Get decent."

"Mmmn," making a moaning sound, as if a field holler had crossed his mind. He called toward her, "You awright?"

I knew only that she had been born in Berlin, that her family home had been shelled and gutted by the Russians, that she, or a sister, had been raped by Russian soldiers (she was evasive), that she had left Germany before the Wall had gone up, and that she liked working in hotels.

"I see what I see in the rooms. People acting who they are, my having not to be seen."

"You know I got to watch out for Sonny," I said. "You know that."

"What you call zis *knowing*, means what?" she asked. She gave me a tight little smile, making it clear she believed that she knew something about knowing that I did not.

When she was dressed in her brown uniform with white piping at the cuffs and collar, she walked over to the bedside table and counted out money for herself from the three small stacks of bills I had laid out the night before. She folded the bills into an apron waist pocket, walked to Sonny, and put two fingers to her lips and pressed the fingers to Sonny's lips.

"These women is killing me," he hooted at me.

As she passed, I said, "Looks like you took a lot of money."

"I take only what I need, what is right."

"Maybe yes, maybe no," I said.

"You want to count?"

"I know that you know that if I thought you were stealing from him, I'd hurt you."

"You do not know how to hurt me," she said. "You ask Sonny."

He'd heard his name and called, "Yeah, what, man?"

"He thinks, Sonny," Gretel said crisply, buttoning her blouse close to her throat, "that maybe I steal from you."

"What she takes is what I owe her, man," he said, getting up from the bed, naked from his T-shirt down to his feet.

"Then that's the way it is," I said, yielding the space to her.

Fisting the cash money deep into her waist pocket, she left.

I again counted out the three small piles of ones, fives, and tens – from left to right – and seeing that Sonny's wax paper from his Banquet Burger was still on the table, along with a slice of onion, a couple of pickle slices, and some ketchup on the paper, I rolled it all into a tight ball and jump-shot it from across the room at the wastebasket beside the bed. It went in.

"Swish," I said.

"What's going on, man?"

"Zis."

"What?"

"Zis, what we're doing," I said as he stood half-naked staring straight ahead into nowhere.

"Swish, from downtown. Perfect."

⌁

SEVERAL YEARS LATER:

Brownie and Sonny were playing a club in Montréal.

Sonny had married again.

"Don't drink no more sky," he'd told me.

His wife, a cautious, caring woman, a retired teacher, was schoolmarmish about keeping Sonny off the whisky bottle. "Gout's gone," she'd said. His sobriety, his restored health, his amiable incurious approach to each performance – playing the same old songs with unrelenting exuberance – *my baby done changed the lock on the door* – nettled Brownie. "I'm stuck," he said sourly, "that man'll be singing 'The Midnight Special' till I die." Brownie had come to like the idea of singing sardonic Randy Newman songs about slavery:

> *In America every man is free*
> *To take care of his home and family*
> *You'll be happy as a monkey in a monkey tree*
> *You're all gonna be American*
>
> *Ain't no lions or tigers – ain't no mamba snake*
> *Just the sweet watermelon and the buckwheat cake*
> *Ev'rybody is happy as a man can be*
> *Climb aboard, little children – sail away with me*

They had, to Brownie's busting-out pride, cut such an album, with Arlo Guthrie on drums, singing "Just a white boy lost in the blues." One night, I'd had a conversation with Muddy, asking him what it was like playing on tour to packed houses of white people lost in the blues, people who, more often than not, sat on their hands in studious appreciation. "Where are your black people?" I asked. "Some black people," he said, "don't want to hear anything about the blues."

"A lot," I said.

"Some," he said.

"No, a lot," I said, and we let it go.

Initial sales of the Randy Newman-rooted album turned out to be disappointing. The record producers who had wanted Brownie and Sonny to continue shining the little light of "The Midnight Special" on the world – Brownie told me – felt justified in resisting any change. Which could only mean more cornbread and molasses songs.

⊰✦⊱

AUGUST, SEVEN OR EIGHT YEARS EARLIER:

They were in Toronto for three weeks, Sonny ensconced in his usual hotel on Jarvis Street – the little Berlin housekeeping lady who took coffee and sex with him in the morning was still working there – and Brownie, having long since abandoned the Hotel California flop, had settled into a bed-sitting room with a kitchen attached in a faux-chic hotel on Charles Street that was known for its upscale hooker-bar. He was eager to cook for himself – turnip greens, okra, chitterlings, ham hocks, grits. He had never in all their years together cooked a meal for Sonny. "The secret to staying together, man, is staying apart."

He had been making notes all afternoon in his journal.

"What you been writing?"

"You can't read that, man," he said, closing the book and taking up a long-handled wooden stirring spoon. "There's secrets

430

there that's never been told," he said, quoting with smiling pleasure from his Daddy song. He was wearing a sleeveless undershirt and tight white boxer shorts, standing in laced-up, heavy oxblood boots, the one sole built up for his shortened leg.

"One day, I'm gonna make you something you never had," he said, wagging the spoon at me, "biscuits with bacon milk gravy."

"Lotta things I never had."

"You'll never eat this till I make it for you."

"I want you to do something for me. I want you to do like you do in your book…write a note in this book of mine."

"What's that?"

"Your father's words. Write 'em down."

He was about to cut the bone out of a ham hock but instead sat down at a round laminated pine table and opened my book to a blank page, saying, "Oh what fools ye mortals be," which is what he always said when he was about to be pleased by his own doings but was at a loss for words.

"What're you gonna do with this?"

"Give it to my son to read some day."

"FARther's Words to A
    Son" B'McGhee
My father, My father
said these words
they followed me
down throughthe years
Believe Half you
see + Nothine that
you Hear,
Theres A many Broken
Heart, that Never
shed's No Tears

Blulvio McGhee
    8-18-90

⊰✦⊱

END TIMES:

I had a Montréal dépanneur bottle of Johnnie Red tucked under my arm.

Brownie and Sonny were coming off stage, doing what they always did, singing "Walk On"…*I got to keep on walking till I make my way back home…*with Brownie on the lead through the crowded tables, Sonny following with his left hand once more on the small of Brownie's back. But Brownie got too many steps ahead of Sonny. Sonny stumbled and almost fell. Brownie did not look back. Hands from the crowd reached for Sonny. It was awkward. Brownie kept going. Helping hands reached out until each ended up by himself at a table in an opposite corner of the barroom. I sat down in front of Sonny and took hold of his forearm.

"Who's 'at, who's sitting there?"

"Man, it's me."

"Who me?"

"Barry."

He gave a *whoop*, his little fox call, and held out his big hands, "Skin, man," he said. I shifted the bottle from under my arm and took his hands in mine. He heard the clunk of the bottle on the table.

"What you got there?"

"Whisky."

"Give it here."

"You drinking again?"

"Give it here," and he reached toward me.

"I got it for Brownie."

"Fuck 'im."

Reaching, he found the bottle and yanked it to himself, settling it down by his shoe.

"How come you here?" he asked.

"You gonna drink that?"

"Naw, and neither's he."

432

"But I want to give it to him."

"You gave it to me."

I had never heard such hardness of tone from Sonny except when he'd told me in New York that he would have shot the kid who'd stolen money from his wife.

"You talking to Brownie?" I asked.

"Naw, we don't talk 'cause we got nothing to say. He wants it that way, so…so do I."

Others crowded in around Sonny. I stood up as he basked in the whisperings in his ear, the hands laid on his shoulders. Then, I leaned in and said quietly, "I'm going over to see Brownie."

"He don't want to play with me," Sonny growled, "but he got to play with me otherwise he don't play at all. You ask him that."

"I'm not gonna ask him. Sorry, man."

Brownie, when he saw me, beamed and opened his arms and cried, "Break clean and come out fighting." Then he closed his arms across his chest.

"So what's with you and Sonny?" I asked.

"The man's a fool. Cain't say too much about it. Cain't get around a fool."

"Come on, man."

The tendons in his forearms, in his neck, were tense. There was something vengeful in his eyes.

(Once, I had seen an old man in my dreams, an old man singing, who had one tooth in his mouth like a nail.

I thought I saw that old man sitting in Brownie's head, singing…

> *got a black snake crawling.*
> *got a black snake sucking on my tongue.*
> *got a black snake crawling, long as my right arm.*)

Brownie had always exuded a powerful sense of himself that most often showed in the jut of his chin, often making him seem ready, not to confront, but to affront the world with a magisterial bearing that gave the lie to his childhood privation, his broken schooling, his broken home, his gimpy foot, his colour. The more he'd brooded on the short-circuiting of his singularity (so it seemed to me), the more he'd come to feel belittled by having to sing the same old black-eyed peas and molasses songs night after night. To nettle him even more, people had begun to say that Sonny was so good that he did not need Brownie.

Soon, Brownie and I were done trying to talk small talk.

On stage again, Brownie and Sonny sat ten feet apart. *There's a many broken heart that never sheds no tears...* When Sonny "blowed on his harp," Brownie rested himself, arms folded over his axe. When Brownie played, strumming more than picking, Sonny drummed his fingers on his knee.

Black snake crawling, the rivers had run dry.

They sang through their sullen paces of disregard, sounding dreadful.

I did not ever see them again.

‹›✦‹›

"I once heard a preacher in Detroit," I told Willie, "give a sermon on the Book of Job, and he called his sermon – 'If it ain't one thing, it's another...'" I laughed. Willie only smiled.

Wearing a freshly laundered white shirt, his tie in a perfect Windsor knot, he buttoned up his dark blue cardigan and draped his heavy arms around the neck of his bass and said, "One thing I do know that concerns the blues: not only are they here, but they're here to stay. Because if you don't have the blues about one thing, then you are gonna have it about another. And the blues is the truth. If it's not the truth, it's not the blues."

2017

A LETTER
FROM THE BLACK
SEPTEMBER WAR, 1970

I was in the area (Cairo, Beirut, Amman, and Jerusalem) trying to report what was going on, and what was going on was deeply chaotic, violent, dangerous. One afternoon in September of 1970 in Shatila Camp in Beirut, I found myself on the wrong street (easy to do, but then, I also had the habit of wearing the right shoe on the wrong foot). I was stopped at gunpoint. I was arrested by Al Saqai, the Syrian branch of the militant Palestinians. Jailed and interrogated in a language I did not understand, I was put on trial before four men. As the sun went down I began to really worry but then was released through the sudden intervention of Ghassan Kanafani, a leader of the Popular Front for the Liberation of Palestine, headquartered in Beirut.

At the noon hour of the next day, knowing that a civil war between the Palestinians in Jordan and King Hussein's Americanized army of Bedouin troops was about to break out, with my partner cameraman, Peter Davis, I flew to Amman and checked into the Intercontinental Hotel in the centre of that desert capital city.

Three days later, on the morning of September 6, as roosters and dogs howled, the battle began.

Within hours, a Russian reporter in the hotel was shot dead in the head by a sniper, and a Swede was wounded in his thigh. The ground floor convention hall rooms of the hotel were shot up and blown apart. The only safe place to sit or lie down was in the hallways. There was no light, little water. American television reporters broke into the basement kitchen and stole the breads, all the chocolate bars, and cigars. At the urging of the British reporters who'd typically formed a sanitation committee, the toilets on all floors were given a last flush.

Since I was housed on the fifth floor of the hotel in the centre of what would come to be known as the Black September War, I decided to close myself into my bathroom when all was dark at night and by light of a candle write an ongoing letter home to my darling Claire in which I would try to make real what I was able to see and hear.

My mind's eye is what I had. And the need to write it down: Looking back, I wonder…what does such a letter from someone who was there actually convey about those twelve days in Beirut and Amman? If the letter does convey any "real" sense of what was happening in the streets — what does that say about reporting? — is it always essentially something going on in the mind's eye of the reporter?

During those nights in the bathroom, eyes burning from candle smoke, I found myself singing lines from the Les McCann protest song of the time: "goddamn, goddamn…trying to make it real compared to what…"

Dear Claire:

With the sun gone down, not even a candle can be lit in the rooms: fear of snipers. Till now, only silence. Tried to sleep on pillows laid out along the corridor. Too tense. Anticipation of the unknown. I've been close to men firing weapons, but never in the centre of a battle. Morning, the wind, the howling and barking of dogs, the sky a gravel colour. From over Hussein hill came the first clattering of automatic rifle fire and the thud of artillery.

In the after-silence of the artillery, cocks crowed and the dogs barked and across the road from the hotel seven commandos, their heads wrapped in *keffiyehs*, appeared out of a side street, passing as shadows into the stone and concrete shell of a building under construction. There are such buildings all through Amman, aborted concrete pillars and exposed structural steel rods. Through the night the commandos angled down from their camps into the alleys and side streets, onto the stone roofs and into these empty houses, crouching into position, to wait. There is more machine-gun fire. The hills of Amman, rust-brown earth and stone rubble, are an echo chamber. Each shot a dry ricochet across the central valley of the city, a drummer's rimshots. Between a *clack clack* in bursts, there is a distant, faint wailing, like hundreds of women keening; it is the hysterical screeching of the thousands of hens of Amman. The screeching stops. Eggs? Are they laying eggs? In this moment of quiet the muezzin makes his morning call to prayer, his broadcast cry lost in rapid machine-gunning. The commandos across the street fire one round. There is no reply. Stillness. The army is not yet on this road.

A cooling breeze rides through the valleys of Amman, a city built on the gentle rise and fall of twelve hills. There is something harsh and half complete about this city of quarried white and grey stone. The buildings, the homes, the three- or four-storey apartment houses, are squat and lumped up the sides of the hills. Homes that seem to be built for siege. Here and there a faded blue shutter, houses painted a washed-out blue. All else is desert-stark. Chiaroscuro is for somewhere else. The shops on South Street, down toward the cramped ruins of the Roman amphitheatre, despite the elbowing crowds and the sidewalk stands of colourful magazines and candy racks and hanging scarves, are gaping black holes over which a steel shutter is rolled at night. The cafés are little more than curbside clusters of Arborite tables. The Philadelphia Hotel by the amphitheatre is built like a barracks and is almost empty. The last group to stay there, a troupe of Korean dancing girls. Children crowd along the alleys hustling cartons of cigarettes. Flashes of colour come from the commandos; some in green-and-yellow battle fatigues, some in red berets, some in cheap "Florida" sports shirts. Others are only dark eyes behind the wrap of black or red chequered *keffieyehs*. All carry a Kalashnikov assault rifle. They are often sullen with outsiders, and can play dangerous: one wheeled me up against a wall, nudging me with his Kalashnikov under my chin. They wear straight-last shoes (like poolroom sharks back home), or Bargain Store running shoes, and a few have combat boots. Over the past three years, they have become the cowboy cops of the streets of Amman. They are tough but not aggressive in the street. They've set up their own roadblocks. Iron sewer pipes and burning tires. They have held the city by default, as Amman itself became a city by default.

Before 1948, this was only a barren town in barren hills. Then, for years bedraggled hordes of refugees slumped east from the Jordan River to these slopes where they have lived without work or hope or dignity, hacking drains out of the harsh earth, using open cesspits for toilets, hauling water in jerrycans for miles, the cans filled at a communal tap – the refugees broiling in their tents during the day, freezing in the wind and rain at night. Ramshackle tents and huts. Corrugated tin roofs. Littered across the hills. Amman is a permanent way station. The Palestinians have not wanted to live here. Yet the Palestinians are more welcome in Amman than anywhere in the world.

Royal Bedouin troops and an armoured car have moved onto our Intercontinental Hotel street. A fifty-calibre machine gun is mounted on the car. Commandos are hunkered down on the roofs. To the southwest are the Nazzal and Ashrafiya hills. The commandos control those two hills. Al-Whedat camp lies in the belly between, a dust-hole. The Dutch hostages from the passenger planes at Revolution Airport, close by Zarqa camp, have been moved to a large house on Ashrafiya hill.

Late last night, before the battle broke out, I rode through the black back alleys of Al-Whedat with two Popular Front leaders, Bassam Abu-Sharif and "Ibrahim." Commando patrols crouched around small fires at roadblocks. Our car, an old Citroën, hardly made it up the steep stone-paved alleys of the camp hills.

Ibrahim, who was driving us, a man usually slow and seemingly indolent, sped through the commando posts. Though almost unknown outside the PFLP, it was he who had helped direct the Front through the hijackings of the three planes, the hostage negotiations, the dynamiting of the BOAC VC-10 at Dawson Field in the desert. It was he, silent and faceless behind his round black, other-side-of-the-moon glasses, who went unnoticed by newsmen. Inside a closely guarded courtyard, we went up narrow concrete stairs. As in all the refugee camps, the sour smell of urine clung to the walls. On the wall at the head of the stairs, a large frame containing many mounted headshot photos, like an assemblage of college graduates: the many dead "commandos" from the camp.

Ibrahim, lean and olive-skinned, with a pencil-line razor-trimmed moustache, sat in a wicker chair. He had long delicate fingers. He spread his legs. A man of weary nervousness. His legs began to flap apart and together like the wings of an awkward, half-alive bird. His right arm hung limp to the floor. He worked his yellow worry beads. He did not listen to either me or Bassam. He leaned back, *flap flap*, detached, preoccupied, aware of us only – so it seemed – as shadows on the other side of the room.

Bassam, with the ease of a young man bred among the bourgeois, a young man educated at Columbia, a man married to the extraordinary Leila Khaled who had hijacked a passenger plane over Greece, asked for *shai bi nana* (hot tea with mint). It came in dirty glasses. It was thick and black and sweet. We drank to the fedayeen. Bassam, not unaware of the effectiveness of his earnest rhetorical facility, explained, "It was the battle of Karameh that had such mythic importance for us. Until then, with the Israelis the fedayeen had always run. But there at Karameh they stood and trapped the Imperialists. It was March of 1968 and they came with their armoured brigade to wipe out the Karameh base, but the fedayeen, the men of sacrifice, did not run. Many tied explosives to their bodies and threw themselves into the Israeli tanks and others carrying explosives lay down in the path of the tanks and blew them up. The Israelis like to strike fast and then clear out but our men had blown the bridges and the fedayeen stood and fought and killed themselves to kill the Israelis. We took heavy losses and the Israelis destroyed the camp of Karameh, but for the first time they lost hundreds and the Israelis do not like to lose one man."

Ibrahim, with his dark close-cropped head resting on the back of his chair, was not listening. There was a curious serenity about his indifference to Bassam's explication of a moment in the Palestinian narrative. Though he had forcefully helped shape the Front policy through the last strung-out days before the battle, the features of his face had a sculpted calmness, the calm of a man given over – either through habit of faith or ideology, or both – to inevitability.

Bassam went on: "You see, after Karameh the masses flooded out of the camps to our ranks. We could not get them Kalashnikov guns fast enough. The men believed that the Israelis could be hurt, that the victory could be won. Now our strength is truly with the masses and we stand against all reactionary regimes. The conflict must come between the masses and the exploiters and here in Jordan it will come immediately, for the King has made a military government. They will move against us and we will stand and the masses will win. There can be no other way. The generals have decided. It must be now. So, let it be. We can afford many deaths. The King's men, like the Israelis, can afford very few. You will see. The masses will win."

The commandos across from the hotel have fired on the Bedouins, who begin riding their mounted machine guns like jockeys. Bullets claw the stone houses, showering orange sparks. A wooden awning cut to pieces falls from its hinges. A wall collapses. Cars parked by curbs have become fireballs, exploding gas tanks, tires, ballooning tunnels of black smoke. There is a pocket of silence. Then. Bombardment has begun on al-whedat hill in east Amman. The machine guns in the distance have a steady engine-chugging sound. The methodical pumping of death's plunger. A sound in which there is nothing human, in which a scream is drowned and lost. Commandos have pulled away from the houses on the hotel street.

The Bedouins have established a mortar position beside the hotel. There are five small tanks in the street. They are pelting the Nazzal and Al-Whedat hillside. Houses have become balls of bone, white smoke, and then…a yellow smear settles over the hillside. The Bedouins have a 105 mm howitzer rocket rifle on a Jeep truck. The howitzer is long and obscene in its thin insect hardness and in the way, so stationary, it casts its recoil as a concussion through all the houses and the hotel. Windows shatter. Bombarded apartments collapse in on themselves. There is no let-up in the firefighting; the light, sterile crackling of machine guns, the howitzer and the mortars, empty thunder thuds, thwacking heavy-calibre guns to the lower right, and up front, the thin, dry whistling of infantry rifles. The air squeezes against the walls. Each hotel room is a cubicle of dead space. Fear comes from not knowing. At the centre of not knowing. A yearning to not only know something, anything, but to write it down. The menace of stillness.

The army assault began yesterday in the north when the army drove past the hotel to a rise in the main valley from where they tentacled out. Al-Whedat hill directly east. Hussein hill and Jabal el-Hussein refugee camp farther east. The amphitheatre and the commercial centre are south, and southwest is Al-Whedat camp. The army, its movements like several lungs, heaving and expanding into and along the main roads. Then, winded, contracting. Al-Whedat hill is blanketed by smoke. The valleys, an underground of death and dying. The sun is high. The houses of Amman gleam through the smoke like chips of bone. With each break in the firing, I hear the hysterical hens, but no human voice, only a vacant calmness that is close to madness. The city has become a sprawl of fires, plumes of black smoke. In the streets, commando bodies are embers and their burial ornaments are brass shell casings. Useless deaths. Martyrdom, in the minds of spokesmen and distraught mothers.

On this the third day, apparently there is a Palestinian spotter in one of the hotel rooms. At five in the afternoon, four troop trucks of Bedouin infantry parked by a row of trees and a stone wall. Within two minutes, Palestinian mortars from Nassal hill blow out the yard beside them. A just miss. The Bedouin gunner reeled around and pumped jackhammer rounds into the hotel. He tore a foot-wide hole in my bathroom wall. Where I've been writing. A percussive smashing whoosh, a shattering thud. Pinned to the ground in the room on my belly. If I thought that death could only come in sanctioned ways, I was wrong. The carpet, prophetic: thick with dust. Waited for the night when I could drag a mattress into the hallway. Try to sleep. A mole.

Once the battle had begun, the French reporters banded together. Their aim: to arrange to get out as a group. This morning, Eric Rouleau, an excellent reporter in the Middle East for *Le Monde* (whom I'd met and become friendly with in Cairo), told me that a deal had been done: the French ambassador to Jordan had persuaded the Bedouins and the King to let a bus take the French to Aqaba, the port city in the gulf. I told Eric it was now time to assert my Canadian/Canadienne *bona fides*: *sympatico* to the Québécois, they should take me with them. He put my case to the group. "Totally humourless," he said sorrowfully. "They dismissed you with a sneer." Within the hour, the French, shameless, loaded up and departed, believing they were taking the story of the year with them.

Night comes. The moon lights up the dead in the streets. A deeper fear comes. Without electricity, without water, I, like the others in the hotel, wait and listen to shell fire and snipers. There can be no candles in the rooms. Both the Bedouins and the commandos will shoot. I bed down in the hall and creep on my belly to the balcony. Red tracers like red cinders streak across the sky. A phosphorous shell explodes on a rooftop on Ashrafiya hill: searing light and then luminous smoke. Heavy machine guns scatter-blast the walls of the house. The house comes alive in the night. A tortured face. The dark windows hollowed eyes. The doorway, a gaping mouth on the hillside. The firing ends. The magic light show dissolves into blackness, into the incessant, dull thudding of mortar fire in Al-Whedat camp. Each shell must kill more mothers and children than commandos. Decades of diaspora have driven these commandos to battle from their homes. Their dream is dying. If not dying, put to savage reckoning.

The hotel is reduced to two dark corridors crammed with men half awake on their mattresses. Shortwave radios splutter lost connections down the corridors. One voice and then another drifts away. Reminds me of when I was a child listening to stations fade in and out on my crystal set. The Fateh radio, earnest and militant, plays Victorian martial music. They announce that the commando positions are secure, that they have destroyed twenty-one tanks on the Webda Road. But I could see the road today and it was open clear. The Army radio proclaims that the commandos have been driven into the camps. But even now they are shelling the American embassy on Webda hill and they control the traffic circle south of the hotel. Perhaps neither knows the truth. No more than I. Voices merge and fall in the darkness. We are bound by uncertainty, submerged beneath what is and is not. Incoming shells shake the hotel. I find myself thinking of birch trees, of yellow cobs of corn, the grotesque childlike drawings of Alexander Calder, of being arrested by those tough Al Saqai Syrian commandos in Beirut, of your breasts, you, the woman I love, and the breasts of a woman I do not love, of my child's hair, and of the day when I was a child and fell off a dock into lake water, and was saved by my grandfather who died a year later in his own blood.

The hotel staff manage one meal a day for us: a bowl of white rice. Every morning, the four or five Italians gather together at the end of the corridor and quietly sing. I keep saying to myself: They're singing. At noon today, an American from ABC News, with whom I'd had an interesting talk about I.F. Stone's weekly journal, about Stone's integrity, appeared standing over me as I lay with other men on the corridor floor. Seemingly unaware that he might be giving offence, he offered me a KitKat chocolate bar from his stolen stash. Somehow the American on-camera men appear well-pressed, shaven, eager every morning. They can't do anything, but they are well-pressed. Meanwhile, the British have grown officious and nasty, fighting among themselves, class against class, as to who will take control of the sanitation committee formed two days ago. A reporter gave us a talk about saving water – having been once stranded at sea for twelve days when he'd thought it only be three. He was put in charge of sanitation. The Russian, of course, got himself shot dead. No one seems to have known him. The Swede, being peripheral, was wounded in the thigh. The French have fucked off, self-serving with that superior air of the maître d' they're so good at. As for me, very Canadian, I am who I am, with nothing obvious to declare – a lone observer force, waiting for whatever is going to happen.

The Palestinian houseboy in the hotel is on his haunches by each mattress, whispering, "The time of the *fedayeen* is of the night."

Three days ago in Beirut, Ghassan Kanafani – born one year before me, in 1936 in Akka, a village now (Acre) inside Israel – who is not only the editor of *Al-Hadaf*, the Popular Front for the Liberation of Palestine newspaper, but an important short storyteller in Arabic (he actually knew who Sherwood Anderson was), and an important spokesman for the Front concerning the hijacked airplane hostages, gave me a remarkable book, a collection of children's drawings. Excellently printed on heavy paper and in full colour, it is a selection of drawings by the children of Baqu'a camp here in Jordan. (I have kept the book in an attaché case that lies exposed on my bed; the case is filled with Cairo jewellery for you, my beloved woman – a gold necklace-bib to cover, a little, your breasts). They are beautiful drawings, sophisticated and yet primitive as the best children's drawings are. But tortured and racked by terror and pain. The drawings are in the colours of innocent delight, yet each is a drawing scarred by death. They speak in their titles of burned flowers and charred oranges: House and Tree and Women Burning – a Child Dead

Among the Grass. Another is: House Burning and an Apple. An eight-year-old girl, Nawal Ahmad, wrote:

> *The trees were laden with fruit.*
> *The enemy's airplanes came and*
> *Bombed the camp and the trees.*
> *The green leaves burned, the roses*
> *Fell, the apples fell, and*
> *The neighbour's daughter also.*

These are the little girls and boys who are nurtured on memories of the roar of Israeli planes, of burned fields, of death, of long treks from camp to camp, and they yearn for a country that their fathers came from, a country that has the reality of a poem and a poem's power in these camps. They yearn while filled with a hatred of these camps – their homes – in which only more hatred festers, and their dreams have become a lived fantasy that they move through daily, studying in tents, training, drilling in mock-military formation. Hoping to be like their grown brothers. Hoping to take up the Kalashnikov. Their brothers are dying today, not in Jerusalem, not Haifa, but in the streets of Amman. In Beirut, in Shatila, one of the largest and ugliest of camps, I was arrested by Al Saqai commandos. With Kalashnikovs levelled at my belly they waved me into a jailhouse. This blockhouse reeked of the urine and excrement in the cess-pails in the cell, a murky room behind floor-to-ceiling bars, and behind the bars, on the floor and hardly looking up, were three slumped men. They spoke no English. They were coldly indifferent and sullen. They loathe intruders. Two days earlier I had been in another section of the camp with Fateh guards. As we walked down the rows of squalid tin shacks, following the line of the open drain, a child spat on my arm. The guard said nothing. Another child hit me with a stick across my back, and when we were leaving that clutch of misery, a child hit me in the back with a rotten tomato. For the first time in my life, I felt no anger, no urge to strike back at being assaulted. After all, I had presumed to walk through their broken lives, "having a look." I had no right to complain. I had never intended to "gawk" my way through this camp, but there is no way around it, the camps are where the Palestinians are, and there I was, arrested by men I did not know, men who shared the anger of those small children. The Al Saqai took me to their headquarters and sat me down in front of four men and interrogated me in a language I did not know. There is a naïve quality about these commandos, even when they are outraged. They have their Kalashnikovs, but beyond that, they are mostly stubborn men, deeply aggrieved, for whom explanations mean little or nothing. They must believe or be assuredly told that you are one with them, and if you are not, then why are you among them?

After an hour of confused talk and translation, I had to confront how dangerous the situation was: they did not know what to do with me and, therefore, they were liable to do anything. I asked that they phone Ghassan Kanafani, dangerous in itself, because there is so much friction between the Al Saqai and the Front (there are at present twenty-one different groups under the umbrella of the PLO). Within half an hour, a four-man negotiating team arrived and talk went on for a long, long time. The sun was going down. It was a lethargic, almost lost feeling that I got while my fate (I presumed) was being decided in their language. Particularly when the negotiators were tense, sometimes abrasive, and quick to be wounded. Suddenly, an Al Saqai man handed me an open bottle of Seven-Up. The mouth of the bottle, used and reused in the camp, was caked with orange grime. I drank it. He'd watched to see if I would flinch at the grime that is their everyday grime. Orange. The commander then explained through a translator that he did not mean to frighten me, that foreigners who were friends were welcome, and I was released into the custody of the Front. Negotiators who were anxious, if not frightened themselves. The Al Saqai had solved their own problem. They presumed the Front would handle me as I deserved.

Kanafani, a very intelligent man of wry humour and a gentle smile, shook his head when I was brought to him. He was relieved and he said, "You know, they had four men blindfolded and ready to be shot the other day until one of them mentioned my name. This is a very dangerous time to be in the camps." Kanafani was tired. Only two nights before, government thugs had tried to kill him. He stood before me with his automatic in his belt. He said, "You know, someone in the government called before the attack on me and warned me that they were going to send three men to beat me up and kill me, and I said that they did not know me, or they would need to send only one." He laughed at his own self-deprecating joke, this small, tough man. Packing his gun. He'd fought the three men off. Tried to kill them.

Kanafani is critically outspoken about the fedayeen fantasy. He has written harshly about the leadership and he has said that the fedayeen achievements are "stagnating, ineffective and in difficulty." He has been caustic with the Arab press, blaming them for irresponsible reporting of fedayeen actions. The press, he has said, is destroying the Palestinian military movement, because the commandos have come to believe in so-called triumphs over Israel. He has accused the leadership of overestimating what the commandos could do in battle. Kanafani has said that despite the fedayeen victory at Karameh, despite the flocking in of recruits, the fedayeen have proven unable to organize an effective resistance movement. Training of recruits, he said, is still in the raw stages, with more attention to propaganda than military expertise. In short, though he is a leader of the extreme Popular Front, Kanafani has cautioned against any move that would thrust the fedayeen into open armed struggle (at the same time, just before this civil war broke out, spokesmen for more moderate Fateh had tried as hard as they could to dissuade other Popular Front leaders from going into battle with King Hussein's army), telling me that the PFLP have been "blinded by a simple-minded, almost mystical faith in the so-called historical, materialistic logic of Marx. They have it all confused with Jesus, how the meek and the poor shall inherit the earth."

The last time I saw Kanafani, at five in the afternoon (it has the ring of Lorca: I used to love reading his poetry), we were in the Amman Front headquarters. He said, "It has begun. Get out, get out. If you stay you will be killed. It begins any moment and you will be killed." I'd gone to the hotel. To stay.

My sleep on the first night of battle had been broken by shelling and machine-gun fire. The Red Crescent ambulance had taken a Swede from down the hall to hospital; he'd been shot in the thigh. A Russian writer had been shot in the head and killed. I've told you that.

It is the fourth night. A ceasefire has been called by the army. But fighting goes on. The Bedouins are lobbing mortars toward Schneller camp. Each explosion is a huge hammer pounding down, dead weight on a mound of earth. There is no tone to the constant thudding. Only a pulsing sense of relentless punishing weight. In the dark, there is a red glow from behind the hills. Stone and tin sheeting have been turned to fire.

On Al-Whedat hill, the army has moved infantry and fifty-calibre machine guns in on three blocks of houses. The commandos held these houses. Under brilliant flares floating like evil flowers of a local apocalypse, the machine guns open up. Red tracers carom off the walls and strike deep into the darkness to arc beautifully and to die suddenly. The chugging of the big guns builds and builds until one house lights up. There is the wallop of mortar from beside the hotel, a pause, and then a direct hit on the lit-up house. After that, there is only sporadic firing. The commandos are either dead or have somehow slipped away to other alleyways.

I have gone to the roof of the hotel- where there was once a supper club. Now, the glass walls are knocked out, bullet-riddled and shattered. Someone is sitting in the dark at the orchestra piano playing "Mary Had a Little Lamb" with one finger, over and over again. I cannot see his face and he does not pause as I pass by.

From the light of the full moon the lines of the hills are clear. In the centre of the city, by the Roman amphitheatre, there is a phosphorous white glow. On the crest of the Al-Whedat camp there is a huge ruby red fire, not blazing, but steadily burning. The mosque on Ashrafiya hill is a silent black shaft into the silent mouth of God. There is neither succour nor peace in this evening silence. Too many are dead. The fury of their fedayeen faith brought them (in place of the world's indifference) the world's contempt and outrage and artillery power. They have come to live by the Kalashnikov. They expect to die by American tanks. Out of the lousy living anguish of the camps has come a commando cult in pursuit of sacrificial death. Here is an idiot tale – full of gunfire and fury, signifying what? The camps remain, and the stricken remain in them. The hatred they have for all outsiders quickens with each commando death, with each mother's child who dies under shelling. A Palestinian in the corridor said to me: "The circle has completely closed. The Hashemite Hussein has come to dance with Menachen Begin. Where is there remorse, or pity, or anger, or outrage at the plight of this people who are told they are not a people?"

The floor-length curtains of the supper club billow with the desert wind. Broken windows and white lace in the moonlight! But the curtains are not beautiful. They do not float freely. They are awkward and crippled and make a flapping noise. They are caught and hooked on the jagged plates of glass that lean into the night.

The barrage begins at dawn. Armoured cars like hard-shelled bugs and small tanks are wedged around the south traffic circle. There are gracious homes there that face the circle and they have gardens down into the brown valley. In the valley there are villas. Commandos have gone into these homes and villages. Methodically, the army machine gunners chew through the stone around the house windows. Rockets are fired into the two-foot thick walls. The commandos hold on. They fire two or three rounds at the gunners and then duck out the back while the army scatter-blasts the walls and drops mortars on the roof. Then, silence, and the commandos creep back in and fire four or five more rounds. In this way, they keep the army occupied, but not pinned into position. The roar of the weaponry finally encloses any fear I have. The roar has become normal. Silence seems arbitrary. Out the window to the east I can see that the army is shelling the roof of the five-storey insane asylum. One pounding eruption after another. Trees fall. A body spins like a rag doll from the roof. I imagine that the insane trapped inside are huddled together along the walls of their corridors (as we reporters are huddled along our corridors), they are calm and unruffled and talk for the first time of days long forgotten. At last they are at ease. The thunder of the outside world matches the thunder inside their heads. Suddenly they know they are sane.

Out of nowhere, a three-hour ceasefire was called. The Army said: Feel free to go out, to leave the hotel. But to go where? At what risk? Snipers, what do they care? I went out and walked through eerily empty streets for four blocks to the British Embassy, picking up and pocketing shell casings as I went. A stroll. Maybe a little mad. A couple wearing cardigans, surprised of course to see me, gave me tea and biscuits. Crazily detached. I asked what they'd been doing through these days and nights. Playing cribbage, they said. After a second cup of tea (the strength of it, the heat, hurt my stomach a little). They warned me that the three-hour ceasefire was almost done. Wished me well while wrapping biscuits in a napkin to take back to the hotel. Which is where I went. Hurrying. Back in my corridor, bone-tired, I felt curiously relieved to be back. Put the casings and the napkin with the biscuits in my attaché case with the Cairo jewellery.

The army has directed its attack toward specific areas: Jabal el-Hussein camp to the far east of Hussein hill; the embassy section to the near east on Webda hill; Al-Whedat camp to the south; and the traffic circles that control the main roads. The commandos control most of Webda hill, which is a residential section tightly packed with homes, narrow streets, and walls. They are returning fire from the camps at Jabal el-Hussein and Al-Whedat, and they still control the centre of the city around the amphitheatre and the Philadelphia Hotel.

The streets of Webda and Hussein hills seem empty, except for the burned-out, charred auto bodies lined up along curbs. Now and then, a shadow slips along a wall, but there seem to be no men in the streets. Yet the firing is incessant and shells heave and belly the air and on the ridge of Hussein hill there are strangely beautiful black bouquets of smoke opening up against the blue sky. Square stone squat houses gleam in the sun, dominate the hillsides. Smoke-scars along our window frames are only another shadow in the late afternoon. The cool breeze clears away the smoke from el-Hussein camp, and for a moment, it is as if the city had been evacuated and some crazed giant child had been let loose with noisemakers in each fist, striding around the hills, whirling the makers. Dumbly amusing himself.

That is only a poor fantasy, bloodless, born from the gap between death in an acrid room and a child who asks how to stop the thunder.

Locked into corridors in the hotel, lying on mattresses, connoisseurs now of rocket recoil and rapid-fire. Human voices wake us and are unwanted. Silence, each of us seeks silence. The steel Kalashnikov casings on the ground must be warm like human skin. The cocks crow, late afternoon is the dawning. Machine guns incessant in the heat, like cicadas. We eat in the dark in the basement. One bowl of boiled rice cooked over a wood fire.

The night passes, through more bombardment and rocket fire, through restless, uncertain sleep, into a dawn in which a new barrage of the camps begins.

The King has sent his troops into the city. The troops are firing on the civilians. Long live the King.

Bitterness wells up as we, removed, watch the slaughter. This is a Palestinian city, nearly two-thirds of the 500,000 people are of Palestinian blood. There are 90,000 Palestinians in Al-Whedat camp alone. There are another 50,000 in Jabal el-Hussein camp. The fires burn all through the night in the camps. Great embers in the night sky. Each shell that has landed in those camps must have collapsed twenty or thirty of the tin shacks, and under the red-hot sheets of tin…round after round of shells has gone into the camps, cannon fire of the King upon the people. The King has turned his troops upon his own city. The Bedouins, wild, erratic, simple-minded gun jockeys turned loose on the people…

If the Arabs say Israel is an artificial nation, imposed from outside on the area, then what is Transjordan and who are the Hashemites on the throne? Churchill boasted that he created the Emirate of Transjordan "one afternoon in Cairo." On these afternoons in the here and now, Hussein the Hashemite has ordered his loyal Bedouins to launch what has become…

TWO DAYS LATER:
I am in Beirut: the Palestinians launched an attack against the hotel, we were given a choice by the Bedouins, stay, take our chances…or get out on a hastily found bus to the airport. Most of us packed into the bus, an old tin coffin on wheels, wheezing. The road through the hills was controlled by commando machine guns: we inched up the incline, waving a white shirt with a red cross painted on the back. Got through to find the promised Red Cross plane long gone, empty. Passed the night in the glass-walled airport, scared, unsleeping, unprotected in any way, armoured cars wheeling around the runways, gun fire…the French maître d's showed up in their stupid bus; they'd been confined to the bus, in the desert, all these days. The port at Aqaba had been closed to them: sheepish, bedraggled. Scorned. Could not bring myself to speak to Eric Rouleau…got out the next afternoon, after drawing lots, by cargo plane to Beirut… Unable to eat here in Beirut, back in the St. George Hotel (astonishing to me there was a letter from you waiting for me at the front desk; you must have written and sent it on ahead to Beirut while I was in Cairo)…also astonishing, two hours after I checked into my

room, a "driver" arrived asking me to come with him…as a guest for supper with Kanafani and his wife in their apartment… I'm afraid that by then I was seeing almost everything "slant"; light-headed, locked in silences, then motor-mouthing manically (or so it seemed to me); his wife, as I remember, is Danish; we talked a little about the civil war, its aftermath(?), but mostly he talked about his short stories, how deeply rooted they were in his home-town history, the eradication of his family, their losses, his willingness to kill…he showed me that along with everything else, he is something of a sculptor… I left, not quite sure what he'd wanted from me, nor was I sure what I wanted from him…back in the hotel, feeling only a strange calm at my core yet I break out in a drenching sweat when there is only silence…manic shake in the nerve linings (men celebrating in Beirut run off midnight clip after clip in the air, machine-gunning the moon clouds over the swimming pool at the hotel, madmen…), I come home fero-ciously calm… I still have all the Cairo jewellery… I need your embrace…never ate the biscuits in their napkin…

1970

NOTES

As I noted in *Raise You Five*, oftentimes, after a piece was published, especially in the years 1967–1971, and having been released from restrictions of space, I added stylistic touches or increases in information to such a piece — while never changing the intent or the spirit of the judgment. The dates attached to each piece indicate first publication, or the year each was written if this is their first publication. A second date indicates the year of revisions and subsequent year and place of publication, if any.

Those poems in "Salt" that deal with the death of Margaret Atwood's father are from *Morning in the Burned House: Margaret Atwood.* McClelland & Stewart, Inc.

The Emily Dickinson quotes are from *The Poems of Emily Dickinson: Variorum Edition*, ed. Ralph W. Franklin. 3 vols, Harvard University Press.

Excerpts in "On a Sunday Morning Sidewalk" are from *Paul Muldoon: Poems, 1968–1998*, Faber and Faber.

The introduction to Marie-Claire Blais' novel is from *The Manuscripts of Pauline Archange*, translated by Derek Coltman and David Lobdell, Exile Editions.

The poems, "Tree" and "Woodchips," are from the works of Latvia's national poet, Imants Ziedonis, *Flowers of Ice*, translated by Barry Callaghan, Exile Editions.

The introduction to Morley Callaghan's non-fiction is from *A Literary Life: Reflections and Reminiscences, 1928–1990*, Exile Editions.

My criticism of Saul Bellow's *Mr. Sammler's Planet* occasioned a feisty ad from his publisher in Canada. Certainly my point of view has not so far prevailed: Bellow was awarded the Nobel Prize for Literature in 1976.

Bellow and I met again in the late '90s, but only for a moment; to my astonishment, he recalled the *Sammler* review and withdrew his hand from our greeting.

"Munich: Fear and Loving in Föhnland" appeared in *Toronto Life* in 1979. A new edition of *Diary of a Man in Despair* by Freidrich Reck-Malleczewen, translated by Paul Rubens, appeared from Duckworth, London, 2000.

"Who Look on War" – As for the writing from World War I: the extraordinary novel, *Generals Die In Bed: A Story from the Trenches* by Charles Yale Harrison, is available from Annick Press, Toronto. Of equal power is *The German Prisoner* by James Hanley, from Exile Editions.

Excerpts in "Céline" are from *Castle to Castle*, translated by Ralph Manheim, Delacorte Press.

The complete text of "In Dedham Jail" [Sacco and Vanzetti] by Bruce Bliven, June 22, 1927 – in which Vanzetti's last written words are recorded – can be found in *The Faces of Five Decades: Selections from Fifty Years of the New Republic, 1914-1964*, Simon and Schuster.

Throughout "They Plenny Zims," fragments of oral stories appear as counterpoint to the Afrikaaner narrative. These are from the *ntsomi* storytelling performance tradition of the Xhosa, peoples whose homelands are in and around Transkei. Each performance has at its center a saying or song or chant that is repeated and expanded upon, so that a "plot" is developed – a story that is improvised upon, involving well-known "clichés" and characters, usually to make a point about current moments of threat and disaster, rescue and resolution. I have quoted from the private *ntsomi* collection of Harold Scheub, author of the introduction to *Tales from Southern Africa*, or from the tales themselves, as translated and retold by A.C. Jordan, University of California Press, Berkeley, Los Angeles, London, 1973.

In 1966, working with and under the brilliant director, R.J. (Paddy) Sampson, I played my part in bringing an 88-minute film (no commercials) to CBC television. It was called simply, *The Blues*. Though the CBC has never re-braodcast the program, it is something of a legend, having been bootlegged around Europe and America. It has been professionally excerpted in several films about the blues in recent years, notably by Martin Scorsese and Clint Eastwood. Several short films about the actual making of the 1966 program have been undertaken over the last couple of years.

In 1970 I made a short film of some 20 minutes about the civil war in Amman, footage shot from within the hotel by my friend and cameraman, Peter Davis. An excerpt from that film can be seen on the website BarryCallaghan.com. It can also be googled under Barry Callaghan Black September War.

Ghassan Kanafani, whose writings are still regarded highly as accomplished and innovative modernism among contemporary writers of short fiction in Arabic, was car-bombed, along with a niece, by Mossad in Beirut in in 1972. It is generally accepted that his assassination was in direct response to the role he played in what has come to be known as the Lod Massacre – the killing of twenty-six people by three members of the Japanese Red Army at Lod Airport (now Ben Gurion International Airport) near Tel Aviv.

Also in 1972, Bassam Abu Sharif survived an attack on his life by Mossad, but lost four fingers, was left deaf in one ear, and blind in one eye after he opened a book that had been sent to him by Mossad. The book, *The Memoirs of Che Guevara*, contained explosives. *Time* magazine, as is their fashion, called him "the face of terror" because of the role he played in the Dawson Field hijackings that triggered the civil war in 1970; the PFLP had seized Pan Am, Swissair and TWA passenger planes and had then blown them up in the Jordanian desert. By 1987, he had become a senior advisor to Fatah leader Yasser Arafat and was party to several proposals agreed to in the Oslo Accords, signed by the Israelis and Palestinians in 1993 and 1995. In that latter year he co-authored the book *Best Of Enemies* with Uzi Mahnaimi, a high-ranking Mossad officer.

I WISH TO EXPRESS MY GRATITUDE TO

At *The Telegram*: Tom Hedley, Ron Evans
At *Saturday Night*: John Macfarlane, Robert Fulford
At *Toronto Life*: Tom Hedley, Marq de Villiers, John Macfarlane
At *idea&s*: Diana Kuprel
At *Leisure Ways*: Jerry Tutunjian

ACKNOWLEDGMENTS

Several selections in this book first appeared in the following publications: *The Telegram, Saturday Night, Toronto Life, idea&s, Leisure Ways.*

A SELECTION OF BARRY CALLAGHAN'S WORKS
ARE NOW AVAILABLE IN DIGITAL FORMATS

BARRELHOUSE KINGS is the unique story of two Canadian writers, each well-known in his own right: Morley Callaghan and his son, Barry. It is a stunningly written recollection of the world in which Barry Callaghan grew up – the world that was Morley's milieu as a writer and became Barry's as their lives dovetailed. Along the road toward that dovetailing, Barry encounters an incredible cast of characters: Becket, Muhamad Ali, Brownie McGee and Sonny Terry, Golda Meir, Pierre Trudeau, mobsters and several song-and-dance men. Unforgettable, this is an autobiography that will stand the test of time.

RAISE YOU FIVE is periodic writing about the most complex ideas, rendered in prose of utter ease and clarity – prose from a man who believes all writing, at its best, whether it is a book review or meditation on evil, is a kind of storytelling, and that storytelling is what keeps it alive.

RAISE YOU TEN As a man of letters, as a poet, novelist, and personal journalist, Barry Callaghan is a singular presence in Canada. Always a storyteller, a *flaneur* "secretly attuned to the history of the place and in covert search of adventure," he is also a public scholar in the tradition of Edmund Wilson (his extraordinary portrait of Wilson concludes this volume). Unflinching before the harsh complexities of our time, *Raise You Ten*, like *Raise You Five*, is, as trumpeted by the *Globe and Mail:* "Literary criticism and cultural history of a high order, in turn joyous, acerbic, celebratory."

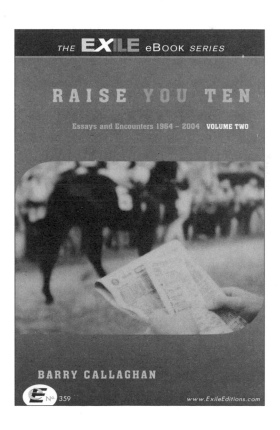

THE **EXILE** eBOOK *SERIES*

R A I S E   Y O U   T E N

Essays and Encounters 1964 – 2004   **VOLUME TWO**

BARRY CALLAGHAN

No. 359   www.ExileEditions.com

ALL THE LONELY PEOPLE Street hustlers, priests, blues singers, Holocaust survivors, cross-dressers, paramilitary snipers, even those we may euphemistically consider the "ordinary" – all of them authentic, and all would subscribe to the maxim that "happiness is overrated." The dialogue is true to speech as it is spoken, shot through with humour, piercing sadness and puzzling beauty. To quote the important American critic, M.L. Rosenthal, "His is one of the few story collections I've seen that even begins to pick up from the method of *Dubliners*. Like Joyce, Callaghan gets so deeply and honestly into the local world that it is the international place we all inhabit."

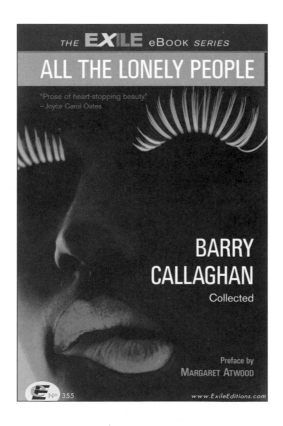

BESIDE STILL WATERS is a passionate love story, with its roots in Toronto and its resolution in the dark heart of contemporary Africa. Adam Waters' search for the woman he loves, who has mysteriously disappeared from their hotel room, takes him from the casinos of Puerto Rico to war-torn Gabon and a leper colony deep in the African bush. Counterpointing Adam's quest are his memories from boyhood, and of his father, wandering jazzman Sweet Web Waters; his experiences as a war correspondent; and the girl who becomes his lover, dancer Gabrielle. Callaghan confronts the pure joy that can be in sexuality and the evil that is inherent in the nature of growth itself, by combining the excitement of an adventure story with the exuberant love of language.

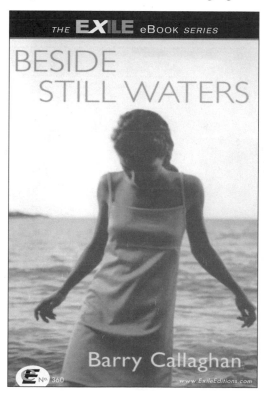

HOGGWASH Barry Callaghan and Joe Rosenblatt, poets of perspicacity, pizzazz, and probity, have been combative, ecstatic compadres for over forty years, with Callaghan donning an array of chapeaus, the man of *belles lettres* and Hogg *flaneur*-on-the-hoof from Smooth City, while Rosenblatt decades ago declared his unconditional allegiance to the buzzzers, chirpers, and purrers of the natural world, and to remain at peace by his pond, aloof from the human horde. This most unlikely pair are conjoined by their shared dedication to the Word, drawn from their nether surreal and noumenal worlds. *Hoggwash* is a convergence by epistle in a tribute not just to their enduring friendship but to the life of the imagination itself.